AMERICAN MUSIC

AMERICAN MUSIC
A PANORAMA

 THIRD CONCISE EDITION

LORENZO CANDELARIA
University of Texas, Austin

DANIEL KINGMAN

 THOMSON

SCHIRMER

Australia • Brazil • Canada • Mexico • Singapore • Spain •
United Kingdom • United States

THOMSON
™
SCHIRMER

American Music: A Panorama, **Third Concise Edition**
Lorenzo Candelaria, Daniel Kingman

Publisher: Clark Baxter
Editorial Assistant: Emily Perkins
Executive Technology Project Manager: Matt Dorsey
Executive Marketing Manager: Diane Wenckebach
Marketing Assistant: Marla Nasser
Marketing Communications Manager: Patrick Rooney
Project Manager, Editorial Production: Trudy Brown
Creative Director: Rob Hugel
Exexcutive Art Director: Maria Epes
Print Buyer: Judy Inouye
Permissions Editor: Joohee Lee

Production Service: G&S Book Services, Melanie Field
Text Designer: Stuart Paterson
Copy Editor: Peggy Tropp
Cover Designer: Janet Wood
Cover Image: Samuel Colman (1832–1920). *Storm King on the Hudson,* 1866. Oil on canvas, $32\frac{1}{8} \times 59\frac{7}{8}$ in. (81.6 × 152 cm). Smithsonian American Art Museum, Washington DC/Art Resource, NY.
Compositor: G&S Book Services
Text and Cover Printer: Webcom

Printed in Canada
1 2 3 4 5 6 7 10 09 08 07 06

Library of Congress Control Number: 2005937010

ISBN 0-495-12839-2

Thomson Higher Education
10 Davis Drive
Belmont, CA 94002-3098
USA

For more information about our products, contact us at:
Thomson Learning Academic Resource Center
1-800-423-0563

For permission to use material from this text or product, submit a request online at
http://www.thomsonrights.com.

Any additional questions about permissions can be submitted by e-mail to **thomsonrights@thomson.com.**

TO GENEVA LEE HIGHLANDER

P A N O R A M A

*T*he panorama

was a popular form of didactic

art in the larger frontier cities of America in the

mid-1800s. It was an exhibition of the painter's

art done on a mammoth scale. A huge canvas, twenty

feet high or more, would slowly pass before the

assembled audience, moving, scroll-like, from one

large roll to another. The paying spectators would

see vast scenes unrolling before their eyes—battle

scenes, or the course of the Mississippi River

between two points—often to the

accompaniment of music.

CONTENTS

C H A P T E R

SECULAR MUSIC IN THE CITIES
FROM COLONIAL TIMES TO THE
AGE OF ANDREW JACKSON 190

C H A P T E R

POPULAR MUSICAL THEATER AND
OPERA FROM THE JACKSONIAN
ERA TO THE PRESENT 203

C H A P T E R

POPULAR SONG, DANCE,
AND MARCH MUSIC FROM THE
JACKSONIAN ERA TO THE ADVENT
OF ROCK 222

AUTHOR'S GUIDE TO THE PANORAMA OF AMERICAN MUSIC

The ordering of the richly complex panorama of American music into distinct streams with their own characters and functions reflects the dynamic nature of American music. Some musical streams are at full flood stage; some have dried to a narrow rivulet. All are constantly changing—overflowing their banks, retreating from them, dividing into separate branches, or yielding their flow to neighboring streams. Three of the streams are broad—folk and ethnic; popular; and classical—and guide the book's organization.

Folk art—including the music of our first stream—tends to thrive within fairly close-knit homogeneous communities possessing a strong sense of group identity. It is music known to and enjoyed by a large proportion of the community who identify it as "their music," made by and for themselves, created for no larger public beyond the artist's own immediate community. Many members of the folk music community—a much higher proportion than in the general population—perform the music themselves, with varying degrees of skill. Ethnic musics share many of folk music's characteristics, but generally originate in societies whose homelands are outside the United States (the notable exception, of course, is American Indian music). Part I covers the various folk and ethnic sources of America's traditional music.

By contrast, popular art (whether secular or religious) tends to be created with the intention of *breaking through* communal and ethnic barriers to reach a mass audience. Thus, popular music is music created for and enjoyed by the vast majority of the people, undefined by region or ethnicity. Produced by skilled professionals making modest demands on a listener's musical knowledge and experience, popular music flourishes whenever and wherever a critical mass of population exists to support a commercial return—the most widely recognized measure of its value. Part II covers the transition that country, blues, and rock music made from folk to popular music, country and blues beginning with the advent of radio and recordings, and rock coming out of both in the early 1950s. Parts III and IV cover America's sacred and secular music that, from the beginning, sought popular status.

Fine art, on the other hand—including the classical music of our third broad stream—tends to have a quality of detachment. It does not try to serve the needs of a community as folk and ethnic musics do, nor does it rely on mass appeal for its existence. Thus, it is not popular. It tends to reward a certain degree of musical experience and historical knowledge in the listener, but its devotees are not defined by any intellectual, social, economic, regional, or racial classification. A full appreciation of classical music requires not only that we assess our own responses to the composer's imagination, but understand some of the creative environment out of which the work grew and the traditions it confronts. Part VI covers the ways American composers have explored classical music.

Jazz, covered in Part V along with its immediate forerunners, is a special case—one that has points of contact with folk, popular, and fine arts, but does not merge entirely with any one of those broad streams. And, finally, Part VII, designed to encourage the reader to get outside the book and engage meaningfully with the diverse music traditions in his or her own backyard, samples the tributaries in two contemporary geographic areas.

FEATURES NEW TO THIS EDITION

Those who have used previous editions will notice an immediate difference in the streamlined text and CD anthology—both tailored to work more effectively with the growing demands on students' time inside and outside of the classroom.

- New Listening Cues, with the line "Listen For . . . ," point the reader to a selection's important musical characteristics and help students manage their use of the CD anthology more effectively.
- A new website devoted exclusively to the text provides detailed Listening Guides, more cultural context for the audio selections, and additional readings for each chapter.
- Nearly 100 new photographs with extensive captions, and viewable in color on the website, enrich the historical context of our story of America's music.

Although streamlining the text and CD anthology have been important goals, we have actually expanded our discussion of some aspects of America's music.

- New material describes Mexican, Asian, and Arabic music, the most recent musical traditions to join the American panorama.
- A new chapter on film music explores a largely unrecognized context in which a significant part of the American population consumes classical music on a regular basis.
- A new focus in the classical music chapters examines the search for an American identity in the Eurocentric world of classical music.
- Wherever possible (and in some cases practical), the CD anthology—with nearly 100 selections—includes complete works that more fully illustrate a topic and make this supplement more attractive on its own.
- Complete lyrics of the vocal works, including translations, appear in the text to clarify the listening and emphasize the importance of word in song.

Seasoned readers will be pleased to find that the suggestions for Projects and Additional Listening, revised from previous editions, have remained. They are intended to give the student an opportunity to investigate further, on her or his own, many different aspects of American music. References are a legal necessity and a scholarly obligation, but here they are more—a point of departure for further investigation of topics covered throughout the book. We encourage the reader not only to take in the panorama, but to explore the single tributaries that feed the larger streams.

A NOTE ON THE MUSIC SELECTIONS

No practical CD supplement can include all the examples relevant to the subject. Furthermore, the profit-oriented (in contrast to education-oriented) policies of much of the commercial music industry made unavailable the rights to many iconic examples, particularly of popular music. Rather than avoid discussing these works altogether, the chapter on rock music takes an innovative approach to this problem by cuing selections that the student can download very inexpensively from iTunes®. We will be interested to receive readers' feedback on this feature of the text. In addition, the complete discussion of every musical selection from the second edition that does not appear in this revision appears in full on the web. Instructors who miss any given piece can play it in class from the second edition's CD set and send their students to the web to read about it.

ACKNOWLEDGMENTS

Several months before Daniel Kingman passed away in Sacramento, California, on May 27, 2003, we had agreed to work together as co-authors on a third edition of *American Music: A Panorama*. That collaboration, unfortunately, never came to pass. But assisting on the second edition and discussing the book extensively with Prof. Kingman, I gained a clear understanding of his goals, his style, and his vision for the third; I have worked with those considerations firmly in mind as I revised the text in some areas and expanded it in others.

I am grateful to Peter Kvetko, ethnomusicologist and lecturer at Tufts University, for our productive discussions regarding rock music and Asian music traditions in the United States. David Neumeyer, my colleague at the University of Texas at Austin, was especially helpful on matters related to film music. Lise Waxer, who passed away unexpectedly in August 2002, contributed much through personal correspondence to the Latino chapter in the last edition. Her efforts have carried forward into this one as well—a testament to her impact as a teacher and scholar. Patricia Shifferd, Program Director of Continental Harmony, a project of the American Composers Forum, was an important source of information and materials related to Philip Bimstein in Chapter 18. Ada Anderson generously provided recordings and materials related to Blind Tom in Chapter 17. Craig Wright allowed me to use some of his pedagogical ideas for the blues chapter. Conversations with Joseph Horowitz also proved influential as I thought about classical music in America. Throughout this project (and many others) Dr. Robert S. Freeman, Dean of the College of Fine Arts at the University of Texas at Austin, has been a valued friend and tireless supporter, a true champion of the arts.

I wish especially to thank the users of this book who consented to write detailed and quite helpful peer reviews: David Borgo, James Madison University, Virginia; Mary Campbell, Las Positas College, California; Michael C. Caputo, County College of Morris, New Jersey; Andrew Connell, James Madison University, Virginia; Julie Dunbar, Edgewood College, Wisconsin; Andrea Dykstra, Grand Valley State University, Michigan; Karen Fosheim, Delta State University, Mississippi; Robert I. Holst, Lewis University, Illinois; Donna Cardamone Jackson, University of Minnesota; Charles Kauffman, Southwest Minnesota State University; Donald C. Meyer, Lake Forest College, Illinois; Carl Moman, Wayland Baptist University, Texas; Jeffrey J. Noonan, Southeast Missouri State University; Kay Norton, Arizona State University; Jennifer S. Peters, McKendree College, Illinois; Paula Savaglio, Hope College, Michigan; David Schiller, University of Georgia; Helena Simonett, Vanderbilt University, Tennessee; Steven Swayne, Dartmouth College, New Hampshire; Gloria J. Thurmond, Seton Hall University, New Jersey. Many of their suggestions have been incorporated in this edition, and consequently quite a few of what I consider to be definite improvements, both small and large, were inspired by the points they made.

One of the most important ties that Daniel Kingman and I have is the privilege of working with our publisher, Clark Baxter. It has also been a special pleasure to work with Trudy Brown, Peggy Tropp, Melanie Field, Diane Wenckebach, and Emily Perkins.

Closest to home, I am deeply indebted to my wife Monique for her patience, support, and assistance at various stages of research and writing. I owe the biggest "thank you" of all to our young daughter Geneva, who cheerfully supported me from start to finish. This book is dedicated to her.

Lorenzo Candelaria
Austin, Texas

AMERICAN MUSIC

FOLK AND ETHNIC MUSICS

A scanning of the vast panorama of American music can begin nowhere more logically than with our folk and ethnic traditions. America's music, throughout its broad spectrum, is so relatively new that it has remained closer to folk sources than is the case in almost any other country. The professional sector of American musical life has never gone for very long without returning to refresh and revitalize itself at the fount of folk culture. Masterpieces as diverse as George Gershwin's *Porgy and Bess* and Aaron Copland's *Appalachian Spring* bear witness to this, as do large amounts of music in popular culture, from Dan Emmett to Bob Dylan.

Yet this very closeness of America's music to its folk and ethnic roots is attended by a paradox. There is probably no other country in the world in which the soil of folk culture has been so thoroughly broken up, and either eroded away or rendered sterile. The all-pervasive media not only have spread commercial urban music exhaustively but also have put music largely into the hands of the professional entertainer. Continuous and extensive migration has broken down and watered down regional character. And affluence, spectacular in comparison with most of the rest of the world, has put the appliances and products of the media into the hands of virtually everyone, so that the need, ability, or desire to make one's own music has lessened, where it has not actually disappeared.

So it would appear that the rich humus of folklore has provided us with nourishment but has proved to be fragile as well. Yet the realization of its fragility has made us more aware of its value and has encouraged us to make efforts not only to conserve it but also to keep its cultivation alive and relevant. And American folk and ethnic musics do live on in the space-and-communications age. Perhaps that is because, faced with the formidable challenge to human values and human scale posed by technology, and with the disorientations of an unstable world, we have come to realize both our need for the sense of community that a living connection with the past provides and the benefits of keeping alive, through adaptation to the world we live in, an oral tradition that is simple, direct, and unflinchingly honest in its expression.

Barely thirty years after George Washington's inauguration as our first president, enough people had crossed the Mississippi to make Missouri our twenty-fourth state. This stylized image shows the self-sufficiency that made isolated frontier life in Missouri possible. Note the hunting rifles and the skinned deer, the tree stumps left from clearing farmland, and the woman churning butter from the cow's milk. Children had games to play, and in many households someone (seen here in the cabin doorway) played the fiddle—the dominant musical instrument of rural America.

THE ANGLO-CELTIC-AMERICAN TRADITION

The Anglo-Celtic-American tradition of folk music, its origins traceable to England, Scotland, and Ireland, is best epitomized in the ballad, that venerable storytelling convergence of poetry and music. The ballad occurs in the United States in three strains: the *imported ballad,* little changed from its old-country forms; the *naturalized ballad,* still recognizable as descended from the old-country versions, in spite of having adopted the trappings of its new cultural surroundings; and *native ballads,* wholly new stories indigenous to the United States.

IMPORTED BALLADS

We begin with one of the most widespread and popular of the imported ballads.

"Barbara Allen" as a Prototype of the Anglo-Celtic-American Ballad

It might seem unlikely that the tale of a man who dies of his love for the woman who spurned him should have so enduringly engaged ballad singers and listeners from the seventeenth century in Scotland (its first recorded emergence) to the twenty-first century in America. Yet that has been the history of "Barbara Allen." Oliver Goldsmith wrote in 1765, "The music of the finest singer is dissonance to what I felt when an old dairy-maid sung me into tears with . . . 'The Cruelty of Barbara Allen'" (Child 2: 276). It had the same effect in 1938 on the singer Bob Brown, an old-timer who lived at the edge of the Big Thicket in east Texas. When Brown came to the line "Young man, I think you're dying," folk-song collector William Owens reports that "tears filled his eyes and he brushed at his wrinkled cheek with the back of his hand."

Owens writes, "If I were asked to name the ballad most deeply ingrained in the heart and thinking of the American folk, 'Barbara Allen' would be my choice. I have heard it up and down the country against backgrounds ranging from expensive nightclubs to sharecroppers' shacks" (Owens 23).

Listening Cue **"Barbara Allen"** H. J. Beeker, vocal and guitar

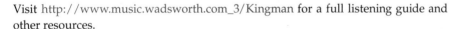

Recorded by John A. Lomax in Boone, North Carolina, 1936 (3:15)
Listen For ▪ strophic form ▪ ballad meter ▪ iambic foot

Visit http://www.music.wadsworth.com_3/Kingman for a full listening guide and other resources.

The tune heard on CD 1/1 resembles in shape if not in note-to-note detail many other tunes associated with this ballad. These tunes constitute a tune family. The addition of a very rudimentary guitar accompaniment (using the three basic chords known to every beginning guitarist) makes this version sound like the conventional idea of folk music.

1. In Scarlet Town where I was born,
   There was a fair maid dwellin'.
   Made ev'ry youth cry well away,
   Her name was Barbara Allen.

2. It was all in the month of June,
   All things there were bloomin'.
   Sweet William lay on his deathbed
   O'er the love of Barbara Allen.

3. And death was painted on his face,
   O'er his heart was stealin'.
   Oh hasten away to comfort him,
   Oh lovely Barbara Allen.

4. He sent his servant to the town
   Where Barbara was a-dwellin'.
   "My master's sick and sends for you
   If your name be Barbara Allen."

5. Slowly, slowly she got up,
   Slowly she came nigh him.
   And all she said when she got there,
   "Young man, I think you're dyin'."

6. "Oh I am sick, very sick,
   Death on me is stealin'.
   No better, no better I never can be
   If I can't have Barbara Allen."

7. "Oh yes, you're sick, very sick,
   Death on you is stealin'.
   No better, no better you never can be
   For you can't have Barbara Allen."

8. "Oh don't you remember in yonder town
   You were at the tavern.
   You drank a health to the ladies all around
   And slighted Barbara Allen."

9. As she was on her highway home
   The birds they kep' a-singin'.
   They sang so clear and seemed to say,
   "Hard-hearted Barbara Allen."

10. Looked to the east, looked to the west,
    Spied his coach a-comin'.
    "Lay down, lay down that corpse of clay
    That I may look upon him."

11. "Oh Mother, Oh Mother, go make my bed,
    Make it long and narrow.
    Sweet William died for pure, pure love,
    And I shall die for sorrow."

12. She was buried in the old church yard.
    He was buried nigh her.
    On William's grave there grew a red rose,
    On Barbara's grew a green brier.

13. The rose and the brier they grew so high
    They could grow no higher.
    They met and formed a true love knot,
    The rose wrapped around the brier.

This version of "Barbara Allen" is a fairly complete one and incorporates most of the events found in other versions. An almost invariable element of this ballad is the "rose-and-brier" motif, with the plants growing up out of the graves to become entwined in a lovers' knot. This sentimental device, rooted in old beliefs that the soul, upon death, either passes into or becomes a plant expressing the character of the dead person, occurs in other ballads as well (Wimberly 39–43).

FEATURES COMMON TO MOST BALLADS

A closer look at this version of "Barbara Allen" can acquaint us with features common to many other ballads, and in fact to much folk music throughout the world. Most ballads are in strophic form; that is, all the stanzas are sung to the same tune. There are as many stanzas as it takes to tell the story, or as many as the singer cares to sing or can remember. The lyrics are also in what is commonly called ballad meter. In ballad meter, we typically find stanzas of four lines each in which eight-syllable lines alternate with six-syllable lines. These syllables are stressed in a very distinctive way too. Indeed, the basic unit of ballad versification is the iambic foot—a unit made up of one unstressed syllable followed by a stressed syllable (ta-**da**). The succession of iambic feet produces a very recognizable lilting pattern for every two lines: ta-**da**-ta-**da**-ta-**da**-ta-**da**; ta-**da**-ta-**da**-ta-**da**a (an extra syllable often latches on at the end of the second line).

Another way to look at this is by the total number of iambic feet per line, which yields a 4+3+4+3 pattern for each stanza as exemplified here (stressed syllables are indicated in bold font and with accent marks):

/   /   /   /
In **Scar**let **Town** where **I** was **born**,
      /   /   /
There **was** a **fair** maid **dwel**lin'.
         /   /   /   /
Made **ev**'ry **youth** cry **well** away,
      /   /   /
Her **name** was **Bar**bara **Al**len.

Ballad meter can be found in many contexts besides that of the ballad. Many hymns, such as "There Is a Land of Pure Delight," are in ballad meter (sometimes called Common Meter). In the informal world of ballad-making and singing, extra syllables are frequently crammed in to accommodate expressive needs. This is particularly noticeable in "John Hardy," the lyrics of which are on page 11.

Ballads are frequently sung without accompaniment, which allows the performer greater rhythmic and emotive freedom. Furthermore, no ballad is apt to have only a single tune indissolubly wedded to it. Neither is any given tune always exclusively associated with only one ballad.

Tune Sources and Scales

Many ballad tunes exhibit characteristics of antiquity, particularly those coming from the Appalachians. Much of this antique flavor can be attributed to the musical scales on which they are based. One scale frequently encountered is the pentatonic—a scale of five notes rather than the seven notes we are more accustomed to hearing in music today. (You can hear the sound of the pentatonic scale by playing only the black keys of the piano.) This scale is the basic building material of much folk and ethnic music worldwide. It occurs in our popular music as well; the first two phrases of two of Stephen Foster's best-known songs, "Old Folks at Home" and "Oh, Susannah," are pure pentatonic, as is the preceding version of "Barbara Allen."

Dispersion and Variation with the Passage of Time

"Barbara Allen" has traveled far and wide. As of 1962, the Library of Congress Archive of American Folk Song contained 243 transcribed versions of this ballad, picked up from twenty-seven states, from Maine to Florida to California. The essence of the story, sometimes referred to as the *emotional core,* endures in all versions. But less vital elements are subject to considerable variation. Traditional folksingers may not intentionally alter a song, but in the course of oral transmission changes become inevitable. Simple forgetting is a constant factor. Another source of change is a misunderstanding of elements of language as the ballad ages.

Difficult or ambiguous words, or words and phrases no longer in current usage, are very vulnerable to change. "The Gypsy Laddie" (see "Gypsy Davy," CD 1/2) is a Scottish ballad in which the lady of the castle, in her lord's absence, is abducted by a band of gypsies who appear at the castle, cast a spell on her, then abduct her. One old version of the ballad, still retaining aspects of the supernatural, says of the gypsy band that as they saw the lady "They coost their glamourie owre her." A later, garbled version says of the gypsies that "They called their grandmother over"! Not only has the word *glamourie* ("glamour") been misunderstood, but also its older meaning as an actual spell to be cast over someone has been lost, to the impoverishment of the ballad.

Interpreting the Ballads

The early attention given to ballads was directed almost exclusively to their texts, and indeed "the ballad as literature" is a prominent branch of study. There are many ways to approach the interpretation of ballads. Using "Barbara Allen" as an example, one could pursue the *historical* context. Was Barbara a real person? One theory is that the ballad was a popular libel on Barbara Villiers, the famous mistress of Charles II of England (1630–1685). Or, to take another road, one could explore the *social-psychoanalytical* dimensions of the ballad, as noted folklorist Alan Lomax (1915–2002) has done, viewing Barbara Allen as a "frigid western woman humbling and destroying the man whom she sees as her enemy and antagonist" (171). The interpretive possibilities for "Barbara Allen" would seem only as limited as the imagination—perhaps another reason for its enduring appeal.

NATURALIZED BALLADS

Old ballads, transplanted in time and place, usually retain their emotional core but become "naturalized" in their details. Changes in place names are common; the "Oxford girl" easily becomes the "Knoxville girl," for example. Other details that surround us in daily life are adapted as well. Nowhere is this more strikingly illustrated than in Woody Guthrie's version of "The Gypsie Laddie," known as "Gypsy Davy"(CD 1/2).

Listening Cue "**Gypsy Davy**" Woody Guthrie, vocal and guitar

Recorded by John A. Lomax in Boone, North Carolina, 1936 (2:46)
Listen For ▪ strophic form ▪ ballad meter ▪ extensions of each stanza

Visit http://www.music.wadsworth.com_3/Kingman for a full listening guide and other resources.

The core of the story is that the lord, on returning to the castle, rides after the gypsies who have abducted his lady. In some versions he is successful in bringing her back; in others he is not. (The ballad has been viewed as a parody on the Greek myth of Orpheus and his attempt to bring Eurydice back from the underworld.) The original Scottish version dates from the time of Shakespeare, when king and parliament sought to drive the gypsies out of Scotland.

A comparison of Guthrie's version with an older Scottish one shows some interesting instances of naturalization as the ballad traveled from the highlands of Scotland to the western prairie of America. The Scottish lord has become the "boss"; his black steed has become the "buckskin horse with the hundred-dollar saddle"; and instead of riding east and riding west in search of the abducted lady, "till they cam' to yonder boggie," the boss finds wagon tracks (as might be expected on the western plains) that lead to a gypsy encampment, and a campfire with gypsies singing to the "sound of a big guitar." Also noteworthy is the presence of a child, the "blue-eyed babe," a typically American addition not in the older Scottish version.

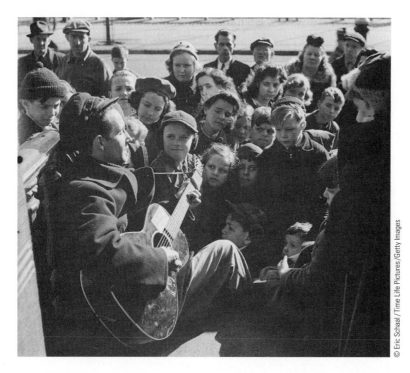

© Eric Schaal / Time Life Pictures /Getty Images

Woody Guthrie—seen here at age thirty in New York City and heard on CD 1, track 2—wrote songs about ordinary working Americans. In his autobiography, *Bound for Glory,* he wrote, "I am out to sing songs that will prove to you that this is your world and that if it has hit you pretty hard and knocked you for a dozen loops, no matter what color, what size you are, how you are built, I am out to sing the songs that make you take pride in yourself and in your work."

1. It was late last night when my boss
   come home
   Asking about his lady;
   The only answer he received:
   "She's gone with the Gypsy Davy
   Gone with the Gypsy Dave."

2. Go saddle for me my buckskin horse
   And a hundred dollar saddle.
   Point out to me their wagon tracks
   And after them I'll travel,
   After them I'll ride.

3. Well, I had not rode 'til the mid-
   night moon,
   Till I saw the campfire gleaming.
   I heard the notes of the big guitar
   And the voice of the gypsy singing
   That song of the Gypsy Dave.

4. There in the light of the camping
   fire
   Saw her fair face beaming,
   Her heart in tune with the big guitar
   And the voice of the gypsy singing
   That song of the Gypsy Dave.

5. "Have you forsaken your house
   and home?
   Have you forsaken your baby?
   Have you forsaken your husband
   dear
   To go with the Gypsy Davy?
   And sing with the Gypsy Dave
   That song of the Gypsy Dave."

6. "Yes, I've forsaken my husband
   dear
   To go with the Gypsy Davy,

And I've forsaken my mansion
high
But not my blue-eyed baby,
Not my blue-eyed babe."

7. She smiled to leave her husband
dear
And go with the Gypsy Davy;
But the tears come a-trickling
down her cheeks
To think of the blue-eyed baby,
Pretty little blue-eyed babe.

8. Take off, take off your buck-skin
gloves

Made of Spanish leather;
Give to me your lily-white
hand
We'll ride back home together
And we'll ride home again.

9. No, I won't take off my buckskin
gloves,
They're made of Spanish leather.
I'll go my way from day to day
And sing with the Gypsy Davy
That song of the Gypsy Dave.
That song of the Gypsy Davy.
That song of the Gypsy Dave.

Words and new music adaptation by Woody Guthrie TRO-© 1961 (renewed) and 1963 (renewed) Ludlow Music, Inc., New York, NY. Used by permission.

The song illustrates a frequently encountered modification of ballad meter: the extension of the last line of a stanza by repeating the sentiment of the words if not the words themselves. There is often only one repetition, but as seen in stanza five on the previous page, longer extensions are possible. Another example of this practice can be heard in the African American ballad "John Henry" discussed on pages 25–27, CD 1/10.

NATIVE BALLADS

Whereas the older English and Scottish ballads, even in adaptation, have not entirely concealed their archaic style (part of their charm for singers of our time, no doubt), the native ballads have more realistic immediacy. They have known authors in many cases, and they are much more likely to be based on actual occurrences. In contrast to the older British ballads, American ballads are less introspective and tend to be more about occupations such as buffalo hunters ("The Buffalo Skinners"), sailors ("The Bigler's Crew"), even criminals ("Jesse James"). Furthermore, they frequently involve fatal disasters ("The Titanic") or a more or less journalistic recounting of murders and executions ("John Hardy"). Much like the lead stories on the evening news, they tend to highlight and even embellish upon the sensational. While the plots and topics are many and varied, one commonly finds in native ballads a sympathetic, even compassionate, approach to their heroes or heroines.

Listening Cue "John Hardy" The Carter Family

Recorded in 1930 (2:50)
Listen For ▪ strophic form ▪ ballad meter ▪ crammed iambic foot

Visit http://www.music.wadsworth.com_3/Kingman for a full listening guide and other resources.

In many respects, the famous ballad "John Hardy" (CD 1/3) presents us with a particularly good example. This recording by the Carter Family spins a rich and riveting account, but very little of the story has any basis in known fact. The only verifiable information relating to this ballad is the existence in the courthouse at Welch, McDowell County, West Virginia, of an order for the execution of one John Hardy on January 19, 1894, for murder. A witness at the trial stated that Hardy worked for the Shawnee Coal Company and that one payday night he shot a man in a crap game over twenty-five cents. (Although both the perpetrator and the victim in "John Hardy" were black men, this murder ballad has ordinarily been sung by white singers in the southern Appalachians.)

1. John Hardy was a desperate little man,
   He carried two guns every day,
   He shot a man on the West Virginia line,
   And you ought to seen John Hardy getting away.

2. John Hardy got to the East Stone Bridge,
   He thought that he would be free,
   And up stepped a man and took him by his arm
   Saying, "Johnny, walk along with me."

3. He sent for his poppy and his mommy too,
   To come and go his bail.
   But money won't go a murdering case,
   And they locked John Hardy back in jail.

4. John Hardy had a pretty little girl,
   A dress that she wore was blue,
   As she came skipping through the old jail's hall
   Saying, "Poppy I've been true to you."

5. John Hardy had another little girl,
   A dress that she wore was red.
   She followed John Hardy to his hanging ground
   Saying, "Poppy, I would rather be dead."

6. "I've been to the East and I've been to the West,
   I've been this wide world around.
   I've been to the river and I've been baptized,
   And it's now I'm on my hanging ground."

7. John Hardy walked out on his scaffold high,
   With his loving little wife by his side.
   And the last words she heard poor John-o say,
   "I'll meet you in that sweet by and by."

The bare and grim facts are relieved by human touches, however, such as the introduction of John Hardy's little daughters into the story, one dressed in blue and the other in red. Such touches would not be found in the more stark Old World ballads. (Remember that Woody Guthrie introduced a "blue-eyed babe" into his naturalized version of the "Gypsy Davy," a gentle touch not found in older versions.) By the time "John Hardy" came into existence, the phrase "sweet by and by" had become commonplace. For more on the very popular gospel song of that name written in 1867, see pages 170–171.

A notable feature of this performance by the Carter Family is what might be described informally as the "crammed iambic foot." In such instances, extra syllables are freely inserted into the basic two-syllable pulse of the iamb (ta-**da**) to accommodate a performer's expressive needs. A mild case is found in the opening line of "Gypsy Davy": "It was late last night when my boss come home" (tata-**da** ta-**da** tata-**da** ta-**da**). But this rendition of "John Hardy" really pushes the limits of the simple lilting pulses so characteristic of ballad meter.

PRINT AND THE BALLAD

Oral tradition still retains its preeminence among folklorists as the *ideal* medium of folk song. Indeed, whether a ballad can be found to be in oral tradition is still regarded as a valid test of its "folkness," regardless of its origins. But print has long had a hand in ballad conservation and dissemination, and more recently so have other media, such as recordings. The older a ballad is, the more likely it is to have been in and out of print over the course of its history. Furthermore, it is likely that its printed versions have had an influence both on the state in which it exists today and on its geographical distribution.

The broadside (a single-sheet, cheaply printed version of the words only) and the songster (a small collection of such texts, also cheaply printed for popular sale) have long figured in ballad history, both here and in the British Isles. Broadside ballads were often hastily written by hacks looking for a quick sale. It was not beneath them to "borrow" liberally from preexisting material or even make up a story to capitalize on current public events, such as hangings. James W. Day, a blind Kentucky musician who used the pseudonym Jilson Setters, told of writing a ballad about a convicted murderer named Simpson Bush. He took it to the hanging and recalled, "I had my pockets plum full of my song-ballet [sic] that I had made up about Bush and that a printer had run off for me on a little hand press at the county seat. I sold every one I had" (Thomas 136–38; Laws 44–45). The broadside appeared in a more up-to-date medium during the famous Scopes trial of 1925, when sixty thousand phonograph recordings of a ballad on the subject were sold on the steps of the courthouse in Dayton, Tennessee, while the trial was going on (Cohen and Seeger).

As 1900 dawned, the new technology of radio attracted thousands of amateurs—like Joseph J. McCrann of Lowell, Massachusetts, seen here—eager to set up their own broadcasting stations. People rushed to buy radios, and by 1928, when the government regulated the use of radio frequencies, broadcasting had become a commercial big business. Listening to the radio for news, drama, comedy, and music—including the old-time music heard in this chapter—became as important a daily ritual in many American families as television became years later.

FIDDLE TUNES

There is probably no form of rural homespun music so indelibly associated in the popular mind with the American folk scene as the familiar *hoedown*. The fiddle and its tunes provided music to dance to, and the fiddle was long the dominant instrument in rural America.

Hoedowns are rapid dance tunes in duple meter, relatives of dance music from the British Isles. In fact, the bulk of Anglo-American fiddle tunes have come more or less directly from the thriving body of reels and hornpipes in Scotland and Ireland. The names and tunes of the most popular hoedowns are well known to any square-dance enthusiast or frequenter of fiddlers' contests. For newcomers, "Lost Indian," "Soldier's Joy," and "Devil's Dream" are a good start.

Listening Cue "Soldier's Joy" Marion Sumner, fiddle, with guitar and mandolin accompaniment

> Recorded in Hazard, Kentucky (1:00)
> Listen For ▪ low strain ▪ high strain ▪ varied repetition of each strain

CD 1

4

Visit http://www.music.wadsworth.com_3/Kingman for a full listening guide and other resources.

We can take "Soldier's Joy" (CD 1/4) as a representative example. Like most fiddle tunes, "Soldier's Joy" is in two distinct strains (or parts) with each strain repeated. Often the first strain is in the middle or low range of the fiddle, while the second strain is higher in pitch and played on the top two strings. These are respectively called the "low strain" and the "high strain." On a first hearing, the piece seems to fly right by. But through careful and repeated listening, we come to appreciate that Marion Sumner—the fiddler in this recording—hardly plays even a single strain twice in exactly the same way. Such is the fluidity and vitality of "oral tradition" (a tradition that does not sing *or play* strictly from written music). Indeed, a performance in oral tradition is like a snapshot of a piece as it exists in the hands of that particular performer at that particular moment.

How, then, does a fiddler think of a fiddle tune that has not been written down? Perhaps as a concept—a basic melodic shape that provides a springboard for the imagination. Or, better yet, as one fiddler put it: "Girl, they ain't no music to them tunes. You jes' play 'em" (Thede 11).

PRINT AND THE FIDDLE TUNE

The complex intertwining of print and oral tradition that we have observed in the case of the ballad has also been at work with the fiddle tune. Despite many fiddlers' independence of, or honest aversion to, written music, the fact is that fiddle tunes have been collected in such form since at least the early nineteenth century—at first in manuscript and later in printed collections. Elias Howe, a New England fiddler, published in 1840 *The Musician's Companion,* a collection of fiddle tunes that he sold from door to door. He published numerous and ever-larger collections over the next half-century, culminating in a joint venture with Sydney Ryan in 1883—*Ryan's Mammoth Collection of 1050 Jigs and Reels*. This was reissued by M. M. Cole in 1940 as *1000 Fiddle Tunes*. Sold initially through the Sears Roebuck stores across the nation, it has since become firmly established as the "fiddler's bible."

PLAY-PARTY SONGS

Play-party songs (also play-party games) offer us a particularly interesting type of Anglo-Celtic-American folk music. These were essentially "sung dances" without instrumental accompaniment that were used at play-parties—organized dancing events for those who followed religious traditions in which dancing was suspicious at best and the fiddle was condemned as an instrument of the devil. At play-parties the word *dance* was discouraged; its chief instrument—the fiddle—was banned outright. Nonetheless, as one writer noted: "The party-games are really dances, of course . . . ; the players furnish their own simple music by singing 'swing-arounds' as they go through their figures, while the spectators clap their hands and stamp their feet as the spirit moves them" (Randolph 394ff).

Listening Cue **"Old Man at the Mill"** Clint Howard, vocal and guitar; Fred Price, fiddle; Doc Watson, guitar

Recorded in 1960 (1:50)
Listen For ▪ dance-like characteristics ▪ calling out of dance steps ▪ various roles of the fiddle

Visit http://www.music.wadsworth.com_3/Kingman for a full listening guide and other resources.

"Old Man at the Mill" (CD 1/5) is a derivative of the play-party song tradition. The ease with which the guitar and fiddle accompany the vocalist demonstrates the extent to which a play-party song is really a dance in all but name. Notice too, how the vocalist is clearly calling out dance steps in the refrain and in the third stanza with the lines "Ladies step forward and the gents fall back" and "First to the left and then to the right." The fiddle shows its prized versatility in this recording. It is foregrounded while beginning the piece, ending the piece, and performing brief interludes, but otherwise fades into the background, occasionally accentuating the underlying rhythms of the guitar as it lyrically doubles the voice part.

Interestingly enough, the miller was traditionally a character of dubious reputation in the community, and the line "One hand on the hopper and the other in the sack" refers to his practice of helping himself to a portion of the meal he was grinding. This song is actually a combination of two others: "The Jolly Miller," a children's game-song that was played over a hundred years ago, and "The Bird Song," collected in the Appalachians in the early years of the twentieth century.

When he was thirteen, Arthel "Doc" Watson learned to play guitar from a Carter Family recording. The song he is playing here—at a concert in October 2005—was probably familiar to the Carter Family and to the fiddler in his Missouri cabin before them. To paraphrase a song he helped preserve and make familiar to modern audiences, in performers like Doc Watson, the circle of traditional American music remains unbroken. Listen for Watson's flat-picking guitar style on "Old Man at the Mill," CD 1, track 5.

Refrain:
Same old man livin' at the mill
The mill turns around of its own free will;
One hand in the hopper and the other in the sack.
Ladies step forward and the gents fall back.

1. "Down," said an owl with its head all white,
   "A lonesome day and a lonesome night.
   Thought I heard some pretty girl say,
   'Court all night and sleep next day.'"
   (Refrain)

2. Then said a raven, and she rue,
   "If I was a young man I'd have two,
   One for to git and the other for to sow,
   And I'll have a little string to my bow, bow, bow."
   (Refrain)

3. My old man's in Kalamazoo
   And he don't wear no—"Yes, I do!"
   First to the left and then to the right
   This old mill grinds day and night.
   (Refrain)

PROJECTS

1. Find an example of a traditional ballad sung by a present-day professional singer and compare it with a version in a printed collection (either words or music, or both).
2. Find some traditional ballads in collections of folk music from your own region. Libraries in your region will emphasize local collections.
3. Make a collection and comparison of ballad refrains, noting the presence or absence of apparently meaningless syllables, words, or phrases.
4. Read Charles Seeger's thought-provoking article "The Folkness of the Non-Folk vs. the Non-Folkness of the Folk," in Jackson Bruce, ed., *Folklore and Society* (Hatboro, PA: Folklore Associates, 1966). Write a brief essay setting forth your interpretation of "folkness" and "non-folkness," drawing examples from the life and culture you see around you.

ADDITIONAL LISTENING

Anglo-American Ballads, vol. 1, Rounder CD 1511.

Anglo-American Songs and Ballads. Library of Congress: AFS L14.

Versions and Variants of Barbara Allen. Library of Congress: AFS L54. A sampling of the many versions of the ballad "Barbara Allen" can be gained from the above archival issues from the Library of Congress (one has been reissued by Rounder Records). Audiocassettes of AFS L14 and AFS L54 are available at http://lcweb.loc.gov/folklife/folkcat.html. Listen to other versions by professional folksingers—for example, Pete Seeger, *God Bless the Grass*, Smithsonian/Folkways CD 37232.

"The Buffalo Skinners" is one of the earliest ballads of the West, predating the advent of the cowboys. Several versions are available. One sung by an actual cowboy is included in *Slim Critchlow: Cowboy Songs*, Arhoolie CD 479; one sung by a famous collector, John Lomax, is on *Cowboy Songs, Ballads, and Cattle Calls from Texas*, Rounder CD 1512; and one sung by a famous professional, Pete Seeger, is on *Industrial Ballads*, Smithsonian/Folkways CD 40058.

THE AFRICAN AMERICAN TRADITION

AFRICAN MUSIC AND ITS RELATION TO BLACK MUSIC IN AMERICA

As we begin our study of African American music, two questions occur immediately: To what extent is it African? What evidence do we have of its African-ness?

In the Western Hemisphere, African survivals are strongest on the north and east coasts of South America, and in the islands of the Caribbean (the latter including, culturally, French-dominated Louisiana until the twentieth century). These were areas of large plantations, with a high percentage of blacks in the population, where minimal attempts were made during slavery to control the activities of blacks when not at work. In what is now the United States, African traits survived less vigorously, for a variety of reasons; among them were the smaller ratio of blacks to whites, their more direct supervision by slave masters, their conversion in fairly large numbers to Christianity, and the attempts to repress African customs by those who regarded them (especially the dancing, which is nearly inseparable from music in African culture) as lascivious, immoral, and pagan.

Nevertheless, African culture unquestionably persisted, and there were early opportunities to observe its survival in the customary celebrations on special occasions. In the South under slavery, Christmas and Easter were traditionally occasions for "jubilees," and before the mid–nineteenth century colorful public festivities such as 'Lection Day in New England (in May or June) and the Sunday afternoon dancing in Congo Square in New Orleans furnished ample evidence of the survival of African music and dance in antebellum America. (For further information on African survivals, see Southern, *Music;* Southern, *Readings;* Epstein; Maultsby.)

One geographical area in the United States noted for its exceptional preservation of African music, language, and customs is that of the sea islands off the coast of Georgia and South Carolina. Here, in relative isolation, numbers of black people, often living in extreme poverty, retained Africanisms in music, speech, and customs well into the twentieth century. This area has been a rich mine for folklorists and anthropologists.

Listening Cue "Music in Praise of a Yoruba Chief" (Nigeria)

Recorded by Moses Asch (2:00)
Listen For ▪ dominance of percussion ▪ steady pulse governing music ▪ rhythmic complexity/diversity

Visit http://www.music.wadsworth.com_3/Kingman for a full listening guide and other resources.

African music is vast and complex. Continentwide it is far from homogeneous. The greatest influence in America has been from West Africa. Certain outstanding traits that have marked correspondences with black music in America are very audible in "Music in Praise of a Yoruba Chief" (CD 1/6). Most obvious is the dominance of rhythm, manifested in a number of ways: the sense of an inexorably steady pulse governing the music; a high degree of rhythmic complexity and diversity; and the corresponding dominance of percussion instruments. Another trait, having to do with musical form, is the use of short vocal phrases, repeated and varied, against a continuous rhythmic background. The choral singing in this example gives further evidence of the predominance worldwide of the pentatonic scale discussed earlier in relation to the Anglo-Celtic-American ballad (see p. 7).

The Yoruba form an important cultural group on the Guinea Coast of West Africa, concentrated primarily in southwestern Nigeria. Their drumming styles, and even versions of the drums themselves, can be found in Cuba and Trinidad, and are a significant influence in the Latin/Caribbean music of New York City (see pp. 57–59).

© National Commission for Museums and Monuments, Ita Yemoo, Ife, Nigeria. Heini Schneebeli/Bridgeman Art Library

This bust of a Yoruba Queen, created some 800 years ago in what is now Nigeria, reflects the dignity and extraordinarily rich culture that centuries of slavery were unable to eradicate. We hear "Music in Praise of a Yoruba Chief" on CD 1, track 6.

RELIGIOUS FOLK MUSIC: THE SPIRITUAL

Listening Cue "Sheep, Sheep, Don't You Know the Road" (excerpt), the Sea Island Singers led by Bessie Jones

> Recorded by Alan Lomax on St. Simons Island, Georgia, 1961 (1:02)
> Listen For ▪ steady pulse in foot taps ▪ offbeat clapping ▪ call-and-response singing

Visit http://www.music.wadsworth.com_3/Kingman for a full listening guide and other resources.

There is no better introduction to the spiritual than "Sheep, Sheep, Don't You Know the Road" (CD 1/7). It illustrates musical traits common to the music of both West Africa and African America. The sense of a steady pulse governing the music is evident, and even though there are no percussion instruments, the basic "drumbeat" is present in the foot tapping that is steadily followed by a clap of the hands. This clapping of the hands on what is called the offbeat (or backbeat) is typical of African American music, especially very rhythmic vocal music. Indeed, offbeat clapping is frequently one way in which an audience can participate in a performance.

Another way is through call-and-response singing—a common trait of both African and African American music. In call-and-response we typically hear a lead vocalist "call out" a statement, or even a question, that is followed by a "response" from a group of participating singers. In this example (the first recording of this spiritual), leader Bessie Jones sings the call "Sheep, sheep, don't you know the road?"; the rest of the group (here, the Sea Island Singers) sings the response "Yes, Lord, I know the road." The religious overtones obviously derive from the biblical imagery of Christ the Good Shepherd watching over His flock (John 10:11).

The term *spiritual* is derived from a shortening of the New Testament phrase "spiritual songs." It has been applied to two related bodies of folk music that began to flourish notably in the nineteenth century—one black and the other white, with a great deal of interchange between them. (An example of a white spiritual, the folk hymn "Wondrous Love," is found on p. 160, CD 2/20.)

The African American spiritual came into being following the conversion of significant numbers of slaves to Christianity. The religious singing of blacks in colonial times is reported in a few contemporary observations. This one, from the mid-1700s, is by Rev. Samuel Davies:

> I can hardly express the pleasure it affords me to turn to that part of the Gallery where they sit, and see so many of them with their Psalm or Hymn Books, turning to the part then sung, and assisting their fellows who are beginners, to find the place; and then all breaking out in a torrent of sacred harmony, enough to bear away the whole congregation to heaven.

Rev. Davies describes the singing of blacks in the context of a formal religious service. But the spiritual itself was born under far less formal circumstances. The real spiritual represents not so much an adaptation of the Methodist and Baptist hymns and formal services as it does a thoroughly African response to them.

Many accounts confirm that the "sperichils" were not at first a part of the formal services but belonged to the *shout* that took place after these services, when the benches were pushed back to the wall and the worshipers stood in the middle of the floor. The shouters were really in a sense dancers, forming a ring in which they circled in a kind of shuffling movement to the sound of singing and hand clapping. The shout could last well into the night, and, not surprisingly, was viewed with disapproval by pious whites, and even by the African Methodist Episcopal Church itself. The shout "Run, Old Jeremiah" (see Additional Listening) is a vivid example of the type of ring-dance music that some tried to curb with the ominous appellation "Voodoo Dance."

The Discovery, Publication, and Adaptation of the Spirituals

The Civil War and its aftermath brought whites from the North, many of them abolitionists, into direct contact with black people on an unprecedented scale. Even before the war's end, events such as the formation of black regiments fighting for the Union cause began the process of acquainting Northerners with an impressive repertory of "slave songs." Written accounts of the singing appeared in northern periodicals, some with the texts of spirituals. In 1867 the first collection of African American spirituals was published in book form, *Slave Songs of the United States* (Allen, Ware, and Garrison). This justly famous collection includes a number of spirituals well known today, including "Roll, Jordan, Roll" and "Nobody Knows the Trouble I've Had."

After the Civil War a number of schools and colleges were established in the South, under the auspices of the Freedmen's Bureau and various church and missionary groups, to begin the great task of educating the newly freed slaves. The Fisk Jubilee Singers, from Fisk University, had an important role in promoting the spiritual, first in their Nashville community, then throughout the northern states, and finally in Europe. Their

Paul Robeson was an All-American football player and Phi Beta Kappa at Rutgers University, a Columbia Law School graduate, a brilliant actor on the Shakespearean and popular stage, and a concert singer. He was also the son of a slave. Seen here singing at a political rally, Robeson's outspoken defense of equal rights for African Americans placed him at constant odds with his government. When the State Department revoked Robeson's passport, it effectively ended his career, and despite his enormous talents, his legacy all but disappeared from popular history. On CD 1, track 8, note that Robeson changes the traditional last line of "Jacob's Ladder" from "We're soldiers of the cross" to "We're soldiers in this fight."

moving story, with its trials and triumphs, inspired other colleges and choral groups (Southern, *Music* 225–28).

Solo singers also performed spirituals. Although white soloists began including them in their programs in the 1920s, it was great black artists such as Roland Hayes, Paul Robeson, and Marian Anderson who sang them with the greatest effectiveness and meaning, and established their stature in the repertoire of solo song.

Paul Robeson (1898–1976) was a noted actor as well as a singer. He played in Eugene O'Neill's *The Emperor Jones* in 1925, the same year he began giving concerts as a bass-baritone. He was famous as an actor for his playing of Shakespeare's *Othello*, and as a singer for his singing of "Ol' Man River" in Jerome Kern's *Show Boat* (see p. 214). But he was of greatest renown for his performances of black spirituals.

Listening Cue "Jacob's Ladder" Paul Robeson, vocal; Alan Booth, piano

Recorded live at Carnegie Hall, May 9, 1958 (3:00)
Listen For ▪ piano accompaniment ▪ deep operatic voice ▪ invitation to join in

Visit http://www.music.wadsworth.com_3/Kingman for a full listening guide and other resources.

The type of spiritual that Robeson popularized might be termed the "concert spiritual." It was written down, harmonized, arranged, and provided with a piano accompaniment for public consumption on the concert stage. Thus, it was quite distinct from the more intimate African American religious folk song that was practiced, and indeed continues to exist down to our own time, in the churches and camp meetings of the South. "Jacob's Ladder," in the version performed here by Robeson, is a good example of the concert spiritual (CD 1/8). Notice that he tips his hat to the spiritual's more intimate, communal origins by inviting others to join him about halfway through the song.

1. We are climbing Jacob's ladder
   We are climbing Jacob's ladder
   We are climbing Jacob's ladder
   We're soldiers in this fight.

2. Ev'ry rung goes higher and higher
   Ev'ry rung goes higher and higher
   Ev'ry rung goes higher and higher
   We're soldiers in this fight.

3. Rise and shine and give God the glory
   Rise and shine and give God the glory
   Rise and shine and give God the glory
   We're soldiers in this fight.

The Words of the Spiritual

Spirituals tend to draw deeply from biblical narrative and symbol. Just as "Sheep, Sheep, Don't You Know the Road" drew on the moving narrative of the Good Shepherd in the Gospel according to John (10:11), so too, "Jacob's Ladder" referenced the powerful symbol of a portal to heaven described in the Book of Genesis (28:10–11). These are but two examples drawn from a repertory of spirituals so immense in number and range that they constitute *in toto* an epic folk recreation of virtually the entire Bible. The texts typically enliven their biblical subjects with pictorial imagery that is vivid and engaging:

> Dark clouds a-risin'!
> Thunder-bolts a bustin'!
> Master Jesus comes a-ridin' by
> With a rainbow on his shoulder.

So who wrote these texts? The general assumption that the authors were anonymous is largely, but not entirely, correct. Indeed, the existence of individual African American "bards" in the late nineteenth century has been documented. James Weldon Johnson, for example, describes an enterprising fellow named "Singing" Johnson who went from church to church making up, singing, and teaching new songs to the congregation (Johnson and Johnson, Preface).

It was once commonly believed that spirituals represented solely an otherworldly view—that they expressed the consolation that African Americans found in religion for their intolerable worldly conditions, and that the promises and hopes referred only to life in the hereafter. Evidence for a contrasting view, however—a view of the spiritual's concrete relationship to contemporary conditions—began to be put forward in the nineteenth century by abolitionist writers and others.

In this view spirituals express in biblical terms not only the wretchedness of slavery but also hopes and plans for an escape from its bondage in this life. This could come about either through northern intervention (thus "de Lord" could stand for a collective embodiment of "de Yankees") or through escape to the North ("heab'n") or to Canada ("Canaan"). The figure of Moses was quite naturally a very central one. The Israelites were the slaves, longing for deliverance; Pharaoh represented the slaveowners; Egypt was the South and slavery. With this understanding, we can appreciate the deeper level of meaning encoded in such famous spirituals as "Go Down, Moses."

> When Israel was in Egypt's land,
> Let my people go.
> Oppressed so hard they could not stand,
> Let my people go.
> Go down, Moses,
> 'Way down in Egypt's land;
> Tell ole Pharaoh,
> Let my people go.

SECULAR FOLK MUSIC

Cries, Calls, and Hollers

Cries, calls, and *hollers* are terms applied to highly personal and intense musical expressions that gave vent to feelings, relieved loneliness, or simply communicated information. Early observers described these occasionally. Frederick Law Olmsted, reporting on a journey through the South in 1853, tells of being awakened in his railroad car in the middle of the night by a group of black workmen enjoying a short break around a fire.

> Suddenly one raised such a sound as I had never heard before, a long, loud, musical shout, rising, and falling, and breaking into falsetto, his voice ringing through the woods in the clear, frosty night air, like a bugle call. As he finished, the melody was caught up by another, then by several in chorus. (Courlander 81–82)

Listening Cue "Quittin' Time Song" Samuel Brooks, vocal

CD 1

9

Recorded in Edwards, Mississippi, 1939 (0:34)
Listen For ▪ intense expression ▪ narrow vocal range ▪ melisma

Visit http://www.music.wadsworth.com_3/Kingman for a full listening guide and other resources.

"Quittin' Time Song" (CD 1/9) is among a few examples that have actually been recorded. It is a cornfield holler, also known as an *arwhoolie* (are-hoo'-lee). The vocal register here is generally high for the male voice. A particular emphasis is placed on the cry "Oh," which is usually sung as the highest note of a phrase and sometimes embellished with a florid, ornate melody called a *melisma* before the rest of the lyrics continue to unfold toward a lower pitch. The vocal range is narrow, but even with just a few notes the performance is quite intense in its mode of expression.

> Oh, the sun's goin' down and I won't be here long
> Oh, the sun's goin' down and I won't be here long
> Oh, then I be goin' home
> Oh, I can't let this dark cloud catch me here
> Oh, I can't stay here long
> Oh, I be at home.

In many ways, the sounds, subjects, and intense individual modes of expression in cries, calls, and hollers bring to mind the more familiar repertory of the blues (see Chapter 8). Is there a connection? Some think so, and consider hollers like "Quittin' Time Song" important forerunners.

Lomax Collection of Folk Music;/© CORBIS

Here we see a South Carolina prison work gang chopping wood in 1934. The angle at which each man wields his ax suggests coordination with the rhythmic accompaniment of a work song such as we hear on CD 1, track 10. Unseen around each prisoner's ankle is a twenty-pound shackle and chain that made it impossible to walk faster than a shuffle. Not until 1962 did South Carolina's Board of Corrections remove chains and striped uniforms and establish inmate education programs.

Work Songs and Ballads

The use of singing to coordinate and lighten physical work, acting as both a coordinator of effort and a lifter of spirits, is practically universal among those who must engage in hard communal labor, on land or at sea. Work songs were prevalent among black laborers during slavery. After the Civil War, work songs were needed wherever gang labor was used, especially in the work of building railroads. There had to be a leader, of course; this called for a special skill involving not only a firsthand knowledge of the work and its pacing as well as a gift for timing, but also the ability to infuse into the work the balm of rhythm and song. A few of the recordings we possess of genuine work songs communicate this sense of rhythm and spirit. With increased mechanization, the work song almost disappeared. The only conditions under which it survived were those that closely duplicated conditions under slavery—that is, in the prisons and on the work farms, where, indeed, practically all the field recordings of work songs were made.

Listening Cue "John Henry" Arthur Bell, vocal

CD 1
10

Recorded by John A. and Ruby T. Lomax at Cumins State Farm, Gould, Arkansas, 1939 (2:54)
Listen For ▪ strophic form ▪ short meter ▪ coordinated hammer strike

Visit http://www.music.wadsworth.com_3/Kingman for a full listening guide and other resources.

The ballad and the work song are dissimilar in function. However, the leader's need to prolong the work song to fit the task at hand often led to the adoption of the ballad, or storytelling, method, with its possibilities for improvisation and its indefinite proliferation of stanzas. "John Henry" (CD 1/10) is the best known of all African American ballads. It is the ballad of a folk hero that has been identified with an actual event: the construction of the Big Bend Tunnel on the Chesapeake & Ohio Railroad near Hilton, West Virginia, in 1870–1872. At a mile and a quarter in length, it was the largest tunnel ever built up to that time. A steel drill had to be hand-driven to make a deep hole in the solid rock for a blasting charge. The construction of the Big Bend Tunnel may have been the occasion for the introduction of a newly invented steam drill to do this work, and a contest between hand driving and steam driving may well have occurred—a contest that the hero won at the cost of his life.

This particular version of "John Henry" is sung as a combination of ballad and work song. It comes from farther west, in Arkansas, and changes the job from that of driving a blasting-hole in a tunnel to lining track. Notice how the worker's hammer strike is carefully coordinated with the steady pulse governing the music.

1. Well, every Monday mornin',
   When the bluebirds begin to
   sing,
   You can hear those hammers a mile
   or more,
   You can hear John Henry's hammer
   ring, O Lordy!
   Hear John Henry's hammer ring.

2. John Henry told his old lady,
   "Will you fix my supper
   soon?
   Got ninety miles o' track I've
   got to line,
   Got to line it by the light of the
   moon, O Lordy!
   Line it by the light o' the moon."

The Granger Collection, New York

The appeal of an individual whose work surpasses that of a machine is universal. John Henry was a former slave hired by the railroads to pound dynamite holes into mountains. In the folk tale, John Henry, working with a hammer and a steel stake, challenges the new mechanical steam drill to a speed contest. He wins, but dies from his heroic effort. We hear two versions of his story: the African American ballad on CD 1, track 10, and the bluegrass version on CD 2, track 9.

3. John Henry had a little baby,
   He could hold him out in his hand;
   Well, the last word I heard that po' child say,
   "My daddy is a steel-drivin' man, O Lordy!
   Daddy is a steel-drivin' man."

4. John Henry told his old captain,
   Said, "A man ain't nothin' but a man;

Before I let your steel gang down
   I will die with the hammer in my hand, O Lordy!
   Die with the hammer in my hand."

5. John Henry told his captain,
   "Next time you go to town
   Uh-jes' bring me back a ten-pound maul
   For to beat your steel-drivin' down, O Lordy!
   Beat your steel-drivin' down."

6. John Henry had a old lady,
   And her name was Polly Ann.
   John Henry took sick and he had to
   go to bed;
   Pauline drove steel like a man,
   O Lordy!
   She drove steel like a man.

7. John Henry had a old lady,
   And the dress she wo' was red.
   Well, she started up the track and
   she never looked back,
   "Goin' where my man fell dead,
   O Lordy!
   Where my man fell dead."

8. Well, they taken John Henry to
   Washington,

   And they buried him in the
   sand.
   There is peoples from the East,
   there's peoples from the West
   Come to see such a steel-drivin'
   man, O Lordy!
   See such a steel-drivin' man.

9. Well, some said-uh he's from
   England,
   And some say he's from Spain;
   But-uh I say he's nothin' but a
   Lou's'ana man,
   Just a leader of the steel-drivin'
   gang, O Lordy!
   Leader of the steel-drivin' gang.

The meter in this rendition of "John Henry" invites comparison with the Anglo-Celtic-American ballads in Chapter 1. In "Barbara Allen" we saw how the stressed syllables per line in a four-line stanza yielded the 4+3+4+3 pattern typical of ballad meter (see p. 6). In "John Henry," however, we find a slightly different underlying pattern of 3+3+4+3 stressed syllables per line. This grouping corresponds to what is called "short meter." The fifth line of each stanza is an extension by repetition as in "Gypsy Davy" (CD 1/2, pp. 9–10).

     /   /   /
Well, **ev**ery **Mon**day **mor**nin',
          /   /   /
When the **blue**birds be**gin** to **sing**,
        /   /   /   /
You can **hear** those **ham**mers a **mile** or **more**,
      /   /   / [extension]
You can **hear** John **Hen**ry's hammer **ring**, O Lordy!
[extension]
Hear John Henry's hammer ring.

Regarding its more general characteristics, commentators on the African American ballad, such as Malcolm Laws (1964), have pointed out the fecundity of invention that manifests itself in improvisation, and also (in contrast to white balladry) the greater emphasis on character and situation, rather than events as such. The propensity for improvisation may account for the inclusion of apparently incoherent additions such as can be noted in the version of "John Henry" above, especially in the last two stanzas. And nowhere is the greater empathy with character and situation more evident than in the number and variety of

African American ballads that were written on the sinking of the *Titanic* in 1912. The text to "The *Titanic*," a song from rural Georgia, is a representative example.

Chorus:
God moves on the water,
April the 14th day,
God moves on the water,
Everybody had to run and pray.

Titanic left Southampton
With all their sport and game,
But when they struck that iceberg,
I know their mind was changed.
(*Chorus*)

Their mothers told their
daughters,
On a pleasure trip they may go,
But when they struck that iceberg,
They haven't been seen anymore.
(*Chorus*)

One man, John Jacob Astor,
A man with pluck and brains,
While this great ship was sinkin',
All the women he tried to save.
(*Chorus*)

He was warned by a freight boat,
Captain Smith would not take heed,
But instead of givin' a warnin'
He ran with greater speed.
(*Chorus*)

He kissed his wife a last time
When the boiler did explode,
He helped her in the lifeboat,
Sayin', "I won't see you anymo'!"
(*Chorus*)

The story of the shipwreck
Is almost too sad to tell,
One thousand and six hundred
Went down forever to dwell.
(*Chorus*)

Well the 14th day April,
It was in nineteen hundred and
twelve,
The ship had a wreck by the iceberg,
It went down forever to dwell.
(*Chorus*)

This observation on the emphasis of character and situation over event serves as a fitting conclusion here, for it underscores the general tendency of the African American folk tradition to evoke, by means of an intensely personal and emotional kind of expression, a unique and characteristic degree of empathy with the subject of song, and indeed with the singers themselves. This survey of the African American tradition has been brief, but it is only a beginning. In subsequent chapters, we will examine further instances of the profound influence that African Americans have had on music culture in the United States, particularly in blues, jazz, rock, and classical music.

PROJECTS

1. Write a short paper on the South Carolina and Georgia Sea Islands as repositories of black folklore, speech, and song. Include whatever you can find out about conditions there today.
2. Review some of the significant studies that have been made of African survivals in American black music. Some of these are by Melville Herskovits,

Alan Merriam, Harold Courlander, Richard Waterman, and Paul Oliver (*Savannah Syncopators*).

3. Write a short paper on textual themes in African American spirituals, including the double meanings they contain. (John Lovell's article in Katz, *The Social Implications of Early Negro Music in the United States,* might serve as a point of departure.)

4. Compare a traditional version of a spiritual (as found in an early collection such as Allen et al., *Slave Songs of the United States*) with a concert version as sung by a recitalist or a trained concert choir. Discuss the advantages and disadvantages of such concert arrangements.

ADDITIONAL LISTENING

"Run, Old Jeremiah." *Afro-American Spirituals, Work Songs, and Ballads.* Rounder CD 1510.s

"The *Titanic,*" *Georgia Sea Island Songs.* New World 80278.

3 THE AMERICAN INDIAN TRADITION

At the time of the first European exploration and colonization, some 3 million people already lived in North America, between 1 and 2 million of them north of what is now Mexico. The population consisted of a thousand different tribal units, each generally having its own language within about sixty distinct language families. The cultural complexity resulting from the 25,000-year history of the aborigines in North America is largely accounted for by the various waves of migration from Asia that were widely separated in time. As a result, the language families are not necessarily identified or coincident with the culture areas. The Navajo and the Apache of the desert Southwest, for example, have a language related to that of the tribes of the far north of Canada and Alaska.

Interestingly enough, the music of the North American Indians has many characteristics shared by all, and this has given some validity to the concept of a generic, or pan-Indian, music. But there are significant distinctions as well—characteristics that can be identified more or less successfully with eight roughly defined culture areas: Southeast and Northeast (both east of the Mississippi), Plains, Southwest (including most of California), Great Basin, Northwest Coast (from northern coastal California up to and including coastal Alaska), Plateau (north of the Great Basin, between the Northwest Coast area and the Rocky Mountains), and North (Arctic and Sub-Arctic, including the Athapaskan and Inuit, or Eskimo, peoples). (See Nettl, *North American;* Nettl, "Indians.")

One chapter cannot possibly do justice to all of these, but we can get a sense of the various roles music played (and continues to play) in Indian life, as well as the features that might subtly distinguish the music of one culture from that of another. As we study Indian music, it is important to keep in mind that we are dealing with the music of indigenous societies that once were aboriginal cultures but are no longer so. In the 300-odd years during which Europeans completed their westward advance across the continent, aboriginal Indian life was thoroughly disrupted. Indigenous societies were dispossessed and their populations drastically reduced by disease and warfare; some tribal groups were destroyed, and most others were relocated or confined on reservations, where they were first treated as a conquered, subject population. As a consequence, large elements of aboriginal cultural ways, including some musical elements, disappeared—destroyed, discarded, lost, or altered beyond modern recognition. One of the most remarkable things about American Indian musical culture is that a significant remnant of it has indeed survived and, in some instances, entered a new phase of cultivation.

MUSIC IN INDIAN LIFE

Among the many ways one might appreciate a work of art, two especially come to mind here. The first is to view it as interesting in and of itself. The second is to understand it contextually as part of the society that brought it forth, and thus as having essential meaning only in that context. These views are never absolutely separate; we can experience every work of art with some mixture of the two. But the closer we get to art in the aboriginal state, the more necessary it becomes to take into account the second view. Though never abandoning the study and apprehension of a work of art intrinsically, we must give a much greater proportion of our effort to understanding what the lives of those who made the art were like, and what place and meaning it had for them. This is in no case more imperative than with the music of the Indian people.

Whatever one's immediate reaction to Indian music, it must be kept in mind that this music was generally not created to be experienced in the essentially passive way we tend to listen to music in the concert hall or on recordings today. Rather, as Willard Rhodes has noted, it "is so inextricably bound up in a larger complex, ceremonial or social, that it is practically non-existent out of its functional context" (132). The following description of a Hopi ceremony that included music (as most Indian ceremonies do) helps illustrate the point:

> With a Hopi acquaintance I drove one July morning to Bakabi, to see the final ritual of the Niman. When I arrived in the village, I found that most of the Hopis had ascended to the line of roof tops, from which they could watch the ceremony in the plaza below. . . . The sky was cloudless and intensely blue. Sunshine flooded everything, illuminating the white walls of the houses along the plaza's farther side. . . . Soon a file of fifteen or twenty men came slowly into the plaza. . . . Each man's body, bare above the waist, was painted brown and marked with white symbols. Behind his right knee was fastened a rattle, made of a turtle shell. With each step that he took, the rattle gave out a hollow, muffled sound. In his right hand he carried a gourd rattle. . . . But the striking feature was the mask that each man wore. This covered his head completely and came down to his shoulders. The front was white and was inscribed with block-like figures, which suggested eyes, nose, and mouth. . . . Immediately, the ceremony began. With measured, rhythmic step the long single file moved slowly forward, in time with a subdued chant. . . . With every step the turtle-shell rattle fastened behind the right knee contributed its hollow accent, sometimes suddenly magnified when all the dancers in unison struck the right foot sharply against the ground. Now and then the gourd rattles were shaken for two or three seconds, giving a curious accompaniment of elevated sound in contrast to

© CORBIS

The Hopi celebrate in dance the renewal of their life pattern. Here, in a 1903 pho-
tograph taken in Shungopavi, Arizona, sacred *katsinam* perform part of their
visitation ceremony in which they bring blessings and messages from the Creator
and return with Hopi prayers for a good life, bountiful harvests, and rain. The
feathers on the dancers' headdresses represent clouds. Because the 10–13 inches
of annual rain or snow that fall in Arizona's high mesa country barely support
crops, virtually everything in the Hopi culture relates to rain. We hear an
agricultural song, the "Butterfly Dance," on CD 1, track 13.

the low, chanting voices. . . . When it was all over, I came away with the feeling that I had witnessed an ancient rite that was rich in symbolism and impressive in its significance. (O'Kane 186–91)

Even if a recording of this music had been made, how much could it convey to us,
abstracted from its context?

THE EXISTENTIAL QUALITY OF SONGS

Music in Indian life has a certain existential quality to it that is largely unfamiliar
in societies more accustomed to experiencing music as a way of enhancing various forms of recreation. In this sense, songs might be considered as something

along the lines of a special tool or a formula that can be owned, passed along, even stolen. Indeed, what matters most about a song is not so much its intrinsic beauty (or lack thereof) but rather its efficacy. As Frances Densmore, one of the pioneering authorities on Indian music, has noted, "The radical difference between the musical custom of the Indian and our own race is that, primarily, the Indians used song as a means of accomplishing definite results" (63). Thus, there are songs that heal, songs that win wars, songs that gain affection, and so forth. Interestingly enough, these tools and formulas can be corrupted too. In a recent recording of songs by the Yurok and Tolowa tribes of northern California, translations of the words could not be made because "to do so would have put the songs' luck in jeopardy" (Heth).

The existential quality of Indian songs is further illustrated by the fact that in many cases they are treated as strictly personal possessions, which may be legitimately transmitted to others only by being sold or given away. One elder, after being persuaded to record a noted war song, said that he would not live long now that he had given away his most valuable possession. This concept extended to the visual medium as well. In the nineteenth century, after an eastern artist had been among the Plains Indians sketching the buffalo, an older Indian complained to a white friend that there were no longer so many buffalo on their range—a white man had put a great number of them in a book and taken them away with him. These examples demonstrate a sense of tangible reality, of magical power— indeed, of presence—in all manifestations of what we would abstractly term *music* or *art*.

With this existential concept in mind, we can better understand not only the value of music in Indian life, but also the customs and rituals used to perform, preserve, and create it. For example, songs of great power, sung chiefly by medicine men or women, would be very carefully passed on in oral tradition. (Indeed, extreme accuracy is crucial to the efficacy of the songs of the Navajo, among others.) New songs were introduced in extraordinary, even supernatural ways. These typically belonged to individuals who had acquired them in the course of "vision quests"—self-imposed ordeals of courage and self-denial known among virtually all tribes. Lonely fasts, often carried out in locations and conditions of extreme discomfort and danger, would last as long as four days. If successful, a vision quest resulted in tangible communication with a spirit dwelling in some animal or, perhaps, in a natural phenomenon. And with that vision would often come the imparting of a new song. Understandably, a clear distinction was made in most tribes between these songs, which had inherent power, and songs that were either borrowed from other tribes or simply made up—consciously composed—for recreation. In recent years, under the pressures of acculturation, many of the older songs have decreased in importance in the repertory of most tribes. Some that are known to have existed have been lost altogether.

TYPES OF SONGS ACCORDING TO PURPOSE

The richness and variety of American Indian cultures make it impractical here to illustrate the form and function of more than just a few songs according to their purposes. Therefore, this very brief survey aims, first, to demonstrate the diverse

We hear a Menominee song for the sick on CD 1, track 11. Here an Indian medicine man, or shaman, prepares a pot of medicine to the accompaniment of a sacred rattle and healing song. Notice the tipi construction. Generally, twelve to seventeen pine poles supported a tipi and approximately thirteen hides covered it. Because the summer buffalo was large, did not have the heavy fat layers of autumn, and its hair could be easily removed, June was the best time to hunt buffalo for their hides. A skin tipi might last two to three years, depending on the amount of traveling and harsh weather it bore.

roles that songs can play and, second, to suggest what one might listen for to distinguish the musical style of one culture from that of another. In addition to the examples highlighted here, one can gain a deeper appreciation of this vast repertory (which includes songs for success in war and hunting, songs to accompany work, and even songs for gambling) by fruitfully exploring various recordings that are now commercially available (see Additional Listening).

Songs to Heal the Sick

"Pigeon's Dream Song" (CD 1/11) forms part of a very important song class in Indian culture—songs to heal the sick. This example is from the Menominee, an Algonquian tribe that, at the time this song was collected in the late 1920s, was still settled along the Menominee River in Wisconsin. (They had inhabited this area for at least three centuries.) It is sung here by tribe member Louis Pigeon. A free translation of the words is "Your tribe will come to you to be cured of sickness."

Listening Cue "Pigeon's Dream Song" Louis Pigeon, vocal; Menominee, Northern Plains

Recorded by Frances Densmore in the late 1920s (0:40)
Listen For ▪ tense vocal style ▪ short phrases ▪ descending terraced melody

Visit http://www.music.wadsworth.com_3/Kingman for a full listening guide and other resources.

Frances Densmore recorded "Pigeon's Dream Song" in the field using portable wax cylinder equipment. Of Louis Pigeon she says that "when he was a boy he sometimes fasted for two days at a time, abstaining from both food and drink. At last he secured a dream that gave him power to treat the sick, and said that his own advanced age showed the power of his dream. Two birds [a crow and a raven] gave him songs in this dream."

The repetition of short phrases as heard in this example is a feature of nearly all North American Indian music. However, the song also shows a subtle but distinctive feature of the Plains style in its descending "terraced" melodic line. Notice, in this regard, how Louis Pigeon's voice begins at a relatively high range and then gradually works its way down to the lower, sometimes scarcely audible range before leaping up and starting the process all over again.

Ceremonial Dances

Listening Cue "Cherokee/Creek Stomp Dance" Eastern Woodlands

Recorded in Oklahoma (1:30)
Listen For ▪ relaxed vocal style ▪ call-and-response singing

Visit http://www.music.wadsworth.com_3/Kingman for a full listening guide and other resources.

The "Stomp Dance" (CD 1/12) formed part of a ceremonial event in the Southeast that was not fundamentally different from the Hopi ceremony described earlier. The recording clearly gives us a sense of measured, rhythmic movement accentuated by rattles. But there are distinctive features here as well. The "call-and-response" singing is typical of music of the Southeast. It is similar in principle to the call-and-response heard in the African American spiritual "Sheep, Sheep, Don't You Know the Road" (CD 1/7) but with shorter phrases or shouts. On a more subtle level, notice that the singing style is more relaxed than that of the Plains tribes exemplified in "Pigeon's Dream Song."

Because of the forcible removal of most of the Cherokee to Oklahoma more than a century and a half ago, we find the music native to the Southeastern United States being performed and recorded in the prairies of the southern Midwest. (See "Indian Music and Acculturation" later in this chapter.)

Songs for Success in Agriculture

The Pueblo Indians of the Southwestern deserts, including the Hopi, the Taos, and the Zuni, have the most complex societies found north of Mexico. Hence, their music also tends to be among the most varied and complex. "Butterfly Dance" (CD 1/13) exemplifies an agricultural song. The text traces the life cycle of the corn plant on which the Pueblo are highly dependent. The butterfly dancer is integral to this song because the butterfly is often associated with water and thus represents a life-giving force and, by extension, fertility.

Listening Cue "Butterfly Dance" San Juan Pueblo, New Mexico (1:30)

Listen For ▪ low vocal tone ▪ longer phrases ▪ changing drum patterns

 Visit http://www.music.wadsworth.com_3/Kingman for a full listening guide and other resources.

A typical feature of Pueblo singing is the consistently low and almost growling tone. (Compare this with the terraced descending melody of "Pigeon's Dream Song.") The musical phrases also tend to be longer and more intricate than those in other Indian music. (Compare these with the short call-and-response phrases and shouts in "Stomp Dance"). The complexity of this example is accentuated by the frequently changing drum and rattle patterns.

Love Songs

Love songs in traditional Indian culture were not for the mere expression of sentimental feelings. Rather, they were "lucky" songs, the means to gain success in love through the invocation of magical power. The Indian flute was associated almost exclusively with these courtship songs, but they could also include singing, as we hear in "Sioux Love Song" (CD 1/14).

Listening Cue "Sioux Love Song" John Coloff, flute and vocal; Lakota Plains (1:42)

Listen For ▪ Indian flute ▪ short phrases ▪ descending terraced melody

 Visit http://www.music.wadsworth.com_3/Kingman for a full listening guide and other resources.

This is another example of the musical style associated with the Plains Indians. It serves well to underscore the distinctive features we heard in "Pigeon's Dream Song" (the Plains song that began this survey). The short musical phrases are a clear contrast to the longer melodies of the Pueblo Indians ("Butterfly Dance"). More importantly, we hear the descending terraced melody not only in the voice but in the flute as well! Here again, as in "Pigeon's Dream Song," voice and flute alike begin in a relatively high range and gradually descend in pitch before leaping up and starting the process all over again.

The making and playing of the traditional Indian flute had, until recently, become a thing of the past. Its revival has been marked by the emergence of concertizing and recording flutists, such as R. Carlos Nakai (an Arizonan of Navajo-Ute heritage), who have expanded its use to include new music composed in a variety of styles from popular to classical. A relatively infrequent instance of the latter can be heard in James DeMars' *Two World Concerto* (see Additional Listening).

CHARACTERISTICS OF INDIAN MUSIC

The preceding examples sought to illustrate diversity in purpose and style. But there are also some shared characteristics of Indian music that can be summed up in the following categories.

Singing Though Indian music is predominantly vocal, singing is usually accompanied by a drum or some sort of rattle, or both. The basic unit for any performance is the song, which may last anywhere from less than a minute to several minutes. When the song accompanies dancing, as it very often does, there is a good deal of repetition. Indeed, it is not uncommon to sing through an entire song four times. Singing in unison is typical. That is, everybody tends to sing together and on the same pitch.

Instruments Indian instruments include drums, whistles, flutes, hand-shaken rattles, and ornaments worn by dancers (made of shell, bone, or some kind of metal), which produce a rhythmic kind of rattling during the dance. The drums range in size from small handheld ones to quite large ones resting on the ground, or suspended between posts in the ground, and played by several people at once. They are made in a variety of ways and are even improvised from inverted baskets, washtubs or kettles covered with skin, or wooden boxes. Flutes are usually fashioned from some straight-grained wood or cane, but in the Southwest they can be made of clay. Rattles are nearly universal, are of many types, and are often worn on the ankles while dancing. The use of drums alone, without singing, is virtually unknown.

Words Since the music is nearly all vocal, the question of the words arises. The songs are very often not in the language of speech. Vocables—simple vocal sounds such as "fa-la-la" in the holiday song "Deck the Halls"—are often either interpolated between actual words or replace them altogether. To call these syllables meaningless is not quite correct; they may have private or ritual significance, or they may be sounds whose original meaning has been lost, either through changes in the language or because they were borrowed from other tribes. Whatever their origin, the vocables are not improvised but belong to the given song and are reproduced with complete consistency.

Painting by Robert Lindneux, 1838. The Granger Collection, New York

President Andrew Jackson and his followers coveted the rich lands occupied by the Cherokee (northern Georgia and parts of North Carolina and Tennessee), Chickasaw and Choctaws (Mississippi), Creeks (eastern Alabama), and Seminoles (Florida). When prospectors discovered gold in northern Georgia, the Jacksonians quickly passed the Indian Removal Act of 1830 to push all tribes across the Mississippi. When 17,000 Cherokee refused to leave, General Winfield Scott led 7,000 troops to drive them from their homes. About a quarter of all eastern Cherokees died in what they called *The Trail of Tears*—pictured above.

INDIAN MUSIC AND ACCULTURATION

Acculturation has gone on continuously since the first contacts with Europeans. The French Huguenots were teaching the Florida Indians to sing psalms in the sixteenth century. Spanish Franciscans who traveled to the Rio Grande Valley with the settlers and their military escorts brought religious festivals and music to New Mexico in the seventeenth century. At the Zuni pueblo of Hawikuh, in western New Mexico, Fray Roque de Figueredo in 1630 was teaching not only Gregorian chant and counterpoint but also bassoon, cornet, and organ (portable organs were brought on expeditions by the Franciscans). Indian musicians proved quite adept in assimilating non-Indian tunes. We even have a Chinook version of "Jesus Loves Me" and a Hopi version of "Dixie" (see Additional Listening).

The length of time that the indigenous Americans have been exposed to European culture varies widely from area to area. We know the least about aboriginal Indian music in the eastern United States, where the cultural pressures, and the dispossessions and dispersions, began earliest and were most severe. A single example of a major uprooting happened between 1830 and 1842, when the Choctaw, Creek, Cherokee, Chickasaw, and Seminole tribes were forcibly moved from the southeastern states to an area west of the Mississippi known as the

In January 1889, Wovoka, a Nevada Paiute, saw a vision of apocalypse and renewal: once again, the Plains Indian homeland, free of white violence and greed, would abound with buffalo and antelope. Word of the vision spread quickly among the starving tribes desperate to regain their independence from disease-ridden reservations. Wovoka encouraged believers to meditate, chant, and perform the ecstatic Ghost Dance—so called by whites because of the religion's belief in the resurrection of Indian ancestors. Here we see an Indian pictograph (late 1800s) of the Cheyenne Ghost Dance. We hear a Pawnee Ghost Dance song on CD 1, track 15.

Indian Territory. The Cherokee movingly refer to their journey during this forced displacement as the "Trail of Tears."

After the Civil War the western portion of the Indian Territory became home for many Indians from the northern and central Plains as well. This kind of dislocation brought tribes from greatly separated regions into contact, and this contact marked the beginnings of the pan-Indian movement. The "Indian Territory" was so designated until its admission to the Union as the state of Oklahoma in 1907.

The Ghost Dance and the Peyote Religion

Two singular developments in the West since the encroachment of European civilization grew out of that cataclysm, directly or indirectly. The first of these was the spread of the Ghost Dance, with its accompanying music. Originating in the Great Basin area between the Sierra Nevada and Rocky Mountains, the Ghost Dance cult represented a kind of messianic religious belief in the appearance of a savior and the expulsion of the white man, accompanied by the resurrection of dead Indian leaders and the return of the buffalo and of the old ways. In the 1880s the Ghost Dance spread rapidly, especially among Plains tribes. It was outlawed by the Bureau of Indian Affairs, and its repression by the United States Army culminated in the tragic massacre of Sioux Ghost Dance devotees at Wounded Knee in South Dakota in 1890. As an active cult and ritual, the Ghost Dance died out as rapidly as it had spread. Its songs persisted, however, and were recorded among Plains tribes as late as the 1940s. A Pawnee "Ghost Dance Song" (CD 1/15) is representative.

Listening Cue *"Ghost Dance Song"* Pawnee Plains (1:07)

CD 1

15

Listen For ▪ short paired phrases ▪ descending melodic line ▪ narrow vocal range

Visit http://www.music.wadsworth.com_3/Kingman for a full listening guide and other resources.

The Ghost Dance was a pan-Indian cultural phenomenon; Ghost Dance songs of various tribes show similar characteristics, apparently of Great Basin origin, that are often markedly different from those of their own indigenous tribal music. Songs of the Great Basin tribes tended to be narrow in vocal range, and to consist of short paired phrases (AA BB CC and so on) chanted in a descending melodic line. These features are readily heard in this example sung by the Pawnee, a Plains tribe.

A second, and not unrelated, development has been the spread of the peyote religion (the Native American Church), the rites of which include the use of the hallucinogenic buttons of the peyote cactus. Originating apparently in pre-Columbian Mexico, it had spread northward into the Rio Grande and Gila River basins by the eighteenth century, where it was known among the Apache. The religion reached the Plains about 1870. Taking on there a somewhat different form, it became a group or community rite, with a well-defined ceremonial that incorporated some elements of Christian theology and symbolism. The spread of the peyote religion has been rather carefully documented, and is still going on; it reached the Navajo in the 1930s, and the Indians of Canada and Florida in the mid-twentieth century. Singing is an integral part of the meetings at which the peyote buttons are consumed, and although any songs, including Christian hymns, may be used, special peyote songs have evolved. These are similar in their musical form to the Ghost Dance.

The relation of the peyote religion to the vanished Ghost Dance, and to the severe upheaval to which the American Indians and their aboriginal culture generally have been subjected in the modern world, is summed up by David McAllester:

The wide spread of the Ghost Dance must have contributed to the receptivity of the Indians to peyote. After the brief currency of the former the

Indians were left with little sense of spiritual direction, although the conditions of radical change and insecurity that fostered the Ghost Dance were intensified after its collapse. . . . In place of resistance a philosophy of peaceful conciliation and escape rose. . . . The vision, all-important on the Plains, was made easily available by the use of the cactus. (85)

Further Instances of Acculturation

Listening Cue "**Rabbit Dance**" the Los Angeles Northern Singers (0:55)

CD 1
16

Listen For ▪ tense vocal quality ▪ descending terraced melody ▪ English lyrics

Visit http://www.music.wadsworth.com_3/Kingman for a full listening guide and other resources.

Acculturation has brought many significant changes to American Indian life. "Rabbit Dance" (CD 1/16) offers a glimpse of its effects on music, language, and culture. This song is a social dance in which men and women are allowed to dance together. After the women choose their partners, couples join hands and dance in a clockwise circle around a drum. Social dancing, with its own music, was originally relatively unimportant in traditional Indian life, but gradually became more prevalent. The singing style in this example is clearly that of the Plains, with its high, tense, pulsating vocal quality and the phrases that are shaped in gradually descending lines. But it was recorded in California during the mid-1970s by The Los Angeles Northern Singers—testimony to the extensive relocation of Indians in recent years to urban centers such as Denver and Los Angeles. The use of English in one section is possibly satirical, but nonetheless a clear result of acculturation.

> Hey, sweetheart, I always think of you.
> I wonder if you are alone tonight.
> I wonder if you are thinking of me.

The greatest degree of integration of Indian and non-Indian elements in music and dance has taken place in the Southwest, especially in New Mexico, where Hispanic and Indian culture, language, and religion exist side by side, sometimes interpenetrating but always distinct. Hispanic influence is evident in the matachines of New Mexico—pageants of dance and drama derived from old Spanish fiestas that were possibly introduced to the Pueblo Indians by the Franciscans as early as the seventeenth century.

A more recent absorption, wholly in the secular domain, is represented by the popular dance music among the Papago, Pima, and Yaqui tribes in southern Arizona known as waila, or more commonly as "chicken scratch." Chicken scratch bands use combinations of such instruments as guitar, accordion, saxophone, and trap set to play waltzes, two-steps, and polkas that show resemblances to Mexican mariachi music, Tex-Mex norteña music, German band music, and even Louisiana zydeco.

The State of Indian Music Today

American Indian music today might be described best as a renovated art—that is, an art renewed in a way that consciously preserves tradition while adapting it in a manner that allows it to survive, and even thrive, in the conditions under which Indians live in the modern world. A major shift in this regard is notable in the perceived function of music. Although its religious function has by no means disappeared, it now coexists with both a recreational and an entertainment function. There exist sizable communities of Indians not only in virtually every small city in the West but also in and around large urban areas, particularly Chicago, Denver, Los Angeles, and the San Francisco Bay area, especially Oakland. These urban Indian communities regularly enjoy large social gatherings, at which Indian songs and dances are performed—in Los Angeles, for example, by such groups as The Los Angeles Northern Singers, made up of members of the Sioux, Arikara, Hidatsa, and Northern Arapaho tribes. At these gatherings, not only are the tribal songs and dances found to be flourishing, but, along with the new emphasis on the social function of the music, there are preserved unmistakable traces of the older attitude toward music as well. These can be seen, for example, in the custom of "sponsoring" an entertainment in honor of a person or an event (which had its aboriginal counterpart in customs such as the *potlatch*) and in surviving manifestations of the concepts that certain songs are private possessions and that certain songs bring luck. The intertribal powwows held annually on the Plains (especially in Oklahoma) are today great social and cultural events as well.

By and large, in spite of tragedy, acculturation, and even commercialization, the music of American Indians retains its dignity as a focal point for cultural identity and revival.

PROJECTS

1. Talk with some people of Indian descent—at least two, if possible—about the current state of Indian culture from their point of view. Should it be preserved, and if so for what reasons? In what ways should the preservation of traditional ways compromise with and adapt to modern society, and in what ways should it retain its distinctness and integrity?

2. Write an essay discussing what you, or what non-Indians in general, might have to learn from the way Indians traditionally used and regarded music.

3. Do some research into the curriculum of one or more Indian colleges (Navajo Community College, for example); try to determine the extent to which traditional Indian music is being studied and taught there.

ADDITIONAL LISTENING

Music of the American Indian Series from the Library of Congress American Folklife Center, Archive of Folk Culture (AFS). The following recordings are available on audiocassette at http://lcweb.loc.gov/folklife/folkcat.html.

Delaware, Cherokee, Choctaw, Creek, L 37 (Peyote songs).

Great Basin: Paiute, Washo, Ute, Bannock, Shoshone, L 38 (Ghost Dance songs).

Kiowa, L 35 (Ghost Dance and peyote songs).

Navajo, L 41 (Peyote songs).

Northwest (Puget Sound), L 34 (Chinook version of "Jesus Loves Me").

Plains: Comanche, Cheyenne, Kiowa, Caddo, Wichita, Pawnee, L 39 (Ghost Dance songs). *Pueblo, Taos, San Ildefonso, Zuni, Hopi*, L 43 (Hopi version of "Dixie").

Sioux, L 40 (Ghost Dance songs, peyote song).

Songs of the Pawnee and Northern Ute, L 25 (Ghost Dance songs).

Spanish and Mexican Folk Music of New Mexico. Smithsonian Folkways CD 04426. Includes two matachines dances.

Two World Concerto. Perf. R. Carlos Nakai. Cond. James DeMars. Canyon Records CR-7016.

Various releases, New World Records: CDs 80246, 80297, 80301, 80337, 80343, and 80406.

CHAPTER

4

LATINO TRADITIONS

Latinos form the largest and fastest growing single ethnic group in the United States. They are also among the most culturally diverse, representing a complicated overlaying and blending of cultures from four continents—North and Central America, South America, Europe (specifically the Iberian peninsula), and West Africa. We begin our exploration of this complex subject with the impact of Spanish conquest and colonization in the Western Hemisphere.

THE LEGACY OF THE SPANISH CONQUEST

The first persistent European presence in America was that of the Spaniards. In the generation following the voyages of Columbus, Spain, the foremost European power of the time, entered upon a period of phenomenal exploration and conquest. By the mid-sixteenth century the Spanish had begun extensive exploration by land and by sea from Florida to the northern California coast, and by 1565 (at St. Augustine, Florida) the first attempts at colonization in what is the present area of the United States had begun. Although Florida was the first point of contact, Spanish influence in what is now the southeastern United States was not destined to be significant in the long term. In the Southwest, on the other hand, it was decisive. Beginning with the earliest missions and small colonial settlements in the upper Rio Grande Valley of New Mexico as early as 1598, and culminating with the high-water mark of Spanish penetration in the California mission period of the late eighteenth and early nineteenth centuries, the foundation was laid for Hispanic influence, which is still of the greatest importance culturally in that part of the country, and which has been reinforced in all periods by almost continuous migrations from Mexico.

SACRED MUSIC FROM MEXICO

The first musical influences were religious. Spanish sacred music reached the highest point of its development in the prosperous sixteenth century, rivaling in its excellence and in the intensity of its cultivation that of Rome itself. It was Span-

Painting by Carl Nebel. Published in *The War Between the United States and Mexico, Illustrated*, 1851/MPI /Getty Images

The Mexican War grew out of a dispute between Mexico and the United States over the southern border of Texas. When the war began (1846), Mexico controlled much of western North America. But then as now, the United States was the richer country—in the words of a Mexican general, "If we had bullets, you wouldn't be here." Shown here is an image of the last major battle (1847), the storming of Chapultepec Fortress that guarded Mexico City. At the end of the war, Mexico ceded control of Texas, California, Nevada, Utah, and parts of Colorado, Arizona, New Mexico, and Wyoming, to the United States—and Mexican music became part of our cultural heritage.

ish sacred music from that era that traveled with the conquistadores, and music was found to be one of the priests' most powerful tools for converting and teaching the Indians. (A survival of this influence into the twenty-first century is the *matachines* dance-drama among the Indians and Mexicans of West Texas and New Mexico.) Before the end of the sixteenth century, vocal and instrumental music were intensively cultivated in Mexico by both Indians and Spanish, accompanied by the manufacture of musical instruments and the printing of music.

New Mexico

New Mexico is the area of the oldest sustained Hispanic influence in the United States. Spaniards began to settle and cultivate the land there at the end of the sixteenth century, and until recently the Hispanic influence has persisted with little interference, especially in the valleys of the upper Rio Grande and the Pecos River. The opening of the Santa Fe Trail in 1821, and the occupation and subsequent annexation of the area by the United States in 1846–1848, had little effect on life in the remote villages, much of which centered on their churches.

During the seventeenth century Spanish religious music, coming by way of Mexico, was almost certainly performed in the missions of New Mexico. However, during the Pueblo Revolt (1680–1692) nearly all records from the missions were destroyed. As a result, the religious music of New Mexico that we know the most about today is the relatively simple folk-like music cultivated and preserved by a devout people worshiping for generations in relative isolation. Of particular antiquity and interest is the music of La Fraternidad Piadosa de Nuestro Padre Jesús Nazareno (The Pious Brotherhood of Our Father Jesus of Nazareth), more familiarly known as Los Hermanos Penitentes (The Penitent Brotherhood), or simply Los Penitentes.

Listening Cue "Al Pie de Este Santo Altar" Luis Montoya, vocal; Vicente Padilla, pito

Recorded in Santa Fe, New Mexico, 1952 (1:35)
Listen For ▪ pito ▪ ornate, unharmonized melody ▪ free meter

Visit http://www.music.wadsworth.com_3/Kingman for a full listening guide and other resources.

The most characteristic form of music cultivated by the Penitentes was the *alabado,* a religious folk song performed with a highly ornamented, unharmonized melody in free meter (without strictly following the constraints of a prescribed tempo). The alabado, whose currency is not limited to the Brotherhood, has indeed been called the "backbone of congregational singing since the sixteenth century" and is still sung in Hispanic Catholic churches throughout the Southwest (Fernández). The alabados of New Mexico are seemingly unrelated to those of Spain, and the origins of neither the words nor the melodies are known at this time. Most of the alabados sung by the Penitentes are lengthy strophic songs commemorating aspects of the Passion of Christ, such as the Stations of the Cross, which are reenacted in pageant form. They are unaccompanied except by the florid improvised interjections of the *pito* (a homemade flute played only during Holy Week), which are said to represent the lamenting cries of the Virgin Mary. These traits are evident in the alabado "Al Pie de Este Santo Altar" (CD 1/17).

Al pie de este santo altar	At the foot of this holy altar
la Virgen quedó llorando	the Virgin stood weeping
por Jesús, su Hijo divino,	for Jesus, her divine Son,
y en su pasión contemplando.	in contemplation of His Passion.
En su santísimo llanto,	In her most holy sorrow,
clama y dice: "¡Ay, mi Jesús!	she calls out and says: "Ah, my Jesus!
¿Qué haré sola en este mundo?	What am I to do alone in this world?
¿Quién lo baja de la cruz?"	Who will bring Him down from the cross?"

Listening Cue "Los Pastores" from *Las Posadas*, Franquilino Miranda and group

Recorded by John A. and Alan Lomax in Cotukkam, Texas, 1934 (1:42)
Listen For ▪ alternating singing groups ▪ simple harmonization ▪ steady pulse
(triple meter)

Visit http://www.music.wadsworth.com_3/Kingman for a full listening guide and
other resources.

A more widespread form of religious folk song is that associated with the
Christmas play *Los Pastores (The Shepherds),* and its related processional drama,
Las Posadas (The Lodgings). Both are related to the mystery plays, liturgical dramas
prevalent in Europe from the ninth through the sixteenth centuries. Possibly
written by the Franciscans in Mexico, they made their ways by separate routes to
California, New Mexico, and Texas. *Las Posadas* (CD 1/18) combines the features
of procession and folk play to reenact the trials of Mary and Joseph as they unsuccessfully seek shelter for the birth of Jesus in Bethlehem (Luke 2:4–7). Traditionally, over nine nights beginning on December 16, the performers of *Las
Posadas* go from one house to another requesting shelter and are refused entrance
until arriving at a predetermined home that will receive them on December 24.

The text of *Las Posadas* reflects a dialogue that alternates between petition and
refusal from one stanza to the next. The sense of dialogue is effectively realized
by the performers in this recording through the use of two alternating singing
groups, the larger one consistently assuming the roles of Mary and Joseph.

1. [Venimos] a casa
   del Ave María,

   pidiendo posada
   por un solo día.

   [We come] to your house
   as a result of the "Hail Mary" [the
   Annunciation, Luke 1:26–38]
   asking for lodging
   but for one day.

2. Y aquí, en esta casa,
   posada no damos,
   que es mucha familia
   y apenas entramos.

   And here, in this house
   we give no lodging,
   for our family is large
   and we barely fit ourselves.

3. Posada pedimos
   por esta ocasión,
   y a mi esposa amada
   tener un rincón.

   We seek lodging
   for this occasion,
   and for my beloved wife
   to have a small corner of the house.

4. Posada no damos
   por esta ocasión;
   pasen adelante,
   que hay otras mejor.
   [This last line sounds different on
   the recording.]

   We give no lodging
   for this occasion;
   Go on ahead,
   for there are better lodgings
   elsewhere.

5. Hermosos los pobres,   Lovely are the poor,
   no tenemos dinero   we have neither money
   ni prendas valiosas   nor valuable garments
   para el mesonero.   for the innkeeper.

Note the simple harmonization in parallel thirds and sixths in this folk rendition. Furthermore, notice that unlike the freer alabado, *Las Posadas* has the feel of a steady underlying pulse (triple meter) governing the music.

California

An echo of the greatness of Spanish church music belatedly reached California in the late eighteenth and early nineteenth centuries. It is now known that during the brief flourishing of the Franciscan missions in California, from 1769 to their secularization beginning in 1834, there was a rather considerable musical culture and that music was integral to mission life. Both vocal and instrumental music was taught to the Indians, who made up the choirs and small orchestras. The range of music extended from folk-like hymns and alabados to elaborate settings of the Mass for chorus with instrumental accompaniment. Inventories made after their secularization show that at least nine of the missions had collections of instruments; Santa Barbara, possibly the most prosperous, had forty-three instruments in 1834, including a fairly large organ.

Spanish California was no cultural backwater. Indeed, the Franciscan missions and their attendant presidios and secular communities, though remote, were for the most part very prosperous centers—prosperous even compared with towns in Spain and in the United States of the time. They were situated in a naturally fertile land with a mild climate, with abundant livestock and food supplies, and with abundant labor supplied by an essentially captive population. It was only after Mexican independence, and with it the secularization of the missions and the departure of the Franciscan priests, that mission music declined and virtually disappeared. What little was preserved of a musical culture was largely passed down through oral tradition.

SECULAR MUSIC FROM MEXICO

Secular folk music from Latin America has been far more widespread and influential in the culture of the United States than has sacred music. To begin to understand the nature and sources of this music, it is important to realize that the mestizo folk culture of Latin America is everywhere a blend of Spanish, Indian, and African elements, the mix varying from region to region. African influence is strongest in the Caribbean (especially Cuba, Jamaica, and Hispaniola) and in the Caribbean and Brazilian coastal areas of South America, though it is not to be discounted in Mexico itself.

In the secular music from Mexico (as indeed from all of Latin America), dance and song are closely associated. Many kinds of music can be used for either. Dancing was a very important pastime from the earliest times in rural Hispanic communities, and there are numerous accounts of *bailes* or *fandangos* (both refer to dances) in the *salas* (halls) of the towns or villages of New Mexico and California, to the accompaniment of fiddle and guitar. Among these were European dances that had arrived either from Mexico itself or, in California, from Anglo-American sailors. Such dances included *el vals* (the waltz), *la polca* (the polka), *el chotís* (the schottische), and *el cutillo* (the cotillion or square dance). Both the waltz and the quadrille (*las cuadrillas*) owe their presence in Mexico to French influence in the nineteenth century, especially during the French occupation of 1862–1867.

Although genuine regional musics, as enjoyed by the mostly rural people in the highly differentiated parts of Mexico, have existed and continue to exist, they have been overshadowed by a kind of "generic" Mexican music, perpetuated as part of a professionalized "cultural front." In the 1880s, for example, during the regime of Porfirio Díaz, *orquestas típicas,* made up of professional musicians dressed in charro costumes, were formed, and were supported by the government as a means of promoting Mexican culture abroad. (The term *charro* refers to the highly skilled rope artists who performed in rodeos, or charreadas, and who wore the distinctive costumes from which the costumes of the mariachi musicians have been adapted.) Orquestas típicas, led by directors such as Carlos Curtí, toured the United States and Europe before the turn of the twentieth century and played important roles as tourist attractions in the large Mexican cities and as exporters of "typical" Mexican music. With the advent of broadcasting and recording, the production of popular music based on folk styles but performed by professional musicians began in Mexico City, in the same kind of development that produced "country music" from regional folk styles in the United States.

© Jan Butchofsky-Houser/CORBIS

Here we see three members of the Douglas Middle School Mariachi Band (Douglas, Arizona) wearing the *charro* outfits that add an impressive visual component to the *mariachi* tradition. The boys hold the trumpets that lend mariachi music much of its distinctive flavor, and a beaming girl holds her guitar. Mariachi programs are now common in the public schools of the American West and Southwest. Mariachi Cobre, the Grammy-nominated band heard on CD 1, track 19—and a driving force promoting mariachi education—began as the youth group *Los Changuitos Feos* (The Ugly Little Monkeys) in Tucson, Arizona.

The Mariachi

The result of this popularization and consequent standardization has been the emergence of two dominant types of instrumental ensemble, used to accompany either dancing or singing. One is the *mariachi*, which in its current popular form consists of trumpets, violins, a *vihuela* (a smaller five-string guitarlike instrument), a guitar, a *guitarrón* (acoustic bass guitar), and optionally a harp of a particular design from the state of Jalisco in western Mexico.

Even though mariachi's country of origin is Mexico, it has become a thoroughly naturalized music of the United States. It is performed, studied, and taught not only in the Southwest, where its cultivation is extensive, but throughout the country and has become something of a convenient symbol for "Mexicanness." Professional mariachis in the United States are highly skilled and versatile show bands, with as many as fourteen musicians who both sing and play. Although they have broadened both their repertory and their musical styles to reach a larger musical public, they have never abandoned their musical roots, to which they consistently pay homage. For example, Mariachi Cobre of Tucson, Arizona, a professional band that has been performing for years at Epcot Center in Disney World, Florida, recently recorded "Las Abajeñas" ("The Lowland Women"), a good example of traditional music from western Mexico, and one of the first examples of mariachi music ever recorded. (The first recording of "Las Abajeñas" was made in 1908 by a group called Cuarteto Coculense.)

Listening Cue **"Las Abajeñas"** ("The Lowland Women") Mariachi Cobre

Traditional arrangement by Vargas-Fuentes (2:21)
Listen For ▪ alternation between triple and duple meters ▪ gritos ▪ stock ending

Visit http://www.music.wadsworth.com_3/Kingman for a full listening guide and other resources.

"Las Abajeñas" (CD 1/19) is a *son jalisciense*. *Son* (sohn) simply means "sound" and refers to the tune as a whole; *jalisciense* (ha-lee-syen'-seh) means "from Jalisco," the state in western Mexico where the mariachi is thought to have originated. What we have here, then, is essentially "a tune from Jalisco."

The traditional core repertory of the mariachi was comprised of *sones jaliscienses*, and these were often complemented by dancers. In "Las Abajeñas" we hear many features that are typical of a *son jalisciense*—the brisk pace, the instrumental introduction, the harmonized singing (often in three parts), the punctuating of stanzas with brief instrumental interludes, and the deft flipping back and forth between triple (3/4) and duple (6/8) meters. (The alternation of meters is heard most clearly in the plucked notes of the guitarrón and in the accented strummings of the guitar and vihuela.) The most distinctive feature is the stock ending that comes just after what seems to be an abrupt halt of all musical activity. This particular musical tag is reserved exclusively for ending the *son jalisciense*. The whistling, whooping, and hollering on the recording are called *gritos* (shouts) and are integral to a performance. Indeed, they are expected of musicians, dancers, and audiences alike.

[Instrumental introduction]

Me gustan las abajeñas	I like the lowland women
por altas y presumidas.	because they are tall and regal.
Se bañan y se componen,	They bathe and they dress up,
y siempre descoloridas.	and always look pale.
(repeat)	

Mariquita, mi alma	Mariquita, my love
yo te lo decía	I told you
que tarde o tempana, mi vida,	that sooner or later, by my life,
habías de ser mía.	you had to be mine.
(repeat)	

[Instrumental interlude]

Me gustan las abajeñas	I like the lowland women
que saben la ley de Dios	who know the law of God
Que largan a sus maridos,	They send their husbands off,
por irse con otros dos.	so they can be with another two men.
(repeat)	

Déjala que vaya	Go ahead and let her leave,
ella volverá	she'll be back
si amores la llevan, mi vida,	for if loves take her away, by my life,
celos la traerán.	jealousies will bring her back.
(repeat)	

[Instrumental interlude followed by a sudden break and stock ending]

Música Norteña

The other dominant Mexican American instrumental ensemble is the *conjunto* of the *música norteña*. This distinctively regional ensemble, coming from the lower Rio Grande Valley shared by Texas and the far northeastern part of Mexico (hence the adjective *norteña*, "northern"), consisted in its early stages of only the button accordion, endemic to the region, with an accompaniment of guitar or *bajo sexto* (a form of twelve-string guitar). Beginning in the 1950s, a saxophone was frequently added, as well as a jazz-type drum set and a bass—more recently an electric one. Música norteña most often has as its rhythmic basis either the quick "**oom**-pah, **oom**-pah" of the adopted polka or the slower, lilting "**oom**-pah-pah, **oom**-pah-pah" of the adopted waltz. The style of música norteña is exemplified in the *corrido* discussed in the next section.

Compared with mariachi music, música norteña is probably the more widely popular of the two among Mexican Americans, especially the younger generation.

OMAR TORRES/AFP/Getty Images

In a contemporary photo, we see the characteristic instruments of *música norteña*: the guitar and, particularly, the button accordion (probably introduced by nineteenth-century German immigrants settling in central Texas and northeastern Mexico). The musicians play in a Mexican cemetery during the festival of *Día de los Muertos* (Day of the Dead, November 2nd), when the Mexican culture honors the resting places of departed family and friends with colorful decorations, flowers (traditionally marigolds), and lively music. We hear an example of música norteña in the *corrido* on CD 1, track 20.

It became a distinctive and regionally very influential style at the hands of accordionists, most notably in the beginning Narciso Martínez—"El Huracán del Valle" ("The Hurricane of the Valley"). The music was spread throughout the Southwest by a more recent generation of performers, including Flaco Jiménez and the guitarist-singers Freddy Fender (Baldemar Huerta) and José María de León ("Little Joe") Hernández (see Additional Listening).

The Corrido

Of all the folk forms now popular, none is more distinctive or more interesting than the *corrido*. The corrido is the equivalent of the folk ballad—a narrative strophic song. It deals with actual people and events, often of immediate and topical concern, and had its origins in Mexico in the turbulent mid-nineteenth century, when it was often political and satirical. Before the advent of recordings and, later, radio, corridos were circulated by itinerant *corridistas* or *trovadores* (troubadours), going from hacienda to hacienda, or singing in marketplaces and on street corners. As with the Anglo-American ballad, corridos were cheaply printed as broadsides, with words only (see p. 12).

The corrido of the southwestern United States is nearly as old as its Mexican forebear. An area rich in the production of corridos and other folklore has been the valley of the lower Rio Grande, from the two Laredos to the Gulf. A fertile valley in the midst of an arid plain, overlooked in early exploration and colonization, largely ignored by Spain and Mexico, and spurned by the United States, it was inhabited by people of a fiercely independent spirit. When in 1836 Texas declared its independence from Mexico, the valley suddenly became a border area, and a period of unrest, oppression, and bloodshed began that was to last intermittently for nearly a century. Like many strife-torn border areas—that between England and Scotland, for example—it bred its heroes and its villains, and its ballads to commemorate them. An early corrido was "El Corrido de Kiansis," known in the border area by 1870. It describes the experiences and hardships of the Mexican *vaqueros* (cowboys) in the cattle drives of the late 1860s and early 1870s from Texas to the western terminus of the railroad in Kansas.

Listening Cue "El Corrido de Gregorio Cortéz" Los Hermanos Banda

CD **1**
20

Recorded in Monterrey, N. L., Mexico, about 1958 (2:42)
Listen For ▪ accordion ▪ simple harmonization ▪ lilting waltz-like meter

Visit http://www.music.wadsworth.com_3/Kingman for a full listening guide and other resources.

One of the most famous corridos, still sung today, is "El Corrido de Gregorio Cortéz" (CD 1/20). This version of the corrido was probably shortened to fit a single side of a 78-rpm recording. Some versions run to twenty stanzas. Following an instrumental introduction, each of the stanzas (customarily of four lines with eight syllables per line) is sparsely accompanied to allow the story to unfold clearly then punctuated by a brief instrumental interlude before moving on to the next stanza. Use of the accordion marks this version as typical of Texas-Mexican border style, or música norteña. Notice here the simple two-part harmonization and lilting waltz-like meter (**oom**-pah-pah, **oom**-pah-pah).

1. En el condado del Carmen
   miren lo que ha sucedido,
   Murió el sherife mayor
   quedando Román herido.

   In Cameron County (Texas)
   look what has happened.
   The sheriff died,
   leaving Román wounded.

2. Otro día por la mañana
   cuando la gente llegó,
   Unos a los otros dicen
   no saben quien lo mató.

   The following morning
   when the people arrived,
   Some said to the others
   they don't know who killed him.

3. Se anduvieron informando
   como tres horas después,
   Supieron que el malhechor
   era Gregorio Cortéz.

   They were investigating
   and about three hours later
   They found out that the wrongdoer
   was Gregorio Cortéz.

4. Insortaron a Cortéz
   por toditito el estado.
   Vivo o muerto que se aprehenda
   porque a varios ha matado.

Cortéz was wanted
throughout the state.
Alive or dead may he be apprehended
for he has killed several.

5. Decía Gregorio Cortéz
   con su pistola en la mano,
   «No siento haberlo matado
   al que siento es a mi hermano.»

Said Gregorio Cortéz
with his pistol in his hand,
"I'm not sorry for having killed him.
It's for my brother that I feel sorry."

6. Decía Gregorio Cortéz
   con su alma muy encendida,
   «No siento haberlo matado
   la defensa es permitida.»

Said Gregorio Cortéz
with his soul aflame,
"I'm not sorry for having killed him,
self defense is permitted."

7. Gregorio le dice a Juan,
   «Muy pronto lo vas a ver,
   anda hablale a los sherifes
   que me vengan a aprender.»

Gregorio says to Juan,
"Very soon you will see,
go and talk to the sheriffs
that they should come and arrest me."

8. Decían los americanos
   «Si lo vemos que le haremos
   si le entramos por derecho
   muy poquitos volveremos.»

The Americans said,
"If we see him what shall we do to him;
If we face him head on
very few will return."

9. Ya agarraron a Cortéz,
   ya terminó la cuestión;
   la pobre de su familia
   la lleva en el corazón.

Now they caught Cortéz,
now the case is closed;
His poor family
he carries in his heart.

The incident described here took place in 1901. Gregorio Cortéz was a young Mexican who, having been falsely accused of horse stealing, shot and killed in self-defense the sheriff who had fatally wounded his brother. After a dramatic chase, he was captured and, after multiple trials, was acquitted of murder. He was convicted of another murder, however, and served time in Huntsville Penitentiary. Given a conditional pardon, he went to Mexico to take part in the Revolution, was wounded, returned to Texas, and died there in 1916. Américo Paredes wrote a book about the man, the legend, and the corrido, titled *With His Pistol in His Hand* (a line from the corrido), and the ballad became the basis for a movie.

In the corrido we encounter a ballad tradition still very much alive. In the days of the 45-rpm single, the common currency of popular music in the 1960s and 1970s, local radio stations could be playing a newly composed and recorded corrido within twenty-four hours of the event it commemorated (often a violent crime or scandal). The almost journalistic immediacy of the corrido resulted in some lawsuits against record companies. Corridos of protest were, and are, common. Many are *homenajes,* lamenting the deaths of popular heroes such as John F. Kennedy and Martin Luther King. Since the 1970s there have been many corridos on César Chávez, Dolores Huerta, and the farm labor movement in California.

The early corridos were performed and recorded as *duetos*—two singers with guitar. Later, by the mid-1940s, they were performed by conjuntos, with their distinctive additions of accordion, and sometimes saxophone, thus becoming part of the norteño repertoire.

The Canción

The *canción* is lyrical and often sentimental, in contrast to the narrative and even epic quality of the corrido. The term *canción* is used to cover a broad range of songs, of which songs about love are only one type. The best-known survivor, probably written for a film by the same name, is "Allá en el Rancho Grande." Other well-known titles include "Cielito Lindo," and "De Colores"; the latter became associated with the farm labor movement under the leadership of César Chávez.

Listening Cue **"Mal Hombre"** ("Cold-Hearted Man") arr. Lydia Mendoza, vocal and 12-string guitar

> CD 1
>
> 21

Recorded in San Antonio, Texas, 1934 (3:29)
Listen For ▪ emotional restraint of the performance ▪ particular resonance of the twelve-string guitar

Visit http://www.music.wadsworth.com_3/Kingman for a full listening guide and other resources.

Lydia Mendoza (b. 1916), "La Alondra de la Frontera" (the Lark of the Border) and "La Cancionera de los Pobres" (the Songstress of the Poor), attained legendary status as a performer of canciones. The story of her life gives some insight into Mexican American music throughout the Southwest, and *tejano* (Texas) border music in particular, and the lives of those who made, and still make, this music. She was a member of a musical family that in the 1920s was traveling from town to town in the lower Rio Grande Valley, trying to make a living from their singing and playing. Like many Mexican families, they had fled the violence and turmoil of the prolonged Mexican Revolution. Lydia was only twelve when La Familia Mendoza made their first recording in 1928, at a time when record companies were first beginning to realize the potential market that existed for recordings of regional folk music. There are many parallels with the Carter Family of Virginia, who began recording what eventually became "country music" about the same time. The hardship and discrimination the Mendozas endured was typical of the experience of most immigrant musicians and their families.

Lydia Mendoza's first success was the recording of a canción titled "Mal Hombre" ("Cold-Hearted Man") in 1934 (CD 1/21). In this recording, she accompanies herself on the 12-string guitar, which has a sound that is richer and more resonant than the standard six-string. (It normally doubles every string of the six-string at the octave.) The singing is beautiful to be sure, but the control and emotional restraint seem curiously at odds with the words themselves. This emotional distance from the subject is fairly typical in the performance of a canción.

Era yo una chiquilla todavía	I was but a young girl
cuando tu casualmente me encontraste	when, by chance, you found me
y a merced a tus artes de mundane	and with your worldly charm
de mi honra el perfume te llevaste.	you crushed the flower of my innocence.
Luego hiciste conmigo lo que todos	Then you treated me like all men
los que son como tu con las mujeres,	of your kind treat women,
por lo tanto no extrañes que yo ahora	so don't be surprised now that I tell you
en tu cara te diga lo que eres.	to your face what you really are.
Refrain:	
Mal hombre,	*Cold-hearted man,*
tan ruin es tu alma que no tiene nombre;	*your soul is so vile it has no name;*
eres un canalla, eres un malvado,	*you are despicable, you are evil,*
eres un mal hombre.	*you are a cold-hearted man.*
A mi triste destino abandonada	Abandoned to a sad fate
entable fiera lucha con la vida,	my life became a fierce struggle,
ella recia y cruel me torturaba	suffering the harshness and cruelty
	of the world
yo mas débil al fin caí vencida.	I was weak and was defeated.
Tú supistes a tiempo mi derrota,	In time you learned of my downfall,
mi espantoso calvario conociste,	how my life had become a road to hell,
te dijeron algunos: «Ve a salvarle»	our friends advised you, "You can help her,"
y probando quien eres te reíste.	but being who you are, you just laughed.
(Refrain)	*(Refrain)*
Poco tiempo después en el arroyo	A short time later,
entre sombras mi vida defendía	I defended my life in a shadowy world.
una noche con otra tu pasaste	One night you passed by with another woman
que al mirarme sentí que te decía:	and upon seeing me, I heard her say:
«¿Quien es esa mujer? ¿Tú la conoces?»	"Who is that woman? Do you know her?"
«Ya la ves—respondiste—una cualquiera.»	and you answered, "You can see for yourself, she's a nobody."
al oír de tus labios el ultraje	When you humiliated me with that insult
demostrabas también lo que tú eras.	you proved once again who you are.

Recordings brought increased personal appearances, and eventually Mendoza became what some consider the most important and historic recording artist in the entire field of Mexican American music. In 1999, President Bill Clinton awarded Lydia Mendoza the National Medal of the Arts and recognized her as "a true

American pioneer" who had paved the way for new generations of Latino performers. Among them was Selena Pérez Quintanilla (1971–1995), a native of southeast Texas and a rising *tejana* star whose promising career ended tragically when she was fatally shot in the back by the founder and manager of her fan club.

THE CARIBBEAN AND SOUTH AMERICA

Music from the Caribbean and South America reached the United States by sea, the chief ports of entry having been New Orleans in the nineteenth century and New York City in the twentieth. It has come from areas as far away as Argentina (which gave us the *tango*) and as close as Cuba (where we got the *mambo*), and from cultures reflecting individually unique mixtures of Spanish, Portuguese, and African influences.

In contrast with the music of Mexico, this music, and especially that from Cuba and Hispaniola, shows much more African influence. This influence is apparent in the greater role of percussion and in the vast array of percussion instruments that are of primary importance. In Latin popular music the *timbales,* a pair of shallow, cylindrical tuned drums, are used extensively and played as featured solo instruments by virtuosos such as New York–born Ernesto Antonio "Tito" Puente, Jr. (1923–2000). In addition to the drums are the smaller handheld percussion instruments, including the *claves* (two hardwood sticks struck together), the *maracas* (gourd-shaped, with seeds or shot in them), and the *campanas* (cowbells), to name just a few. This mere sampling will suffice to convey the importance not only of rhythm, but also of percussive timbre in this music.

Latin-Derived Influences in American Popular Music

There are two key aspects to these importations from the Caribbean and South America. The first has been their impact on American popular music by way of popular dance. The Cuban *habanera* (its name derived from the capital city of Havana) was all the rage around the turn of the twentieth century, and was followed in the 1910s and 1920s by the *tango,* which arrived from Argentina by way of Paris. In the 1930s came the *rumba* (Afro-Cuban), and after this the *samba* (Afro-Brazilian), the *mambo* (Afro-Cuban), the *chachachá* (Cuban), the *merengue* (Dominican), and in the 1960s the

Frank Driggs Collection/Getty Images

Ernesto Antonio "Tito" Puente performs here in 1955, three years before recording his best-selling album *Dance Mania* that popularized the Cuban mambo. Puente played the *timbales* (drums) standing at the front of the stage, rather than in the traditional sitting position at the back. The cymbal suspended on the left and the cowbell mounted just above the timbales add a variety of percussive sounds so important to this music. Puente plays a mambo on CD 1, track 22.

bossa nova (Brazilian). These successive waves of popular Latin genres have been initiated mostly as professional musicians, steeped in their own traditions, moved into the arenas of American jazz or popular music, bringing their traditional styles with them but adapting them to cater to broad popular taste. The term *salsa,* so commonly heard in relation to the Latin music of New York City, is basically a marketing label (much like *soul* in African American popular music) that includes under its broad umbrella a variety of Latin-tinged popular music.

Indigenous Music of the Caribbean Immigrants

The second aspect of the importation of Latin music to the United States is its meaning to Latin immigrants, in their own lives and communities, as a focal point for defining and maintaining cultural identities. New York City has long been a magnet for emigration from the Caribbean, and its Latin populations make up small cities within the supercity. Emigration from Puerto Rico (ceded to the United States after the Spanish-American War in 1898 and given commonwealth status in 1952) has been significant ever since United States citizenship was granted to Puerto Ricans in 1917, and it reached a peak in the 1940s and early 1950s. Emigration from Cuba has been less extensive, but an important ingredient in *la salsa* of New York City has been the presence of Cubans of the poorer classes, especially black Cubans who came to the United States before the Revolution of 1959. Thus for two generations New York has echoed with the strongly flavored music of the Caribbean: the Spanish-derived forms of the *danza,* the *seis,* and the *aguinaldo,* the African-influenced *plena* and *bomba* of Puerto Rico, the Cuban *son* and *guajira,* and the Afro-Cuban *rumba,* among others.

The Rhythms of Caribbean Music

To highlight the primary importance of rhythm in Latin music, this final section will focus on a fundamental rhythmic ingredient of Cuban music: the *clave* (kla'-veh). The clave is a rhythmic pattern whose constant repetitions unify a piece. (This pattern is often, but not exclusively, played on the *claves*—two hardwood sticks that are struck together for percussive effect.) At its simplest, the clave is two measures in length, and consists in its skeletal form of five percussive strokes grouped as either "3 + 2" (long-long-long, short-short) or "2 + 3" (short-short, long-long-long). So important is the clave in Cuban music that all melodic lines, accented notes in various instruments, and even the syllables of the lyrics themselves must line up with it.

Listening Cue "**Para los Rumberos**" Tito Puente, 1956 (3:23)

CD 1
22

Listen For ▪ prominent role of percussion ▪ virtuosic drumming (on timbales) ▪ 3 + 2 clave

Visit http://www.music.wadsworth.com_3/Kingman for a full listening guide and other resources.

For the uninitiated, the clave might seem an elusive figure. But with careful, repeated listening, one can often lock onto the distinctive pattern underlying even the most rhythmically complex piece. It will take practice, but a good starting point is Tito Puente's "Para los Rumberos" (CD 1/22), which uses a clearly defined 3 + 2 clave that is constantly present and explicitly stated by the horns at 0:15–0:22 and 0:29–0:35, and by the drums and horns together at 2:49–3:02. Begin by listening to those sections and clap along with the instruments that are explicitly stating the clave. The first grouping of three long claps might feel slightly uneven. This is due to an irregular grouping of rhythmic values called *syncopation*—a common feature in Latin music. Once you have mastered the 3 + 2 groove, start "Para los Rumberos" from the beginning and try to clap the clave all the way through. If you remain consistent, you will immediately notice that no matter how complicated the music gets, the musicians tend to emphasize the notes that line up with the clave.

"Para los Rumberos" ("For the Party-goers") is a salsa standard. Specifically, it is a mambo, but more generally, it presents an excellent example of the diverse percussive timbres and rhythmic variety that are hallmarks of Caribbean and South American music. It also showcases the virtuosic drumming and keen rhythmic sense for which Tito Puente—a composer, arranger, performer, and dominant figure in both Latin and jazz in New York for fifty years—was rightly famous. The mambo is a popular, upbeat Cuban dance genre of the 1940s and 1950s that emphasizes dynamic brass and energetic dancing. The term possibly comes from an African (Bantu) word meaning "to speak." Interestingly enough, the mambo had a bigger impact in North America than in its native Cuba, crossing over into mainstream American society to become a huge dance craze of the 1950s. It is thus a fitting close to this brief look at the Latin tinge in American music.

PROJECTS

1. Attend a concert by a professional mariachi show band, and write a review. Comment on, among other things, the makeup of the audience, the things the audience reacted most strongly to, and the relationship of the music played to traditional Mexican music.
2. Write a paper on the state of some aspect of Latino music today. Include a discography and a list of poet-musicians active in Latino circles. The periodicals *Aztlán* and *Latin American Music Review* may be helpful.
3. In *Listening to Salsa*, Frances Aparicio writes that the conflicting views on salsa "dramatize the central role of popular music as a site for the formation and definition of national identity" (66). In a short essay, develop your own opinion as to whether or not popular music can form and define national identity. Explain why, in your opinion, it either can or cannot. If you believe it can, give other examples of popular music defining national identity (of the United States or any other country).
4. Identify and write a brief informative paragraph on three female performers of Latin-Caribbean music. The books by Aparicio, Steward, and Waxer (see

References) should be helpful. Present the facts and your opinions; do not quote flowery press-agent-like prose. Include two songs each that you think show them at their best, and explain your choices.

ADDITIONAL LISTENING

The Best of Flaco Jiménez. Arhoolie CD 478.

Dark and Light in Spanish New Mexico. NW 80292. Includes alabados and bailes.

Caliente = Hot: Puerto Rican and Cuban Musical Expression in New York. NW 244.

Freddie Fender: Canciones de Mi Barrio. Arhoolie CD 366.

Mexican-American Border Music, Vol. 1. Arhoolie Folklyric CD 7001. Includes "Que me gano con llorar" and is a good additional example of the early phases of música norteña.

Mexican-American Border Music, Vol. 3. Arhoolie CD 7016. Includes Narciso Martínez.

Mission Music of California: A 200-Year Anthology. Mission San Luis Rey, (760) 757–3651.

Spanish Mexican Folk Music of New Mexico. Smithsonian/Folkways P-426. Includes a polka and a waltz.

DIVERSE TRADITIONS: FRENCH, SCANDINAVIAN, ARAB, AND ASIAN

American music is richer and far more diverse than the Anglo-Afro-Latino canon that tends to be foregrounded, in part, because of racial demographics, and equally so, by the commercialism that taps into those large and growing demographic markets. Indeed, we have already seen one example of that broader diversity in the music of American Indians. This chapter highlights the impact of four traditions—French, Scandinavian, Arab, and Asian—but only as a mere starting point for further inquiry into the multitude of cultures that comprise the broad panorama, and reality, of American music. (See the final chapter for an example of what such an inquiry might look like.)

THE FRENCH INFLUENCE IN LOUISIANA

French people began settling Louisiana early in the eighteenth century, some coming directly from France, and others arriving after a stopover of a few generations in the West Indies. Many were families of means and belonged to the aristocracy, and they soon constituted a wealthy planter class. Their cultural inclinations were urban and elite; this was manifested in the establishment of French opera in New Orleans as early as the 1790s.

At the other end of the economic scale was the French-descended refugee population that came to Louisiana from Acadia (now Nova Scotia) in the latter part of the eighteenth century. A few Acadians had reached Louisiana before the Expulsion, but the great flow took place after 1755, when the victorious English, in a cruel episode known as the Dérangement, began to expel all Acadians who would not take an oath of allegiance to the British crown. The Acadians began arriving in Louisiana some ten years later, after stopovers in France and in the American colonies. These people, mostly farmers and fishermen whose families had come from Brittany and Normandy, were regarded with contempt by the upper-class French, who excluded them from New Orleans but allowed them to settle upstream, along a stretch of the right bank of the Mississippi that became known as the "Acadian coast." The "Cajuns" (a corruption of "Acadians") were regarded as inferior, but the colony benefited from the presence of these industrious people, in their raising of crops and livestock to feed New Orleans and their ability to construct the all-important dikes to control the rivers and bayous.

The Cajuns suffered a "second expulsion" after the Louisiana Purchase in 1803 and the coming of the Americans, when it was found that the land they occupied was ideal for raising sugar. They moved farther south and west, into the bayous and swamps of the coastal regions, and into the prairies of the west. Thus they came to occupy the "French triangle," with its base along the Gulf coast and its apex around Alexandria. Tracing their lineage back two centuries to the first Acadian families (the Moutons, the Arceneaux, the Bernards, the Broussards, the Guidrys), they occupy the largest area of French-derived culture and language in the United States. Approximately 1 million people, roughly a quarter of the population of Louisiana, identify themselves as Cajuns.

Louisiana Folk Songs from France

Among the repertory of folk songs in Louisiana, some have been determined to come directly from France. "Sept ans sur mer" ("Seven Years on the Sea"), an old, possibly medieval, sailor's ballad, is very widespread. It is sung in French Canada as well as in Louisiana. Originating in Brittany and Poitou, and following the seacoasts, it is found in versions in Icelandic, Norwegian, Danish, Catalan, Spanish, and Portuguese. John and Alan Lomax recorded a version in New Iberia, Louisiana, as late as 1934 (see Additional Listening).

Cajun Music

Cajun music began to be recorded in the 1920s, at a time when major record companies had begun to realize the potential market for regional folk musics. In recent years, it has enjoyed a resurgence in popularity thanks to musicians such as Michael Doucet and his group Beausoleil, featured here in a performance of "Le Two-Step à Midland" ("The Midland Two-Step," CD 1/23). As the long instrumental passages suggest, this is music for dancing. The "two-step" in the title indicates a dance in quick duple meter, but lilting triple meter waltzes are also common. An example of the latter is "J'ai passé devant ta porte" ("I passed in front of your door"; see Additional Listening). The text for "Le Two-Step à Midland" (given on the next page) is representative of the predilection for sentimental love themes in Cajun songs.

Listening Cue "Midland Two-Step" Beausoleil (Michael Doucet, fiddle and vocal; David Doucet, guitar and vocals; Errol Verret, single-row accordion; Billy Ware, triangle, spoons; Tommy Alesi, drums)

CD 1
23

Recorded in Lafeyette, Louisiana, 1981 (3:20)
Listen For ▪ quick duple meter ▪ accordion and fiddle ▪ Cajun vocal style

 Visit http://www.music.wadsworth.com_3/Kingman for a full listening guide and other resources.

O chère bébé, gardez donc mais quoi tu m'as fait	O darling, look what you've done to me
T'as fait la misère, o chagrin	You've caused me misery, oh pain
Ouais chagrin que moi j'ai eu	Oh, the pain that I've felt
O hé 'tit coeur, 'y a pas personne qui veut les voir.	Oh little heart, nobody knows.
Mais moi j'ai seul à la maison	I'm all alone at my house
Veux t'en allez ouais avec moi?	Do you want to go with me?
O, mais gardez donc le chagrin que tu m'as fait	Oh, look at the pain you've caused me
Chère bébé, mais je mérite pas ça	Babe, I don't deserve that
Oui catin malheureux	Heartless woman
O ouais plus belle t'es plus belle	Your beauty isn't pretty any more
Pourquoi faire mais les misères	Why do you make me miserable
Mais ouais dans moi	Oh me
Et moi tout seul je t'espérais.	All alone I waited for you.
O 'y a pas longtemps, 'y a pas longtemps	It wasn't long, it wasn't long ago
Que moi je t'ai vue, chère bébé	That I saw you, baby
Mais moi t'ai donc emmenée	But I'd like to take you with me
Pour aller ouais ensemble.	To go away together.

The distinctive sound of Cajun music can be attributed to its instrumentation and, even more so, to its unique vocal style that is at once lyrical and tends to sound as if shouted from the back of the throat. It might be described more generally as having a very tense, hoarse quality with a timbre that alternates between grainy in the lower extremes and nasal in the upper register. A Cajun ensemble is typically comprised of the fiddle, accordion, guitar, and some type of background percussion instrument such as a drum, triangle, or spoons that are clicked together to keep time. The fiddle was the basic Cajun instrument from the earliest times; the accordion began to be adopted in the 1920s, around the time the music was first being recorded. From the perspective of recorded history, then, the accordion is integral to the Cajun band.

Zydeco

An extension of the French influence in Louisiana can be found in an interesting blues-inflected translation of Cajun music by African Americans called *zydeco* (or *zodico* or *zarico*). The term *zydeco* (pronounced with the accent on the first syllable) is said to have come from the pronunciation of "les haricots" (snap beans) in the early Cajun song "Les haricots sont pas salés" ("The Snap Beans Are Not Salty"). Zydeco music features the accordion typically heard in Cajun songs, and sometimes adds the fiddle. Other instruments in a zydeco band include the piano, the electric guitar, the electric bass, drums, and occasionally saxophones. The most characteristic instrument, however, is the *frottoir*: a rub board of corrugated sheet metal that hangs across the chest (it looks like a vest from the front) and is rhythmically scraped with hand-held metal objects.

In an image taken at a 1988 festival in Lafayette, Louisiana, Clifford Alexander strums on a zydeco *frottoir*—a metal wash-board-like instrument—that we hear on CD 1, track 24. On the left, Nathan Williams plays the accordion.

© Philip Gould/CORBIS

Listening Cue "Zydeco sont pas salé" Clifton Chenier, accordion and vocal; Cleveland Chenier, rub board; Madison Guidry, drums

Recorded in Houston, Texas, 1965 (3:10)
Listen For ▪ *frottoir* (rub board) ▪ Cajun vocal style ▪ imitation of train sounds

Visit http://www.music.wadsworth.com_3/Kingman for a full listening guide and other resources.

Clifton Chenier (1925–1987), the "king of zydeco" (he had many publicity photos taken wearing an actual crown), was a versatile musician who in the 1960s and 1970s performed both zydeco, singing in Cajun-French, and out-and-out Gulf Coast rhythm-and-blues, which he sang in English. Chenier's "Zydeco sont pas salé," from about 1965, is representative of early zydeco (CD 1/24). The throaty vocal style is pure Cajun. Furthermore, notice the characteristic sound of the *frottoir* (frah-'twahr), which teams up with the drums and accordion to imitate the sound of a train—a clear nod in the direction of the early blues tradition. (The train is an important motif in the blues and reflects the traveling careers of early bluesmen.)

THE SCANDINAVIAN INFLUENCE IN THE UPPER MIDWEST

Scandinavian immigrants began settling in Wisconsin in the 1840s, and in Minnesota in the 1850s. The Swedes, the most numerous group, began as farmers but later moved to the cities, to be outnumbered in farming by the Norwegians, the next most numerous. Other immigrant peoples, also from northern or central Europe, were the Germans (notably in Wisconsin), the Danes, the Finns, the Poles, and the Czechs. But by the last quarter of the century it was the Scandinavians whose presence was decisive in determining the cultural makeup of the upper Midwest. Among them, the largely rural and conservative Norwegians have striven the most consciously to preserve their language and culture. This is reflected in part by such staunchly nationalistic organizations as the Sons of Norway, which until 1942 continued to publish its official newsletters in Norwegian.

The kind of regional music most in evidence in the upper Midwest is music for dancing. The oldest dances from Norway, such as the *halling* (in which the dancer

In front of the cookshack of Bill Landahl's lumber camp in Beltrami County, Minnesota, in 1917, Clara and Martha Steve pose with a fiddle and a wooden *lur,* a long Scandinavian trumpet with roots in the Middle Ages. Notice that the women have come outside to pose while snow remains on the ground. Winter in northern Minnesota (as in Scandinavia) can last into April, reach minus 50° or lower, making music an ideal way to pass the time. We hear a Scandinavian polka on CD 1, track 25.

kicks a hat off a vertically held pole), the *springer,* and the *gangar,* belong to a by-gone era and are encountered only in deliberate and costumed revivals. The same is true of the instruments that were associated with these dances. Chief among them was the Hardanger fiddle (*Hardangfele*), an instrument that has four strings that are played with a bow and an additional set of strings that vibrate sympathetically to enrich the tone.

As the old dances and the old instruments gradually fell out of general use, they were replaced by the three dances most popular among Scandinavian Americans today: the polka (quick duple meter), the waltz (lilting triple meter), and the schottische (essentially a slow polka). The most popular instruments for these dances now are the modern fiddle and accordion, along with the guitar, piano, or banjo, as available. In rural areas, dances took place at house parties in homes, or in the cleared-out second-floor lofts of roomy barns. More recently, barns that have never housed hay or cattle have been built especially for "barn dances." In the towns and cities, public dances are held in various social halls.

Listening Cue "Banjo, Old Time" LeRoy Larson and the Minnesota Scandinavian Ensemble (1:25)

CD 1

25

Listen For ▪ quick duple meter ▪ accented offbeat in the accordion ▪ dry, percussive sound of the banjo

Visit http://www.music.wadsworth.com_3/Kingman for a full listening guide and other resources.

"Banjo, Old Time" (CD 1/25) is an example of a polka. It is performed here by the Minnesota Scandinavian Ensemble, a popular group that was formed in 1974 by LeRoy Larson while he conducted extensive research into the Scandinavian folk music of the Midwest. In this recording, we hear the quick "oom-pah" meter that is characteristic of the polka, but the accordion tends to accentuate the offbeat, adding some variety to the musical texture. The broader "airy" sound of the accordion also provides a contrast to the dry, percussive sound of the banjo in the foreground. The banjo is not a particularly resonant instrument, so longer notes demand that the player restrike the string multiple times to keep the sound going. All of these elements combine to create a vibrant musical experience for dancers and wallflowers alike. The banjo and accordion central to this music today were taken up after the arrival of Scandinavian immigrants in America.

Professional and semiprofessional bands began to make commercial recordings of Scandinavian music in the first years of the twentieth century. As early as 1915, the Swedish immigrant musician and entertainer Hjalmar Peterson (who adopted the stage name "Olle i Skratthult") recorded his love song "Nikolina," which became immensely popular and was performed in many variants both as a song and as an instrumental piece. The impact of recordings, radio, the jukebox, traveling vaudeville (Olle i Skratthult himself was "on the road" for years with his band of entertainers), and movies was to force changes in Scandinavian

American music, and a decline in home music-making. But it was, ironically, through the very medium of the old recordings that the "old-time" styles of the early twentieth century were ultimately preserved.

ARAB AMERICAN TRADITIONS

Some of the least-studied musical traditions in the United States are those of Arab Americans, who number in the neighborhood of 2.5 million people representing twenty different nations of the Arab world, including Morocco, Egypt, Lebanon, Somalia, Saudi Arabia, and Iraq. The earliest Arab immigrants arrived in the mid-nineteenth century, with significant waves coming between 1870 and 1925, then between 1965 and the present. Many Arab immigrants settled in the urban areas of California, New York, and Michigan. Indeed, one of the largest Arab American populations in the United States can be found in the Detroit area, with a major concentration situated in the adjacent city of Dearborn, Michigan, where the first Arab American National Museum opened its doors in May 2005 (visit their website at www.theaanm.org).

The Arab American population of the Detroit area forms part of what is believed to be the largest Arab-speaking community outside of the Arab world. The roots of this community extend back to the nineteenth century, but it experienced a major growth spurt with the arrival in 1903 of the Ford Motor Company and the nascent mass-production automotive industry, which offered many new jobs that required few English-language skills and little or no previous technical training. In 1965, the lifting of restrictions that had been placed on Arab immigration more than thirty years earlier stimulated further growth, which continues to this day. For cultural historians, the result has been a windfall of sorts. Anne K. Rasmussen (one of only a few historians studying Arab American musics) has noted: "There is no place in America, and perhaps in the world, that better approximates the ideological notion of the Arab world mosaic than Detroit and the adjacent city of Dearborn" (Lornell and Rasmussen 81). It is a

© Ed Kashi/CORBIS

Children from the Islamic Institute of Knowledge in Dearborn, Michigan, recite a Ramadan prayer, December 15, 2001. Greater Detroit and neighboring Dearborn are home to an estimated 270,000 Arab Americans, the second largest (after Paris) Islamic population outside the Muslim world. With attention focused on the radical elements of Islam, it is easy to misperceive a peaceful population, only half of whom practice Islam, as they adapt their traditions to life in the contemporary West. We hear an Iraqi American selection, recorded in Detroit, on CD 1, track 26.

testament indeed to the diversity of American music that after studying the Scandinavian musical heritage of Minnesota one need only visit a neighboring Midwestern state to learn something about the music of Iraq, to which we now turn.

The Iraqi Americans in the northern suburbs of Detroit are generous and steady patrons of musical groups, which are engaged regularly for various social functions. To quote one professional musician in the know: "You've got to play Iraqi [music]. Everybody plays Iraqi. If you don't play Iraqi you starve" (Lornell and Rasmussen 90). The music performed in Iraqi American communities is an exciting fusion of traditional sounds re-created on modern instruments that include keyboard synthesizers, drum machines, and other technical equipment. The result is what Rasmussen aptly describes as a "digitized ethnic sound" (Lornell and Rasmussen 91).

"Zaffat al-Hilu" ("The Procession of the Beautiful Bride," CD 1/26), presents us with an example of Iraqi American music. It is performed in this recording by the Bells Band, a Detroit group made up of Majid Kakka, Salam Kakka, and Johny Sana, three musicians of Iraqi heritage. The context for this performance is an Iraqi–Italian wedding documented in 1995 by Anne Rasmussen; a translation of the lyrics describes the occasion.

> Tonight we do the Zaffah for the bride and groom of the black eyes [a sign of beauty]. The ring that she's wearing is shining all over her dress; there is nothing else like it in the market. Congratulations to you [two], the beloved ones.

Listening Cue "Zaffat al-Hilu" (excerpt) the Bells Band (Majid Kakka, director, lead singer, and keyboard; Salam Kakka and Johny Sana, percussion synthesizers)

Recorded at an Iraqi–Italian wedding, Detroit, 1995 (1:27)
Listen For ▪ "digitized ethnic sound" created on synthesizers and drum machines

Visit http://www.music.wadsworth.com_3/Kingman for a full listening guide and other resources.

The Gulf Wars along with the attacks of September 11, 2001, and subsequent acts of terrorism throughout the world have given rise to an unfortunate swell of anti-Arab and anti-Arab American sentiment. At a time when the media and pundits of every political persuasion tend to focus on cultural differences, we might do well to recall individuals of Arab descent who have been central fixtures in various facets of American life: activist Ralph Nader; Energy Secretary Spencer Abraham; quarterback Doug Flutie; Indy racer Bobby Rahal; musicians Frank Zappa and Paula Abdul; radio and television personality Casey Kasem; schoolteacher and astronaut Christa McAuliffe; actors Danny Thomas and Salma Hayek, to name a few. Examples of the rich, but largely unknown musical repertory of Arab Americans can be enjoyed in a recent compilation by Anne K. Rasmussen (see Additional Listening).

THE ASIAN INFLUENCE

The Asian influence is probably most readily perceived in American popular and classical musics that draw from the courtly and religious musical traditions of India and Indonesia.

George Harrison (1943–2001) promoted an awareness of Indian music in Western popular culture during the 1960s through recordings with the Beatles such as "Love You To" (*Revolver,* 1966) in which he performed the *sitar*. The *sitar* is an instrument with roots in elite courtly circles; it is a large, fretted lute with a long neck that has as many as twenty-seven strings, some of which are performed upon while others vibrate sympathetically to provide a drone. Harrison publicly embraced Indian culture and philosophy, studying the *sitar* with renowned virtuoso Ravi Shankar, who, at 85, continues to perform throughout Europe and the United States.

Indonesian music, particularly from Java and Bali, is widely performed in American academic circles on the *gamelan,* an ensemble traditionally tied to ceremonial or religious rituals that basically consists of a variety of gongs and metal slab instruments that are struck with mallets. American composers such as Henry Cowell (1897–1965) and Lou Harrison (1917–2003) played important roles in acquainting music listeners in the United States with Indonesian as well as other Asian musics. Indeed, Harrison even built instruments for the *gamelan* himself. Beginning in the 1950s, American colleges and universities began establishing *gamelan* performance programs as an attractive way to involve students with music from other parts of the world, and the *gamelan* has since become something of an academic music tradition.

The impact of Indian and Indonesian traditions is significant to be sure, but they do not directly reflect the lives, cares, routines, and concerns of Asian communities in the United States as such, and might be looked upon instead as Western appropriations of Eastern art. The case is decidedly different, however, with the folk musics emanating from two of our largest Asian American groups today, those of Chinese and Japanese origin, and, specifically, the manner in which these folk musics have been transformed into powerful messages of identity and resistance by activist composers and performers such as Fred Ho and Nobuko Miyamoto. To view their works from a proper perspective, we will begin by considering briefly some relevant points in the histories of Chinese and Japanese Americans, and Asian American activism in the 1960s and 1970s.

The Chinese and Japanese in America

The earliest Asians to arrive in significant numbers were the Chinese, attracted to California by the gold rush of 1849, and subsequently by employment prospects in the building of the transcontinental railroad. With the completion of the railroad in 1869, a large number of Chinese laborers began moving into urban areas, where they were exploited as sources of cheap labor in the manufacturing and service industries. Once members of the established working class began to perceive the Chinese as a threat to their jobs, it was not long before legislators responded with such measures as the Chinese Exclusion Act of 1882, which curtailed further immigration of Chinese laborers and prohibited their naturalization as United States citizens. Such legislative acts merely formalized the intense racism that society had exercised upon the Chinese. We find symptoms of its pervasiveness in popular culture in such examples as Bret Harte's poem "The Heathen Chinee" (1870) and Harte's collaboration with Mark Twain to stage the derived play *Ah Sin* (1877), in which the title character is unflatteringly described as a "moral cancer," a member of "that godless race," a "slant eyed son of the yellow jaunders," and an "unsolvable political problem" (Garrett 126). It is under these circumstances of marginalization and outright racism that communities of Chinese began to coalesce into culturally insulated cities-within-cities called "Chinatowns," first in San Francisco and later in Los Angeles, Chicago, Boston, and New York.

The Japanese did not arrive in large numbers until the 1890s, primarily because of laws that prohibited laborers from leaving Japan to work in another country. When emigration was legalized in 1884, an increasingly steady stream of Japanese immigrants arrived in the United States, settling largely on the West Coast. Though subjected to many of the social injustices that affected the Chinese immigrants before them, perhaps none stands out so sharply today as the internment of more than 100,000 Japanese and Japanese Americans during World War II (1939–1945). This was effectively authorized by President Franklin Delano Roosevelt's Executive Order 9066, issued in the wake of the bombing of Pearl Harbor on December 7, 1941. The order was not formally rescinded until 1976, by President Gerald Ford.

Although early Chinese and Japanese immigrants held fast to native cultural traditions as a source of comfort in a strange land, anti-immigration sentiments and legislation in the United States would prompt them to become increasingly detached from them in an attempt to assimilate, only to have a subsequent generation try to reclaim a part of that heritage. Nowhere is this process of detachment and recovery more clearly illustrated than among the Japanese, who distinguish three important cultural generations: *issei, nisei,* and *sansei.* The *issei* (first generation; born between the 1890s and the mid-1920s) maintained the language and cultural practices of their native Japan. The *nisei* (second generation; born between 1910 and 1940) maintained some of their cultural heritage but more fully embraced American customs, accepting English as their language and Christianity as their religion. The *sansei* (third generation; entered high school and college in the 1960s) are more thoroughly assimilated but tend to strive to reclaim their heritage by recovering certain cultural and religious aspects of Old Japan.

Asian American Activism

By the time the *sansei* began to enter college in the late 1960s, Asian Americans of various backgrounds had started to come together with an activist agenda to reclaim their suppressed heritage and engage in new acts of cultural production that would at once assert their collective identity and subvert what they perceived to be the myth of a mainstream American culture. Part of the strategy involved creating a new type of music that fused traditional Asian instruments and performance practices with what were accepted as quintessentially American

Shane Sato

While many of the 120,000 Japanese-Americans imprisoned in camps during World War II left the United States after their release, Nobuko Miyamoto—whom we hear on CD 1, Track 27—became an early voice of the Asian-American cultural movement. In 1973, she, Chris Iijima, and Charlie Chin created the first album of Asian American songs, *A Grain of Sand* (recently reissued by Bindu Records). Believing in the power of art to transform oneself and society, Nobuko founded Great Leap, an organization that, twenty-five years later, is a thriving, multicultural, performing arts group (www.greatleap.org) that gives voice not only to the experiences of Asian-Americans, but to those of African-Americans, Latinos, Native Americans, Arab-Americans, and others, as Nobuko continues to build understanding among cultures through music.

styles, such as jazz. These fusions not only asserted an Asian cultural presence, but they unsettled accepted notions of what precisely constituted American music. To construct Asian identities, folk musics presented themselves as natural tools. In this regard, Asian American activist composers and performers drew inspiration not only from the Black Arts movement, which emphasized a return to one's native culture as a source of empowerment, but also the social commentary styles of folk singers such as Woody Guthrie, Pete Seeger, and Bob Dylan (see Chapter 6). We will conclude this chapter with a look at two composer/performers who grew out of this movement.

Nobuko Miyamoto and Fred Ho

Nobuko Miyamoto (b. 1939), a Japanese American, is a Los Angeles–born musician/activist of the *sansei* generation. Her collaboration with Chris Iijima and Charlie Chin on the album *A Grain of Sand: Music for the Struggle by Asians in America* (1973) produced some of the first Asian American songs with a social and political bent. Her more recent "Tampopo" ("Dandelion," CD 1/27), from 1995, offers us a sense of the various components involved in an act of cultural production that brings together traditional Japanese and American elements. The context for this particular performance is an O-Bon festival observed at the Senshin Buddhist Church in Los Angeles, California, in July 1995. An O-Bon festival commemorates the departed souls of one's ancestors, and as Susan M. Asai notes: "The traditional context of the O-Bon festival requires a strict interpretation of Japanese folk music as accompaniment to folk dancing" (Lornell and Rasmussen 269). Yet, amid the sounds of traditional Japanese folk instruments such as the *shamisen* (a plucked lute), *shakuhachi* (bamboo flute), and *taiko* (barrel drum), we clearly hear that some of the text is being sung in English. The result is one that would likely sound just as "foreign" to Americans as it would to Japanese. Such is the essence of true Asian American music.

Listening Cue "Tampopo" (Dandelion) by Nobuko Miyamoto, text by Nobuko Miyamoto and Rev. Mas Koda; Nobuko Miyamoto, vocals; Saron Koga, shamisen; Danny Yamamoto, taiko; Taii Miyagawa, acoustic bass; Rev. Mas Koda, spoken vocals

CD 1

27

Recorded in Los Angeles, California, 1995 (3:01)
Listen For ▪ *taiko* heard at the beginning ▪ dry, percussive sound of the *shamisen* ▪ intermingling of Japanese and English lyrics

Visit http://www.music.wadsworth.com_3/Kingman for a full listening guide and other resources.

Tampopo Tampopo kiosuke-yo
moshi kaze fukeba aaa. . . .
. . . aaahhhh

The seed of the dandelion
Scatters in the sky (Tampopo,
Tampopo, hai hai)
A wind-blown weed, a wildflower
Watch it fly (Tampopo, Tampopo,
hai hai)
Dancing on the wind, spinning from
a world it leaves behind
Dancing on wind
New life begins

Yare yare sore
Okagesama de
Yare yare sore
Okagesama de

Through all the forces
(Okagesama de)
Through the shadows and the light
(Okagesama de)

The unknown forces
Dandelion
Hai, hai, hai, hai, hai, hai, hai
Hai hai
Aaaahhhh....

The seed of the dandelion
Scatters in the sky (Tampopo,
Tampopo, hai hai)
A wind-blown weed
A wildflower
Watch it fly (Tampopo, Tampopo,
hai hai)
Dancing on the wind, spinning from a
world it leaves behind
Dancing on wind
New life begins

Yare yare sore
Okagesama de
Yare yare sore
Okagesama de

On this special night (Okagesama de)   Hai, hai, hai, hai, hai, hai, hai
Past and present are one   Hai hai
(Okagesama de)   Aaaahhhh . . . .
On this night of Obon
Dandelions return

Lyrics written by Nobuko Miyamoto and Reverend Mas Koda. Used by permission.

Another notable artist in this vein is Fred Ho (b. 1957), a Chinese American musician and composer born in Palo Alto, California, but raised largely on the East Coast in Amherst, Massachusetts. Fred Ho (born Fred Wei-han Houn) was profoundly influenced by folk songs he came to learn as a social worker in Boston's Chinatown. His subsequent compositions would draw deeply from these and combine them with elements of jazz to produce what Ho refers to as an "Afro-Asian multicultural music expression . . . neither American nor Asian but quintessentially Asian American" (Asai 97). In compositions such as "Uproar in Heaven" from his ballet series *Journey Beyond the West*, Ho combines a jazz sextet and the harmonies and rhythms of jazz with such traditional Chinese instru-

As composer of the first contemporary Chinese American opera, *A Chinaman's Chance*, and leader of the Afro-Asian Music Ensemble and the Monkey Orchestra, saxophonist Fred Ho signals a ground-breaking combination of traditional Chinese and Western instruments. He once told an interviewer: "Music stirs emotions, the intellect, and the imagination. And if we as artists can have an impact that increases the possibilities for compassion, resistance to hype and lies, and an imagination and desire for our planet's ecological health, then all power to us! But if all we want is to make careers, to increase our consumerist consumption, to become celebrities, then we are simply mediocre and mainstream, predictable and banal in the aspirations we place upon our art."

ments as the *erhu* (a two-stringed fiddle), *p'ip'a* (a plucked lute), and an array of percussion instruments. At the heart of the ballet itself is a Monkey King, a popular traditional character in China that represents a "hero of the people, powerful, wise, faithful to his mission, vigilant against evil spirits, and above all, defiant toward the Heavenly ruling powers but sympathetic to the weak and downtrodden" (Zhang 97). In Susan Asai's reading of the character, "The Monkey King can be thought of as the equivalent of a working-class hero defying the capitalist, bourgeois forces that oppress the masses" (Asai 98).

An especially interesting example of Fred Ho's work is his martial arts ballet *Once Upon a Time in Chinese America,* which needs to be experienced in its entirety (see Additional Listening). Briefly, it unfolds the story of a renegade monk who has allied with the enemy to destroy the sacred Shaolin Temple, and five surviving monks who eventually defeat the traitor. Though set in China around the 1600s, according to the website maintained by Fred Ho's Big Red Media production company, the ballet really aims "to serve as a radical allegory about the betrayal of late-20th century activism in the Asian American Movement by the role of sell-outs internal to that movement" (www.bigredmediainc.com/ VOD.htm). In an interesting twist, then, protest music has been used to confront individuals within a movement itself!

Having broached the topic of folk music as an instrument of advocacy, we explore the subject more fully in the following chapter.

PROJECTS

1. Find out about any holidays or festivals that are celebrated by ethnic groups in your community, and attend and report on them. Consider the role music plays in projecting cultural identity.
2. Find out about and report on the support your own state government gives to folk, ethnic, or regional arts through a state folklorist or through a state arts board or arts council.
3. Write an essay that considers what musics are foregrounded as representative of American culture, either domestically or abroad. Who makes these decisions and why? (Compare your answers with a classmate.)

ADDITIONAL LISTENING

"Sept ans sur mer," *A Treasury of Library of Congress Field Recordings* (Rounder 1500).

"J'ai passé devant ta porte," *Arhoolie's American Masters* Vol. 3: 15 Louisiana Cajun Classics (Arhoolie 103).

The Music of Arab Americans: A Retrospective Collection (Rounder 1122).

Fred Ho, *Once Upon a Time in Chinese America* (Innova Recordings 550)

FOLK MUSIC AS AN INSTRUMENT OF ADVOCACY

The use of music in the service of a cause is nothing new. John Powell, American composer and folk-music scholar, has called attention to an anecdote about the ingenuity and zeal of Saint Aldhelm, a seventh-century monk of Malmesbury, England (about 95 miles west of London):

> According to this story, the Saint would station himself on a bridge in the guise of a gleeman and would collect an audience by singing popular songs. He would then gradually insert into his entertainment the words of the holy scriptures and so lead his hearers to salvation. (Jackson vii)

From Saint Aldhelm in the seventh century to the labor union organizer, the civil rights advocate, the environmental activist, or the war protester in the twenty-first, the method is the same—adapting an already known and accepted song, or song style, so as to transform it into an instrument of advocacy. "Protest songs," the name frequently applied to songs of advocacy, have been sung in the United States since colonial times. The opening verse of the "Junto Song" of 1775, satirizing what was seen as British avarice in taxing the colonists ("'Tis money makes the member vote, And sanctifies our ways; It makes the patriot turn his coat, And money we must raise"), is startling in its applicability to today's debates on reforming politics! (For the entire song, see pp. 200–201 and CD 3/6.)

Listening Cue "The Farmer Is the Man That Feeds Them All" Fiddlin' John Carson, vocal (3:01)

CD 1

28

> Listen For ▪ simple and direct vocal style ▪ fiddle unobtrusively doubling the voice part

Visit http://www.music.wadsworth.com_3/Kingman for a full listening guide and other resources.

Engraving by Frank Bellow for *Leslie's Illustrated Newspaper*/Photo © Bettmann /CORBIS

In this 1873 cartoon, an iron horse—the Railroad Monopoly—consumes a farmer's livelihood—the corn in his bin. Most crops went to market on the railroads, which charged farmers exorbitant shipping fees. In 1885, at the beginning of a farm depression, the Farmers Alliance organized the Populist (or People's) Party—a third party targeting the corruption it saw throughout industry and government. We hear the song that arose from this movement, "The Farmer Is the Man That Feeds Them All," on CD 1, track 28.

The plight of the farmer has seldom been the subject of protest songs, but the Populist movement in the 1890s produced "The Farmer Is the Man That Feeds Them All" (CD 1/28). Fiddlin' John Carson was the first musician to record commercially what was at first called "old-time music," and later "country music."

If you'll only look and see, I know you will agree,
That the farmer is the man that feeds them all.
While the women uses snuff, and they never get enough,
But the farmer is the man that feeds them all.
When the farmer come to town, with his wagon broken down,
The farmer is the man that feeds them all.

Chorus:
Farmer is the man, Farmer is the man,
Buys on credit until fall.
Then they'll take him by the hand, then they'll lead him through the land,
Then the merchant he's the man that gets it all.
If you'll only look and see, I know you will agree,
That the farmer is the man that feeds them all.

While the judge on his bench, he will scratch his head and wink,
But the farmer is the man that feeds them all.
And the lawyer, I'll declare, will tell a lie and swear,

But the farmer is the man that feeds them all.
If you'll only look and see, I know you will agree,
That the farmer is the man that feeds them all.
(Chorus)

Oh, the doctor hangs around, while the blacksmith whups his iron,
But the farmer is the man that feeds them all.
And the preacher and the cook, they'll go trolling on the brook,
But the farmer is the man that feeds them all.
If you'll only look and see, I know you will agree,
That the farmer is the man that feeds them all.
(Chorus)

The lyrics sometimes resemble a litany as they run through the various individuals dependent on the farmer. Notice that there is little artifice in Fiddlin' John Carson's performance here; even the fiddle part comes across as subdued. But the voice is firm and emphatic, pointed and direct. Say what we might about the performance, its message is clear: the farmer is the man that feeds them all. And in the art of protest song, there is nothing more important than the message.

THE URBAN FOLK SONG MOVEMENT OF THE 1930S AND 1940S

The Depression period of the 1930s ushered in a new era of American folk song as an instrument of advocacy. As D. K. Wilgus said, "The use of folksong for political purposes is an old device: what is new is the use of the folk concept, the magic term *folk*" (228). The "magic" inherent in the term *folk* has been described by R. Serge Denisoff as "Folk Consciousness."

> Folk Consciousness refers to an awareness of folk music that leads to its use in a foreign (urban) environment in the framework of social, economic, and political action. The addition of social and organizational themes to traditional tunes, the emulation of rural attire, and the idealization of folk singers as "people's artists" are all aspects of Folk Consciousness. (99)

When northern labor organizers went into the South to organize mine and textile mill workers, they found that the tradition of folk singing, which was still vital in the rural South, was already at work providing songs to rally the workers in the bitter struggle. In Harlan County, Kentucky, scene of violent labor disputes in the coal mines in 1931, Aunt Molly Jackson (born Mary Magdalene Garland, 1880–1960), a midwife, union organizer, and ballad singer for the coal miners who had lost her brother, husband, and son in the mines, sounded a rallying cry with "I Am a Union Woman" (CD 1/29). In the lyrics that follow, CIO stands for the Congress of Industrial Organizations, which was established in 1938 and has since joined with the American Federation of Labor to create the AFL-CIO. NMU

Before the legalization of labor unions in 1935, coal companies fired and blacklisted union miners at will. In this photo, destitute strikers look on as National Guardsmen escort miners who have forsaken the union and returned to work in Kentucky's "Bloody Harlan" County coal fields—site of a shootout on May 4, 1931, between union miners and coal company hired thugs. Not seen are 800 additional soldiers guarding the forty-two mines. On CD 1, track 29, Aunt Molly Jackson refers to the "dear old NMU"—the National Miners Union, which was in fact sponsored by the U.S. Communist Party—and "the CIO," which was not.

stands for the National Miners Union. The references to "Rooshian Red" (Russian Red) indicate attempts to undermine Jackson by painting her as a sympathizer with Communist Russian ideals. In short, her detractors aimed to portray her as "un-American."

Listening Cue "I Am a Union Woman" Aunt Molly Jackson (1:22)

Listen For ▪ vocal timbre that alternately signals exhaustion, strain, and determination

Visit http://www.music.wadsworth.com_3/Kingman for a full listening guide and other resources.

I am a union woman, just as brave as I can be.
I do not like the bosses and the bosses don't like me.
Join the CIO, come join the CIO.

I was raised in Kentucky, in Kentucky borned and bred.
And when I joined the union, they called me a Rooshian Red.
Join the CIO, come join the CIO.

When my husband asked the boss for a job, this is the words he said:
"Bill Jackson, I can't work you, sir, your wife's a Rooshian Red."
Come join the CIO, join the CIO.

If you want to join a union as strong as one can be,
Join the dear old NMU and come along with me.
If you want to join a union, step in and come along.
We'll all be glad to have you, we're many thousand strong.
Come join the CIO, join the CIO.

One of the most notable features of this recording of Aunt Molly Jackson is the timbre of her voice, which alternately signals exhaustion, strain, and determination. Though the voice might falter in one verse, it regains its strength in the next as she struggles to get her message out under trying circumstances. There is no better example on record of a passionate amateur trying to use the art of music to persuade. The song's lyrics and its performance by Aunt Molly Jackson remind us of the hardships that confronted early union organizers as they tried to empower the exploited working classes.

When the union organizers and their supporters and chroniclers, such as John Dos Passos and Theodore Dreiser, returned to the North, they brought with them not only many of the songs but also some of the singers, including Aunt Molly Jackson herself, who had been banished, in effect, from Kentucky. Thus began the urban phase of the urban folk song movement. In addition to singers from the Kentucky coal mines, there was Leadbelly (Huddie Ledbetter, 1885–1949), whose talents were discovered in a Louisiana prison by folklorists John and Alan Lomax, who secured his parole and brought him to New York. There was Harvard dropout and durable activist Pete Seeger, son of the distinguished ethnomusicologist Charles Seeger. And there was Woody Guthrie.

Woody Guthrie

Woody Guthrie (1912–1967) was a highly individual and somewhat enigmatic figure. His Oklahoma background was certainly folk in any sense of the term, and his absorption of this heritage is evident in his early recordings of traditional ballads, including "Gypsy Davy" (CD 1/2) encountered in Chapter 1. The broad and varied experiences of his life, the first thirty years of which are so colorfully set forth in his somewhat fictionalized autobiography, *Bound for Glory,* gave him abundant contact with the common people. His identification with them, and his sympathies for them, resulted in a spontaneous flood of songs (only a small proportion of which have been preserved) as well as poems and sketches. Many of the songs, even those that became broadly popular, had a hard and determined edge of protest to them, though that edge was somewhat muted in popular versions. "So Long, It's Been Good to Know Ya," for example, reveals its original context, as a song about the Dust Bowl, only in its spontaneous, rambling, talking-and-singing version by Woody himself. (See Additional Listening.) Certainly songs like this and "Hard Travelin'" have their roots in his personal experience. But some of the songs, especially the ones he wrote on commission, such as those written for the Bonneville Power Administration and the set on the famous Sacco and Vanzetti case, show the effects of their separation from a definable folk community. This is seen in the broadly inclusive "This Land Is Your Land." The Dust Bowl Ballads, written after the fact, were neither sung nor known by the migrant workers themselves who left the area for California in the 1930s. Yet his enormous talent, when brought to bear on an immediate event, could produce a truly great song, through his faculty of making us sense at once the human dimension. "The Sinking of the *Reuben James*," about the seamen lost in the first American ship torpedoed in World War II, was probably the best ballad to come out of that conflict. (See Additional Listening for versions by both Woody Guthrie and Pete Seeger.)

A man of shrewd intelligence and diverse talents (he read voluminously and was a very prolific writer apart from his songs, and an artist as well), Guthrie was no simple "man of the soil." Yet he often found himself having to deny his own acute perceptions and conceal his intellect behind a mask of simplistic doggerel in trying to fulfill his most difficult job of all—which was largely thrust upon him—that of being a kind of universal "folk poet" of the common man.

Pete Seeger and the Almanac Singers

Pete Seeger (b. 1919) along with his sister Peggy and brother Mike are prominent folk performers and scholars. Pete himself, the quintessential folk activist, has been engaged in many of the urban folk-song movement's phases. Early in 1941 Seeger assembled a group of folk song enthusiasts then active in New York's left-wing circles and formed a group called the Almanac Singers. (See Additional Listening.) From time to time Woody Guthrie joined this group. On a trip together that happened to take them through Pittsburgh, Guthrie and Seeger came up with one of the earliest political/environmental songs, "Pittsburgh." True to protest song tradition, the lyrics were sung to the then-familiar children's song titled "Crawdad." What we have here, then, is another example of protest music's habitual method of appropriating existing folk tunes for the production of new songs. Although sung to the tune of a children's song, the message of "Pittsburgh" is quite serious. As one line goes: "All I do is cough and choke from the iron filings and the sulphur smoke." The song also takes a stab at corruption in the city's famous steel industry. But a solution is just over the horizon. As the lyrics note in the optimistic final stanza: "From the Alleghany to the Ohio, they're joining up in the CIO in Pittsburgh, Lord, God, Pittsburgh." The CIO that had been central to the refrain in "I Am a Union Woman" is thus promoted once again. As anyone who has ever closely followed a political campaign knows well, repetition and "staying on message" are key weapons in the arsenal.

Pittsburgh has now officially cleaned itself up, and all is forgiven, because the song is now popular in an official version, with phrases such as "Pittsburgh town is a smoky old town" replaced by the more salutary "Pittsburgh town is a great old town."

PROTEST AND FOLK SONG IN THE 1960S
Bob Dylan

The protest song movement was somewhat muted in the decade and a half following World War II. When it reemerged in the 1960s it presented a marked contrast to the movement of the 1930s and 1940s. The career of Bob Dylan (Robert Zimmerman, b. 1941) is illustrative. Dylan emerged into prominence from the same Greenwich Village milieu that had launched his idol, Woody Guthrie, into the role of protester and "folk poet." But the men, their backgrounds, and their times were different. As a folk musician, Guthrie never seemed preoccupied with adopting or changing styles. One gets the impression that he just played as the spirit moved him. Dylan, coming along at a later and more self-conscious period for folk music, had already gone from rock 'n' roll to acoustic folk by the time he went to New York. He was to change his style, his sound, and his type of material many times thereafter, sometimes alienating fans who had grown accustomed to experiencing him in a certain way.

Dylan created some memorable songs and ballads of protest, especially in his early career. Some are explicit as to the issues: "The Lonesome Death of Hattie Carroll" and "Seven Curses" (the corruption of justice); "Only a Pawn in Their Game" and "Oxford Town" (the machinations of racial prejudice); "Masters of War" and "With God on Our Side" (war). He also produced some very realistic ballads that are not overt protest songs but reflect upon a general human condition such as poverty ("North Country Blues"). Others are more highly distilled and convey more generalized feelings about the future ("Blowin' in the Wind" and "The Times They Are a-Changin'").

Listening Cue "**Masters of War**" Bob Dylan (4:38)

Listen For ▪ strained vocal quality ▪ ostinato in the guitar accompaniment ▪ clear projection of the lyrics

Visit http://www.music.wadsworth.com_3/Kingman for a full listening guide and other resources.

"Masters of War" (CD 2/1) is from the album *The Freewheelin' Bob Dylan,* originally released in May 1963. The song is an intense Dylan experience, one that

© Jay Dickman /CORBIS

Bob Dylan, shown here performing at George Harrison's 1971 Bangladesh Benefit Concert, is one of the preeminent songwriters of the last half of the 20th century. Classic phrases from his lyrics—"You don't need a weatherman to know which way the wind blows"—entered popular culture and his "The Times They Are A-Changin'" became a rallying cry. At a time when the American musical culture rested on boy-meets-girl songs, when the roles of singer and song-writer were separate professions, Dylan stunned listeners by combining an eccentric, often aggressive, but always authentic, vocal style with lyrics that used poetic imagery, humor, and surreal absurdity to illuminate political, social, and personal concerns. Expanding the vocabulary of popular music, Dylan also stretched the limits of popular radio with his 6-minute hit single "Like a Rolling Stone." In 2004, *Rolling Stone* named it #1 on its list of the 500 greatest songs of all time, and his 1966 album *Blonde on Blonde* has been called one of the greatest in American popular music. We hear Bob Dylan's "Masters of War" on CD 2, track 1.

even seemed to cause the poet/musician some level of discomfort, undoubtedly because of the raw aggression expressed in its closing stanza.

Come you masters of war	You that never done nothin'
You that build the big guns	But build to destroy
You that build the death planes	You play with my world
You that build all the bombs	Like it's your little toy
You that hide behind walls	You put a gun in my hands
You that hide behind desks	And you hide from my eyes
I just want you to know	And you turn and run farther
I can see through your masks	When the fast bullets fly

Like Judas of old
You lie and deceive
A world war can be won
You want me to believe
But I see through your eyes
And I see through your brain
Like I see through the water
That runs down my drain

You fasten all the triggers
For the others to fire
Then you sit back and watch
When the death count gets
higher
You hide in your mansion
While young people's blood
Flows out of their bodies
And is buried in the mud

You've thrown the worst fear
That can ever be hurled
Fear to bring children
Into the world
For threatening my baby
Unborn and unnamed
You ain't worth the blood
That runs in your veins

How much do I know
To talk out of turn
You might say that I'm young
You might say I'm unlearned
But there's one thing I know
Though I'm younger than you
Even Jesus would never
Forgive what you do

Let me ask you one question
Is your money that good
Will it buy you forgiveness
Do you think that it could
I think you will find
When your death takes its toll
All the money you made
Will never buy back your soul

And I hope that you die
And your death'll come soon
I'll follow your casket
By the pale afternoon
And I'll watch while you're
lowered
Down to your deathbed
And I'll stand over your grave
'Til I'm sure that you're dead

Although the lyrics are a broad swipe at bureaucrats, the military industrial complex, and those who profit from it, one cannot help recalling the tragic coincidence of President John F. Kennedy's assassination just six months after the album's release. "Masters of War" was written in response to the nuclear arms race of the Cold War, but it transferred quite readily to the Vietnam War just a few years later, and equally so to the recent wars in the Middle East. Indeed, on Veteran's Day 2002, Dylan performed "Masters of War" at Madison Square Garden following a Fifth Avenue parade that the president had dedicated to those fighting what has been coined "the war on terror." According to David Boucher, "The audience roared in recognition and approval when he sang the lines, 'And I hope that you die, and your death'll come soon'" (Boucher 157), a sign of the raw emotion it continues to trigger even four decades after it was written.

Unlike Aunt Molly Jackson's "I Am a Union Woman" (CD 1/29) and to a much greater degree than Fiddlin' John Carson's "The Farmer Is the Man That Feeds Them All" (CD 1/28), the highly polished studio quality of "Masters of War" smacks of commercialism. Indeed, Mike Marqusee notes that Dylan once irritated folksinger Joan Baez (b. 1941) "by telling her he wrote 'Masters of War' for the money" (Marqusee 50). Whatever actually motivated Dylan, he was clearly

Here, a large crowd demonstrates on April 24, 1971, against the "Masters of War" (CD 2, track 1) in Washington. While President Lyndon Johnson vowed "We will not be defeated. We will not withdraw," protest against the Vietnam War spread throughout American society. In 1968, Republican Richard Nixon, campaigning for the presidency, vowed to make "law and or-der" (against such civil unrest as this demonstration) his first domestic priority while bringing "peace with honor" in Vietnam. Nixon won the election, but the war dragged on. After U.S. withdrawal in 1975, the North Vietnamese, against whom we had fought so hard, unified Viet-nam under a communist government. Of the 8 million Americans who served in the war, nearly 58,000 died.

following the "protest song" model to the letter. For one, the tune itself is bor-rowed from a haunting Appalachian song titled "Nottamun Town." We also hear a stylized strain in Dylan's voice that attempts to convey the sense of authentic-ity heard so clearly in Jackson's "I Am a Union Woman." Finally, notice the un-obtrusive repeating pattern (called an *ostinato*) in the guitar accompaniment, which allows us to focus on the song's message all the way through to its startling turn at the end.

FREEDOM SONGS AND THE CIVIL RIGHTS MOVEMENT IN THE SOUTH

For all of the differences between the 1930s and the 1960s, there was an interest-ing parallel. In the 1930s, labor sympathizers who went into the South to help organize the miners found a sturdy singing tradition already at work furnishing

The Student Nonviolent Coordinating Committee—SNCC (pronounced "snick")—was at the center of the civil rights movement. Here, John Lewis (front in light coat), then SNCC chairman and now a U.S. Representative from Georgia, wards off a state trooper's billy club in Selma, Alabama, on March 7, 1965. "We Shall Overcome"—the song we hear from a SNCC reunion concert on CD 2, track 2—became the unofficial anthem of the civil rights movement. When on March 15, addressing Congress to urge passage of the 1965 Voting Rights Act, President Lyndon Johnson said, "What happened in Selma is part of a far larger movement . . . Their cause must be our cause too. . . . All of us must overcome the crippling legacy of bigotry and injustice. *And we shall overcome.*"—most members roared their approval. That August, Johnson signed the bill into law.

songs for the workers. So too, in the early 1960s, protest folksingers from the North who went into the South at the time of the early civil rights struggle also found a southern tradition. In this case, however, it drew from a repertory of African American religious music, which was already furnishing songs for those engaged in marches, mass meetings, sit-ins, and prayer vigils, and for those in jails.

Listening Cue "We Shall Overcome" Freedom Singers of the Student Nonviolent Coordinating Committee (SNCC) (2:07)

Listen For■ harmonization■ lining out■ audience participation

Visit http://www.music.wadsworth.com_3/Kingman for a full listening guide and other resources.

"We Shall Overcome" (CD 2/2) is the best known among these. It is based on the African American church song "I'll Overcome Some Day," with words by the gospel hymnodist C. Albert Tindley, and sung today all over the world. "We Shall Overcome" had been adapted from its religious song model as early as 1945 by union workers in Charleston, South Carolina. It was the "theme song" of Highlander Folk School, in Tennessee, and from there became introduced into the civil rights movement. Like Dylan's "Masters of War," it does not fail to arouse an immediate response from the listener. In this case, however, the state of mind is decidedly more tranquil, and, indeed, hopeful. As many times as we have heard or sung this song before, it continues to move us with its simple yet poignant message. The warmth and richness of sound in this performance is due to a combination of the harmonies created by the principal singers and the audience's participation through communal singing. Notice that some of the lyrics are distinctly shouted out to the audience in advance to let participants know what will be sung next. This practice, called "lining out," will be encountered again in Chapter 10. The present recording was made at a reunion concert of the Freedom Singers in Washington, D.C., in 1988.

We shall overcome,
We shall overcome (my Lord),
We shall overcome someday.
Oh, deep in my heart (my Lord),
I do believe,
We shall overcome someday.

We are not afraid,
We are not afraid (my Lord),
We are not afraid today.
Oh, deep in my heart (my Lord),
I do believe,
We shall overcome someday.

PROJECTS

1. Attend a meeting or a rally (either as participant or as observer) and note what role, if any, is played by actual songs (as opposed to chanted slogans). If their role is minimal or totally absent, speculate as to why this is so, and what might make gatherings devoted to advocacy different in the 2000s from those in any period in the past you might choose (the civil rights movement, for example).
2. R. Serge Denisoff has contrasted what he called the "magnetic" song—that is, the song that advocates a specific action ("join the union" or "join the march," for example) with the "rhetorical" song, which simply dramatizes an issue. Look through past issues of folk music periodicals such as *Broadside* or magazines such as *Sing Out!* to find one song of each type, and analyze and contrast their stances.

ADDITIONAL LISTENING

Dust Bowl Ballads. Smithsonian/Folkways CD FH 2481. By Woody Guthrie.

Pete Seeger and the Almanac Singers. Smithsonian/Folkways CD FH 3864.

Sing for Freedom: Civil Rights Movement Songs. Smithsonian/Folkways CD 40032.

"The Sinking of the *Reuben James*" (reissue). By Woody Guthrie. *Woody Guthrie. That's Why We're Marching: World War II and the American Folk Song Movement*. Smithsonian/Folkways CD 40021.

"So Long, It's Been Good to Know Ya" (reissue). By Woody Guthrie. *Woody Guthrie. That's Why We're Marching: World War II and the American Folk Song Movement*. Smithsonian/ Folkways CD 40021.

Voices of the Civil Rights Movement. Smithsonian/Folkways CD 40084.

THREE OFFSPRING OF THE RURAL SOUTH

The South has been the largest and richest reservoir of folklore we have. In the second half of the twentieth century, great changes came to this region, so that it is no longer what it once was. But if we are seeking the origins of its folklore, we have to look at the South not as it is now but as it existed for three centuries before our own time. The two key words are *isolation* and *conservatism*. The isolation was not only geographic (of the lowlands as well as the highlands) but also demographic—an isolation of the southern people, largely, from the greater mass of the American people. For once the frontier had passed through and moved on west, there was emigration from the South but, until our time, little significant immigration to the South. The conservatism owed a good deal to this isolation but also to the almost exclusive farming economy; to the hierarchical (if not actually aristocratic) social and political structure; to the defensive attitude assumed almost monolithically by southern whites toward the institution of slavery and its equally problematic sequel, white supremacy; and, last but by no means least, to the prevailing orthodox religious modes of thought. Out of this soil, then, sprang the two most pervasive forms of rural music America has ever produced and, as a second generation, a citified but visceral amalgamation that has revolutionized popular music throughout the world.

No one seems more typically American than a cowboy. But cowboy culture came to North America in the 1500s with the Spanish colonists: the ranch (rancho), the cowboy (vaquero), the clothing (hat copying the sombrero; pointed-toe boots with 2½-inch heels; chaps, chaparreras), the tools (lariat, la reata), the herding techniques (branding and open range grazing; the rodeo roundup, al rodear; the cattle drive to market), and even the first cattle. The invention of barbed wire (1873) made fencing inexpensive, closed the open range, and ended the great cattle drives to railroad towns in Kansas and Missouri. But the cowboy— a symbol of American individualism and self-reliance that country singers freely borrowed—had entered American folklore.

COUNTRY MUSIC

The latent popularity of "hillbilly" music, fully revealed only after it had spread beyond its original geographical limits in the 1930s and 1940s, was one of the surprises of the twentieth century, at least to city-bred entrepreneurs and savants of popular culture. Its base of popularity was found not only in the rural South and, as might be expected, among its people who had immigrated to the cities and to other parts of the country, but also among rural white people elsewhere who had no cultural ties with the South at all. We are dealing, then, with the closest thing to a universal "people's music" that rural white Americans have had.

The term *hillbilly,* like so many labels in art that have stuck, was originally derogatory. The first recorded use of the term appeared in a New York periodical in 1900: "A Hill-Billie is a free and untrammelled white citizen of Alabama, who lives in the hills, has no means to speak of, dresses as he can, talks as he pleases, drinks whiskey when he gets it, and fires off his revolver as the fancy takes him" (Green 204–28). The term *old-time music,* an early euphemism for marketing purposes, was used for a time, before the adoption of the now-universal designation *country music.*

ENDURING THEMES

Words are of paramount importance in country music. They exhibit certain pervasive traits that have consistently characterized this genre through its half-century of change.

A fundamental characteristic of country music is its paradoxical blend of realism and sentimentality. The realism reveals itself in a readiness to treat any human situation in song and to deal unflinchingly with any aspect of life that genuinely touches the emotions. Consider, for example, the unsparing realism and grisly details of the lyric "There was whiskey and blood all together / Mixed with glass where they lay" in the Dorsey M. Dixon song "Wreck on the Highway," recorded in 1949 by Roy Acuff (see Additional Listening).

Yet, on the other side of this realism is a tendency toward sentimentality that may often strike one outside the tradition as excessive and tainted with self-pity.

The sentimentalization of objects is also common. These traits are found, for example, in the lyric "Send me the pillow that you dream on / So darling I can dream on it too" from the 1949 Hank Locklin song, recorded as recently as 1988 by Dwight Yoakam (see Additional Listening).

The subjects of country songs are diverse, but tend to revolve around certain recurring themes: love, death, religion, nostalgia, traveling, patriotism, and current events. Songs on important happenings of the day reveal country music's relation to the earlier ballad tradition. Indeed, many songs and ballads collected by Cecil Sharp in the southern highlands in 1916–1918 appear in country music recordings of the 1920s and 1930s. The ballad "John Hardy" (CD 1/3), heard in Chapter 1, was collected by Sharp in 1916 and subsequently recorded commercially by the influential Carter Family in 1930. The ballad tradition was kept alive in country music as event songs continued to be written. With the coming of commercialism, it became vital to hit the market as soon after the event as possible. A song based on General Douglas MacArthur's speech before Congress in 1951, after President Harry Truman removed him from command in Korea, was written and recorded by Gene Autry within hours of the event. And the tradition continues to this day. Shortly after the terrorist attacks on September 11, 2001, Alan Jackson wrote, recorded, and released the moving song "Where Were You" (see Additional Listening).

Eric Schaal / Time Life Pictures/Getty Images

In this photo of the original Carter Family, (l. to r.) Sara Carter sings alto lead and plays autoharp, Sara's husband, Alvin Pleasant "AP" Carter, sings bass, and his sister-in-law, Maybelle Addington Carter, sings harmony and plays guitar. AP was the driving force, securing a contract from Victor Records in 1926. The Carter Family pioneered country music with their recordings of folk songs, gospel hymns, and old ballads (such as "John Hardy," which we heard the Carter Family sing on CD 1, track 3). Records and radio would help country music find a mass audience and give rise to musical celebrities like the Carter Family.

THE "COUNTRY SOUND"

Several factors have traditionally come together to create the distinctive "country sound." Three of the most important are dialect and regionalisms, the instruments, and the style of singing.

Dialect and Regionalisms

One of the most characteristic traits of the "country sound" is the use of a regional southern accent. The early country singers naturally retained in their songs not only their regional accent but their dialect as well, with such usages as "a-going," "a-coming," "rise you up," and "yonders." With the first wave of commercial success and the broadening of country music's public, there was a tendency (on the part of singers such as Jimmie Rodgers) to drop the dialect and substitute standard English. In more recent country music, a few vernacular survivals such as "ain't" and the dropping of the final *g* of the *-ing* suffix ("ramblin'," "cheatin'"), have become clichés. The loss of an authentic vernacular, together with the introduction of such devices as more sophisticated rhymes ("infatuation," "sensation," "imagination"), has introduced an artificial conventionality to latter-day country music, which has already lost many of its distinctive regional characteristics in the general process of transforming itself to appeal to a broader audience.

The Instruments

Country music is basically music for string band, originally played on those stringed instruments that were easily portable. The dominant instrument in traditional country music is the fiddle, which takes the lead not only in dance music but often also in the instrumental passages that come between the lyrics in country songs. The mountain dulcimer and the autoharp belong more to the folk origins of this music, and with a few exceptions did not survive long in the country music tradition. The banjo (possibly acquired in the lowlands, through contact with African Americans and black-face minstrels) became an early mainstay of country music. In the second quarter of the twentieth century, it was almost supplanted by the guitar, a more resonant instrument with a greater range. The mandolin entered country music in the 1930s, being at first associated with Bill Monroe and subsequently with the whole style known as "bluegrass," which also introduced a revival of the banjo. With its thin but penetrating tone, the mandolin competes with the banjo for the lead parts. Less easily portable is the string bass (always plucked rather than bowed), but it became established in country music as early as the 1930s and has been essential in the bluegrass band since the 1940s.

An exotic addition to the hillbilly band came from as far west as Hawaii, probably by way of the Hawaiian bands that were so popular in the United States in the early decades of the twentieth century. The Hawaiian steel guitar, with its sliding, wailing sound, was appropriated by country musicians as far back as the 1920s and 1930s. A guitar with a built-in resonator, which served to amplify the sound mechanically before the advent of the electric guitar, was known as the dobro.

The piano, drums, saxophones, and trumpets, essentially alien to country music, were introduced in the country/jazz hybrid "western swing" in the 1930s. With "rural electrification" came the electric guitar in the 1940s (primarily associated with the need for a louder sound in honky-tonk music) and eventually, in the late 1960s, electric keyboards. Acoustic stringed instruments, however, remain the basis for any country music committed to its tradition.

The Style of Singing

Much traditional country music is characterized by a particular manner of singing. A direct carryover from the folk singing of the rural South is a vocal timbre best described as high, nasal, and somewhat strained. The "lonesome," impassive manner of delivery is suited to the impersonality of the ballad tradition. The melodic range for most songs tends to be narrow, with few dramatic leaps from one note to the next. The vocal ornamentation is very conservative, consisting largely of short slides leading up to a note. These factors play into what many consider country music's greatest appeal: its down-home unvarnished sincerity that just tells it like it is. Indeed, essential to any consideration of vocal style is that utter sincerity of delivery without which country music is not genuine. Hank Williams, Sr., expressed it vividly when asked about the success of country music:

> It can be explained in just one word: sincerity. When a hillbilly sings a crazy song, he feels crazy. When he sings, "I Laid My Mother Away," he sees her a-laying right there in the coffin. He sings more sincere than most enter-tainers because the hillbilly was raised rougher than most entertainers. You got to know a lot about hard work. You got to have smelt a lot of mule manure before you can sing like a hillbilly. (Malone 242)

With these general characteristics of the "country sound" in mind, we now turn to an overview of the history of country music.

COMMERCIAL BEGINNINGS: EARLY RECORDINGS, RADIO, AND THE FIRST STARS

We first encounter country music proper as it emerged from folk tradition into the realm of popular music in the 1920s. Although commercial phonograph recording was established before the turn of the century, its application to jazz, blues, and hillbilly music did not come for another two decades, principally because recording executives either were only dimly aware that those genres existed or were unsure as to whether there was a market for such recordings at the time. When recording companies did move into the area of hillbilly music (camouflaging it at first under such names as "old-time music" or "old familiar tunes"), they did so at least partly in response to growing competition from that other powerful new medium of the day, radio. Thus the roles of radio and phono-graph recording in the dissemination and popularization of country music were elaborately intertwined from the start.

In 1923 Georgia moonshiner, circus barker, and political campaign performer Fiddlin' John Carson (1868–1949), who had recently become a locally popular radio performer, recorded "The Little Old Log Cabin in the Lane" and "The Old Hen Cackled and the Rooster's Going to Crow" as the A and B sides of a record that proved to be phenomenally successful. (For an example of Fiddlin' John's style, listen to "The Farmer Is the Man That Feeds Them All," CD 1/28.) With that, the move to record hillbilly music was on. Recording companies made ex-cursions into the South, set up temporary studios, and began recording country musicians by the score, either as individuals or in groups. In other cases, the new-found artists were brought to New York to record. A few who were recorded in the 1920s became the stars of the ensuing period. These included Uncle Dave

Macon (from Tennessee), the Carter Family (from Virginia), and Jimmie Rodgers (from Mississippi).

Radio broadcasting, until then an amateur's plaything, suddenly came of age in the 1920s. As receiving sets came within the economic reach of more and more Americans, broadcasting stations appeared and multiplied, and with them grew the demand for performers to cater to the new invisible audience. Some stations in the South began almost immediately to broadcast country music by local musicians. In 1925, WSM in Nashville began a show, with two unpaid performers and without a commercial sponsor, that was to evolve into the Grand Ole Opry. The early radio programs, like the early recordings, presented a highly traditional country music, still close to its folk origins. But its very popularity generated winds of change.

Of the three stars of early country music mentioned earlier, the first two are representative of performers who never essentially changed their style or material to appeal to a larger audience. David Harrison ("Uncle Dave") Macon (1870–1952), a wagoner from Tennessee, got his professional start playing banjo and singing in local fairs, tent shows, and traveling medicine shows, and the basis of his style and repertory was his background in nineteenth-century minstrel, circus, and vaudeville songs and routines. He was a favorite performer on the Grand Ole Opry from 1925 to 1952.

The Carter Family (Alvin Pleasant, 1891–1960; his wife, Sara, 1898–1979; and his sister-in-law Maybelle, 1909–1978) came from a Virginia mountain background. Their varied repertory (which included not only nineteenth-century parlor songs but also early Tin Pan Alley songs and gospel hymns, as well as ballads and other folk material) made them very influential, as did their distinctive sound and style, with Sara Carter playing autoharp and Maybelle Carter playing the melody on the bass strings of the guitar and the harmony and the rhythm on the upper strings. We have already heard an example of the artistry that helped make them famous in the ballad "John Hardy" (CD 1/3).

Jimmie Rodgers, by comparison, was in a class by himself.

The Granger Collection, New York

A muleskinner drove a team of mules carrying provisions or coal and ore from the mines. (Teamsters now drive trucks instead of mules.) Muleskinners used salty language, told tall tales, and developed an expertise cracking the whip to get stubborn mules to move. Here we see mules loaded with winter provisions for the Revenge Mines, a miner's camp in Colorado, 1880. The man with the whip is the muleskinner. We hear two versions of "Muleskinner Blues," a country version by Jimmie Rodgers (CD 2, track 3) and a bluegrass version by Bill Monroe (CD 2, track 8).

JIMMIE RODGERS: THE FATHER OF COUNTRY MUSIC

Jimmie Rodgers (1897–1933), the "Father of Country Music," was born in Meridian, Mississippi. He based his career on music he had actually grown up with, but he contributed enormously to the popularization of that music, and in the process wore a number of different country hats. Rodgers recorded many types of songs: sentimental love songs, melancholy nostalgic songs, cowboy and railroad songs, and white blues, for example. With such an eclectic repertory, he was bound to bring something new to the traditional country style. And indeed he did. Rodgers' role as an innovator is probably best remembered by the trademark "blue yodel" he introduced into country music. Some of his songs even bore the generic title "Blue Yodel" followed by a number to distinguish one from another. An example is "Muleskinner Blues," also known as "Blue Yodel No. 8" (CD 2/3).

Listening Cue **"Muleskinner Blues"** ("Blue Yodel No. 8") Jimmie Rodgers, vocal and guitar (2:55)

Listen For ▪ falsetto ▪ blue yodel ▪ changing role of the guitar

Visit http://www.music.wadsworth.com_3/Kingman for a full listening guide and other resources.

Good morning, captain
Good morning shine (falsetto)
Do you need another muleskinner
Out on your new mud line
(yodel)

I like to work
I'm rolling all the time (falsetto)
I can pop my initials
On a mule's behind
(yodel)

Hey little water boy
Bring that water round (falsetto)
If you don't like your job
Set that water bucket down
(yodel)

Workin' on the good road's
A dollar and a half a day (falsetto)
My good girl's waiting on a Saturday night
Just to draw my pay
(guitar passage)

I'm going to town, honey
What you want me to bring you back?
Bring a pint of booze
And a John B Stetson hat (bring it to me, honey)
(yodel)

I smell your bread a-burning
Turn your damper down (falsetto)
If you ain't got a damper, good gal
Turn your bread around
(yodel)

In "Muleskinner Blues," we notice that the famous blue yodel plays a very clear structural role in the pacing of the music, punctuating the end of every stanza. It is only in the fourth stanza that it does not. At that point, the guitar steps out of its background role as a strumming accompaniment to present a melody of its own. Another notable feature is Rodgers' very clean break into *falsetto*—an unnaturally high voice—at the end of the second line of almost every stanza. It is no wonder that songs such as "Muleskinner Blues" were generically marketed as "Blue Yodels." For indeed, at some point we forget the lyrics altogether in anticipation of Rodgers' next feat of vocal gymnastics, coming predictably at the end of every stanza. In essence, then, the attention is shifted away from the music and its message to the antics of the performer himself. This is an important part of what made Jimmie Rodgers the first country music superstar.

With the advent of Jimmie Rodgers, the attention and emphasis in country music shifted to the solo singer. The "Singing Brakeman"—a nickname derived from Rodgers' early days as a railroad worker—had an extremely short career as a performing and recording artist. But in a mere six years (from his first trial recording in 1927 to his death in 1933), he recorded 111 songs, sold 20 million records, became internationally famous, and led country music into greener pastures than it had ever dreamed existed.

The interaction between the commercial country music of the 1930s and what was held to be "folk music" shows how complex the relationship between the two had become after the advent of radio and recordings. Folklorists traveling through the South in the 1930s, in the first wave of collecting on behalf of the Library of Congress and others, "discovered" and collected songs that their singers had learned from the commercial recordings of Jimmie Rodgers!

THE WEST: COWBOYS, HONKY-TONKS, AND WESTERN SWING

Hillbilly music's native soil was the upland South, and it is the music from this hill country that has come to be unmistakably identified with the "country music" of the Southeast. But meanwhile the West was being heard from as well. America has long pursued a love affair with its own romantic conception of the West and the image of the cowboy. The western branch of country music has played its part in the propagation of this romanticism. For just as the Southwest is in large degree a cultural extension of the South, so is "western music" an extension and adaptation of hillbilly music.

The link between the eastern and western strains of country music is Texas. Here the southern influence, especially in east Texas, is notably strong. The country was settled primarily by southern planters, and slavery and the raising of cotton flourished, along with southern religion, culture, and folklore. But Texas is also where the West begins. The dry and spacious topography, the open range and the raising and transporting of cattle to the new railroads, and ultimately the industrialization following the oil boom, produced a distinctive Texas economy. The influence of Mexican, Louisiana Cajun, and midwestern American culture further distinguished Texas from the old South.

Authentic Cowboy Music

There is a rich store of authentic cowboy and frontier songs that were actually sung in the old West. "The Buffalo Skinners," a pre-cowboy song from the days of the buffalo, is one of the oldest (see Additional Listening). These were among the first folk songs, after African American spirituals, to be collected and published in the United States, the earliest dating from 1908. Early singers such as Jules Verne Allen and Harry "Haywire Mac" McClintock, who really had been cowboys, made recordings of these songs in the 1920s. But the cowboy image did not loom large in American popular culture until the advent of western movies and the "singing cowboy."

The Cowboy Image on Records and Film

The "western" part of the trade designation "country-and-western" was added as cowboy life began to be romanticized. Ken Maynard was perhaps the first singing cowboy; he sang two traditional songs in *The Wagon Master* as early as 1929. The genre—and the image—was well launched in the 1930s. Jimmie Rodgers, already a star as the "Singing Brakeman" from Mississippi, adopted the ten-gallon hat, Texas as his home state, and the role of singing cowboy. Native Texans such as Gene Autry, Ernest Tubb, and Woodward Maurice "Tex" Ritter soon capitalized further on this image. The Sons of the Pioneers, which included Leonard Slye (later Roy Rogers), was among the earliest singing groups. Rubye Blevins moved from her native Arkansas to California and became, as Patsy Montana, the first singing cowgirl. Her own song, "I Want to Be a Cowboy's Sweetheart," became very popular and marked a significant entry of women into the ranks of country singers.

Few actual cowboy songs found their way into the country-and-western repertoire. Nonetheless, the country music entertainer adopted cowboy dress (often in fancy and exaggerated form) and continued to sing country songs. Cowboy films made in Hollywood spurred the writing of popular songs based on western themes. Curiously enough, songs such as "Tumbling Tumbleweeds" by the Canadian Bob Nolan, and "The Last Roundup," by Bostonian Billy Hill, born and raised in Boston, became prototypes of the "western" song.

Honky-Tonk Music

The occupation of cowboy has not gone out of existence. But the open range, with its freely roaming cows and cowboys, was largely fenced and gone by 1900, and the great cattle drives ended more than a century ago. A more realistic ambience of the West for the greater part of the last half century, particularly in Texas, has been that of small farm towns and oil-boom towns, of truck stops and bars; its more realistic heroes and heroines the oil "boomers," the truck drivers, and their roaring eighteen-wheelers.

A new kind of "western" music evolved to fit one of the chief social institutions of this more modern environment—the honky-tonk. *Honky-tonk* was a generic term for the neon-light-emblazoned bars, saloons, dance halls, ballrooms, and nightclubs that grew up, generally on the outskirts of towns. The music adapted for the lively honky-tonks had to emphasize louder and more incisive instruments; thus, the electric guitar began to be used in the 1940s, as did that distinctly urban instrument, the piano. County music historian Bill Malone has pointed out that country musicians "found receptive audiences in the oil communities," but in the absence of live performers the music reached its consumers by means of the jukebox.

Thematically, the music was no longer concerned with nostalgia for rural life, home, and family, or with traditional religion or mores. Rather, it dealt with harsh realities, preeminently loneliness and infidelity ("slippin' around"). "Walking the Floor Over You," as recorded by Ernest Tubb, with its use of the steel guitar and the addition of a honky-tonk piano, typifies the genre (see Additional Listening). Texans have been the main purveyors of honky-tonk. In the 1970s and 1980s, country-and-western musicians in Austin, Texas, including Willie Nelson, reincarnated the honky-tonk sound, style, subject matter, and spirit as an alternative to the more mainstream "Nashville sound."

Western Swing

Texas, at the crossroads of a variety of influences, was hospitable to bands that were more innovative and eclectic in their instrumentation and repertory than those of the more traditional Southeast. It is not surprising, then, that Texas was the locale where hybridization took place between country music and big-band jazz. The introduction of such hitherto alien instruments as saxophones, drums, and later trumpets into the string band of fiddles, mandolins, and guitars began as early as the 1930s.

Bob Wills (1905–1975), the figure most closely associated with this development, started his famous Texas Playboys in 1934. His "Cotton-Eyed Joe" has been described as the "meeting of frontier fiddle and big-band swing." Based on an old square-dance fiddle tune, it is framed by Wills' fiddling over a very steady "boom-chuck" accompaniment. The instrumental passages between the lyrics introduce, successively, a steel guitar and a jazzy piano, before the return of the fiddle.

© Bettmann/CORBIS

Bob Wills and His Texas Playboys—whom we hear on CD 2, track 4—helped introduce western swing to a national audience. Originally played by string bands (fiddles, mandolin, banjo, acoustic six-string guitar, and a baritone ukulele), western swing was always dance music—simple two-steps and Mexican waltzes—played in dance halls, roadhouses, and country fairs. Wills added drums, horns, a big-band swing style, and a pedal steel guitar to create an exuberant new sound. Here we see Bob Wills, Laura Lee, and Tommy Duncan at the mike, and Joe Ferguson with his fiddle, before 20,000 people in the Aragon Ballroom in 1944.

Listening Cue "Cotton-Eyed Joe" Bob Wills and His Texas Playboys (2:36)

CD 2

4

Listen For ▪ fiddle ▪ steel guitar ▪ "boom-chuck" accompaniment

Visit http://www.music.wadsworth.com_3/Kingman for a full listening guide and other resources.

Don't you remember, don't you know
Daddy worked a man they called Cotton-eyed Joe
Daddy worked a man they called Cotton-eyed Joe

Refrain:
Hadn't oughta been for Cotton-eyed Joe
I'd-a been married a long time ago.
I'd-a been married a long time ago.

Down in the cotton patch down below
Everybody's singing the Cotton-eyed Joe
Everybody's singing the Cotton-eyed Joe
(Refrain)

I know a gal lives down below
Used to go to see her but I don't no more
Used to go to see her but I don't no more
(Refrain)

I fell down and I stubbed my toe
Called for the doctor Cotton-eyed Joe
Called for the doctor Cotton-eyed Joe
(Refrain)

Git my fiddle and rock my bow
Gonna make music everywhere I go
Gonna play a tune they call Cotton-eyed Joe
(Refrain)

A key feature in this recording is the sound of the steel guitar, which Bob Wills helped to make prominent in country music, especially in honky-tonk, with songs like "Steel Guitar Rag" and the better-known "San Antonio Rose." By the early 1940s the popularity of this eclectic blending of styles and repertory allowed Wills to move the band's base of operations from Texas to California, and from there, he began touring and recording extensively. The mix became known as "western swing," and other bandleaders, such as Milton Brown, Tex Williams, and Hank Penny, cultivated it as well. Though the roots of western swing might have been Texan, it was California that really nurtured this hybrid genre. Merle Haggard (b. 1937) of Bakersfield, California, among others, has been responsible for its more recent popularity.

POSTWAR DISSEMINATION AND FULL-SCALE COMMERCIALIZATION

The migrations and upheavals that attended both the Depression in the 1930s and World War II in the 1940s had the effect of spreading country music far beyond the rural South, dispersing its devotees to the cities and their suburbs, and to all parts of the country. This regional music thus acquired nationwide popularity, and became altered—de-regionalized—in the process. This set the stage for its full-scale commercialization in the decades that followed.

Mainstream Stars of the 1950s and 1960s

The use of the suspect term *mainstream* here is prompted by the fact that the country music stars mentioned below clearly came out of, and continued to cultivate, the dominant characteristic traditions of country music.

Of these, Alabama-born Hank Williams (1923–1953) probably shone the brightest and cast the longest shadow—all the more remarkably since his career, like that of Jimmie Rodgers twenty years earlier, was brief (essentially 1947–1952). The pervasiveness of the western image is seen in the name Williams gave his band—the Drifting Cowboys—and the stylized cowboy costume he sometimes wore, even though he had virtually no cowboy songs in his repertory. Nonetheless, the Drifting Cowboys had a traditional instrumentation of fiddle, guitars, steel guitar, and bass, with the occasional mandolin. His vocal style could be relaxed and rhythmic or highly intense, depending on his material, and his

In this candid shot, Hank Williams plays at a square dance in 1947, two years before recording "Lovesick Blues." The recording was so popular that it convinced the Grand Old Opry to overlook his reputation for recklessness (he liked to play with guns) and unreliability (he missed performances)—probably arising from his dependence on alcohol and painkillers to dull his chronic back pain. Williams died at 29 of heart failure in the back of his new Cadillac while being driven to a performance. The original caption to this photo called Williams the "king of the hillbillies"; today, many know him as one of the fathers of country music. We hear him sing "I'm So Lonesome I Could Cry," on CD 2, track 5.

technique included such traditional effects as a modified yodel and an almost-sobbing break in the voice on emotion-laden songs. The latter is heard on "I'm So Lonesome I Could Cry" (CD 2/5), consistently in the last line of every stanza (most often on "lonesome," once on "hide"). The extended steel guitar solo after the second stanza provides us with a good sense of the distinctive sound Bob Wills had helped to introduce into country music (see above).

Listening Cue "I'm So Lonesome I Could Cry" Hank Williams (2:45)

CD 2
5

Listen For ▪ extreme sentimentality ▪ sobbing break in voice ▪ extended steel guitar solo

Visit http://www.music.wadsworth.com_3/Kingman for a full listening guide and other resources.

Hear that lonesome whippoorwill,
He sounds too blue to fly.
The midnight train is whining low,
I'm so lonesome I could cry.

I've never seen a night so long
When time goes crawling by.
The moon just went behind the clouds
To hide its face and cry.

Did you ever see a robin weep,
When leaves began to die?
That means he's lost the will to live,
I'm so lonesome I could cry.

The silence of a falling star
Lights up a purple sky.
And as I wonder where you are
I'm so lonesome I could cry.

"I'm So Lonesome I Could Cry" presents a striking example of an extreme
form of the sentimentality noted previously as an attribute of country music. An-
imals—the whippoorwill or the robin—or even inanimate objects such as a train,
the moon, a star—are endowed with the capacity for human feelings and even
the ability to manifest them visibly.

Many of Williams' songs reflect his own very troubled life. In spite of that, his
range was broad. Williams excelled as a song writer. Some of his most memorable
songs include "Your Cheatin' Heart," "Honky-Tonkin'," and "Hey, Good
Lookin'." Also placing him in the mainstream of country musicians is the fact that
he wrote and recorded religious songs, including his well-known "I Saw the
Light," based on an earlier gospel song. Other stars who worked in an essentially
traditional vein during country music's postwar surge of popularity were Johnny
Cash (1932–2003) from Arkansas, Tennessee Ernie Ford (1919–1991) who actually
was from Tennessee, and the "Coal Miner's Daughter" Loretta Lynn (b. 1935).

Patsy Cline (1932–1962), born Virginia Patterson Hensley, in Winchester, Virginia, is arguably the figure with whom the modern era of female country singers
began (Malone 263). Patsy Cline had a versatility of style that enabled her, in the
late 1950s and early 1960s, to fuse country and pop styles in a manner that appealed
to a broader audience. She was, in essence, what we would recognize today as a
"crossover artist"—someone like Shania Twain, who plays equally well on country and pop stations. And this without particularly wanting to be; she dressed as a
cowgirl and always wanted to yodel on her records. Patsy Cline's vocal power and
expressive flexibility are showcased in "I'm Blue Again" (CD 2/6). The accompaniment is in a kind of halfway mode between country and pop; the steel guitar reminds us of Hank Williams, but the use of vocal backup group and drum set are
distinctly pop. Her career was cut short by a plane crash that took her life on
March 5, 1963.

Frank Driggs Collection/Getty Images

This full-length studio portrait of Patsy Cline, in fringed western dress and cowboy boots, coincides with her 1956 appearance on the nationally televised *Arthur Godfrey Talent Show,* where she sang "Walkin' After Midnight"—her first big hit. Cline credited her singing voice to a timbre change after surviving rheumatic fever in childhood. When, after her second marriage in 1957, Godfrey reportedly asked her, "Are you happy?" Patsy replied, "Just as happy as if I had good sense." We hear Cline sing "I'm Blue Again" on CD 2, track 6.

Listening Cue "I'm Blue Again" Patsy Cline (2:04)

CD 2
6

Listen For ▪ pop vocal group ▪ pop drums ▪ country steel guitar

Visit http://www.music.wadsworth.com_3/Kingman for a full listening guide and other resources.

I'm blue again
My friends all said I'd be
I'm blue again
Because you're leavin' me

This heart of mine
So well remembers you
Although I've lost your love
To someone new

The nights are long
So long my darlin' hear me
I pray that dawn will come
And somehow, you'll be near me

I'm blue again
My heart is filled with tears
I'm blue again
As I think of wasted years

The nights are long   I'm blue again
So long my darlin' hear me   My heart is filled with tears
I pray that dawn will come   I'm blue again
And, somehow, you'll be near me   As I think of wasted years

Rockabilly and a New Generation of Performers and Fans

The influence of African American musical styles has never been absent from country music; blues have been in the repertory from the beginning, and the debt of performers such as Jimmie Rodgers, Bob Wills, and many others, to blues and jazz is clear. In the 1950s a few white performers then in their twenties, including Elvis Presley and Jerry Lee Lewis, began copying the material and style of black blues and rhythm-and-blues singers such as Arthur Crudup, Little Richard, and Otis Blackwell. The nascent rock 'n' roll had a heavy impact on country music itself, splitting its constituency (many fans and performers alike left traditional country for rock, some to return later) and leaving its mark on Nashville and commercial country music in the form of the rock beat, the electrification of the instruments, and the studio-produced sound.

The immediate progeny of this cross-fertilization was rockabilly—"an amalgamation of honky-tonk, country, blues, gospel, and boogie-woogie jackhammered by white performers . . . [and] largely the creation of Sun Records, operated by Sam Phillips" (Giddins). This complex mixture of musical ingredients had an overwhelming appeal for youthful fans. Indeed, the persistent influence of rock on subsequent commercial country music is attributable in large part to the historic background and tastes of many country fans who grew up in the rockabilly era of the 1950s and 1960s. A somewhat different, and largely urban, generation of youth brought up on the folk rock of Bob Dylan were introduced to country music when Dylan visited it briefly in the late 1960s in the albums *John Wesley Harding* (1968) and *Nashville Skyline* (1969, with Johnny Cash).

Nashville and the Pop Sound

The major changes in the move toward pop music had to do with the sound of the instrumental accompaniment—changes that were primarily associated, for a variety of reasons, with Nashville, Tennessee.

Nashville had an early lead in establishing itself as a center for the commercial production and dissemination of country music, thanks to the presence there since 1925 of radio station WSM and the Grand Ole Opry. Recording began as a sideline in conjunction with the station in the 1940s. The availability of talent in the area, together with the increasing market for country music, caused major record companies to begin recording there instead of in New York or Chicago, and ultimately to establish their own studios in Nashville. Independent record companies also sprang up, and as more and more records were produced there, the city acted as a magnet for performers from all over the South. The cycle of growth went on, and the combination of superbly equipped studios and an abundance of skilled engineers and versatile musicians available as session players led to the expansion of the Nashville recording industry to include all types of popular music. The city is also the home of a number of television studios, publishing houses, and booking agencies. The new Grand Ole Opry House is in the center of a huge amusement park.

The characteristics of the "Nashville sound," which began to be evident in the 1950s, include the regular use of drums (which, except in the jazz-hybrid western swing, had been foreign to country music), electric bass (sometimes pounding out a fairly heavy beat reminiscent of rock or boogie), a background of elegantly played strings with a sound more refined than the rustic fiddle style, and the use of singers (often tightly disciplined gospel groups) to provide an impersonal, anonymous kind of vocal backup. Some of these features were heard in Patsy Cline's "I'm Blue Again" (CD 2/6), recorded in 1959.

Studio techniques such as echo effects and overdubbing (adding material in later recording sessions) became standard. A common device for sustaining interest in popular arrangements—bumping the performance pitch up by a half step when material is repeated—was also adopted in Nashville productions. The occasional whine of the steel guitar, the very occasional faint sound of a fiddle or a banjo (often overdubbed), and, above all, the lyrics that still exude an inbred and ineradicable sentimentality are virtually all that remain to distinguish thoroughly "Nashville-ized" country music from any other kind of "easy listening" fare. Nonetheless, the Nashville sound was a tried and true formula for commercial success. And in the business world, that made the "Nashville sound" the law of the land.

Austin, Texas: "Outlaws" and Honky-Tonk

Just as the West had its share of romanticized outlaws, so did its music. The "outlaws" of country music were musicians who resisted conforming to the dictates of Nashville's influential recording industry. An

Here, Willie Nelson sings at the first Farm Aid concert on September 22, 1985, in Champaign, Illinois. The idea for the benefit apparently arose at the Live Aid concert (for African relief) when Bob Dylan said on stage, "Wouldn't it be great if we did something for our own farmers right here in America?" With a recession forcing many farmers into foreclosure, Willie Nelson, Neil Young, and John Mellencamp raced to stage the first show in six weeks. We hear Nelson sing "Blue Eyes Crying in the Rain" on CD 2, track 7.

alternative to the Nashville sound and concept is the neo-honky-tonk (sometimes called "cosmic cowboy") music emanating from Texas, where honky-tonk began.

Austin in the 1970s had a unique ambience that combined ranchers and cowboys with college students at the University of Texas. One result of this diverse mix was a style of music that embraced it all; a style that "reflected a curious combining of images and symbols: hippie, Texan, and, above all, cowboy" (Malone 394). No one embodied that new image better than Willie Nelson (b. 1933).

After his move to Austin in 1972, Willie Nelson abandoned his symbolic Stetson for his trademark hippie headband, earrings, and long hair and embarked on performing and recording a brand of uncomplicated, pre-Nashville honky-tonk music. The combination of image and music, not to mention his resistance to the authority of Nashville, could not help but ensure his appeal to ranchers, cowboys, and hippie college students alike. Nelson's recording of "Blue Eyes Crying in the Rain" (CD 2/7), from his classic album *Red Headed Stranger* (1975), is representative of the music produced by the "outlaw" counterculture. It had been recorded thirty years earlier by Roy Acuff, one of the first country music stars after Jimmie Rodgers. The song was thus distinctly "old school," and Nelson responded by keeping his performance style very simple.

Listening Cue "**Blue Eyes Crying in the Rain**" Willie Nelson, vocal and guitar; bass, harmonica (2:19)

CD 2
7

Listen For ▪ simple performance style ▪ absence of heavy instrumentation and background singers

Visit http://www.music.wadsworth.com_3/Kingman for a full listening guide and other resources.

In the twilight glow I see her
Blue eyes crying in the rain
When we kissed goodbye and parted
I knew we'd never meet again

Love is like a dying ember
And only memories remain
And through the ages I'll remember
Blue eyes crying in the rain

Someday when we meet up yonder
We'll stroll hand in hand again
In the land that knows no parting
Blue eyes crying in the rain

Lyrics reprinted by permission of Paul E. Johnson, dba Tompaul Music Co.

The simplicity of "Blue Eyes Crying in the Rain," and indeed many of the songs on *Red Headed Stranger,* contributed to making the album both different and controversial for its time. Record executives accustomed to the tried and true success of the "Nashville sound," were highly skeptical of its "underproduced," "unfinished" qualities, and recommended lush strings and studio effects. But Nelson held his ground and, with the help of fellow outlaw Waylon Jennings (1937–2002), secured its release on the Columbia label. The album went multiplatinum. "Blue Eyes Crying in the Rain" was a number one hit on the country charts, climbed to twenty-one on the pop charts, and earned Willie Nelson the Grammy award for Best Male Country Vocal Performance.

Country Music's Identity Crisis

The tremendous commercial success of country music over the past thirty years or so has been something of a mixed blessing. While country music has entered the consciousness of many more Americans than it had as a southern regional music, something has been lost too. In short, modern country music is suffering from an identity crisis. Its cause boils down to pure economics, for the country music industry has "discovered that its best interests lie in the distribution of a package with clouded identity, possessing no regional traits . . . a music that is all things to all people" (Malone 369). As the music itself has become more bland and less regional, many of its performers have tended to move out and away from both the context and the material of country music. Tammy Wynette, Barbara Mandrell, and Dolly Parton achieved superstar status in crossing over into pop styles and into the media of television and movies. In the other direction, pop singers such as Kenny Rogers successfully crossed over and achieved a measure of identification as country singers—though exactly what that designation now means, and to whom, is no longer as clear as it once was, because the identity of the audience for country music has also undergone a considerable shift.

At the dawn of the twenty-first century, there is little left to distinguish what is marketed as country from what is marketed as pop except for the occasional trace of a rural accent, cliché regionalisms, and, with decreasing frequency, the way the singers are dressed. Indeed, many country singers are beginning to turn more and more to "urban chic" as the marketing demographics shift to a younger, more hip crowd. Long gone are the unposed photos of fiddlers in denim overalls and of old wooden rockers on dilapidated porches. These have been replaced by carefully crafted publicity shots featuring the stylish, sexy designer look of Shania Twain, or the contrived grunge look of Keith Urban. A symbolic death knell of "pure country" (if such a thing ever existed) might well have been sounded in 2005 when, for the first time in its history, the Country Music Association held its annual awards show outside of Nashville, Tennessee. The show took place that year in New York City.

From a musical perspective, it is telling that more traditional styles such as bluegrass (to which we turn next) have been moved into a separate marketing category. Banished from modern country is the sound of the folk fiddle or the banjo; even the acoustic guitar and steel guitar are becoming increasingly rare.

THE PERSISTENCE AND REVIVAL OF TRADITIONAL STYLES

Bluegrass

The strongest bastion of the musical tradition of the rural southeastern United States is bluegrass music. Yet bluegrass music as we know it today is scarcely fifty years old. Its origins, well documented, are within the living memory of many, and some of its originators are still playing and singing. It is less a literal revival of an older style than it is a new, highly demanding, highly professional virtuoso style derived from the music of the old string bands. The term *bluegrass* refers to an acoustic string band sound (fiddle, mandolin, banjo, guitar, and bass) and a singing style that stresses a high-pitched, straight tone. There is a pronounced blues influence, palpable not only in the presence of blues numbers in the repertory but also in the frequent blues inflections in fiddle and banjo passages. Although one occasionally comes across slow, mournful bluegrass songs, its most characteristic tempo is fast—often breathtakingly so. Bluegrass shares with bebop jazz (a revitalization of jazz by virtuosos that began to develop around the same time) the distinction of being the fastest vernacular music we have—pushed to its limits by phenomenal players.

The one man who, more than any other, was responsible for the rise of bluegrass, and whose group, the Blue Grass Boys, gave it its name, was Bill Monroe (1911–1996). Monroe was a gifted mandolin player, guitarist, and singer who began his professional career performing with his two brothers and proceeded to develop a style that was true to the old-time music. Monroe was not from the bluegrass country but from farther west in Kentucky. His signature sound came into being slowly, by degrees, in Atlanta (where the Blue Grass Boys were first assembled) and in Nashville (where they became part of the Grand Ole Opry). Monroe's high, clear singing style and his mandolin playing were important hallmarks of the genre, as was the reinstatement of the fiddle. His most requested piece, and the first one he performed on his debut on the Grand Ole Opry in 1939, was his famous rendering of Jimmie Rodgers' "Muleskinner Blues" (CD 2/8). Notice that Bill Monroe has prominently retained the use of *falsetto* and the famous "blue yodel," occasionally adding a weeping inflection to both. The mandolin, with its somewhat faint percussive timbre, is heard at the outset. The fiddle assumes a prominent role throughout the recording, and is played in a highly virtuosic style.

Listening Cue "**Muleskinner Blues**" Bill Monroe and His Blue Grass Boys (2:44)

Listen For ▪ virtuosic fiddle playing ▪ weeping blue yodel

Visit http://www.music.wadsworth.com_3/Kingman for a full listening guide and other resources.

Good morning, captain
Good morning, shine
Do you need another muleskinner
Out on your new mud line
(yodel)

I like workin'
I'm rolling all the time
I can pop my initials
On a mule any ole time
(yodel and extended fiddle passage)

I'm going to town
What you want me to bring you
back?
Bring a walkin' cane
And a John B Stetson hat
(yodel)

Hey little water boy
Bring that bucket around
If you don't like your job
Set your water bucket down
(yodel)

A trademark of bluegrass in the popular mind is the incisive tone of the five-string banjo, which, like the fiddle, is also played with a virtuoso technique. The banjo had all but disappeared in country music by the 1940s, but it had a dramatic revival in a "picking style" (as opposed to a simple strumming style) native to western North Carolina. This picking style is exemplified in the phenomenal playing of Earl Scruggs (b. 1924). Scruggs joined the Blue Grass Boys in 1945, and although his tenure with them was brief, in his three years of playing with Bill Monroe, Lester Flatt (guitarist and singer), Chubby Wise (fiddler), and Howard Watts (bassist), the "bluegrass sound" was essentially established.

© Henry Horenstein /CORBIS

In 1952 the Lilly Brothers—shown here at a 1978 reunion—went north from Beckley, West Virginia, and, along with Don Stover, a bluegrass banjo picker, played for eighteen years at Boston's honky-tonk Hillbilly Ranch. Generally a little seedy and usually located on the outskirts of town, honky-tonks were havens for bands to hone their skills entertaining occasionally rowdy customers. We hear the Lilly Brothers play a bluegrass version of "John Henry" on CD 2, track 9.

Flatt and Scruggs left in 1948 to form the Foggy Mountain Boys. That group, along with the Stanley Brothers and the Lilly Brothers, among others, continued to cultivate and push the limits of bluegrass music, which sometimes drew from the repertories of the African American ballads as well as blues.

"John Henry" (CD 2/9) is a fast-paced rendition of the African American ballad "John Henry" studied in Chapter 2 (CD 1/10). It is performed here by the Lilly Brothers. The three hammer strikes at the beginning are a nod in the direction of the John Henry story, but they also set the brisk pace for this rendition. To get a sense of the breakneck speed that the musicians are following, snap your fingers to the bass line. The "tinny" sound of the mandolin is heard prominently at the beginning. The banjo, with its somewhat deeper tone, is played in "picking style" and initially assumes a background role. It is foregrounded in the extended instrumental passage after the first stanza, but with careful listening you can hear that even when it fades behind the voice or mandolin, it never lets up on the pace of its virtuosic picking. (If you are snapping along, notice that the banjo regularly manages to play four notes in the time it takes you to get from one snap to the next.) The hammer strikes check in again about halfway through the piece, marking the downbeat of every measure.

Listening Cue "**John Henry**" The Lilly Brothers (2:38)

Listen For ▪ mandolin ▪ banjo in "picking style" ▪ use of hammer strikes

Visit http://www.music.wadsworth.com_3/Kingman for a full listening guide and other resources.

John Henry, he was a little bitty boy, no bigger than the palm of your hand.
His mammy looked down at John Henry and said,
"Johnny gonna be a steel-drivin' man, lord, lord,
Johnny gonna be a steel-drivin' man."

John Henry, he said to his captain,
"Captain, you're goin' into town.
Bring me back a nine-pound hammer,
For I want to see that railroad down, lord, lord,
I want to see that railroad down."

John Henry said to his shaker,
"Shaker, you better pray,
For if I miss that little piece of steel,
Tomorrow be your dyin' day, lord, lord,
Tomorrow be your dyin' day."

John Henry went up on the mountain.
He looked down on the other side.
The mount was so cold, John Henry was so small,
He lay down that hammer and he cried, lord, lord,
He lay down that hammer and he cried.

John Henry, he had a purty little woman.
Her name was Polly Ann.
John Henry took sick and had to go to bed.
Polly drove the steel like a man, lord, lord,
Polly drove the steel like a man.

Bluegrass has for some time, possibly because of its strict loyalty to acoustic instruments, had an existence independent of the more mass-audience-oriented country music. But the style has also by this time spawned substyles, branching off in several directions. The group Seldom Scene has purveyed a smooth honky-tonk bluegrass (as in "Bottom of the Glass," 1974), and the Osborne Brothers were already producing in the 1960s a kind of neo-bluegrass (as in "Rocky Top," 1967), adding piano and drums, complex harmonies, and lyrics that, with their corny references to such stereotypical images as moonshine, were pseudo-hillbilly. (See Additional Listening.) But traditional bluegrass flourishes as well, especially in the many summer festivals that have been taking place since the early 1960s and that encompass all the many styles the genre has produced.

PROJECTS

1. Interview a number of people, from varied backgrounds, on the subject of country music, with a view to ascertaining the degree of correlation (if any) between a like or dislike of country music and a basically rural or urban background and orientation. It may be well to play some recorded examples as part of the interview. Include yourself as one respondent if you wish.
2. Review the film *O Brother Where Are Thou* with regard to the music. Do you know any of the songs? In what ways does the use of "old-time music" contribute to the atmosphere and sense of place?

ADDITIONAL LISTENING

Classic Country Music: A Smithsonian Collection. Smithsonian Collection of Recordings RD042. This is an important basic collection that includes examples for many of the trends and artists discussed here, including "Bottom of the Glass," "Rocky Top," and "Walking the Floor Over You."

"Buffalo Skinners." *Slim Critchlow: Cowboy Songs.* Arhoolie 479.

"Send Me the Pillow You Dream On." Dwight Yoakam, *Buenas Noches from a Lonely Room.* Reprise/WEA 25749.

"Where Were You." Alan Jackson, *Drive.* Arista 67039.

"Wreck on the Highway." Roy Acuff, *The Essential Roy Acuff.* Sony 90906.

THE BLUES

Like country music, the blues has exercised a strong presence in American culture, and the range of its influence has been even broader, as we shall see in the next chapter. The origin of the blues, however, is unclear. It seems to have originated as a form of black folk song in the South during the closing decades of the nineteenth century, and might have had important antecedents in the cries, calls, and hollers visited briefly in Chapter 2. Much like the field holler, the early folk blues was not a communal expression. It was the intensely personal lament or reflection of the solitary individual facing the hardships of what can often seem an indifferent world. Yet long before our time, this lament had become an entertainment, the solitary singer's comment had crystallized into a form that could be printed and sold, and the lone cry of the despondent individual had become a commodity. The folk blues, in other words, had become popular music—even before the first blues recordings appeared.

The early blues were propagated by a class of black musicians who were to a degree outcasts, even within the black community. They were rejected, at least, by its more settled and established members, especially the devoutly religious, who referred to the blues as "devil songs." Among the early propagators of blues were the down-and-out who had gravitated to the larger cities to make the street music that became their prime means of livelihood and independence. As the blues gradually shifted from its folk roots to its popular form, it established characteristics that we regard now as hallmarks of the blues tradition.

CHARACTERISTICS OF THE BLUES

Numerous characteristics typify the blues: the way the voice is handled, the instruments used, the range and treatment of its subjects, its distinctive musical form, and the basic feel that has its roots in a solitary experience and view of life. Of these, we will do well at the outset to concentrate on three: its treatment of subjects, its musical form, and instruments that contribute to the blues style. Other traits will be addressed as they pertain to specific examples discussed in this chapter.

Frank Driggs Collection / Getty Images

In a performance portrait from 1923, we see blues singer Gertrude "Ma" Rainey (1886–1939) and her Georgia Jazz Band, a pickup group in Chicago, Illinois. At the piano (right) is Thomas A. "Georgia Tom" Dorsey, bluesman and gospel singer (see Chapter 11). On CD 2, track 10, Rainey performs with then studio musicians Fletcher Henderson on piano and the great Louis Armstrong on the cornet. Few can point to an important blues singer before Ma Rainey, billed as the Mother of the Blues.

Blues Subjects

The subjects treated in the blues encompass a wide range. Indeed, no area of commonly shared human experience would seem to be excluded. Some blues speak of a nameless depression, work (or lack of it), poverty, and gambling; others of crime, prisons, addiction, and even homosexuality and prostitution. Here, for example, are the unflinching lyrics to Gertrude "Ma" Rainey's (1886–1939) "Hustlin' Blues," a song about prostitution:

> It's rainin' out here and tricks ain't walkin' tonight,
> It's rainin' out here and tricks ain't walkin' tonight,
> I'm goin' home, I know I've got to fight.

> If you hit me tonight, let me tell you what I'm going to do,
> If you hit me tonight, let me tell you what I'm going to do,
> I'm gonna take you to a court and tell the judge on you.

I ain't made no money, and he dared me to go home,
I ain't made no money, and he dared me to go home,
Judge, I told him he better leave me alone.

He followed me up, and he grabbed me for a fight,
He followed me up, and he grabbed me for a fight,
He said, girl do you know, you ain't made no money tonight.

Oh, Judge, tell him I'm through,
Oh, Judge, tell him I'm through,
I'm tired of this life, that's why I brought him to you.

The greatest number of blues lyrics, however, are in some way about the relationship between a man and a woman. As the blues singer Robert Pete Williams said, "Love makes the blues. That's where it comes from" (Cook 40). The man–woman relationship is displayed in the blues in a great variety of aspects—from a comment on the power of a woman's attraction or the exhilaration of being in love, to a scornful comment on infidelity, the painful fact of separation, or the most bitter rejection. The following lyrics from the "Lost Your Head Blues," recorded by Bessie Smith in 1926, present us with a good example:

I was with you baby when you did not have a dime
I was with you baby when you did not have a dime
Now since you got plenty money you have throw'd your good gal down

Once ain't for always, two ain't for twice
Once ain't for always, two ain't for twice
When you get a good gal, you better treat her nice

When you were lonesome, I tried to treat you kind
When you were lonesome, I tried to treat you kind
But since you've got money, it's done changed your mind

I'm gonna leave you baby, ain't gonna say goodbye
I'm gonna leave you baby, ain't gonna say goodbye
But I'll write you and tell you the reason why

Days are lonesome, nights are long
Days are lonesome, nights are so long
I'm a good gal, but I've just been treated wrong

As these and other blues lyrics demonstrate, the blues language is keen, apt, colorful, and given to the use of irony, metaphor, and double entendre. No subject is off limits, but with the prevalent treatment of interpersonal relationships, it is no wonder that the blues have had such a broad appeal. The only requirement one often needs in order to connect with this music is to have loved—and, preferably, lost.

From a strictly formal point of view, notice that the lyrics are customarily arranged as a succession of three-line stanzas and that the second line tends to repeat the first. This arrangement is due to the now-standard musical form that is used to set blues lyrics, called "twelve-bar blues" form.

Musical Form

Although the lyrics and the styles of performance from one blues singer to the next are often enough to keep our attention riveted, an understanding of the basic musical form of the blues enhances the enjoyment and understanding of the music as well.

The blues are typically sung to a musical form called the *twelve-bar blues,* a standard pattern of chord changes that is applied to each stanza of text in blues lyrics. Here are the essentials for understanding how it works. First, each and every three-line stanza gets twelve bars (or measures) of music in a moderately slow 4/4 time. Another way to think about this is that each bar will accommodate four toe taps or finger snaps that are evenly spaced at a moderately slow speed. Second, the twelve bars of music that set every three-line stanza incorporate a predictable series of chord changes consisting of the three most basic chords in any musical key: I (tonic), IV (subdominant), and V (dominant). These chords are typically arranged in the predictable pattern of I-IV-I-V-I, and with careful listening the basic changes are quite audible. A third essential ingredient is the *break,* a brief instrumental passage that comes at the end of every line in a three-line stanza. The alternation between the vocal line and the break that, in effect, "responds" to it produces a call-and-response pattern that is an important distinguishing feature of the blues. (Incidentally, the break itself is not unique to the blues. The term can be applied to instrumental passages that come between the lyrics in bluegrass and jazz, for example.)

The following diagram illustrates how the vocal lines and breaks for one stanza of blues lyrics might unfold over the predictable chord changes in a standard twelve-bar blues pattern.

Vocal Line:	Line 1		break	Line 2		break	Line 3		break	
Chord:	I———————————————IV———I———V———I———									
Bar (measure):	1	2	3	4	5	6	7	8	9	10	11	12

Of course, the proof is in the listening. To get a better idea of how the twelve-bar blues form is actually applied, listen carefully to the first stanza of Ma Rainey's "Countin' the Blues" (CD 2/10), recorded in 1924, while following the chord changes mapped out on the next page for every line. To help lock onto the chord changes, listen carefully to the piano part, which also steadily marks the four moderately slow beats in every bar. The lyrics are preceded by an instrumental introduction (with Ma Rainey talking over it). This introduction sets the mood for the audience, but it also provides Ma Rainey with her musical bearings in terms of the key and pacing of the song. Blues songs typically begin with this type of instrumental introduction. As the recording plays out, notice in particular the distinctive call-and-response pattern that results from the instrumental breaks following every line that Ma Rainey sings.

Listening Cue "Countin' the Blues" Ma Rainey, vocal, and Her Georgia Jazz Band

Recorded in New York, New York, 1924 (3:20)
Listen For ▪ twelve-bar blues form ▪ breaks ▪ call-and-response pattern

 Visit http://www.music.wadsworth.com_3/Kingman for a full listening guide and other resources.

Line 1:   Layin' in my bed this mornin' face turned to the wall (break)

Chord: (I)——

Line 2:   Layin' in the bed this mornin' face turned to the wall (break)

Chord: (IV)——————————————————————————(I)——————————

Line 3:   Trying to count these blues so I could sing them all (break)

Chord   (V)————————————————————(I)——————————

The same pattern applies to each of the subsequent stanzas:

> Memphis, Ramport, Beale Street, set them free
> Memphis, Ramport, Beale Street, set them free
> Braveyard, 'Bama Bound, Lord, Lord, come from stingaree
>
> Lord sittin' on the Southern, gonna ride, ride all night long
> Lord sittin' on the Southern, gonna ride all night long
> Downhearted, Gulf Coast, they was all good songs
>
> Lord, 'rested at midnight, jailhouse made me lose my mind
> Lord, 'rested at midnight, jailhouse made me lose my mind
> Bad Luck 'n' Boll-Weevil, made me think of old Moonshine
>
> Lord, goin' to sleep for Mama just now got bad news
> Lord, goin' to sleep now, just now got bad news
> To try to dream away my troubles, countin' these blues

This now-standard form was perhaps first crystallized in the published blues that began appearing as early as 1912. But while it has become commonplace to describe the blues as though it were invariably conventionalized, it bears mentioning here that the blues can also be found in musical forms that might strike us as surprisingly free. In other words, the sung portions do not always arrange themselves into three-line stanzas, but may consist of a varying number of lines, often unequal in length. So, too, performers are not always caged in by the strict twelve-bar blues pattern but turn instead to a more fluid, even rhapsodic style, singing as the mood strikes them. Consider, for example, the unconventional "Prison Cell Blues" (CD 2/11) recorded in 1928 by Texas bluesman Blind Lemon Jefferson (1897–1929).

Hulton Archive/Getty Images

Blues singer and guitarist Blind Lemon Jefferson issued this studio portrait (a standard and relatively inexpensive publicity tool in the early 1900s) in 1925, around the same time that he recorded "Prison Cell Blues," which we hear on CD 2, track 11. A one-time resident of Dallas, Texas, where he met and performed with Leadbelly, Jefferson traveled widely around the South and recorded forty-three songs in Chicago before dying mysteriously in his early thirties.

Listening Cue "Prison Cell Blues" Blind Lemon Jefferson, vocal and guitar

CD 2

11

Recorded in Chicago, Illinois, 1928 (2:45)
Listen For ▪ unconventional form (not twelve-bar blues) ▪ fluid performance style

Visit http://www.music.wadsworth.com_3/Kingman for a full listening guide and other resources.

Getting' tired of sleeping in this lowdown lonesome cell
Lord, I wouldn't have been here if it had not been for Nell
Lay awake at night and just can't eat a bite
Used to be my rider but she just won't treat me right
Got a red-eyed captain and a squabbling boss
Got a mad dog sergeant, honey, and he won't knock off
I'm getting tired of sleeping in this lowdown lonesome cell
Lord, I wouldn't have been here if it had not been for Nell
I asked the government to knock some days off my time
Well the way I'm treated, I'm about to lose my mind
I wrote to the governor, please turn me a-loose
Since I don't get no answer, I know it ain't no use
I'm getting tired of sleeping in this lowdown lonesome cell
Lord, I wouldn't have been here if it had not been for Nell
I hate to turn over and find my rider gone

Walking across my floor, Lordy, how I moan
Lord, I wouldn't have been here if it had not been for Nell
I'm getting tired of sleeping in this lowdown lonesome cell

Instruments and the Blues Style

The guitar is perhaps the instrument most often associated with the blues, and over time, performers have developed their own individual sounds and techniques, some of which passed into general currency. One of the most common and recognizable techniques in the blues is that of "bending" the pitch. Bending is a technique that guitarists use to make a note temporarily higher in pitch by pulling or pushing on the guitar string while a note is sounding. (This type of inflection is also commonly heard in the voice part.) Another technique produces the effect of a vibrating slide from one note to the next. This is accomplished by sliding the back of a knife blade on the strings of the guitar or, more often, by doing the same with the broken top of a bottle that is worn on the little finger. (The jagged edge is always smoothed down first.) This "bottleneck" style overrode the rigid tuning imposed by the frets of a guitar and provided a flexibility that made it possible for a skillful performer to match the sliding and wailing of the voice. The playing of Delta bluesman Robert Johnson (1911–1938) in "Preachin' Blues (Up Jumped the Devil)" (CD 2/12) illustrates the vibrating slide of the "bottleneck" style. The effect invites comparison with the sound of the steel guitar heard in "Cotton-Eyed Joe" (CD 2/4) and "I'm So Lonesome I Could Cry" (CD 2/5), both of which were discussed in Chapter 7.

Robert Johnson—seen here in a dime store photo taken in the 1930s—recorded only twenty-nine songs and died before he turned thirty. But the influence of his dazzling guitar technique is heard in such performers as Eric Clapton and Keith Richards. Speculation abounded that Johnson had sold his soul to the devil to acquire his great talent, but this rumor, like so many others about Johnson, cannot be confirmed. We hear this legendary Delta bluesman on CD 2, track 12.

The Granger Collection, New York

Listening Cue "Preachin' Blues (Up Jumped the Devil)" Robert Johnson, vocal and guitar

Recorded in San Antonio, Texas, 1936 (2:49)
Listen For ▪ "bottleneck" style on the guitar

Visit http://www.music.wadsworth.com_3/Kingman for a full listening guide and other resources.

Mmmmm mmmmm
I's up this mornin', ah, blues walkin' like a man
I's up this mornin', ah, blues walkin' like a man
Worried blues, give me your right hand
And the blues fell mama's child, tore me all upside down
Blues fell mama's child, and it tore me all upside down
Travel on, poor Bob, just cain't turn you 'round
The blues, is a low-down shakin' chill
(spoken: Yes, preach 'em now)
Mmmmm mmmmm, is a low-down shakin' chill
You ain't never had 'em, I hope you never will
Well, the blues, is a achin' old heart disease
(spoken: Do it now, you gon' do it? Tell me all about it)
Let the blues, is a low-down achin' heart disease
Like consumption, killing me by degrees
I can study rain, oh, oh, drive, oh, oh, drive my blues
I been studyin' the rain and, I'm 'on' drive my blues away
Goin' to the 'stil'ry, stay out there all day

Other instruments were used as auxiliaries to the ubiquitous guitar. The harmonica, for example, was fairly cheap and very portable. In this tradition it was dubbed the "blues harp," and in the hands of virtuosos such as Sonny Terry (1911–1986), it became a very flexible and expressive instrument, capable of shadings and bendings that approached the subtlety of the voice (see Additional Listening). Improvised instruments were also common. The jug served as a kind of substitute tuba. The washboard, fitted out with auxiliary metal pans and lids attached, was a whole rhythm section. The inverted washtub, with a piece of rope stretched between a hole through its center and a broom handle, was a substitute bass. Jug bands and washboard bands incorporating these instruments were sometimes even recorded commercially.

EARLY PUBLISHED BLUES

It was inevitable that a type of music being sung and played in cities and small towns in the lowland South from Piedmont to Texas should eventually find its way into print. This happened first in 1912 when, by coincidence, within a period of two months, blues were published in St. Louis ("Baby Seals Blues"),

Oklahoma City ("Dallas Blues"), and Memphis ("Memphis Blues"). "Memphis Blues" had been widely played in that city for three years before its publication by the enterprising composer-bandleader who, more than any other early professional, was to promote the blues as popular music and bring it to a wide public—William C. Handy (1873–1958). Handy's early experiences with the performance and publication of these compositions are interestingly set forth in his autobiography, *Father of the Blues*. In the beginning, "Memphis Blues" netted him fifty dollars, with the real profits for years going to others. But Handy was to learn quickly. If the nickname "father of the blues" is something of an exaggeration (Bruce Cook has said that a more accurate one would be "rich uncle"), his place in blues history is still important, and his ties with its roots are perfectly genuine (Cook 122).

CLASSIC BLUES

The blues as a more or less standardized form of popular music for a large public (mostly black, but with a growing white element) enjoyed what has been called its "classic" period from 1920, when the first recordings were made and sold, until the onset of the Depression in the early 1930s. Personal appearance tours (mostly on vaudeville circuits) and nightclub appearances were a mainstay for the more popular blues singers, and there were some radio performances and even some films. But the principal medium for the propagation of the blues was the phonograph recording. In a development parallel to that of instrumental jazz and white hillbilly music, thousands of blues performances by hundreds of singers were recorded, and millions of copies sold.

The period of the classic blues was dominated by the female blues singer. Various reasons have been advanced for this, but the most likely ones have to do with the nature of show business at the time and the success of the female singers in tent and vaudeville shows. The recording of blues was regarded at the outset as a risky venture. The first singers recorded were not really blues singers but professional entertainers with experience in cabaret and vaudeville singing in styles much like those of popular white singers. Mamie Smith (1883–1946) made the famous first recording ("That Thing Called Love" and "You Can't Keep a Good Man Down") in 1920. After that recording's promising success, she recorded the hit "Crazy Blues," and the potential became unmistakable. Real blues singers in the southern tradition began to be recorded a few years later. Of these, by far the best known and most influential were Gertrude "Ma" Rainey (1886–1939) and Bessie Smith (1894–1937), both of whom began recording blues in 1923.

Gertrude "Ma" Rainey

Ma Rainey's early career sheds light on the milieu in which the classic blues evolved. Both her parents were in the minstrel-show business, and she herself was singing on the stage by the time she was 14. She acquired her familiar nickname "Ma" when, at age 18, she married William "Pa" Rainey, a minstrel performer, and they began touring with their song-and-dance routine. (She actually preferred to be called "Madame" Rainey.) Thus she had had more than twenty years of professional experience in touring circus, variety, and minstrel shows by the time she made her first blues recording. Of all the classic blues singers, she remained closest to the rural folk blues tradition. She never sang professionally outside the South, except to make recordings in New York and Chicago during a four-year period that ended in 1928. By then, a recording executive is said to have expressed the opinion that Ma's "down-home" material had gone out of fashion. During that brief period, she recorded with some of the leading jazz musicians, but also with a traditional southern jug, kazoo, washboard, and banjo band.

The charismatic "Madame" Rainey recorded in Chicago and New York with a pickup group that included many of the important blues and jazz performers of the time. In "Countin' the Blues," studied earlier in this chapter (CD 2/10), her Georgia Jazz Band includes Louis Armstrong (1901–1971) on the cornet and Fletcher Henderson (1897–1952) on the piano.

Bessie Smith

Bessie Smith, eight years younger than Ma Rainey, began her career as the latter's protégée, though she declined to acknowledge that in later years. She and Ma Rainey began recording about the same time, but Bessie Smith eventually became far better known and was undoubtedly a more versatile singer. If Ma Rainey's "down-home" style had more in common with the blues in its rural, folk phase, Bessie Smith became identified wholly with the sophisticated city blues tradition, and her material was tailored largely for that market.

Like Ma Rainey, Bessie Smith worked with leading jazz musicians and recorded with piano (with Fletcher Henderson, for example), with piano and one instrument (quite often with Joe Smith or Louis Armstrong playing muted blues cornet), with a small jazz combo, and even with a choral background in some early "production numbers." Her mastery of the idiom and the forcefulness and directness of her delivery are undisputed. But Bessie Smith, too, was out of fashion by the time she made her last recordings in 1933.

Other singers in the classic blues tradition included Ida Cox, Clara Smith, and Victoria Spivey, all of whom performed with major jazz musicians of the 1920s and 1930s. It was the day of the female blues singers, and although there have been eminent black female popular singers since (Ella Fitzgerald, Billie Holiday, Aretha Franklin), none after the classic period has been so exclusively identified with the blues. The dominant role in blues singing has since passed largely to men.

BLUES AND JAZZ

As we have seen in discussing musical form, by the early 1920s the blues had evolved structurally in such a way as to demand the complementing role of an answering voice (or instrument) at the end of each sung line. This manifestation of call-and-response is a distinguishing feature of the blues. The solitary blues singer filled in his own breaks on his guitar; in more organized ensembles, it was taken up by the piano or some other collaborating instrumentalist. Curiously enough, we find an interesting example of distinctive *jazz* breaks provided by the small combo that can be heard in Ma Rainey's "Countin' the Blues" (CD 2/10), in which each break in the three-line blues form is taken in turn by cornet, clarinet, and trombone. Indeed, these collaborations provide some of the finest moments in early jazz.

At this time "blues" and "jazz" were taken by some to be one and the same. Although they are distinct traditions, their parallel development is a rather complex history of periodically strong influence and identification. At the same time that the blues was slowly taking shape in rural areas before migrating into the cities, something like its urban counterpart was having a hand in the early formation of jazz. By 1900 there were bands in New Orleans (and possibly in Memphis and other cities as well) playing music that was called "blues." We will never know what the blues played by these early bands sounded like. But the identification of blues with jazz remained exceptionally close through the classic blues period we have been examining. Then, in the 1930s, began a gradual divergence; the blues declined somewhat, and jazz moved ahead in other directions. Although the blues as a harmonic and formal design can be heard in all ages of jazz, the blues references, as we advance through the so-called modern period, become increasingly attenuated. Recently, under the impact of the reenergized urban blues (discussed later in this chapter), jazz has been forcibly pulled back to a closer relation with its blues roots. But the blues, in both form and feeling, has never been wholly absent from jazz. (Jazz will be discussed in greater detail in Part V.)

BOOGIE-WOOGIE

Boogie-woogie is essentially a solo piano form with roots in the blues tradition. Its sound is pure energy—a driving left hand plays the lower-sounding notes of the piano with a repeated pattern called an *ostinato*; the right hand takes the higher-sounding notes, often insistently repeating figures of its own. Underlying it all, we hear the form and harmony of the blues. It was spawned as piano entertainment in bars, nightclubs, and related establishments. Early boogie-woogie soloists would often sing along, or talk to their audience, while they were playing. Generically, boogie-woogie was probably an adaptation of the intricate, sometimes ostinato-like accompaniments that blues singers had been providing themselves on the guitar for some time.

Boogie-woogie, transferred out of the environment of its origins, went through a period of short but intense popularity in the late 1930s. But this tends to obscure the fact that it is a much older phenomenon. Indeed, Jelly Roll Morton (1890–1941, see p. 253) said that in his early days, shortly after the turn of the twentieth century, many pianists played in what must have been something like this style of piano blues, with a heavy ostinato-like left hand. Furthermore, W. C. Handy mentions adopting and orchestrating for his group a type of piano music played in the bordellos of the Mississippi delta region about the turn of the century. It was a style referred to as "boogie-house music."

Although the craze for boogie-woogie subsided somewhat in the 1940s, it remained a potent musical style. With its driving ostinato and blues form, it was

Frank Driggs Collection/Getty Images

Meade "Lux" Lewis helped move boogie-woogie into the mainstream of American music and toward its eventual use in early rock and roll. In a photo of Lewis at the piano in the 1950s, we catch a sense of the style that we hear on CD 2, track 13.

to emerge as a major influence on rock 'n' roll in the 1950s. We will see an example of this influence in Wynonie "Blues" Harris' "Good Rockin' Tonight" (CD 2/15) in the next chapter.

Boogie-woogie's resources are limited. Nevertheless, within those limitations a considerable amount of variety is found—in its speed (not all boogie is fast), in its left-hand patterns, and in its general feeling. In "Mr. Freddie Blues" (CD 2/13), a boogie-woogie treatment by Meade "Lux" Lewis (1905–1964) of an earlier blues by J. H. Shayne, the typical ostinato bass and the twelve-bar blues form are exceptionally clear. The telltale boogie-woogie ostinato that enters at 0:06 marks the start of the twelve-bar pattern. Each bar still gets four beats, and these are clearly marked by the bass line as it climbs up and down the musical scale. But if you are going to count bars here, stay sharp—this boogie is fast.

Listening Cue "Mr. Freddie Blues" Meade "Lux" Lewis, piano

CD 2

13

Recorded in Chicago, Illinois, 1936 (2:56)
Listen For ▪ driving *ostinato* in the left hand (lower sounding notes) ▪ repeated figures in the right hand (higher sounding notes) ▪ underlying twelve-bar blues form

Visit http://www.music.wadsworth.com_3/Kingman for a full listening guide and other resources.

SELLING THE COUNTRY BLUES

Recordings of the "classic blues" by female singers such as Bessie Smith in the early 1920s were very successful, especially in the cities. But as the business of selling records by mail grew, it became apparent that a large market existed among the black people of the rural South for recordings of their own singers. The ice was broken for male blues singers when Papa Charlie Jackson (1890–1938) recorded his "Lawdy Lawdy Blues" in Chicago in 1924. Ironically, the piece was not really a blues, nor was Jackson a blues singer. Rather, he was a minstrel- and medicine-show performer from New Orleans who accompanied himself on a six-string banjo. Nevertheless, when this recording yielded an encouraging amount of commercial success, the search for traditional country blues performers was on, and there soon followed recordings by singers from across the entire South, from Florida (Blind Blake) to Mississippi (Robert Johnson) to Texas (Blind Lemon Jefferson).

Race records was the trade term used for several decades for recordings by black musicians intended for black consumers. For the earliest recordings, singers were brought to Chicago, where they worked in makeshift studios that were often primitive even by the standards of the time. But expeditions through the South with recording equipment were also undertaken. The engineering and production of the records were for the most part as cheap as the promotional material was crass, and usually little attempt was made to preserve the masters. The records themselves, especially those made in the 1920s, became very rare indeed. Although a few country-blues singers, such as Leadbelly (Huddie Ledbetter, 1885–1949), did eventually become well known and frequently recorded, many of the singers were exploited and treated with disdain.

URBAN BLUES

Though the blues is rural at its core, city environments and city life have provided for its most significant growth as a musical style. And indeed, there is no music that better epitomizes the harsher aspects of urban life, especially for African Americans, than the urban blues.

The move toward modern urban blues was signaled by the introduction of that quintessentially urban instrument, the piano, into the ensemble. The combination of piano and guitar was used by the influential team of Leroy Carr and Francis "Scrapper" Blackwell in the 1930s, and the piano almost invariably figured in Chicago blues recordings of the period. The style of piano playing was, not surprisingly, essentially that of the blues-related boogie-woogie, with its heavy and incessant left-hand ostinatos clearly presaging the main features of early rock 'n' roll. Also to be noted was the addition of drums to many of the Chicago groups. But this was a transitional period in the citification of the blues; some recordings still included such down-home instruments as the harmonica and even the washboard. The blues, just before World War II, had one foot in the city and one still in the country.

In the 1950s and 1960s, a number of blues singers born in the South, and with strong blues roots there, began recording, mostly in Chicago, a brand of hard-driving blues with a strong beat, backed by electric guitar (which they often played themselves), bass, drums, and sometimes electric organ and/or piano. This blues was strongly influenced by the gospel tradition, a background from which many of the singers came. These include Howlin' Wolf (born Chester Arthur Burnett, 1910–1976), Muddy Waters (born McKinley Morganfield, 1915–1983), and John Lee Hooker (1917–2001), all from Mississippi, and Willie Mae "Big Mama" Thornton, from Alabama (1926–1984). Such artists defined a type of urban blues that was very influential on later blues and rock musicians, especially in England, where many of them toured.

Meanwhile in the West, typically Kansas City, blues singers were often backed by jazz bands, with heavily pounding rhythm sections, and featuring prominently the wind instrument that became the blues singer's alter ego, the saxophone. The wailing, honking, screaming saxophone often took a complete chorus after the singer had sufficiently established the mood. That in turn affected vocal style. The modern blues singer has a microphone, of course, but the shouting style that Midwest blues singers such as Joe Turner (whose "Shake, Rattle and Roll" became a musical icon of nascent rock 'n' roll) and Jimmy Rushing had to adopt to be heard, unamplified, over the big-band sounds of Kansas City, remains as a characteristic of much blues singing today. So, too, the guitar, by now invariably electric, remains as an element of continuity in the blues band.

BLUES AT THE TURN OF THE CENTURY

Many changes have affected the blues in the 1990s and into the new century. The recordings that are being produced are both fewer and technologically and stylistically slicker. Live concerts have become more expensive and more gargantuan. Gender and racial shifts are noteworthy as well. White male blues singers such as Johnny Winter and William Clarke have come into prominence, as has the interracial women's group Saffire: The Uppity Blues Women.

Stevie Ray Vaughan (1954–1990), a native of Dallas, Texas, was particularly influential in the 1980s and '90s, and continues to stand out as one of the great bluesmen of our time. His 1982 recording of Larry Davis' "Texas Flood" (CD 2/14), a blues song written in the 1960s, reveals Vaughan's conservative taste in music and progressive approach to the electric guitar. Indeed, his highly virtuosic guitar playing in the breaks between lyrics is almost always the most notable feature of his recordings. In addition to using stock blues techniques such as bending and the "bottleneck" style (the latter can be heard on his recording

One of *Rolling Stone* magazine's top ten guitarists of all time, Stevie Ray Vaughan, performs on stage shortly before dying in a 1990 helicopter crash. Often playing simultaneous lead and rhythm parts, Vaughan said in a 1985 interview with *Guitar World*: "Now, I use heavy strings, tune low [inspired by Jimi Hendrix], play hard, and floor it. . . . Getting that passion, that's what I try to do." We hear Vaughan's passion on CD 2, track 14.

of "Boot Hill"; see Additional Listening), Vaughan also took advantage of effects that could be produced by pedals, switches, and a lever (whammy bar) that were part of his electric guitar setup, or even the feedback that was produced by moving too close to an amplifier. The overall sound and style of his playing might be described as a fusion of the heavy blues style of Albert King and the rock virtuosity of Jimi Hendrix. Like Hendrix, Vaughan was known for stage gymnastics that included flipping the guitar behind his back in the middle of an extended and difficult solo without missing a note.

The lyrics for "Texas Flood," given below, are set to a slow and straightforward twelve-bar blues form. The foregrounding of the guitar is evident in the structure of this recording. After a four-bar guitar introduction, the equivalent of the first stanza is taken up by the guitar itself. The guitar is also subsequently given two stanza-lengths of virtuosic solos. Rather than simply providing background during the vocals and short fillers during the breaks, the guitar assumes the role of an equal partner here. The technique of bending is especially prevalent in this recording. Notice, too, the distinctive urban elements in the use of electric bass (played by Tommy Shannon) and, especially, the drums (played by Chris Layton).

Listening Cue **"Texas Flood"** Stevie Ray Vaughan, vocal and electric guitar, and Double Trouble (Tommy Shannon, bass; Chris Layton, drums)

Recorded in Los Angeles, California, 1982 (5:21)
Listen For▪ virtuosic guitar technique▪ urban sound of bass and drums▪ twelve-bar blues form

Visit http://www.music.wadsworth.com_3/Kingman for a full listening guide and other resources.

[4-bar guitar intro]

[12-bar guitar solo = 1 stanza]

Well it's floodin' down in Texas, all of the telephone lines are down [break]
Well it's floodin' down in Texas, all of the telephone lines are down [break]
And I've been tryin' to call my baby, Lord and I can't get a single sound [break]

Well dark clouds are rollin' in, man I'm standin' out in the rain [break]
Well dark clouds are rollin' in, man I'm standin' out in the rain [break]
Yeah flood water keep a rollin', man it's about to drive poor me insane [break]

[12-bar guitar solo = 1 stanza]

[12-bar guitar solo = 1 stanza]

Well I'm leavin' you baby, Lord and I'm goin' back home to stay [break]
Well I'm leavin' you baby, Lord and I'm goin' back home to stay [break]
Well back home there no floods or tornados, baby the sun shines every day
[closing tag]

Stevie Ray Vaughan's career ended tragically in a fatal helicopter crash near East Troy, Wisconsin, on August 27, 1990. But here at the dawn of the twenty-first century, the blues mantle is carried on by artists from every corner of the United States, including such commercially successful and critically acclaimed musicians as Marcia Ball (b. 1949) from Orange, Texas; Keb' Mo' (Kevin Moore, b. 1951) from Los Angeles, California; Susan Tedeschi (b. 1970) from Boston, Massachusetts; and Jonny Lang (b. 1981) from Fargo, North Dakota (see Additional Listening). Whatever the present and future state of the blues, there can be no doubt of its importance up to this point. Blues authority Paul Oliver has called it "one of the richest and most rewarding of popular arts and perhaps the last great folk music that the western world may produce" (168).

PROJECTS

1. Collect recorded examples of at least three blues guitarist-singers. Describe and compare their original guitar techniques and styles, especially their treatment of the "breaks."
2. Collect recorded examples of blues illustrating at least four of the textual themes identified and treated in this chapter or, alternatively, in Paul Oliver, *The Meaning of the Blues.*
3. Using W. C. Handy's autobiography, *Father of the Blues,* and any other sources you can find as your basis, describe in a brief essay what life was like for a black musician in the Deep South in the first quarter of the twentieth century.
4. Assemble a list of at least five male and five female blues singers (besides Ma Rainey and Bessie Smith) who recorded between 1920 and 1930, with a brief biographical sketch of each. Cite at least one recording for each, and listen to as many others as you can.

ADDITIONAL LISTENING

Marcia Ball. *Presumed Innocent.* Alligator Records 4879.

"Boot Hill," Stevie Ray Vaughan, *The Sky Is Crying.* Sony 47390.

Jonny Lang. *Lie to Me.* A&M 640.

Keb' Mo'. *Keep It Simple.* Sony 86408.

Susan Tedeschi. *Just Won't Burn.* Tone Cool 51109.

Sonny Terry. *The Folkways Years, 1944–1963.* Smithsonian Folkways 40033.

9 ROCK MUSIC

The label "rock" covers a broad range of music traditionally marketed to young, white audiences since the 1950s. Depending on whom you ask, "rock," in its current usage, can apply to anything from Elvis Presley's "Love Me Tender" and The Beach Boys' "Good Vibrations" to Madonna's "Like a Virgin" and Green Day's "Boulevard of Broken Dreams." Indeed, rock music might fairly be described as a panorama in and of itself.

This chapter starts by looking at the origins of "rock and roll" in the 1950s as an offshoot of rural southern traditions—namely, blues and country music—then briefly surveys the diverse trends in rock music from the 1960s to the present. From a consumer's perspective, rock music is difficult, and perhaps impossible, to pin down in stylistic terms. But it is less elusive when considered from the vantage points of those who make it and those who sell it. In many ways, the performer's ideology and the businessman's marketing lie at the heart of the rock tradition. Those topics in particular will reemerge throughout this chapter.

There is perhaps no more immediate lesson regarding the central role of marketing than the licensing fees and restrictions that have prohibited the inclusion in our CD anthology of commercially successful musical examples to illustrate this chapter. Nonetheless, the recordings cited here are very likely owned by your school or public library; many are probably also in your own personal collections. If not, every highlighted example can be downloaded legally for a modest fee from iTunes®, which like the jukebox of years past, has become one of the latest outlets for this music.

ROCK'S TIES TO RHYTHM AND BLUES

Rock and roll was born in the 1950s—at least as a commercial brand name. The music itself, however, had been around since the 1940s in a twelve-bar blues form that was faster and infused with livelier rhythms and more pronounced beats. This was in essence "blues with rhythm"—or, as the music industry would call it after 1949, "rhythm and blues." Wynonie Harris' "Good Rockin' Tonight"

(CD 2/15), recorded in 1947, presents many of the key characteristics of the music marketed as "rhythm and blues": the up-tempo boogie-woogie bass line, the honking saxophone, the straightforward twelve-bar blues form, and, importantly, the heavy emphasis on beats two and four of every measure. These are the "backbeats," and they are clearly marked in this recording by a clapping of the hands. (To review the twelve-bar blues form that is a key feature of this music, see Chapter 8, pp. 115–116.) The instrumentation is that of the urban blues in the 1930s and 1940s (pp. 124–125). In addition to the saxophone, we hear the drums, bass, piano, and, at the very outset, a jazzy muted cornet.

Listening Cue "**Good Rockin' Tonight**" Wynonie Harris, vocal with group (2:42)

Listen For ▪ twelve-bar blues form ▪ boogie-woogie bass line ▪ backbeats

Visit http://www.music.wadsworth.com_3/Kingman for a full listening guide and other resources.

(Introduction)
I heard the news, there's good rockin' tonight.
Oh, hold my baby tight as I can; tonight she'll know I'm a mighty man.
I heard the news, there's good rockin' tonight.

Have you heard the news? Everybody's gonna rock tonight.
Gonna hold my baby tight as I can; tonight she'll know I'm a mighty man.
Have you heard the news? There's good rockin' tonight.

So meet me in the alley behind the barn. Don't be afraid, I'll do you no harm.
Baby, bring my rockin' shoes, 'cause tonight I'm gonna rock away all my blues.
Have you heard the news? There's good rockin' tonight.

(Rock, oh, we're gonna rock.)
(Saxophone break)

I got the news. Everybody's gonna rock tonight.
I'm gonna hold my baby as tight as I can. Tonight she'll know I'm a mighty man.
I got the news. Everybody's rockin' tonight.

Well Ezra Brown, Deacon Jones; they've even left their happy home.
They'll be there, just you wait and see, a-jumpin' and a-stompin' at the Jubilee.
Hey man, there's good rockin' tonight.

Sweet Lorraine, Sioux City Sue, Sweet Georgia Brown, Caledonia too.
They'll be there jumpin' like men. Hey sister ain't you glad,
We got the news? There's good rockin' tonight.
Hoy hoy hoy, there's good rockin' tonight. Hey hey hey.

Interestingly enough, the key characteristics of rhythm and blues heard in "Good Rockin' Tonight" are also heard in the first bona fide rock and roll hit,

© Topical Press Agency/Getty Images

Here, Bill Haley and His Comets (Haley kneeling in the foreground with his guitar) rehearse for a promotional tour of the film *Rock Around the Clock* (1956), a fictional account of how rock and roll was discovered. It was their performance of "(We're Gonna) Rock Around the Clock"—heard on CD 2, track 16—in the 1955 film *Blackboard Jungle* that made rock 'n' roll history.

"Rock Around the Clock" (CD 2/16), recorded by Bill Haley and His Comets in 1954. Notice in particular the boogie-woogie bass line, the straightforward twelve-bar blues form, and the emphasis that the drums give the backbeat (beats two and four of every bar). Here, with its saxophone, heavy drums, bass, and electric guitar, the ensemble recalls the urban blues bands of the 1950s.

<table>
<tr><td>CD 2
16</td><td></td></tr>
</table>

Listening Cue **"Rock Around the Clock"** Bill Haley and His Comets (2:09)

Listen For ▪ twelve-bar blues form ▪ boogie-woogie bass line ▪ backbeats

Visit http://www.music.wadsworth.com_3/Kingman for a full listening guide and other resources.

(Spoken Introduction)
One, two, three o'clock, four o'clock, rock,
Five, six, seven o'clock, eight o'clock, rock,
Nine, ten, eleven o'clock, twelve o'clock, rock,
We're gonna rock around the clock tonight.

Put your glad rags on and join me, hon,
We'll have some fun when the clock strikes one,
We're gonna rock around the clock tonight,
We're gonna rock, rock, rock, 'til broad daylight.
We're gonna rock, gonna rock, around the clock tonight.

When the clock strikes two, three and four,
If the band slows down we'll yell for more,
We're gonna rock around the clock tonight,
We're gonna rock, rock, rock, 'til broad daylight.
We're gonna rock, gonna rock, around the clock tonight.
(Electric guitar break)

When the chimes ring five, six and seven,
We'll be right in seventh heaven.
We're gonna rock around the clock tonight,
We're gonna rock, rock, rock, 'til broad daylight.
We're gonna rock, gonna rock, around the clock tonight.

When it's eight, nine, ten, eleven too,
I'll be goin' strong and so will you.
We're gonna rock around the clock tonight,
We're gonna rock, rock, rock, 'til broad daylight.
We're gonna rock, gonna rock, around the clock tonight.
(Saxophone and electric guitar break)

When the clock strikes twelve, we'll cool off then,
Start a rockin' round the clock again.
We're gonna rock around the clock tonight,
We're gonna rock, rock, rock, 'til broad daylight.
We're gonna rock, gonna rock, around the clock tonight.

The similarities between "Good Rockin' Tonight" and "Rock Around the Clock" extend to the lyrics as well, particularly in their mischievous play on the word "rock" which since the 1920s was slang for "sex" (so was "roll"). In light of all of these similarities, then, what makes one song "rhythm and blues" and the other "rock and roll"? In a word: audience. More specifically, "rhythm and blues" refers to music that was marketed to a black audience; "rock and roll," to music directed at a white audience. In fact, until the influential *Billboard* charts began using the term "rhythm and blues" in 1949, the particular blues-based style it came to designate was referred to as "race" music and tracked on the "race charts."

REACHING WHITE AUDIENCES

Alan Freed (1922–1965), a white disc jockey on Cleveland radio station WJW, is credited as the first to apply the term "rock and roll" to music that was essentially rhythm and blues. Though probably not the first to use it in this way, Freed and his *Moondog Rock 'n' Roll Party* radio show, which regularly played black rhythm and blues for a largely white audience, were undoubtedly key factors in making the term stick. The intent behind masking rhythm and blues with the term "rock and roll" lay in part with a need to reach a wider audience in the 1950s, when racial politics had begun to reach a fever pitch in segregated American society. Rob Bowman has noted of Freed: "He decided to use rock and roll as a euphemism for rhythm and blues in an attempt to disassociate the music from any and all racial stigma" (349). In the final assessment, then, the earliest commercial uses of the term "rock and roll" had less to do with a distinctive musical style than with marketing strategies that were grounded in the social and racial politics of the day.

A cynic might dismiss Freed's switch from "rhythm and blues" to "rock and roll" as mere opportunism in pursuit of profits, and certainly it was to some extent. But at a time when race relations between whites and blacks had become so incredibly strained, his regular programming of "rock and roll" accomplished something quite remarkable for a younger generation of Americans. As Robert Walser has observed: "Black and white audiences were not just listening to the same music; they were listening together. While parents, police, and government authorities could and did strive to maintain racial boundaries in night clubs, juke boxes, dance halls, and record stores, it was impossible to segregate the airwaves" (353).

While history tends to like singling out its heroes, Freed was not alone in taking the music of black Americans into the homes of white audiences. A more important, if indirect, phenomenon in this regard was the relatively new medium of television. As major networks such as NBC (National Broadcasting Company) and CBS (Columbia Broadcasting System) became increasingly convinced of television's viability in the late 1940s, they began to sell off many of their radio stations at bargain prices to focus their attention and financial resources on the newer visual medium. This created opportunities for enterprising individuals who were eager to tap into new advertising markets, and thus began structuring their programs to appeal to African Americans, a demographic that had been overlooked during radio's heyday. William Barlow has dubbed these new outlets "black appeal radio stations," and by 1956, there were 400 of them, the most famous being WDIA in Memphis and WLAC in Nashville. Of this phenomenon, Bowman notes: "Once stations such as WDIA began programming black music from dusk to dawn, any white teenager who chose to could spin his or her radio dial and consume an unending diet of all forms of rhythm and blues" (350).

THE INFLUENCE OF COUNTRY MUSIC

Early rock and roll is virtually synonymous with black rhythm and blues. But with the added influences of white country music around the mid-1950s, rock and roll began to take on a distinctive sound of its own. The country influence can be attributed in part to white musicians who began recording rhythm and blues numbers as the industry began to realize the potential market for this variety of music. The country infusion came perhaps most notably with Elvis Presley (1935–1977), "The King of Rock and Roll," in his early recordings for Sam Phillips (1923–2003) and Sun Records. Rob Bowman has observed: "Elvis Presley's first five releases on Sun Records in 1954 and 1955 all combined one rhythm and blues song with one country song. In all cases Presley modified the songs, adding substantial rhythm and blues elements to his recordings of country material and, similarly, adding country and pop elements to his versions of rhythm and blues songs" (353). The result of this fusion has been called "rockabilly" in some circles. Presley's recording of "That's All Right" for Sun Records in 1954 exemplifies the country-inflected rhythm and blues number.

Presley's landmark "That's All Right" (iTunes® 1) is a cover version of a rhythm and blues number by the black Mississippi bluesman Arthur Crudup (1905–1974). ("Cover version" refers to the fairly standard practice of one artist recording his or her own interpretation of a song originally recorded by another artist.) Were it not for the emotion-laden bluesy inflections of Presley's voice, the occasional flourish on the electric guitar, and the rare hint of a boogie-woogie bass in the background, the music would be virtually indistinguishable from a country tune. The absence of heavy backbeats and rhythmic complexity is immediately noticeable; in their places we find the guitars and percussion emulating the simple, even, unobtrusive strumming we might expect to hear in old-school country music, before the overproduced Nashville sound became the norm (see Chapter 7, pp. 104–105).

Here we see Elvis Presley enthralling teenage girls at a 1956 concert in his hometown of Memphis, Tennessee. Mocked at the time as "Elvis the Pelvis" for his provocative hip movements on stage, later earning the title "The King of Rock and Roll," Elvis became an American cultural icon. His cover of Arthur Crudup's rhythm-and-blues number "That's All Right," iTunes® 1, was one his earliest recordings.

Listening Cue "That's All Right" Elvis Presley

Single, recorded in 1954 (1:55)
Listen For ▪ no emphasis on backbeats ▪ simple rhythmic background ▪ bluesy inflections in the voice

Visit http://www.music.wadsworth.com_3/Kingman for a full listening guide and other resources.

If Presley's "That's All Right" presents us with a good example of country-inflected blues, an equally good example of blues-inflected country can be found on the flip side of that record with his cover of Bill Monroe's "Blue Moon of Kentucky." Presley's innovative fusion of blues, country, and pop would go on to influence future white rock and roll stars including Carl Perkins (1932–1998) and Buddy Holly (1936–1959).

The country influence did not always come by way of white musicians. One of rock and roll's earliest and most influential black stars, Chuck Berry (b. 1926), played a role in the blues-country fusion as well. His 1955 recording of "Maybellene," which became a hit with black and white audiences alike, was nothing other than an ingeniously reworked version of the country standard "Ida Red," previously recorded by Bob Wills and His Texas Playboys, among others.

Oddly enough, one of the best examples of an early country influence in rock and roll takes us right back to "Rock Around the Clock" (CD 2/16). In terms of its overall sound, we have already heard how the song plays out as straight-ahead rhythm and blues. But a closer look at one of its components reveals a hidden country influence. Indeed, the music setting the first line of every stanza was borrowed almost note for note from one of Bill Haley's favorite tunes, a 1949 country hit by Hank Williams titled "Move It on Over" (Dawson 82). The country repertoire is one with which Bill Haley was intimately familiar. For, in his early career, he had been "Bill Haley the Rambling Yodeler," posing for publicity shots as a country musician with western wear that was topped off with a Stetson hat. And before repackaging his group as "Bill Haley and His Comets" in 1952, he and his fellow musicians had made their way in the musical world as a western swing band that called itself "Bill Haley and the Saddlemen." Although the country influence in 1950s rock and roll is somewhat less pronounced, its presence forms an important part of its early history.

TRENDS FROM THE 1960s TO THE PRESENT

As we have seen, the earliest trends in rock coalesced tightly around the blues and country music. In the period from the 1960s to the present, however, we find trends (and countertrends) emerging in such rapid succession that "rock" becomes an umbrella term for a broad variety of amplified musics marketed for young white audiences: folk rock, bubblegum, psychedelic rock, punk rock, heavy metal, glam rock, grunge, hard rock, progressive rock, soft rock, and thrash metal, to name just a few.

The Early 1960s

By the start of the 1960s, many of the brightest stars in the American rock and roll galaxy of the 1950s had faded. Elvis Presley was drafted into the Army in 1958. On February 3, 1959, Buddy Holly (b. 1936) was killed in a plane crash near Mason City, Iowa, that also took the lives of J. P. Richardson ("The Big Bopper," b. 1930) and Ritchie Valens (Richard Steven Valenzuela, b. 1941), the first Latino rock and roll star. Later that year, Chuck Berry, who set a new standard for rock and roll guitar playing, was arrested for transporting a minor across state lines (purportedly for sexual purposes), and spent the better part of the early 1960s in prison.

From a musical perspective, the early 1960s was a bland period of carefully groomed and packaged "teen idols" such as Ricky Nelson (1940–1985), Fabian (Fabiano Bonaparte, b. 1943), Frankie Avalon (Francis Thomas Avallone, b. 1939), and Bobby Rydell (b. 1942). Yet these crafted "teen idols" are key indicators of an emerging teen market to which the music industry was intent on catering. To take advantage of the now-proven market while bypassing mainstream critics, there was a particular emphasis on promoting a wholesome, clean-cut look as the new face of rock. Another indicator was the success of Dick Clark's (b. 1963) youth-oriented rock and roll dance show *American Bandstand,* which ran daily on ABC television from 1957 until 1963. (From that point, it ran on a weekly basis until 1987, retaining Dick Clark as host.) *American Bandstand* created a dance sensation in the early 1960s with "The Twist"—a song that made its singer, Chubby Checker (Ernest Evans, b. 1941), a household name.

In 1964, the Beatles and other bands of the "British Invasion," including the Rolling Stones and the Who, reacquainted America with music that was more analogous to the energetic rock and roll of the 1950s. Before bursting on the scene with such hits as "I Want to Hold Your Hand" (1964), the Beatles had been greatly influenced by American rock and rollers and in their early years had focused on performing covers of tunes recorded by Chuck Berry, Carl Perkins, and Buddy Holly. Similarly, the Rolling Stones, who became well known with "(I Can't Get No) Satisfaction" (1965), had started out as a cover band with an affinity not only for rock and rollers like Chuck Berry, but also for bluesmen such as Howlin' Wolf (Chester Arthur Burnett, 1910–1976) and Muddy Waters (McKinley Morganfield, 1915–1983). These American rock and roll and blues artists were known in England not only from their recordings but also from personal tours. The "British Invasion," in fact, brought with it much that was already our own. As Muddy Waters put it to an American college audience: "I had to come to you behind the Rolling Stones and the Beatles. I had to go to England to get here!" (Shaw, *Honkers* 526).

The Beach Boys

As the British invaded, America's most significant and lasting contributions to rock music in the 1960s were coming by way of the Beach Boys, a band from Hawthorne, California. The Beach Boys, formed by Brian Wilson (b. 1942) in 1961, emerged as the best-selling American group of the 1960s, and their influence has extended well beyond the period. As late as the 1980s, performers such as David Lee Roth, former lead singer with the heavy metal rock group Van Halen, were covering their songs, and in 1988, the Beach Boys themselves produced the number one hit "Kokomo."

Much of the Beach Boys' popularity rests on songs such as "Surfin' USA" (which borrows heavily from Chuck Berry's 1958 hit "Sweet Little Sixteen"), "Surfer Girl," "Surfin' Safari," and "California Girls," songs that celebrate idealized visions of surfing and carefree beach life. Less well remembered,

The theremin, which we hear the Beach Boys use in "Good Vibrations," iTunes® 2, originated with Leon Theremin, a Russian engineer shown here demonstrating his instrument in Paris, France, in 1927. The movement of his right hand around the vertical antenna determines the pitch (high or low) of a note. The movement of his left hand over the round horizontal antenna changes the note's amplitude (loud or soft). The theremin has also provided eerie background music for movies ranging from Alfred Hitchcock's *Spellbound* (1945) to Tim Burton's *Mars Attacks!* (1996).

© Bettmann /CORBIS

however, is that they were one of the most experimental and innovative groups of the 1960s. Their *Pet Sounds* (1966) may be rock music's first *concept album*—"an album conceived as an integrated whole, with interrelated songs arranged in a deliberate sequence" (Starr and Waterman 260). Though only a modest success commercially, *Pet Sounds* exerted a powerful influence on other musicians, most notably the Beatles, who responded in 1967 with a concept album of their own, *Sgt. Pepper's Lonely Hearts Club Band.*

Listening Cue "Good Vibrations" The Beach Boys

The Beach Boys: The Greatest Hits, Vol. 1–20 (Capitol, 1999) (3:37)
Listen For ▪ contrasting soundscapes ▪ polished vocal harmonies ▪ theremin

Visit http://www.music.wadsworth.com_3/Kingman for a full listening guide and other resources.

"Good Vibrations" (iTunes® 2), also from 1966, encapsulates the creative and innovative spirit of Brian Wilson and the Beach Boys. While marketed now as pop—possibly because it comes across as relatively innocent compared with the hard-edged rock we have since come to know—"Good Vibrations" is nonetheless "widely acknowledged as one of rock music's greatest masterpieces" (Harrison 34). Brian Wilson took special pride in it, calling it his "pocket symphony"

(Starr and Waterman, 262–63). From a formal point of view, "Good Vibrations" does not unfold in the generally predictable patterns of pop music, or even of rock and roll based on the twelve-bar blues. Instead, it moves (sometimes jarringly) from one musical texture to another, driving forward, teasing with the promise of returning to a familiar area (but never really settling), then fades out just as it appears to move onto something new. The contrasting "soundscapes" are as much a result of the complex vocal arrangements and performance styles as they are of the instruments used in this recording: organ, flutes, percussion, cello, and theremin. The theremin (which makes its entrance at 0:26) is probably the wildest instrument ever used on a hit record and produces the spooky, vibrating background noise that recurs throughout the song. It was invented in 1919 by the Russian Leon Theremin (Lev Sergeyevich Termen, 1896–1993) and is one of the earliest fully electronic instruments, a box with projecting antennas that are "played" by moving the hands closer or farther away, but never touching them. The polished vocal harmonies on this recording are heard consistently throughout the group's career and are integral to the classic "Beach Boys sound."

The Late 1960s

Rock in the late 1960s began to experience a fragmentation into a variety of diverse styles, a signal development. "By 1966 and 1967, new styles began to emerge that were different enough from the roots of rock and roll to be designated under the short form rock" (Bowman 347). If anything held these various styles together, it is the broader ideological tenets to which they adhered— politically, morally, and culturally. In this sense, issues such as America's involvement in the Vietnam War (1965–1972), and the perceived mainstream American culture of adult, white, middle-class values and artistic production provided key focal points.

As rock music turned to deal more directly with the issues of the day, groups such as the Byrds, from Los Angeles, California, turned to folk singers who used music as an instrument of advocacy. Their "Turn, Turn, Turn" (1965), popularly interpreted as an antiwar "folk rock" song, is essentially a cover of a folk tune that Pete Seeger (see p. 80) had based on a passage from the Old Testament (Ecclesiastes 3:1–8). In San Francisco, singers such as Texas-born Janis Joplin (1943–1970) and groups like the Grateful Dead and Jefferson Airplane catered to the disaffected white youths of the "hippie" movement, centered (at least symbolically) in the Haight-Ashbury district. Theirs was a music identified with liberation from social restraints (including sexual), a rejection of mainstream commercial pop, and heightened states of awareness brought on by psychedelic substances that prominently included LSD—lysergic acid diethylamide, or "acid" for short. Appropriately enough, "psychedelic rock" and "acid rock" were often applied to the music that grew out of San Francisco's hippie counterculture. Jefferson Airplane, with its charismatic singer Grace Slick (b. 1939), emerged as the leading band of the San Francisco psychedelic scene. Its first national hit came in 1967 with "Somebody to Love." Although the term "psychedelic rock" (like the term "rock" itself) encompasses a variety of styles, its bands collectively added at least

© Douglas Kent Hall/ZUMA/CORBIS

Shortly before appearing at the legendary 1969 Woodstock Music and Art Festival—where
he played his highly personal and politically charged version of "The Star-Spangled Banner"
(iTunes® 3)—Jimi Hendrix (shown here) performed at a live street concert in Harlem.
Although he was left-handed, Hendrix played a right-handed guitar held upside down
and restrung to suit his nonconformist style—yet another example of the skill and original
imagination that made him one of the most influential rock guitarists.

three identifiable elements that have become mainstays of rock culture: an increased use of amplification, sound distortion by manipulation of electronic
equipment, and, importantly, the light shows without which modern-day rock
concerts would not be complete.

The Woodstock Music and Art Festival marks the end of the 1960s, chronologically and symbolically. The "Three Days of Peace and Music" on August 15–17,
1969 (it actually spilled over into the morning of the 18th), were originally to take
place in the town of Woodstock in Ulster County, New York, but because of local
opposition actually ended up taking place on a dairy farm in the neighboring
town of Bethel. Nonetheless, the name "Woodstock" stuck and the festival itself
has come to represent the climax of 1960s counterculture. One of the most famous
(and subsequently controversial) events at Woodstock was the improvised performance of America's national anthem, "The Star-Spangled Banner," by Jimi
Hendrix (1942–1970). In Hendrix's "Star-Spangled Banner, Live at Woodstock"
(iTunes® 3) we hear a number of elements that characterized "psychedelic rock" at
the end of the 1960s. The distortion of sound is immediately notable at the outset.
There is also a good example of conceptual play with "authority" as Hendrix im-
provises upon the national anthem at the height of the Vietnam conflict, inserting
sonic references to bombs, screams, machine guns, and even a brief funerary
quotation from "Taps" (at 2:35).

Listening Cue "The Star-Spangled Banner (Live at Woodstock)"
Jimi Hendrix

iTunes®
3

Experience Hendrix: The Best of Jimi Hendrix (3:46)
Listen For ▪ distortion of sound ▪ imitation of war sounds ▪ quotation from "Taps"

Visit http://www.music.wadsworth.com_3/Kingman for a full listening guide and other resources.

James Marshall ("Jimi") Hendrix, born in Seattle, Washington, was the most influential electric guitarist of the 1960s, and possibly in the history of rock music. Though his performance of "The Star-Spangled Banner" at Woodstock is culturally significant, it does not show his accomplished musicianship in the best light. (Few "inspired" moments ever do.) Larry Starr and Christopher Waterman offer the best summary of his guitar legacy: "Jimi Hendrix's creative employment of feedback, distortion, and sound-manipulating devices like the wah-wah pedal and fuzz box, coupled with his fondness for aggressive dissonance and incredibly loud volume—all of these characteristics represented important additions to the musical techniques and materials available to guitarists" (301). In the previous chapter, we heard how some of these techniques were taken up in "Texas Flood" by Hendrix disciple Stevie Ray Vaughan (see pp. 125–127). But not all of Hendrix's music was loud and brash. His gifts as a sensitive musician and lyricist are exemplified in such songs as "Little Wing" and "Bold as Love" (both from 1967).

Hendrix's early musical background was rooted in the blues, but as he moved decidedly into the psychedelic rock scene, he would find a more receptive atmosphere in England. The move was likely motivated by racial stereotypes in the United States. As Starr and Waterman have observed, "It was arguably difficult for an African American musician who neither fit into nor cared much about popular definitions of black musical style to find acceptance in the American popular music scene" (302).

The 1970s

The fragmentation of rock in the late 1960s was largely driven by the experimentation of various performers. In the 1970s, the fragmentation continued. This time, however, it was largely driven by marketing considerations within the commercial music industry. As the industry doubled in size from 1973 to 1978, "It increasingly relied on genre labels and strict radio formats to make marketing more efficient, helping to fragment the rock community of the previous decade" (Walser 368).

Hard Rock, Heavy Metal For practical purposes the market would eventually define the mainstream "rock" of the 1970s as music played on FM radio stations that was "aimed primarily at young white males aged thirteen to twenty-five" (Starr and Waterman 307). The format was referred to as "AOR" (album-oriented rock) and favored aggressive "hard rock" and "heavy metal," both essentially off-shoots of the heavy blues-inflected style of British groups such as the Rolling Stones and Cream (with Eric Clapton). The distinction between hard rock and heavy metal would seem to be a fine one, but Joe Stuessy describes it as follows:

> If hard rock was loud, heavy metal was louder; if hard rock was simple and repetitive, heavy metal was simpler and more repetitive; if hard rock singers shouted, heavy metal singers screamed; if hard rockers experimented with distortion and feedback, heavy metalers distorted everything; if hard rock favored long instrumental improvisations, heavy metal offered longer, louder, and more dazzling instrumental solos; if hard rock was countercultural, heavy metal would come to specialize in the anticultural. (306)

The British seemed to lead in this development with groups such as Led Zeppelin, whose "Whole Lotta Love" of 1970, with its heavy bass riff and obsessive repetition in the main sections, its electronic manipulation and sound effects in a middle section, and the explicit sexuality of its lyrics, is representative. Led Zeppelin's musical "borrowings" in "Whole Lotta Love" and "You Shook Me" from American bluesman Willie Dixon's (1915–1992) "You Need Love" and "You Shook Me," reveal the persistent influence of African American blues on rock music into the 1970s.

Led Zeppelin along with other British groups, principally Black Sabbath and Judas Priest, took heavy metal a further step out of the mainstream by introducing and capitalizing on occult themes of black magic, witchcraft, and devil worship, as well as the darker aspects of Celtic and Greek mythology and medieval lore, all of which were more familiar to British youth, who grew up surrounded by castles and whose cultural heritage included dark myths and legends, than to Americans, for whom the scariest themes were those from horror movies. These themes were exaggerated, of course, in the fanciful art found on their album covers as well as promotional posters and advertising. American heavy metal groups of the 1970s included Van Halen and the Blue Öyster Cult. In light of the targeted audience, it probably comes as no surprise that the prominent hard rock and heavy metal groups were almost exclusively male and white.

Although heavy metal, to qualify as such, incorporates the loudness, the pounding beat, and the distortion that are its trademarks, these frequently mask musical sophistication and virtuosity, especially on the electric guitar. In Blue Öyster Cult's "(Don't Fear) The Reaper" (the Grim Reaper being death) of 1976, there can be heard, over and between the statements of the obsessive four-note bass riff, guitar solos of considerable complexity. After Jimi Hendrix (who was entirely self-taught), classically trained Edward "Eddie" Van Halen (b. 1955) brought a new level of performance to the electric guitar; all of the Van Halen albums illustrate this, but the famous "Eruption" of 1978 (iTunes® 4) is an astounding display of virtuosity, which includes at 0:31 a transformed quote from a famous study piece by the classical composer Rudolphe Kreutzer (1766–1831) that is known to every student of the violin.

Listening Cue "Eruption" Van Halen

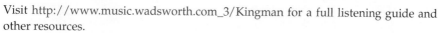

Van Halen (Remastered) Warner Bros. (1:42)
Listen For ▪ display of virtuosity ▪ quote from a classical study piece

Visit http://www.music.wadsworth.com_3/Kingman for a full listening guide and other resources.

With its brief quotation of Kreutzer's classical study piece, "Eruption" flirts with another style of rock music in the 1970s—"progressive rock" (or "classical rock"), which aimed at creating increasingly complex musical forms, in part by quoting from classical icons such as Johann Sebastian Bach (1685–1750) or Johannes Brahms (1833–1897). The progressive rock movement was spearheaded most notably by British groups such as Yes and Emerson, Lake, and Palmer.

Glam Rock A notable contribution of the 1970s had more to do with "look" than "sound." Here, we can start to see the marketer's push to try to break through and distinguish one group from another in an increasingly crowded market. Black leather and elaborate hardware, including chains, became familiar in costuming. So too, makeup contributed to the creation of fantastic and abnormal stage personae. Alice Cooper (the name of the band, as well as the stage name of the lead singer, Vincent Furnier) featured black eye makeup. Kiss, another group, used full character makeup, personifying what one observer has identified as "the bloody, ghoul-like image of a cat, a lover, a spaceman, and a devil" (Charlton 164). The New York Dolls featured all of its white male members in drag. The fascination among groups with a theatrical presence can be traced back to the sensational packaging of androgynous stage personae such as David Bowie's Ziggy Stardust. Bowie (David Robert Jones, b. 1947), a British rock musician, is perhaps the most influential pioneer of the "glam (short for glamour) rock" movement, which emphasized elaborate stage presence and costuming. The success of this particular marketing strategy is reflected in the fact that while most Americans would be hard pressed to name three songs by the rock group Kiss, there are few who would not recognize their trademark look.

Punk Rock The end of the 1970s saw a rebellion of sorts within the rock community against earlier trends of the decade. The rebellion was as much against the musical artifice and glittery stage presence of rockers themselves as it was against the commercial forces and music corporations shaping them. The "punk rock" movement signaled a return to the basics, and one of the earliest American groups to embody that attitude was the Ramones, formed in New York City in 1974.

The Ramones posed a stark contrast to the heavily made-up and costumed glam rockers with their blue jeans, leather jackets, and grungy urban look that reflected an attitude of carefree abandon. In their music, they cast aside the corporate model of expensive, heavily produced albums for deliberately simple, straightforward, and unvarnished recordings. Their song "Sheena Is a Punk Rocker" (iTunes® 5), from 1977, presents us with an interesting example.

The Ramones' grungy urban look, seen here, and raw recordings—such as "Sheena Is a Punk Rocker," iTunes® 5—offered a clear alternative to the glam rockers and overproduced studio albums of the 1970s. Their trademark black leather jackets, T-shirts, ripped jeans, and disheveled hair projected a disregard of convention that their fans still emulate. According to some observers, the Ramones did for punk music in England what the Beatles had done for rock 'n' roll in America.

Listening Cue "Sheena Is a Punk Rocker" The Ramones (2:47)

Rocket to Russia (Expanded & Remastered) Rhino/Warner Bros. 2005
Listen For ▪ simple, unvarnished style ▪ absence of virtuosity ▪ heavy emphasis on backbeats

Visit http://www.music.wadsworth.com_3/Kingman for a full listening guide and other resources.

In "Sheena Is a Punk Rocker," the pared down production style and simplified musical approach are immediately apparent. At the beginning of the song, we hear the very end of a countdown (a quick "1, 2, 3, 4") to start the song. The full "1, 2, 3, 4" count is often heard at the start of many of their recordings, and gives the impression of a "do-it-yourself," underproduced quality. It suggests, for one, that the recording studio's audio engineers, who would normally count a song down before setting a track, have had a minimal hand in the recording process. Furthermore, the fact that the countdowns were not erased in production suggests the recording's "authenticity"—no studio tricks here, this is the "real deal." The music itself is a very simple progression of sustained chords on heavily strummed electric guitars that never take on extended or virtuosic solo passages (not even during the breaks). The drums bang away heavily on the backbeats as typically heard in the "rhythm and blues" and "rock and roll" of the 1950s. The vocals are also very simple, with the possible exception of an occasional attempt to emulate the more complex and polished harmonizations of the Beach Boys.

In this case, the allusion to the Beach Boys' characteristic harmonization is tied directly to the lyrics which, Starr and Waterman note, "announced that the center of the rock 'n' roll universe had shifted from the beaches of southern California to the lower east side of Manhattan" (350): "She had to break away / Well New York City really has it all."

The Ramones proved to be especially influential in England. "Sheena Is a Punk Rocker" made the Top 40 in the U.K. (it only reached number 81 in the U.S.), and their concerts throughout England had a major impact on musicians there. British groups such as the Clash, the Damned, and the Sex Pistols can attribute their early influences to the Ramones, an American group that "staged a British Invasion in reverse" (Starr and Waterman 350). The "punk aesthetic" would reemerge in the United States with the "grunge" movement of the 1990s, again a reaction to the glam-like visual excesses of the 1980s.

As a brief side note here, it bears mentioning that as much as the music and image of the Ramones strive toward "real deal" rock and roll, the group itself is a fabrication of sorts. Contrary to popular belief, the "Ramones"—Joey Ramone, Johnny Ramone, Dee Dee Ramone, and Tommy Ramone—are not related. These are merely the stage names adopted by Jeffrey Hyman, John Cummings, Douglas Colvin, and Tom Erdelyi, the band's members. Then, as now, even a counterculture of "authenticity" within the commercial rock industry needs its gimmicks.

The Last Quarter of a Century

If anything has characterized rock music over the past quarter of a century, it has been the application of gadgetry and new technologies. In the 1980s, just about every hit had a synthesizer somewhere in the background. In the 1990s, affordable and portable computer technology created even more possibilities for innovative soundscapes and the manipulation of pitches and timbres. Lasers and artificial smoke at live concerts today make the light shows of the psychedelic era appear clean and sober by comparison. However, while technology has advanced creative possibilities on some fronts, it has also diminished them on others. For example, in the age of digital sound that can be downloaded from the Internet and manipulated in a variety of ways, it will never again be possible for a recording artist to ensure the integrity of a "concept album" or even of a hit single. (With regard to the latter, consider the "mixes" heard on many FM radio stations today which seamlessly weave one song into another to create a "hit potpourri" of sorts.)

The central role of video in modern rock—whether on MTV, VH-1, or *American Idol*—has continued to make it essential (and perhaps even most important) that musicians remain visually appealing according to the shifting ideals of popular culture. It is tempting to say that "Video Killed the Radio Star," by the English group the Buggles, was sounding a prophetic message when it became the first video aired on MTV, at 12:01 A.M. August 1, 1981. But in many ways video did that the moment *American Bandstand* had every teenager doing "The Twist" in 1960. What has changed in recent years, however, is the accessibility of video. You don't have to be in front of the only TV in your neighborhood anymore to access images. These can now be streamed online or even viewed on a cell phone. More so than ever before, America has become a visual culture, and before too long the rock star's music and image will become inseparably fused. Future generations will no longer be content to listen to music, they will need to watch it too.

With the high-tech turns of the past twenty-five years or so, rock music would seem to be at its farthest remove from its roots in blues and country music. Yet, as we have seen, the Beach Boys reemerged with "Kokomo" in 1988, their first rock hit in twenty-two years. And in 2005, the Rolling Stones launched a highly successful tour to promote a brand-new rock album titled *A Bigger Bang*. But whether it is the grunge of the 1990s rehashing the punk of the 1970s, or the Stones of the 2000s reaching back to the style that made them famous in the 1960s, rock music—even with all of its technical gadgetry—appears to have fallen into an endless loop. The bottom line is that, while rock trends have renewed (or recycled) themselves periodically, the music no longer seems to go anywhere.

At the dawn of the twenty-first century, it may be that rock has run its course as the music of white youths in America. Increasingly, it has come to be supplanted by hip-hop (or rap), an African American genre of popular music that emerged in New York City during the 1970s. Hip-hop has caught on not only because of its energetic and complex play with rhymes and rhythmic declamation of lyrics, but also with an attendant dance culture and an authentic social outlook that has generated a mass popular appeal among young people today. Indeed, one of the core appeals of rap music and hip-hop culture is their attempt at an honest social commentary which resonates with many young people across America. A difficulty lies, however, in the fact that lyrics are often more important than the music. This means that audiences need, first, to understand the lyrics (often hard for whites), and then to align with them in a common cause (*very* difficult for whites). Nonetheless, the music industry is taking notice. Indeed, hip-hop culture's growing domination of airtime on MTV was noted at the 2005 MTV Music Awards by Billie Joe Armstrong, lead singer of the punk group Green Day, who, upon receiving a video award, quipped: "It's great to know that rock music still has a place at MTV." It remains to be seen whether black hip-hop artists will suffer the same fate as black "rhythm and blues" artists as the music industry increasingly tries to market hip-hop to a broader audience.

Projects

1. Interview a local disc jockey, and produce a paper profiling the job (both positive and negative aspects) and recording his or her opinions on current trends in popular music, the influence and responsibilities of the disc jockey, and related issues.

2. Interview the manager, or a knowledgeable employee, of a local record store, and produce a paper on a topic such as (a) the buying habits of the local public (for example, percentages buying rock, hip-hop, country, classical, folk, and other types of music); (b) any recognizable characteristics (such as apparent age, occupation, dress, or behavior) of the various buying publics; (c) the effect of rock videos on the sales of specific albums; (d) the presumed impact on record sales of the iPod®; (e) his or her experiences in handling hit albums (the predictability of hits, the buying rush—how strong, how long, etc.); or (f) some other topic/approach of your own choosing.

3. Tipper Gore's *Raising PG Kids in an X-Rated Society* (Nashville: Abingdon Press, 1987) and Robert Walser's *Running with the Devil: Power, Gender, and Madness in Heavy Metal Music* (Hanover & London: Wesleyan Univ. Press, 1993), Chapter 5, present opposing views on a topic of importance to parents. Read both, make up your own mind, and then present your own views in a paper.

4. Write a brief "History of Rock" from the 1980s to the present. What five or six pieces would you highlight as important and why? What trends do they signal?

5. Investigate the recent history of hip-hop music. Who are the major artists? How is the music industry packaging them? Who is the intended audience?

ADDITIONAL LISTENING

Best of Chuck Berry: 20th Century Masters. MCA 11944.

Led Zeppelin. Atlantic/WEA 82632 ("You Shook Me").

Led Zeppelin II. Atlantic/WEA 82633 ("Whole Lotta Love").

Pet Sounds (The Beach Boys). Capitol 26266.

Sgt. Pepper's Lonely Hearts Club Band (The Beatles). Capitol 46422.

Surrealistic Pillow (Jefferson Airplane). RCA 50351.

Willie Dixon: The Chess Box. Chess 16500 ("You Need Love," "You Shook Me" performed by Muddy Waters).

POPULAR SACRED MUSIC

America is too young to have been able to nurture such highly cultivated worship music as is represented, for example, by the rich flowerings of Gregorian chant, elaborate settings of the Roman Catholic Mass, or the Lutheran cantata. Nor, the question of age aside, have the conditions been present that could have produced such flowerings. The reasons are many—America's broad spectrum of religious denominations, her inbred distrust of the ecclesiastical organization and wealth that are indispensable for building a tradition of religious art, and her increased secularization. America has lacked the type of patronage and focus on religious art that in Europe produced, at its apex, original but highly contrived works along the lines of Handel's *Messiah* and Mozart's *Requiem*. Instead, the most significant of America's religious music is that which has remained closest to folk sources. As such, it draws its significance not primarily from its aesthetic value but, rather, from its meaning in the lives of those who sing it and from the response it evokes from those who experience it.

In this 1740 engraving, singing colonists process into church at the height of the Great Awakening—America's first religious revival. Responding to worries that the descendants of the devout founders of Massachusetts were "profane Drunkards, Swearers, Licentious scoffers at the power of Godliness" (Increase Mather, 1678), evangelical ministers began to preach a personal interpretation of scripture aimed at producing an emotional response— an Awakening from sin to God's grace—a new birth. Because the revival arose in many different faiths, and personal conversion meant individuals could find salvation in any religion, the Great Awakening encouraged religious pluralism and the separation of church and state in the United States.

10 FROM PSALM TUNE TO RURAL REVIVALISM

PSALMODY IN AMERICA

Rendering the 150 psalms of the Old Testament in song (psalmody) is one of the most venerable traditions in the history of Western music. Probably the first musical sounds from the Old World that the indigenous inhabitants heard in what is now the United States were the simple, unharmonized psalm tunes sung by Protestant settlers and sailors. French Huguenots were singing psalms from their Psalter (a book containing psalm tunes) in Florida half a century before the landing of the English Separatists at Plymouth. At the other edge of the continent, the California Indians were fascinated by the psalm singing of Sir Francis Drake's men in 1579. When the first permanent settlements in Massachusetts were established, Psalters were an important part of the few precious possessions brought over. The Separatists (Pilgrims) who founded the Plymouth Colony in 1620 brought with them the Psalter (*The Book of Psalmes: Englished both in Prose and Metre*) that Henry Ainsworth had published for the Puritan exiles in Amsterdam in 1612. Other Psalters used by the early colonists include the older Sternhold and Hopkins, and especially the Psalter by Thomas Ravenscroft (London, 1621), used by the Puritans of the Massachusetts Bay Colony.

Psalm tunes were the most important body of religious music in constant use throughout those colonies founded by the English and the Dutch, almost until the time of the Revolution. Subsequently, they were largely replaced by other types of devotional music such as hymns, anthems, and fuging tunes that, though religious in character, did not necessarily set a psalm text. But many of the old psalm tunes have survived, and tune names such as "Old 104th," "Old 120th," and the famous "Old 100th" (familiar to many as the Doxology) bespeak their presence in songbooks for modern worship.

Calvinism and the Psalms

A glance at a map of Europe, together with some understanding of the situation there at the time of the Reformation, will make clear why it was the psalm tune, rather than the Lutheran chorale or the venerable and cultivated music of the

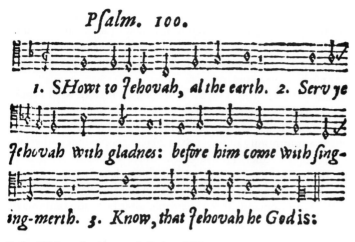

Psalm 100 from the Ainsworth Psalter, 1612

Roman Catholic Church, that dominated early religious music on the eastern seaboard of the United States and, with its related progeny, left its mark on American sacred music for 300 years. We cannot here fill in the background; suffice it to say that most of the earliest permanent settlers there brought with them not only their Psalters and their psalm tunes but also their pronounced aversion to state religion and temporal ecclesiastical hierarchy and power—all of which, to them, was summed up in one word: "popery." This was to have a profound effect on the development of American consciousness and culture.

Calvinism, a Reformed Church movement named after its leader John Calvin (1509–1564), dominated the religious practices of a large portion of the early settlers on the east coast of the United States. Music in the Calvinist churches was rather severely limited to the unaccompanied unison singing of metrical versions of the psalms. This was but one manifestation of the ancient and ever-present dichotomy that exists between the musician and the theologian on the question of music in worship. The musician wishes to use the utmost skill and craft, and give the music free rein; the theologian wishes to keep music simple and ensure its subordination to the worship itself. The controversy is nearly as old as the Christian church, and the history of church music is the history of the swinging of the pendulum back and forth between the two positions. It so happened that in the sixteenth century the pendulum swung decisively to the side of strict control of music, in both the Roman Catholic Church and the new Reformed Church, but much more drastically and completely in the latter. In the Reformed Church, the new broom had no weight of musical tradition to encumber it. Psalm singing, then, was the product of a musical simplicity enforced on theological grounds.

Psalm Tunes and Psalters

With John Calvin's exhortation to psalm singing came the need for metered and rhymed versions of the psalms, and tunes to which they could be sung by entire congregations and not by trained choirs. This need was met by a series of

Psalters, the first published in Strasbourg in 1539. The sixteenth century thus saw the establishment of two great bodies of sacred tunes, the Lutheran chorales and the psalmody of the Reformed Church. The two traditions share similar characteristics (as well as some of the same tunes); most importantly, they are easily singable melodies of fairly simple construction.

The most significant Psalter, for us, was the first book printed in what is now the United States, *The Whole Booke of Psalmes Faithfully Translated into English Metre*, published in Boston in 1640 and nicknamed the Bay Psalm Book. It was no mean achievement for a community of fewer than 20,000 people that had established itself on the edge of the American wilderness scarcely more than a decade before. The preface of the Bay Psalm Book reinforces the key dictum of "substance over style," citing nothing less than the authority of the Book of Exodus, Chapter 20, where the Lord demands that His proper altar be made of unhewn stone.

> If therefore the verfes are not alwayes fo fmooth and elegant as fome may defire or expect; let them confider that Gods Altar needs not our pollifhings: Ex. 20. for wee have refpected rather a plaine tranfla-tion, then to fmooth our verfes with the fweetnes of any paraphrafe, and foe have attended Confcience rather then Elegance, fidelity rather then poetry, in tranflating the hebrew words into englifh language, and Davids poetry into englifh meetre;
>
> that foe wee may fing in Sion the Lords fongs of prayfe according to his owne will; untill hee take us from hence, and wipe away all our teares, & bid us enter into our mafters ioye to fing eternall Halleluiahs.

Preface of the Bay Psalm Book, 1640: "If therefore the verses are not always so smooth and elegant as some may desire or expect, let them consider that God's altar needs not our polishings (Exodus 20), for we have respected rather a plain translation than to smooth our verses with the sweetness of any paraphrase, and so have attended conscience rather than elegance, fidelity rather than poetry, in translating the Hebrew words into [the] English language, and David's poetry [The Psalms] into English meter; that, so we may sing in Zion the Lord's songs of praise according to His own will, until He takes us from hence, and wipes away all our tears, and bids us enter into our Master's joy to sing eternal Halleluiahs."

Two Divergent "Ways"

By the 1720s a hundred years of psalm singing in America had produced two discernible traditions, simultaneous but widely divergent. They amounted to one practice that was written and another that was oral. In the written practice, the tunes would be sung as they were notated in the psalmbooks of the time. But psalmbooks were few, and few in the congregations, especially in rural areas, could read music. This led to the practice of "lining out," in which the deacon, or precentor, sang or recited each line before it was sung by the congregation. This oral practice, called the Usual Way, led to a severe shrinking in the number of tunes in common use. It also encouraged a much slower performance of the music in order to allow the congregation to keep up. The slow pace proved exasperating for some. As one observer noted, "I myself have twice in one Note paused to take Breath."

Two aspects of the Usual Way have persisted to the present, especially in rural areas. The first is the independence of, or even the absence of, a printed hymnal—hence singing from memory. In some traditions knowing the tunes "by heart" is felt to be essential.

The second is the persistence of "lining out." This practice is preserved in rural areas of the South, especially in the Appalachians. A performance of "Amazing Grace" (CD 2/17) recorded in a Baptist church in Kentucky, illustrates the survival of this practice. Notice here the "lining out" of verses and the slow pace of the singing.

Listening Cue "**Amazing Grace**" (one verse) Congregation of the Old
Regular Baptist Church in Jeff, Kentucky (1:07)

Listen For ▪ lining out ▪ very slow pace of the song

Visit http://www.music.wadsworth.com_3/Kingman for a full listening guide and other resources.

> Amazing Grace, how sweet the sound,
> That saved a wretch like me.
> I once was lost but now am found,
> Was blind, but now, I see.
> T'was Grace that taught my heart to fear . . .

Reform and Instruction

Opposition to the Usual Way on the part of a more musically literate portion of the populace grew more outspoken as time went on and came to a head in the 1720s. What the reformers, or proponents of what was called Regular Singing, wanted to make happen could be accomplished only by teaching people to read music. This is exactly what they set out to do. Instruction books such as *An Introduction to the Singing of Psalm Tunes in a Plain and Easy Method*, by Rev. John

Tufts, appeared in the 1720s and went through many editions. As intimated in their titles, these books represented only the first of a long series of assaults by American ingenuity on the perennial problem of how to make music easier for the uninitiated. From *An Introduction to the Singing of Psalm Tunes in a Plain and Easy Method* through the recent *Guitar for Dummies*, this elusive goal has been pursued—often with some success.

But no one has ever learned to perform music just by reading a book. The need for instruction by a "master," and for practicing together under his tutelage, produced one of the most important and pervasive musical and social institutions in our early history—the singing school.

THE SINGING-SCHOOL TRADITION

That uniquely American institution, the singing school, may have had its beginnings in New England, but ultimately it spread far and wide. In the cities its descendants are represented by the numerous choral societies, great and small. In rural areas it retained its original characteristics longest; here, as a social as well as a musical gathering, it brightened the routine of lives that were otherwise all too often harsh and dreary. The firm place and meaning of the singing school in rural American life before the twentieth century can hardly be better attested to than by the following excerpt from the reminiscences, in folk-verse form, of a pioneer woman writing of her life in Sangamon County, Illinois, in the mid-nineteenth century.

> We had so few things to give us pleasure
> The memories of such times I love to treasure.
> Our singing school, where we looked forward to meet
> Our beloved teacher, and his pupils to greet.
> Our singing books, few here now, ever saw
> The old patent notes, fa, sol, la, sol, fa, me, la.
> There were some good voices to lead the rest,
> All long since gone to the home of the blest.
> I seem to hear their voices now singing, loud and clear
> And almost feel their presence hovering near.

How the Singing Schools Worked

From the 1720s on, the singing-school movement gradually picked up momentum, and the period 1760 to 1800, encompassing the Revolution and the founding of the new nation, saw its greatest activity, especially in New England. The singing school was a private venture, taught by an itinerant master. The school would be advertised in advance in the community, and subscriptions taken. The singing school itself was not a denominational institution, and in fact the instruction did not always take place in the church; a room in a schoolhouse or local tavern was sometimes used. Two or three meetings a week for three months seems to have been a common schedule. If the singing master had published a tunebook, the pupils would be expected to buy and use it, thus somewhat augmenting his income, which was seldom large. There is evidence that singing masters sometimes took their pay in produce—Indian corn, for example. At the close of the term, there was almost always a public concert, or "exhibition." The pupils thus got a chance to show off what they had learned; the singing master then moved on to another community.

Contemporary accounts show that the pupils were mostly young people. It seems, from the directions for the conduct of a singing school that have survived, that the teacher's ability to keep order was at least as important as his ability to teach music—an observation that has a familiar ring. Yet there is little doubt that the singing schools generally accomplished their objectives very well. After the term was over, one or more of the ablest pupils might start teaching themselves, or even try their hand at composing psalm settings, anthems, or fuging tunes. Thus the singing schools, in addition to raising the general level of musical literacy and expanding the repertory of music available, played a vital part in encouraging the development of native composers.

William Billings and His Contemporaries

Not every singing master became a composer, but the number that did is substantial. In fact, the singing-school movement gave us our first school of indigenous American composers, who worked under the most fruitful conditions a composer can experience: writing music for which there is a clear demand and appreciation on the part of a well-defined public. This fruitful period for America's first native composers did not last long, but the productivity was intense. By 1800 there were more than 1,000 compositions in print in American tunebooks, most of them by native composers.

The singing masters and composers were for the most part humble craftsmen, artisans, or small businessmen, who composed and taught in addition to working within their trades. The names and trades of these native pioneers read like a litany of eighteenth-century New England names and occupations, and perhaps help to give the flavor of the singing-school movement in a way nothing else can: Supply Belcher, tavern keeper; David Belknap, farmer and mechanic; William Billings, tanner; Amos Bull, storekeeper; Oliver Holden, carpenter; Jeremiah Ingalls, cooper; Jacob Kimball, lawyer; Abraham Maxim, farmer and schoolteacher; Justin Morgan, horse breeder; Timothy Swan, hatter.

William Billings (1746–1800) of Boston, Massachusetts, was the best known among these. He was also the most prolific, inventive, and enthusiastically dedicated. In 1770, at the age of 24, he published the first tunebook in America consisting entirely of music by a single composer; his *New-England Psalm-Singer* contained more than 120 compositions. In the next quarter-century he brought out five more books, whose titles give something of their flavor and usage: *The Singing Master's Assistant* (1778), *Music in Miniature* (1779), *The Psalm-Singer's Amusement* (1781), *The Suffolk Harmony* (1786), and *The Continental Harmony* (1794).

Billings became quite well known in his time. Yet he was never able to give up his tanning trade permanently. In fact, records show him to have held down several civil posts to help make ends meet for himself and his family. In spite of every good effort, he died in severe poverty.

William Billings' "Chester"—which we hear on CD 2, track 18—appeared in his 1770 publication, *The New England Psalm Singer,* a virtual declaration of independence from European music. This engraving (by Paul Revere) in the book's frontispiece shows a group of colonists seated in the round while singing a round, or *canon,* in which each successive voice, singing the same melody, enters at a different time (as in "Row, Row, Row Your Boat"). A musical circle also surrounds the lyric of "Wake Ev'ry Breath," the first piece printed in *Psalm Singer.*

> Wake ev'ry Breath, and ev'ry String,
> To bless the great Redeemer King,
> His Name thro' ev'ry Clime ador'd.
> Let Joy and Gratitude, and Love,
> Thro' all the Notes of Music rove;
> And Jesus sound on ev'ry Chord.

Listening Cue "Chester" by William Billings; The Old Sturbridge Singers (1:53)

Listen For ▪ strophic form ▪ lyrical melody ▪ clear, balanced phrases

Visit http://www.music.wadsworth.com_3/Kingman for a full listening guide and other resources.

A friend of Samuel Adams and Paul Revere, Billings was an ardent patriot, and his patriotic song "Chester" (CD 2/18) was one of the most popular songs of the Revolution. The lyrical melody reveals Billings' appreciation for catchy tunes and clear, balanced phrases. With its first stanza, it appeared in 1770 in *The New-England Psalm-Singer*. During the Revolution, further stanzas were added, with the names of five British generals (William Howe, John Burgoyne, Henry Clinton, Richard Prescott, and Charles Cornwallis) and the boast that "Their Vet'rans flee before our Youth, / And Gen'rals yield to beardless Boys"—and it was in this form that it appeared in *The Singing Master's Assistant* of 1778. Because of its strophic form, stanzas can be added to this song indefinitely without ever corrupting Billings' melody. (Every stanza just gets the very same music.) They can be taken out too. And, indeed, our recording does not include stanzas two and three below. The melody here has been fleshed out with additional voices and instruments. It can be heard most clearly, however, in the clarinet at the start of the recording. It is later taken up by the tenor voice.

Let tyrants shake their iron rod,
And Slav'ry clank her galling chains;
We fear them not, we trust in God,
New England's God forever reigns.

Howe and Burgoyne and Clinton, too
With Prescott and Cornwallis join'd,
Together plot our overthrow,
In one infernal league combin'd.

When God inspired us for the fight,
Their ranks were broke, their lines were forc'd,
Their Ships were Shatter'd in our sight,
Or swiftly driven from our Coast.

The foe comes on with haughty Stride,
Our troops advance with martial noise;
Their Vet'rans flee before our Youth,
And Gen'rals yield to beardless Boys.

What grateful Off'ring shall we bring,
What shall we render to the Lord?
Loud Hallelujahs let us Sing,
And praise his name on ev'ry Chord.

In addition to being a singing master and composer, Billings was a colorful and energetic writer of prose as well—as the salty, conversational, and sometimes lengthy prefaces to his tunebooks attest. His philosophical approach to music (as well as to politics) was one of independence and self-reliance. Oft-quoted statements of his resonate with the fiercely independent spirit of Americans today: "Nature is the best dictator"; "I don't think myself confin'd to any rules for composition laid down by any that went before me"; and "I think it best for every composer to be his own carver." Perhaps the best summation of Billings as man and composer is contained in a diary entry of the Rev. William Bentley of Salem, made a few days after Billings' death. Bentley, one of America's best-educated men of his time (Thomas Jefferson had thought of him for the presidency of the University of Virginia), moved in circles unfamiliar and even inaccessible to Billings. Nevertheless, his insight into Billings' work and importance moved him to write, "Many who have imitated have excelled him, but none of them had better original power. . . . He spake and sung and thought as a man above the common abilities."

Yankee Tunebooks by the Hundreds

Billings was but one among many. An examination of the singing-school period during its golden age gives an impression of tremendous activity and vitality. By 1810, about 300 of the distinctive tunebooks, homely in appearance and typography, had been published. Their oblong shape gave rise to the terms "long boys" and "end-openers." The titles of these old books tell us much. Some show the classical education or aspirations of their compilers: *Urania, Harmonia Americana*. Some of the titles show clearly the books' use and purpose: *The Musical Primer, The Easy Instructor, The Psalmodist's Assistant, The Psalmodist's Companion, The Chorister's Companion*. Many bespeak their particular locale: *The Massachusetts Compiler, The Vermont Harmony, The Harmony of Maine, The Worcester Collection of Sacred Harmony, The Essex Harmony*. The word "harmony" was widely used: *The American Harmony, The Northern Harmony, The Union Harmony, The Federal Harmony, The New England Harmony, The Christian Harmony*, and as a final distillation, *The Harmony of Harmony*. To close the list, there appeared (with singular appropriateness to their environment) *The Rural Harmony* and *The Village Harmony*.

The Music of the Tunebooks

The venerable psalm tunes are well represented in some of the earlier collections (*Urania*, for example), but along with these appear tunes for short nonscriptural hymns to original texts, and also larger and more ambitious anthems—more elaborate settings of texts that could be scriptural, adapted from scripture, or entirely original. It is evident that by this time hymnody—the singing of texts that were not necessarily psalms—had fairly well succeeded in replacing psalmody—the stricter practice of singing psalm texts specifically.

Whether we are dealing with psalmody or hymnody, the poetic and musical principles tend to be very similar. Like the ballads discussed in Chapter 1, settings of these religious texts are in strophic form. Every stanza (which typically consists of four lines) gets the exact same music. As for the texts themselves, these are distinguished by the number of syllables in each line. Stanzas with four lines of eight syllables per line, yielding the pattern 8:8:8:8, are designated as being in Long Meter. The first stanza of Psalm 100 as set in the *Ainsworth Psalter* of 1612 presents an example of Long Meter:

Showt to Jehova, al the earth
Serv ye Jehovah with gladnes
before him come with singing-merth
Know, that Jehovah he God is.

Texts with the metric pattern of 8:6:8:6 syllables per stanza are in Common Meter, which, incidentally, is identical with "ballad meter" (see p. 6). The text for the hymn "Amazing Grace" (see previously) exemplifies Common Meter. The only other meter used with sufficient frequency to be given a name is Short Meter, which follows a pattern of 6:6:8:6 syllables per stanza. For an example of a secular text that observes this pattern, see "John Henry" in Chapter 2 (pp. 25–27).

Of particular interest are the famous *fuging tunes*. (The term, though derived from *fugue*, was very possibly pronounced "fudging" in contemporary usage.) Alan Buechner describes it simply as a piece that "begins like a hymn and ends like a round." It was the second section, or *fuge*, that was distinctive, with its rather informally constructed homespun imitative entrances of the voices. The fuging tune was very popular in its day; the effect of hearing the successive entrances coming from different parts of the U-shaped meetinghouse gallery must have thrilled singers and congregation alike. Billings describes these pieces as being "twenty times as powerful as the old slow tunes." Although he composed many himself, there were other composers of the time who favored them even more, and more than 1,000 were published by 1810. The fuging tune later fell into disfavor among reformers of church music, who argued that it was both too crude and too lively as music for worship. But its appeal among the rural folk persisted, and fuging tunes in considerable numbers appear in the shape-note songbooks of the nineteenth century. "Amity," by Daniel Read (1757–1863), a Revolutionary War soldier who became a storekeeper and maker of combs, is an excellent example of this popular form (CD 2/19).

Listening Cue "Amity" by Daniel Read; The Old Sturbridge Singers (0:43)

Listen For ▪ successive entrances of voices

Visit http://www.music.wadsworth.com_3/Kingman for a full listening guide and other resources.

How pleasant is to see
Kindred and friends agree,
Each in their proper station move,
(Fuging section)
And each fulfill their part,
With sympathizing heart,
In all the cares of life and love.

A number of the larger anthems and set pieces were written for specific occasions or observances—for Thanksgiving, for a Fast Day, for Ordination, for Easter, for thanksgiving "after a victory," to commemorate the landing of the Pilgrims, and so on. Some were of a still more topical nature, as illustrated by Billings' famous "Lamentation Over Boston," a spirited paraphrase of Psalm 137 commemorating the British occupation of the city during the war.

The End of an Era and the Suppression of the Indigenous Tradition in the Urban East

America's expansion, which began in earnest with the opening of the nineteenth century, manifested itself in two directions at once: in the growth of her cities in size, complexity, and sophistication; and in the continuous rolling westward of her frontier. Both had profound effects on American thought, life, and art—including indigenous religious music. By 1810 an "anti-American" reform movement had successfully established a trend away from the native, unschooled, innocent art of the pioneer tradition, and toward the closer imitation of European models. The fuging tune especially was castigated. In 1807 the preface of a new compilation characterized the fuging tunes as "those wild fugues, and rapid and confused movements, which have so long been the disgrace of congregational psalmody." The reformers prevailed, to the extent that the editor of the *Boston Courier* lamented in 1848 that "the good old days of New England music have passed away, and the singing-masters who compose and teach it, are known only in history as an extinct race" (Stevenson 85n).

THE FRONTIER AND RURAL AMERICA IN THE NINETEENTH CENTURY

That the music of the New Englanders was in fact far from extinct is now clear to us. As is often the case, in the rural areas the "old ways"—and the old music—were tenaciously clung to long after they had been replaced in the cities. And the frontier, southwestward into the long valleys of the Appalachians and beyond into the broad river valleys of the Ohio and the Tennessee, was an extension of rural America. We can follow the movement of the singing-school tradition along these paths just by tracing the continued appearance of its odd oblong books of tunes. Moving out of Boston and Philadelphia, we find compilations being made in Harrisburg, Pennsylvania; in the Shenandoah Valley of Virginia; in Hamilton, Georgia; in Spartanburg, South Carolina; in Lexington, Kentucky; in Nashville, in Cincinnati, in St. Louis. The titles tell a story of both continuity and movement. As lineal descendants of *The New England Harmony* and *The Harmony of Maine,* we find *The Virginia Harmony, The Kentucky Harmony, The Knoxville Harmony, The Missouri Harmony, The Western Lyre, The Southern Harmony,* and finally, the famous *Sacred Harp.* These books clearly revealed their ancestry—in their shape and appearance; in their prefatory introductions to the "Rudiments of Music"; in their repertories and manner of musical notation. Pieces by Billings himself were almost invariably included. Far from being "extinct," as the editor of the *Boston Courier* had lamented in 1848, William Billings and some of his contemporaries have turned out to be the most continuously performed composers in American history. Indeed, their music has already entered its third century. The singing schools continued to flourish in the nineteenth century, fulfilling their dual musical and social function much as they had done in New England in colonial times. Later came the institution of annual gatherings, or "singings," some lasting two or three days, with "dinner on the grounds" a fixed feature.

Thus we see that the "old ways" did not die. Two important additions were made, however, as the native tradition moved out of the East into the South and the West. One was the development of the famous shape notes, and the other was the infusion of the folk element into the music.

The Shape Notes

John Tufts' *An Introduction . . . in a Plain and Easy Method* in the early eighteenth century was only the first of many attempts to simplify and speed up the process of teaching people to read music. There appeared in 1801 a book by William Little and William Smith called, appropriately, *The Easy Instructor,* which introduced a simple but ingenious device that proved to be eminently practical. This consisted of the use of differently shaped notes for each of the four syllables (fa, sol, la, mi) then in use to indicate pitches of a musical scale.

The device appears to have caught on rather quickly and well. *The Easy Instructor* was reissued in various editions for thirty years; by the time it ceased publication, there were at least eighteen other songbooks in print using the same device. *The Easy Instructor* was first published in the urban East (Philadelphia). The shape-note method was so readily adopted by the compilers of the traditional rural songbooks, however, that its vast literature—for so long all but unknown to outsiders—has taken on the name "southern shape-note hymnody."

Infusion of the Folk Element

Another important development as this rural hymnody moved southwest at the beginning of the nineteenth century was a fresh infusion of the folk element into the tune collections. Folk or folkish tunes of Anglo-Celtic cast, given sacred words and spare, austere harmonic settings, were found in the new books, alongside the established hymn tunes, anthems, and fuging tunes. This process had already begun in New England. The "borrowing" of folk tunes to supply the needs of sacred music—"plundering the carnal lover"—is a venerable practice. The great body of Lutheran chorale tunes, for example, contains its share of melodies that began life as folk or popular tunes, in some cases love songs.

The harmony of these hymns abounds in austere open consonances (octaves, fifths, fourths). The simplicity and spare openness of the harmonic texture contributes a distinct, antique touch to this music. This style is nowhere better illustrated than in the three-voice setting of the famous folk hymn "Wondrous Love,"

Here we see shape notes illustrating three voices (three-part harmony) for the hymn "Wondrous Love," which we hear on CD 2, track 20. The melody is in the middle voice above the words.

as found in *The Southern Harmony* (CD 2/20). The folk tune is in the middle, or tenor, voice.

Listening Cue "Wondrous Love" Anonymous 4 (2:35)

Listen For ▪ simple texture ▪ austere open consonances ▪ initial vocalization on syllables

Visit http://www.music.wadsworth.com_3/Kingman for a full listening guide and other resources.

(Introductory vocalization on syllables)
la la sol mi sol la. . . .

. . . .

What wondrous love is this! oh my soul! oh my soul!
What wondrous love is this! oh my soul!
What wondrous love is this
That caused the Lord of Bliss,
To bear the dreadful curse for my soul, for my soul,
To bear the dreadful curse for my soul.

When I was sinking down, sinking down, sinking down,
When I was sinking down, sinking down,

When I was sinking down
Beneath God's righteous frown
Christ laid aside his crown for my soul, for my soul,
Christ laid aside his crown, for my soul.

Ye winged seraphs fly, bear the news, bear the news,
Ye winged seraphs fly, bear the news,
Ye winged seraphs fly
Like comets through the sky,
Fill vast eternity, with the news, with the news,
Fill vast eternity with the news.

And when from death we're free, we'll sing on, we'll sing on,
And when from death we're free, we'll sing on,
And when from death we're free,
We'll sing and joyful be
And in eternity we'll sing on, we'll sing on,
And in eternity, we'll sing on.

Revivalism and the Camp Meeting

Successive waves of religious revivalism have swept America since 1800. Their impact on our indigenous religious music was most pronounced in the period of the expanding frontier before the Civil War, for it was on the frontier that revivalism nurtured its most striking manifestation: the camp meeting. The camp meeting in turn nurtured, for its own needs, one of our most distinctive forms of religious music: the revival spiritual. To understand the origin, nature, and function of the revival spiritual, let us turn our attention briefly to the camp meeting itself.

The colonial South was far from being a devout society. The fundamentalist faith that later became so ingrained there was established as a result of two factors. One was the hardship of what amounted to a frontier existence throughout the antebellum South for the "plain folk" who made up the bulk of the population—mostly white subsistence farmers, who were continually forced to move and take up less arable land as the large slave-worked plantations spread into the fertile lowlands. This kind of existence bred a need for the reassurance and consolation that could be supplied by an evangelical religion—a religion that held out the promise in the hereafter of all the good that was so elusive and pitifully transient in the here and now. The other factor was the unremitting effort of the three most popular denominations after the Revolution: the Presbyterians, the Baptists, and the Methodists (the last most especially, with their organized hierarchy and their corps of indefatigable circuit-riding preachers). These two factors set the stage for the Great Revival of the early nineteenth century.

At its beginning it was called the Kentucky Revival, for that state was its fertile seedbed. Of all the newly opened territories west of the Appalachians, Kentucky was the first to attract settlers, and it acted as a kind of staging area for

With the aid of one of fifty clergy, worshipers at this 1851 Methodist camp meeting in Eastham, Massachusetts, pray with great piety. As Henry David Thoreau described it: "10,000 people might arrive on a Sunday by boat from Boston to hear the ministers. . . . They have an oven and a pump, and keep all their kitchen utensils and tent coverings and furniture in a permanent building. . . . I saw the heaps of clam-shells left under the tables . . . and supposed it the work of the unconverted, or the backsliders and scoffers. It looked as if a camp-meeting must be a singular combination of a prayer-meeting and a picnic" (*Cape Cod*, 1865).

those who were eventually to move on. By 1800 it was a "boom" state, having a greater population (more than 200,000) than all the other states and territories outside the original thirteen colonies combined. It was at about this time that revivalism in its most sensational form came to this raw frontier state.

The early camp meetings of the Kentucky revival were huge, chaotic, turbulent affairs. Many people traveled for days to get there. One camp meeting of August 1801 at Cane Ridge, in the gently rolling country of Bourbon County northeast of Lexington, lasted six days; estimates of the number in attendance ran between 10,000 and 25,000. The preaching, praying, shouting, and singing went on day and night. According to one of the many eyewitness accounts:

The noise was like the roar of Niagara. The vast sea of human beings seemed to be agitated as if by a storm. I counted seven ministers, all preaching at one time, some on stumps, others in wagons, and one . . . was standing on a tree which had, in falling, lodged against . . . another. Some of the people were singing, others praying, some crying for mercy in the most piteous accents, while others were shouting most vociferously.... A strange supernatural power seemed to pervade the entire mass of mind there collected. . . . Soon after I left and went into the woods, and there I strove to rally and man up my courage.

After some time I returned to the scene of excitement, the waves of which, if possible, had risen still higher. The same awfulness of feeling came over me. I stepped up on to a log, where I could have a better view of the surging sea of humanity. The scene that presented itself to my mind was indescribable. At one time I saw at least five hundred swept down in a moment as if a battery of a thousand guns had been opened upon them, and then immediately followed shrieks and shouts that rent the heavens. (Johnson 64–65)

There was many a strange and disquieting sight to be viewed on the American frontier, and none more so at times than the camp meeting. But in spite of the undenied excesses of the early ones, their emphasis on emotionalism, and the dubious significance of many of the "conversions," most careful observers now conclude that the positive influence of the camp meetings outweighed the negative. As Charles Johnson has summed it up, "Among all of the weapons forged by the West in its struggle against lawlessness and immorality, few were more successful than the frontier camp meeting. This socioreligious institution helped tame backwoods America" (Johnson vii).

The Revival Spiritual

Singing was a vital part of revivalism from the beginning. Another account of Cane Ridge tells of the powerful impulse of song: "The volume of song burst all bounds of guidance and control, and broke again and again from the throats of the people." Still another eyewitness reported that at the camp meetings the "falling down of multitudes, and their crying out . . . happened under the singing of Watts's Psalms and Hymns, more frequently than under the preaching of the word" (Johnson 57). All agree that the singing was loud. "The immediate din was tremendous; at a hundred yards it was beautiful; at a distance of a half a mile it was magnificent" (Chase 204).

What was sung at the camp meetings? Since it was for so long a matter of purely oral tradition, evidence must be pieced together. The reference above to "Watts's Psalms and Hymns" refers to an important publication of texts by Isaac Watts (1674–1748), the "Father of English Hymnody," whose works were obviously being used. Though pocket-sized "songsters" with just the words began to appear about 1805, the tunes were not written down and published until the 1840s. From these later collections we can form some notion of the camp meeting repertory, since we know what the hallmarks of the true "revival spiritual" were. The tunes had to be lively and easily learned. There was an almost unvarying reliance on the verse-chorus form; everyone could at least join in on the choruses, even if they didn't know the verses, or if the leader introduced unfamiliar ones or even made them up on the spot. A further development along the line of what has been called "text simplification," for the sake of mass participation, was the single-line refrain, interpolated after a couplet of original text or even after every line. With the crowds joining in on the refrains, this turned the singing into the familiar call-and-response pattern. Indoor church hymns could be transformed into revival spirituals by this process.

The revival spirituals were distinguished, in part, by the import of their texts. These emphasized the basic themes of the prevailing theology—especially salvation, its attendant joys, and the glories of a heaven that was far removed from the present life. Along with descriptions of heaven and its joys is a dissatisfaction with this present life that is so pronounced as to amount at times to a rejection of the world and, if not actually a wish for death, at least a poignant anticipation of the joys and release from pain it would bring to the righteous saints who had been converted.

> Our bondage it shall end, by and by, by and by.
> I am a stranger here below.
> This world is not my home.
> How blest the righteous when he dies!
> How gently heaves the expiring breast,
> How mildly beams the closing eyes
> When sinks a weary soul to rest.
> Sweet home! Oh, when shall I get there?

Parallel Traditions: White and Black Spirituals

The African American spiritual was treated extensively in Chapter 2. Parallel traditions of these "spiritual songs" existed among blacks and whites, as has been documented, for example, by George Pullen Jackson, who included in his *White and Negro Spirituals* a comparative list of 116 tunes from both. Thus white rural hymnody—folk hymns and especially revival spirituals—may have furnished some of the material for black spirituals. Much heated controversy as to which tradition influenced the other has been generated. Yet even the most polemical arguments will stop short of denying that some degree of mutual influence was involved.

Though there is still some controversy over where and how this blending of white and black spiritual traditions might have occurred, it seems reasonable to assume that it did not happen in the large slave-holding areas of the South or through the master-slave relationship, but precisely in those regions and under those conditions that nurtured the folk hymn and the revival spiritual among whites—in the uplands and on the frontier, among the plain folk and at the camp meeting. Whether it was a matter of black singers listening to white singers or the other way around, both were present, and the camp meeting, a frontier institution, was probably the site of as uninhibited a meeting of the races as could be encountered in that time. Many of the early camp meeting preachers, such as

© CORBIS

Because early members trembled while the Holy Spirit purged sin from their bodies, the United Society of Believers in Christ's Second Appearing became known as the Shakers. Here, the Shakers perform a sacred march with intricate floor patterns and a simple marching step designed to allow older members to worship. The dancers made a solid sound by striking their feet firmly on the floor, clearly the intent of the raised legs in this 1836 engraving of a Shaker Meeting in New (Mt.) Lebanon, New York. Dancing—to unaccompanied singing—was at the center of Shaker worship, which, along with their inclusion of all races (note the figures on the right), placed them on the fringes of American religion. We hear "'Tis the Gift to Be Simple" on CD 2, track 21.

Lorenzo Dow and Peter Cartwright, preached against slavery and were, in fact, among the earliest abolitionists.

MUSIC AMONG SMALLER INDEPENDENT AMERICAN SECTS

Conditions in America have been such as to nurture from the beginning, despite glaring episodes of intolerance and persecution, a lively tradition of religious independence and nonconformity. Many sects either have been transplanted to the United States or have sprung up here, finding, especially in the eighteenth and nineteenth centuries, the space necessary to provide the measure of isolation and self-sufficiency they so deeply desired. Mention must be made at least of the Moravians (of central European origin, with a strong classical music tradition) and the Shakers (originating in the English Midlands, with a self-generated tradition of folklike music). It is fitting to close this chapter on early American religious music with one of its great masterpieces, the Shaker spiritual "'Tis the Gift to Be Simple" (CD 2/21).

Listening Cue "'Tis the Gift to Be Simple" The United Society of Shakers (1:08)

Listen For ▪ simplicity of the tune ▪ humble performance style

Visit http://www.music.wadsworth.com_3/Kingman for a full listening guide and other resources.

> 'Tis the gift to be simple, 'tis the gift to be free,
> 'Tis the gift to come down where we ought to be,
> And when we find ourselves in the place just right,
> 'Twill be in the valley of love and delight.
>
> When true simplicity is gained,
> To bow and to bend we shan't be asham'd.
> To turn, turn will be our delight,
> 'Till by turning, turning we come round right.

This song (the melody of which was borrowed by Aaron Copland for his *Appalachian Spring*, CD 4/5) gives expression to the basic Shaker themes of simplicity and humility. It stands as a consummate achievement of a religious art that shuns self-indulgence and elitism.

PROJECTS

1. Find three psalm tunes (besides "Old 100th"!) that are still in use and appear in modern hymn collections in this country. Find out as much as you can about the origins of the tunes, and in which early Psalters they appeared. Find and consult early versions of the tunes if possible. (Most hymnals have a good index of composers and sources, which can help, as can the index of tune names. The *Hymnal of the Protestant Episcopal Church in the United States of America*, for example, is rather rich in tunes from the old Psalters of the sixteenth and seventeenth centuries.)

2. Read William Billings' prefaces to his *Continental Harmony* (see Additional Reading)—both "To the several Teachers of MUSIC, in this and the adjacent States" and "A Commentary on the preceding Rules: by way of Dialogue, between Master and Scholar." Comment on what these treatises seem to say about Billings himself: his sense of humor, his ability and ingenuity as a teacher, and his views on music, especially vocal music.

3. Find three revival spirituals in present-day hymnals. Find out what you can about the tunes and put together a brief commentary. The Lorenz book in the reading list may be helpful.
4. Write a brief paper comparing the camp meetings of the Kentucky Revival with the large outdoor rock festivals of the 1960s such as Woodstock.

ADDITIONAL LISTENING

Early Shaker Spirituals. Rounder 0078.

The New England Harmony: A Collection of Early American Choral Music. Smithsonian/Folkways 32377.

11 URBAN REVIVALISM AND GOSPEL MUSIC

The opening decades of the nineteenth century witnessed the beginnings of a growing cultural cleavage between the city and the country. The products of America's native school of church composers were progressively cast aside by those dedicated to what they saw as the improvement of church music, who turned to Europe not only for "rules" as to what was correct but also for actual tunes. *The Boston Handel and Haydn Society Collection of Church Music*, compiled by Lowell Mason and published in 1822, was a landmark. Gone were the fuging tunes; there was not a single piece by Billings. Instead, there were European hymn tunes, as well as adapted tunes by Handel, Mozart, Haydn, and Beethoven. The inexorable divergence between "highbrow" and "lowbrow" in American tastes after 1800 applied to religious music as well. For the worship services of the urban churches that had a pronounced liturgical bent, coupled with a substantial tradition and an intellectual, even aesthetic, dimension to their appeal (Episcopal, Lutheran, Presbyterian to some degree, as well as Roman Catholic), a hymnody continued to develop along the lines Lowell Mason helped to establish—cultivated and eclectic, selecting and adapting from a wide range of traditions. Any recent hymn book of these denominations (such as *The Hymnal of the Protestant Episcopal Church in the United States of America*) will illustrate this. Here medieval plainchant, Lutheran chorales, Calvinist psalm tunes, and melodies by classical and modern composers rub shoulders with American folk hymns such as "Kedron."

On the other hand, after 1800 the broadly popular evangelical denominations and sects continued to demand a popular type of song, particularly for special occasions such as revival meetings, which incorporated many features of the old camp meeting spiritual.

URBAN REVIVALISM AFTER THE CIVIL WAR: THE MOODY-SANKEY ERA OF GOSPEL HYMNS

Robert Stevenson has called hymn tunes "pre-eminently the food of the common man," and nineteenth-century America had a seemingly insatiable hunger for that food. In the period following the American Revolution, the demand for

In this 1877 woodcut, Dwight L. Moody preaches to a crowd of 6,000 at a revival meeting in Boston. Ira D. Sankey stands behind Moody near a choir of some 250 voices—who may well have sung the then popular "In the Sweet By-and-By," which we hear on CD 2, track 22. Conducting crusades across the country, Moody said, "I look upon this world as a wrecked vessel. God has given me a lifeboat and said to me, 'Moody, save all you can.'"

popular hymnody was met by drawing upon the wealth of folk music in the possession of the rural people, thereby creating the folk hymn. After the Civil War, folk music, no longer a very vital part of the lives of a much larger and increasingly citified populace, could not be drawn upon to satisfy that demand. Instead, it was met by a large number of hymn writers and composers, most of whom had only a modest amount of formal training but had an instinctive feel for what would best appeal to the great numbers of Christian believers, many of them new converts. These hymn writers and composers maintained a prodigious output of what have come to be known as gospel songs or gospel hymns. The production of these became especially copious after the revivalism of Dwight L. Moody (1837–1899) and Ira Sankey (1840–1908) swept the country beginning in 1875. In that year Sankey published, with P. P. Bliss, a volume called *Gospel Hymns*. This was followed by five sequels, culminating in *Gospel Hymns Nos. 1 to 6 Complete* in 1895, a compendium of more than 700 hymns and songs that typify the genre. As comprehensive as such a collection might seem, it represents only a small fraction of the simple, homely songs and hymns produced.

The models for these gospel songs did not come from the European-influenced collections of Mason and others; rather, their lineage was from the earlier camp meeting song through the Sunday school songs for children that began to be published in the mid-nineteenth century. Their optimistic stance is revealed in the titles of collections such as *Happy Voices, The Sunny Side,* and *Golden Chain.* A new feature of revivalism was that singing the gospel became as important as preaching the gospel; therefore, to reach the masses the gospel hymn had to be of the utmost simplicity, governed by a conventionality that virtually amounted to a formula. With extremely rare exceptions, all the tunes were written in musical keys that project a bright and cheerful soundscape. Part of their aim, after all, was to reinforce the optimistic millennial spirit of the revivalist preaching of the day—preaching that replaced the grim pessimism and preoccupation with death and eternal judgment that had characterized antebellum "hellfire" preaching and the songs that went with it. The tunes were harmonized with the three most basic chords, embellished occasionally with added notes between them to give the impression of gliding smoothly from one chord to another—a style of harmonization that has since become associated with barbershop quartets (see Chapter 14, pp. 236–237).

The form of the gospel song is nearly always that of verse and chorus. The chorus is a feature that not only shows a direct descent from the earlier revival spiritual but also relates the music to the commercial secular songs of Tin Pan Alley (see Chapter 14, pp. 233–235). This chorus often embodies a sort of polyphony even more rudimentary than that of the old fuging tunes; the lower, or men's, parts simply trade off short repeated phrases with the upper, or women's, parts. The chorus of "In the Sweet By-and-By" (CD 2/22), one of the best known hymns of the 1895 collection *Gospel Hymns Nos. 1 to 6 Complete,* illustrates this feature.

Listening Cue "In the Sweet By-and-By" The Harmoneion Singers (1:08)

Listen For ▪ men and women trading off short, repeated phrases in the chorus ▪ optimistic sentimentality

 Visit http://www.music.wadsworth.com_3/Kingman for a full listening guide and other resources.

Verse:
There's a land that is fairer than day,
And by faith we can see it afar;
For the Father waits over the way
To prepare us a dwelling place there.

Chorus:
In the sweet by and by,
We shall meet on that beautiful shore;
In the sweet by and by,
We shall meet on that beautiful shore.

We shall sing on that beautiful shore
The melodious songs of the blest;
And our spirits shall sorrow no more,
Not a sigh for the blessing of rest.
(Chorus)

To our bountiful Father above,
We will offer the tribute of praise
For the glorious gift of His love
And the blessing that hallow our days!
(Chorus)

Music by Joseph P. Webster, lyrics by Sanford F. Bennett, 1868.

The words, as might be expected, show the same preoccupation with the central theme of salvation as did those of the revival spiritual, though there is less gloomy dwelling upon death and, with the increased cheerfulness that pervaded popular theology, a great deal more sentimentality.

THE BILLY SUNDAY–HOMER RODEHEAVER ERA: FURTHER POPULARIZATION

The turn of the century saw further popularization and even secularization of evangelical song. There was a greater emphasis on informality and entertainment in revival meetings; the piano replaced the old reed organ, and Homer Rodeheaver (1880–1955), associated from 1909 to 1929 with the famous evangelist Billy Sunday (1862–1935), added trombone solos to his singing and piano playing to liven up the proceedings. In mid-career Rodeheaver made full use of the new media of radio and recordings; he also published extensively, through the Rodeheaver Company of Winona Lake, Indiana. His *Christian Service Songs* (for which practical orchestrations were available) went through many editions. It is best known for the popular sacred and semi-sacred songs that characterized the era, among them "In the Garden" (C. Austin Miles, 1912), "The Old Rugged Cross" (George Bernard, 1913), and "Brighten the Corner Where You Are" (CD 2/23).

Listening Cue **"Brighten the Corner Where You Are"** Homer Rodeheaver, vocal and brass band

Recorded in 1915 (2:30)
Listen For ▪ cheerful sentimentality ▪ enlivening role of brass instruments

Visit http://www.music.wadsworth.com_3/Kingman for a full listening guide and other resources.

The Granger Collection, New York

After a career in professional baseball, William Ashley "Billy" Sunday turned to evangelism. As this 1920s drawing shows, he brought athleticism and theatrics to tent-meeting revivals, and people came in droves to hear his dramatic sermons. In calling listeners to conversion, Sunday would ask, "How many of you men and women will jump to your feet and come down and say, 'Bill, here's my hand for God, for home, for my native land, to live and conquer for Christ?'" Homer Rodeheaver—whom we hear on CD 2, track 23—joined Billy Sunday's revival tour in 1909.

Verse:
Do not wait until some deed of greatness you may do,
Do not wait to shed your light afar;
To the many duties ever near you now be true,
Brighten the corner where you are.

Chorus:
Brighten the corner where you are!
Brighten the corner where you are!
Someone far from harbor you may guide across the bar;
Brighten the corner where you are!

Just above are clouded skies that you may help to clear,
Let not narrow self your way debar;
Though into one heart alone may fall your song of cheer,
Brighten the corner where you are.
(Chorus)

Hulton Archive/Getty Images

Evangelist and Southern Baptist minister Billy Graham—whom we see here at a religious rally in 1955—has said about his calling, "My one purpose in life is to help people find a personal relationship with God, which, I believe, comes through knowing Christ." Crisscrossing the country and the world since 1946, preaching the gospel to more live audiences than anyone before, and reaching millions more through television, webcasts, and his fifty-year-running Sunday radio program *Hour of Decision*, Graham has become synonymous with a muscular Christianity.

Here for all your talent you may surely find a need,
Here reflect the bright and Morning Star;
Even from your humble hand the Bread of Life may feed,
Brighten the corner where you are.
(Chorus)

Music by Charles H. Gabriel, lyrics by Ina D. Ogden, 1913.

After a decline during the Depression era, urban revivalism again began attracting attention with the activities of Billy Graham. The music accompanying his meetings was conservative, with a return to the repertoire represented in the Moody-Sankey *Gospel Hymns*. With the advent of television evangelism, the emphasis, as in the Sunday-Rodeheaver era, is again on entertainment, eclecticism, and commercialism.

GOSPEL MUSIC AFTER THE ADVENT OF RADIO AND RECORDINGS

Following the course of jazz, blues, and country music, what Charles Wolfe has called "the fourth great genre of grass roots music"—gospel music—entered the commercial arena of the radio and the phonograph in the mid-1920s, and was profoundly influenced by both media. In the eighty years since, two parallel traditions, black and white, have developed, both drawing to a significant degree on the same reservoir of nineteenth-century gospel hymnody, but each reacting in its own way to popular secular currents of the times—white gospel music to those of white country music, and black gospel music to those of blues and jazz.

Southern White Gospel Music

Twentieth-century white gospel music in the South had its musical roots in the rural shape-note tradition described in the preceding chapter and, instrumentally, in the folk music of that region. Its religious roots were in evangelical revivalism and in the Holiness and Pentecostal movements that about the turn of the century began to sweep across the whole country, taking root especially in the South, the Midwest, and California, where they made converts among the poor, both black and white.

The commercial process has been a major factor in the story of twentieth-century gospel music. In white gospel music, the process reached a new level in the early part of the century. Publishers whose business was to sell songbooks found many "worldly" ways to promote their wares, including the formation of professional male quartets that toured churches and conventions, recorded, and received airtime on radio stations. Dominant players in the increasingly competitive business of publishing gospel included James D. Vaughan of Lawrenceburg, Tennessee, and the Stamps-Baxter firm of Dallas, Texas. In light of the decidedly commercial aspect, it is not surprising to find the influence of popular music in the singing of the many male quartets that publishers sponsored. Recordings of the famous Stamps Quartet from the late 1920s show the addition of piano accompaniments that introduce ragtime figures in the breaks. The choruses often indulged in tricky instrumental-like afterbeat effects. Sometimes whole choruses were repeated with the voices imitating banjos, as heard in the very popular "Give the World a Smile" (CD 2/24). Note the cheerful optimism of the lyrics.

Listening Cue **"Give the World a Smile"** The Stamps Quartet

Recorded in Atlanta, Georgia, 1927 (3:08)
Listen For ▪ cheerful lyrics ▪ vocal imitation of banjo-style ▪ afterbeats in the chorus

Visit http://www.music.wadsworth.com_3/Kingman for a full listening guide and other resources.

Verse:
Are you giving to the world a smile (sunny smile),
Helping lessen someone's dreary mile (dreary mile)?
Do you greet the world with song as through life you pass along,
Cheering those whom you may meet along life's way?

Chorus:
Give the world a smile each day,
Helping someone on life's way;

From the path of sin bring the wand'rer in,
To the Master's fold to stay;
Help to cheer the lone and sad,
Help to make some pilgrim glad,
Let your life so be that all the world may see
The joy of serving Jesus with a smile (a bright sunny smile).

Just a bright and sunny smile will win (it will win)
Many souls from dreary paths of sin (paths of sin),
Lift them up on higher plain, where they hear the glad refrain
Of the smiling band of workers on life's way.

(Chorus)

(voices imitating plinking sound of banjos)

Music by M. L. Yandell, lyrics by Otis Deaton, 1925.

The popularity of bass soloists in gospel music, still apparent in 1980s recordings of male gospel groups, goes back to this period of the publishing house
quartets. As Bill Malone has put it, "The gospel singers learned much of their
four-part harmony from the shape-note singing schools, but they also picked
up elements from the barbershop quartets, the black gospel quartets, and other
popular quartets of their day" (69). In fact, the banjo imitation heard in "Give the
World a Smile" is the kind of onomatopoeic effect for which black barbershop
quartets had been famous for years.

Charlie D. Tillman (1861–1943), composer of "Old Time Religion" (a song associated more than any other in the popular mind with southern white gospel
music), was among the first to broadcast this music, in 1922 in Atlanta. Record
companies, discovering the sales potential of secular hillbilly music and the
blues, were also looking for artists to record gospel music. Performers who already had a reputation for doing mostly secular songs and ballads also recorded
some gospel songs—among them Uncle Dave Macon, the Carter Family, and the
Stanley Brothers. Since then virtually all country singers have included some
gospel songs in their repertory.

In the face of a persistent trend toward the commercialization of white gospel
music since the 1930s, a few groups continued to perform it with a more traditional simplicity. One of these was a mixed quartet (originally a father, son, and
two daughters) from Texas that had the somewhat misleading name of the Chuck
Wagon Gang thrust upon them. From the late 1930s to the early 1970s, they
achieved considerable and enduring popularity, on radio and recordings, singing
mostly old songs such as "The Church in the Wildwood" to a conservative accompaniment; only in the late 1950s was an electric guitar sometimes substituted.
By the 1960s, with the rewards of commercial success becoming ever larger, as the
careers of successful country and rock groups showed, two distinct motivations
for performing gospel music had emerged. As Malone puts it, "The sense of
religious mission no doubt still burned brightly in the lives of many gospel

singers, but an increasing number viewed the music as just another facet of popular music, or as an avenue for entrance into different kinds of performing careers" (113).

In the 1980s, popular commercial gospel groups such as the Florida Boys, a male quintet, were typically purveying a slick, studio-produced product, with a large pop/soft-rock backup group with drums and a mixture of electric and acoustic instruments, strangely at odds with the conservative old-line evangelical message of the words. More recently, a return to tradition is evidenced in the work of "Christian bluegrass" groups such as Doyle Lawson and Quicksilver. With their unaccompanied traditional arrangements, they are reviving, as in their *Heaven's Joy Awaits,* some of the Stamps-Baxter and James D. Vaughan songs (see Additional Listening).

Black Gospel Music: The Roots

African American gospel music had its religious roots in the turn-of-the-century Holiness movement that had influenced white gospel (see above). The Holiness sects are based on a highly personal, vivid, and emotional religious experience— an experience that involves, ultimately, possession by the Holy Spirit. This possession shows itself in emotionally charged expression and movement— moaning, singing, speaking in tongues, and dancing (the term *shout* can refer to a dance as well as a song). This seemingly unbridled expression—the one and only outlet for pent-up emotions in the lives of the poor of both races, who made up the majority of adherents of the Holiness sects—elicited amusement and scorn from the world at large. The derogatory term "Holy Rollers" was frequently heard. As these believers were already among the outcasts of society, the contempt only strengthened the sense of community they felt in their worship. Though the Holiness and Pentecostal adherents were always in a minority numerically among church members, the freedom of expression that they encouraged, especially in music, had a special appeal and gave them, eventually, an influence disproportionate to their numbers. The singular fact is that it was just these scorned modes of worship, this rejected music of the disinherited, that ultimately came to influence not only a large segment of American religious music, white and black, but indirectly a broad spectrum of popular music as well.

We cannot go very far in understanding the conditions under which black gospel music developed unless we understand something of the role of the black preacher. W. E. B. Du Bois said, "The Preacher is the most unique personality developed by the Negro on American soil. A leader, a politician, an orator, a 'boss,' an intriguer, an idealist—all these he is, and ever, too, the center of a group of men, now twenty, now a thousand in number" (Oliver 140). In the Holiness church, all that was required to be a preacher was that one have the combination of qualities enumerated by Du Bois and that one feel the "call" to preach. An indispensable gift was the ability to elicit a response from the congregation. As, in the course of his exhortation, the responses became more frequent and more intense, the sounds of preacher and congregation together gradually merged into song. Early entrepreneurs recorded many of these sermons-into-songs, in conditions not unlike those of the storefront churches where the actual services took place. It is estimated that more than 700 "sermons" were recorded in the 1920s and early 1930s. Recordings in archival collections, such as "Jesus the Lord Is a Savior," give some flavor of what the Sanctified services were like (see Additional Listening.)

The black Holiness churches welcomed the use of instruments. There were the characteristic percussion instruments (the tambourine, the triangle, and later the drums) as well as the guitar and its urban replacement, the piano. But the services could also include, especially on the recordings of the 1920s, the trumpet, the trombone, and the string bass. The music, in fact, often has the sound and feel of early jazz. To conclude, however, that jazz influenced the music of the Sanctified churches is to get the picture as much backward as forward; they grew up together, and jazz may well owe as much to the music of the Holiness churches as it does to the streets and brothels of New Orleans. One small clue is that the traditional jazz standard "When the Saints Go Marching In" is actually a Sanctified shout. Early gospel singers such as guitar-playing Rosetta Tharpe, who came out of the Church of God in Christ, recorded "Daniel in the Lion's Den" with bass, drums, and boogie-woogie piano; and Sister Ernestine Washington recorded, among other pieces, "Does Jesus Care?" with Bunk Johnson's jazz band (see Additional Listening).

Black gospel music, unlike its white counterpart, was a music of the cities. Its roots can be found not only in what preachers and their congregations were doing in many humble storefront Holiness churches but also in the music of many blind street evangelists. Blind Willie Johnson (1902–1950) was a street singer in Dallas. His "God Moves on the Water," one of many songs based on the sinking of the *Titanic* in 1912, shows him to have been the religious counterpart, in terms of style and guitar technique, to blues singers such as Blind Lemon Jefferson (see Additional Listening). Memphis, world headquarters of the Church of God in Christ, the largest black Sanctified denomination, was a center for Sanctified music in the 1920s. For further evidence of the influence of Sanctified singing on jazz, listen to Sister Bessie Johnson, who, together with Sister Melinda Taylor as the Memphis Sanctified Singers, recorded the traditional "He Got Better Things for You" (CD 2/25). The growling, rasping vocal quality is exactly what jazz musicians were imitating on trumpet and trombone.

Blind Street Evangelists

Listening Cue "He Got Better Things for You" Memphis Sanctified
Singers, Sisters Bessie Johnson and Melinda Taylor, vocal duet with guitar

> Recorded in 1929 (3:10)
> Listen For ▪ rowling, rasping vocal quality

CD 2

25

Visit http://www.music.wadsworth.com_3/Kingman for a full listening guide and other resources.

Verse:
Kind friends I want to tell you
Because I love your soul
No doubt you've been converted
But this ain't ever been told
Some people they'll try to fool you
There's nothing else to do
But, Jesus Christ, my saviour,
He's got better things for you.

Chorus:
He's got better things for you,
And no one on earth can do.
He's got the Holy Ghost, and the fire
Sure can make you true.
He's got better things for you,
No one on earth can do.
Oh place my mind on Jesus;
He's got better things for you.

Cornelius he was humble
He prayed to God always
But that was not sufficient
He had to give Him praise.
God sent to him an angel
And he told him what to do
'Cause there he's awaitin' in glory with
Better things for you.
(Chorus)

Mary was a virgin
She birthed the Son of God
But that was not sufficient
She had to be well-shorn.
God sent her to Jerusalem
And there He made her new
'Cause there she's awaitin' in glory
With better things for you.
(Chorus)

The Methodist minister and composer Charles Albert Tindley (1851/59–1933) has been called the "progenitor of black-American gospel music." In the first decade of the twentieth century he was writing songs in what became the prototypical form and style of gospel music—simple melodies and harmonies, in verse-and-chorus form. Among these was "I'll Overcome Some Day" of 1901, the chorus of which entered, by a circuitous route, the civil rights struggle a half-century later as "We Shall Overcome" (CD 2/2, p. 85). Another was "What Are

They Doing in Heaven," also from 1901, one of several songs to cross over into the white gospel tradition. The center of Tindley's work was Philadelphia, where he wrote songs for "new arrivals in the North who poured in daily, most of them poor and illiterate, and who valued highly the simple, direct, and emotional life style of which Tindley spoke" (Boyer, "C. A. Tindley" 113).

By the 1920s the gospel music indigenous to the Holiness churches was beginning to be introduced to other African American denominations as well. But the phenomenal growth of modern gospel music as it is known today did not begin until the 1930s.

Modern Black Gospel Music's First Phase: The 1930s, 1940s, and 1950s

The one person most responsible for the initial propagation of modern gospel music was Thomas A. Dorsey (1899–1993). After an early career as a blues singer, composer, and pianist—as "Georgia Tom" he had played and recorded blues with Ma Rainey—he was first drawn to gospel music in 1921. For a while he

© Ted Williams/CORBIS

Here, Mahalia Jackson, perhaps the best-known gospel singer of her time, sings at a revival meeting on Chicago's South Side in the 1950s. Jackson stuck firmly to her gospel roots and rejected lucrative crossover opportunities. In her autobiography *Movin' On Up*, she recalled that when Louis Armstrong offered her a job in the late 1930s with the words, "I know what you can do with the blues," she responded, "I know what I can do with it too, baby, and that's not sing it. Child, I been reborn!"

continued to play and record blues, but from 1932 on he devoted himself wholly to the blues' sacred counterpart. It was in that year, a year of personal tragedy, that he wrote his most famous song, "Precious Lord." Dorsey proved to be an indefatigable promoter, organizer, and manager, as well as composer, of gospel music. He published his own compositions, and went from church to church in Chicago, and later from city to city, with singers such as Sallie Martin (1895–1988) and later Mahalia Jackson (1911–1972), performing and promoting gospel music. Dorsey published his songs not in book collections, as had been the case with popular sacred music up to that time, but rather as sheet music. In his capacity as organizer and promoter, he started with Sallie Martin the National Convention of Gospel Choirs and Choruses. "I'll Tell It Wherever I Go," which Sallie Martin recorded with Dorsey at the piano, illustrates the seminal style of "gospel blues" in its early stages (see Additional Listening.)

The Era of the Gospel Divas   Thanks in part to Dorsey's promotional activity, the solo gospel singer began to assume more importance. Female singers dominated during this first phase of modern gospel music, just as in the 1920s female singers had dominated the classic urban blues. In fact, the two greatest influences on the first two generations of female gospel soloists were the singing styles of blues singers such as Ma Rainey and Bessie Smith, and the music of the Holiness churches. Of the female singers prominent in the first three decades of gospel music, Mahalia Jackson, Rosetta Tharpe, Marion Williams, and Ruth Davis either came out of Holiness backgrounds or were strongly affected by the music, and Willie Mae Ford Smith joined a Holiness church in 1939, at the age of 33.

The first generation of singers included Roberta Martin (1907–1969), who began as the pianist for Dorsey's chorus; Mahalia Jackson, with whom Dorsey toured as pianist from the mid-1930s until about 1950; Willie Mae Ford Smith (1906–1994); and Sister Rosetta Tharpe (1915–1973). The second generation included such singers as Clara Ward (1924–1973), Marion Williams (1927–1994), Ruth Davis (1928–1970), and Albertina Walker (b. 1930). These women developed distinctive styles that were individual blends of certain enduring characteristics of gospel singing: their inflections ("bending") of notes, the sliding into or between pitches, the repetition of syllables or words, the interpolation of extra words or exclamations, and a range of vocal effects that included shouting, falsetto, and a hoarse, rasping, or growling vocal quality. Roberta Martin's "Ride On, King Jesus" and Mahalia Jackson's "Didn't It Rain" are illustrative of their distinctive styles.

In the beginning the basic accompanying instrument was the piano, played in a "gospel" style, which, quite unlike the accompaniments played for congregational hymn singing, owed a great deal to ragtime, stride piano, and other popular styles. Soon it was common to add bass and drums to the piano; in the 1950s, the electric organ became an indispensable part of the ensemble. A small vocal group (mostly female, but occasionally including men) was frequently added, but the soloist tended to dominate; the vocal backup group merely added support, and reiterated key phrases of the soloist for emphasis. When gospel music began to enter the commercial arena with recordings, radio appearances, and tours, many soloists formed their own groups, such as the Roberta Martin Singers, the Davis Sisters, the Clara Ward Singers, and later the Caravans.

The Gospel Quartets The foregoing capsule description helps to define the traditional gospel group led by the female "diva," but the other type of group important in gospel music's first phase was the male ensemble—usually a quartet that sang unaccompanied, dressed in suits and ties. The unaccompanied male gospel quartet predated modern gospel music; early quartets in what Boyer has termed the "folk" phase, up until 1930, were built on the nineteenth-century tradition of the Fisk Jubilee Singers and others (Boyer, "Black Gospel Music"). In the period 1930–1945, termed by Boyer the "gospel" or "jubilee" period, groups adopted mannerisms from the more rhapsodic aspects of Holiness singing and from the

Frank Driggs Collection/Getty Images

In a 1938 photo, Willie Johnson (baritone lead), Orlandus Wilson (bass), William Langford (tenor), and Henry Owens (second tenor)—the Golden Gate Quartet we hear on CD 3, track 1—sing around a microphone. That same year, the quartet began regular appearances at the New York City nightclub Café Society, which opened to showcase African American talent and took pride in treating black and white customers equally. Advertising itself as "The Wrong Place for the Right People," Café Society was the venue most responsible for bringing gospel groups to the attention of white audiences.

rhythmic aspects of jazz; a characteristic number would start slowly, with florid improvisation, and then work up to a highly rhythmic ending. Characteristic of this "jubilee" period is the 1946 recording by the Golden Gate Quartet of the traditional "Swing Down, Chariot" (CD 3/1). Notice the tight, instrumental quality of the vocal accompaniment in the verses.

Listening Cue "Swing Down, Chariot" Golden Gate Quartet, vocal quartet
with piano, guitar, string bass, and drums

CD 3

1

Recorded in 1946 (3:29)
Listen For ▪ slow chordal introduction with florid solo interjections ▪ rhythmic vitality of choruses ▪ tight, instrumental quality of vocal accompaniment in verses

Visit http://www.music.wadsworth.com_3/Kingman for a full listening guide and other resources.

Introduction:
Swing low, swing low, sweet chariot
Comin' comin'
Over in Zion, comin'
I'm tellin' you chillun, she's comin' to carry me home.
Well, well, well, well, well
Look over yonder what I see?
Seems like the chariot comin' after me.

Chorus:
Why don't you swing down sweet chariot
Stop and let me ride
Swing down chariot
Stop and let me ride
Rock me lord, rock me lord, calm and easy
I've got a home on the other side

Verse:
Well, Ezekiel was out in the middle of the field
He said he saw an angel with a chariot wheel
He wasn't so particular 'bout the chariot wheel
He just wanted to see how a chariot feel
(Chorus)

Well, Ezekiel went down and got on board
The chariot went bumpin' on down the road
Zeke wasn't particular 'bout the bumpin' of the road
He just wanted to lay down his heavy load
(Chorus)

Well I got a Father in the promised land
I won't stop until I shake His hand
Rock me lord, rock me lord, calm and easy
I got a home on the other side
(Chorus)

The black gospel quartet is in some ways the sacred counterpart of the black barbershop quartet (see Chapter 14, pp. 236–237). In fact, the Golden Gate Jubilee Quartette, which later became the Golden Gate Quartet, originated in Eddie Griffin's Barber Shop in Norfolk, Virginia, in 1930 (Abbott 292).

The "jubilee" period male quartet merged imperceptibly into Boyer's next phase, that of "sweet" gospel, in which a lead singer emerged as dominant, with the rest of the group forming a close-harmony background and responding to the lead. The Dixie Hummingbirds' "When the Gates Swing Open" is representative (see Additional Listening).

Styles in Black Gospel Music Since Midcentury

Since the mid-twentieth century, and especially beginning in the 1970s, gospel music has evolved along two fairly distinct lines: "contemporary" and "traditional." Underneath the difference in style and sound, the basic distinction between the two types lies in the way each regards its public. For contemporary gospel, the public is an audience to be entertained, and perhaps soothed and comforted; for traditional gospel, it is a congregation to be charged with religious ecstasy.

Traditional gospel music, even on recordings, always conveys the ambience of an actual service. Even though the location may be Carnegie Hall (and it is much more apt to be an actual church), the congregation is palpably there, and participating. The "sermonette" before the song (an innovation evolved out of the old recorded preachers' sermons by Willie Mae Ford Smith, Dorothy Norwood, Inez Andrews, and other old-line gospel singers) or the pastor's exhortation is delivered over an instrumental background that merges into the next song. The instrumentation of piano, electric organ, electric guitar, electric bass, and drums is in the direct line of the tradition that has evolved since the 1930s. The choir, singing in an altogether homophonic texture, is an important element. Numbers now appear for chorus alone, representing a resurgence of actual choral singing in gospel music. More frequently, the chorus is used for

Perhaps the greatest preacher of our time because of the clarity of his thought, his steadfast courage, and his incandescent moral leadership, the Reverend Martin Luther King, Jr., led blacks and whites to a common understanding of freedom and justice. Here, Dr. King addresses Atlanta's Ebenezer Baptist Church in 1964. That same year he became the youngest recipient (at thirty-five) of the Nobel Peace Prize; four years later, he was assassinated in Memphis, Tennessee. But his evocative speech "I Have A Dream," delivered in 1963 at the Lincoln Memorial in Washington, D.C., inspired millions, became the iconic statement of the American civil rights movement, and left an indelible legacy.

backing up the soloist, singing a verse or a chorus of the song, or sometimes repeating short phrases, in the background, under the soloist's improvisation. The soloists tend to sing in a "hard gospel" style, highly charged emotionally. The fast numbers, driven by the accompaniment (all the instruments except the organ can be considered a rhythm section), are highly rhythmic and syncopated, and often incorporate hand clapping on the backbeats.

The intensity and momentum that build up during a performance have to be heard live to be appreciated fully. During the vamps (sections of music that can be repeated over and over) the leader may go down and circulate among the congregation, and the congregation may respond to the highly charged emotional momentum established by the music and go into a shout, dancing or moving rhythmically. In a live situation this may go on for as long as half an hour before leader and ensemble bring it to a close; recordings obviously must edit these vamps which, theoretically, can go on indefinitely.

Although there is a considerable overlap between traditional and contemporary gospel music, the latter tends to sound as if it is more at home in the concert hall than in church, and often more in the recording studio than either. The singing style and the vocal quality of both soloists and choir tend to be smoother, more polished, and more pop-oriented, with less of the emotion-driven "edge" that characterizes traditional gospel singing. Solo cuts may have a soft rock or soft rhythm and blues background, with velvet-voiced studio backup singers replacing the incisive and committed voices of the historic gospel choir. Instrumentally there is a heavy reliance on a battery of electronic keyboards and on

© Gary Hershorn/Reuters/CORBIS

Outspoken hip-hop artist Kanye West performs "Jesus Walks" during the gospel segment of the 47th Annual Grammy® Awards in 2005. "Jesus Walks" won the Grammy® for Best Rap Song, and the album on which it appeared, *The College Dropout*, won the Grammy® for Best Rap Album of the year. A lyric from the song asks, "If I talk about God, my records won't get played, huh?"

studio electronic manipulation. Brass instruments and even a full orchestra augment or replace the basic piano-organ-drums sound of traditional gospel. Heilbut has summed it up in these words: "The eclecticism of 'contemporary gospel' derives from several sources: the academic training of many young choir directors; the example of the highly complex recording techniques of a Stevie Wonder or Michael Jackson; and the simple financial lure" (Ferris and Hart 113). Contemporary gospel is a product in which there is indeed a fine line, often subtly crossed, between the sacred and the secular. The secularization of which Heilbut speaks sometimes involves not only adopting the "highly complex recording techniques of a . . . Michael Jackson" but also imitating, in a muted way, the sex appeal of mainstream recording artists as well, as album photos of Al Green or Edwin Hawkins, with open shirt and necklace, show.

In live performances and on live recordings, "audience" has replaced "congregation." Perhaps the trend toward multiracial concert audiences accounts in part for Boyer's observation that the congregational response during many contemporary gospel concerts consists of smiling, soft weeping, and clapping, most often on a primary rather than a secondary beat—that is, shunning the "back-beat" so traditional in black music. Where a section of a song would have previously elicited a moan, shout, or vocal utterance, the audience response is only applause at concerts of contemporary gospel. Boyer goes on to note the loss of "participation"—a passive role has replaced the formerly active one ("A Comparative Analysis" 143).

Andraé Crouch, one of the leaders of contemporary gospel, goes so far in the lyrics of one of his songs as to disown gospel's roots in the worship of the Holiness churches:

> You don't have to jump no pews,
> Run down no aisles,
> No chills run down your spine;
> But you know that you've been born again.
> Don't you know my hands didn't shake,
> The earth didn't quake,
> No sparks fell from the sky;
> But I know that I've been born again.

Secularization and Commercialization in African American Gospel Music

The evolution of contemporary gospel style, so briefly described above, is only one manifestation of what has been happening to African American gospel music since midcentury. In 1961 two significant events occurred: Mahalia Jackson sang at one of John F. Kennedy's inauguration parties, and Clara Ward and the

Ward Singers started singing in nightclubs. Mahalia Jackson's appearance symbolized the widespread acceptance of gospel music, Clara Ward's its secularization. Recent developments include black gospel's move from shabby storefront churches to concert extravaganzas; the appearance of black gospel stars and groups at jazz festivals and in nightclubs; a secularizing of the material, whereby "message" songs, expressing optimistic or altruistic sentiments but avoiding the word "God" or "Jesus," could be sung to a broader audience, and thus earn both popularity and money; and a "song exchange" between gospel and secular pop music, wherein pop songs could be "gospelized" and their popularity appropriated.

Gospel music today presents a pluralistic picture. In its commercial aspect, as represented by contemporary gospel, it now accounts for a significant segment of the American popular music industry. At the grassroots level of church and community choirs, on the other hand, traditional gospel music is flourishing; ensembles such as the New Jerusalem Baptist Church Choir in Flint, Michigan, and the Sacramento Community Choir in California are giving live performances and producing "live" recordings that have a resounding authenticity. Gospel has become multiracial, and other Christian denominations, including such liturgically conservative ones as the Roman Catholic Church, have instituted gospel choirs, as have many colleges and universities. A network of teachers, workshops, and conventions (especially the large Gospel Music Workshop of America) is active in propagating and offering instruction in gospel music, not only in the United States, but in other countries as well. Gospel music, following jazz and rock and roll, now belongs to the long succession of exports of American popular music—all of which have stemmed from African American roots.

PROJECTS

1. Make a survey of "Christian music" in the urban churches today, with emphasis on your own area if you live in a city. For each church you survey, characterize the basic repertory as being, for example, "revivalist," "traditional, with strong European influence," "folk," "pop," "ethnic," "consciously multiethnic," or whatever. Determine whether there is more than one constituency for music in the same church, and hence more than one distinct repertory, with perhaps even separate services for each.

2. Using W. E. B. Du Bois' description of the African American preacher in *The Souls of Black Folk* as a point of departure, carry this into our own time by writing a paper on the social and political roles of the black preacher since the mid-twentieth century. Has the relationship of preacher to congregation carried over into the relationship of speaker to audience? In what ways?

3. Make a study of the music in the black churches in your area. How does it relate to the gospel music described in this chapter? What part do older hymns or spirituals play in the repertory? Are there differences in musical preferences between one denomination and another?

ADDITIONAL LISTENING

"Does Jesus Care?" Perf. Sister Ernestine Washington with Bunk Johnson's band. *The Asch Recordings 1939–1947.* Smithsonian/Folkways AA001.

"God Moves on the Water." Perf. Blind Willie Johnson. *Country Gospel Song.* Smithsonian/Folkways RF019.

Heaven's Joy Awaits. Perf. Doyle Lawson and Quicksilver. Sugarhill 3760.

"I'll Tell It Wherever I Go." Perf. Sallie Martin, vocal; Thomas A. Dorsey, piano. *Precious Lord: The Great Gospel Songs of Thomas A. Dorsey.* Sony 57164.

"Jesus the Lord Is a Savior." *An Introduction to Gospel Song.* Smithsonian/ Folkways RF005. Includes three more sermons. *The Anthology of American Folk Music* (Smithsonian/Folkways 40090) includes two sermons by the Reverend Gates and one each by the Reverend McGee, the Reverend Moses Mason, and the Reverend D. C. Rice.

"When the Gates Swing Open." Perf. The Dixie Hummingbirds. *The Essential Gospel Sampler.* Sony 57163.

POPULAR SECULAR MUSIC

*P*opular music refers to a music produced for masses of people by specialists. It is distinct from *folk music,* which is made for people in smaller groups, or cultural "villages," by people who are themselves members of the village. The distinction is not always so clear; but this will suffice as a working definition.

Popular music requires a certain critical mass of population to support the commercial process devoted to its production. It will emerge whenever sufficient numbers of people are willing to pay for an art that has the look or sound of the familiar, that is made easily available by the mechanisms of its commercial distribution, and that adds something desirable and even necessary to their lives without being too difficult to understand. Its primary purpose is to entertain us, not necessarily to impress us with sheer artistry.

Except for the products of the singing-school composers described in Chapter 10, Americans did not begin to make their own distinctive kind of popular music until the Jacksonian era—an era of cultural as well as political populism. It was not until the end of the nineteenth century that the making of popular music became an industry—an industry in which the United States remains a leader.

Because of the vast market, those who can successfully create this kind of music are very well paid for it. The superlative popular song, the "evergreen"—the one song in perhaps a hundred thousand that transcends the ephemeral nature of the genre, that has that imponderable property of resonating in the memory and feelings of generation after generation—is surely one of the glories of American music. But the gift of creating something that many people will regard as memorable, and that will be immediately and widely in demand, is mysterious and rare; few possess it in spite of the number of books on the market that promise to teach you how to write the next hit for the ages.

Once dismissed by scholars, "serious" musicians, and snobbish consumers as beneath them, popular art is no longer ignored by observers and students of culture. Indeed, popular music (as a component of popular culture) is an important and sensitive indicator of the temperament and preoccupations of a people at any given time and place.

© CORBIS

At a Friday afternoon band concert, many of the immigrants shown here at the tip of Manhattan, New York, could look across the water to Castle Garden (right background) where they first entered the United States at its earliest immigration center (1830). On the bandstand, notice the many brass instruments (well suited to playing outdoors), and the large drum to the rear of the conductor. Outdoor concerts, unrestricted by race or gender, less formal than indoor concerts, and requiring no tickets, have been a feature of American music from the 1700s—perfect settings for the popular music we hear in this section.

SECULAR MUSIC IN THE CITIES FROM COLONIAL TIMES TO THE AGE OF ANDREW JACKSON

Musical life in the largest American cities (Philadelphia, New York, Boston, Charleston, and Baltimore) during the colonial and federal periods was by no means primitive or dull. Music historians, together with performers specializing in the re-creation of early music, have illuminated the existence of a lively and varied musical culture in our growing urban centers. To re-create a sense of what this musical life was like will be the purpose of this chapter.

CONCERTS AND DANCES

The giving of public concerts for which people pay admission presupposes a certain critical mass of population that will include enough people with the means, the leisure, and the inclination to support such endeavors. For the first hundred years of eastern-seaboard settlement, that was not the case. But by the middle of the eighteenth century, public concerts were being given fairly regularly in Philadelphia, New York, Boston, and Charleston. Oscar Sonneck (1873–1928), pioneer historian of American music, determined that the first "concert of music on sundry instruments" was given in Boston in 1731.

What were these concerts like? Many of the early ones would hardly fit our notion of a formal concert of classical music; the music itself was varied and popular, but in addition the program could include dramatic recitations, card tricks, and balancing acts ("a dance upon wire"), among other spectacles. Another pleasurable aspect of concert life was the outdoor concert in the summer months, modeled after English practice. Two attractions existed then that have been familiar to patrons of outdoor summer concerts ever since—fireworks and ice cream!

Dancing in the Eighteenth and Early Nineteenth Centuries

That the range of pleasures offered by these events was agreeably broad is demonstrated by the fact that the concert proper was nearly always followed by a different type of music "to wait upon such ladies and gentlemen, as may choose to dance." "The concert will terminate by a ball" was the pleasant and in fact nearly obligatory promise put forth in most advertisements. The kind of dancing that would have gone on at these balls varied with time and place. In colonial times, especially among the landed gentry of the southern colonies, it is likely that the elegant *minuet*, and possibly also the more intricate *gavotte*, would be danced. After the Revolution, these dances, with their suggestions of monarchy and aristocracy, fell out of favor. The *country dances*, on the other hand, enjoyed the widest popularity throughout the period. Of English origin, they were done in all the colonies and states, by all classes of society, in urban as well as rural settings. A French importation, the *cotillion*, became the *quadrille* (which in time gave rise to the more typically rural *square dance*). Both the country dance, with its typical lining up of dancers in opposing rows (as in the later *Virginia reel*), and the quadrille, with its square set of eight dancers, were social dances, as contrasted with later couples dances such as the *waltz* and the *galop*.

The music for country dances came from a variety of sources. Fortunately some of it has been preserved in manuscript books, mainly for the use of the fifers and fiddlers who played for dancing. Many tunes used for eighteenth-century dancing are still familiar to us today, including "The Irish Washerwoman," "Soldier's Joy" (which in its countless variants became a staple in the fiddler's repertory; see p. 13 and CD 1/4), and "The College Hornpipe" (CD 3/2), better known to us today as "The Sailor's Hornpipe." In "College Hornpipe," the two-part form (called binary form) is exactly that of "Soldier's Joy": an eight-bar first strain, repeated, followed by a contrasting strain, repeated, then the whole thing played again. Notice that the fiddler is accenting the backbeats in the course of his performance. This is a very difficult thing to do consistently, and particularly so in fluid passages. His foot stomps on the beat (barely audible here) add yet another rhythmic component to enliven this performance.

Listening Cue "The College Hornpipe" Rodney Miller, fiddle (1:09)

Listen For ▪ binary form ▪ contrasting strains ▪ backbeat accents

Visit http://www.music.wadsworth.com_3/Kingman for a full listening guide and other resources.

The Performers

Who were the musicians that furnished the music for the first hundred years of American urban musical life? Contemporary advertisements show those who plied the trade of "music master" to have been of a hardy, resourceful, and versatile breed. In addition to being music masters, many were also dancing masters and fencing masters; they were thus equipped to minister to more than one need of the polished aristocrat of the day, especially in the southern colonies. Many also offered a variety of musical instruments for sale—as well as tobacco and other sundries. It is known that a great many African Americans were accomplished musicians and played for dances in the northern as well as the southern colonies and states. Some of the scant information we have on this subject comes from contemporary newspapers, in advertisements about slaves—either "for sale" or "runaway." These indicate that the most common instrument played was the fiddle, but the fife, the drum, the flute, the banjo, and the French horn also appear in the lists (Southern).

The child prodigy was evidently a great attraction at concerts, promoted by parents who were professional performers and who seized the opportunity to capitalize on the public's curiosity and eagerness to be amazed. The ages of such children were naturally featured in their announcements. Thus we find, for example, a concert by "P. Lewis, Professor of Music," who presented an entire program in Boston in 1819 featuring his children, ages eight, seven, and four.

The century 1730–1830 was a period of gradual transition from the amateur to the professional. Though the word "amateur" does not appear at first, his identity was made plain by the use of the word "gentleman," as distinguished from the professional, who was designated as "professor." By this means the "gentleman amateur" not only maintained his distinction of class but also insulated himself from judgment by professional standards. An advertisement of a concert in Charleston in 1772 makes both these points plainly: "The vocal part by a gentleman, who does it merely to oblige on this occasion." After the privations of the Revolution had passed, the flow of professional immigrants increased, mostly on account of the increased appetite for musical theater in the cities. This resulted in the gradual reduction of the amateur, "gentleman" or not, to a distinctly subordinate role in the growing musical life of the cities (Crawford).

The Composers

Who were the composers of this music? Late in the eighteenth century it began to be common to print programs, especially in the newspapers. We find, as might be expected, that the composers were mostly European; Haydn, Pleyel, Handel, Stamitz, and Corelli appear frequently. After the Revolution, with the coming into prominence of the professional musician, we find the names of those, either immigrants or native-born, who must be recognized as the first American composers. Included among the native-born were Francis Hopkinson, Samuel Holyoke, and Oliver Shaw, and among the immigrants, Alexander Reinagle, James Hewitt, and Rayner Taylor.

Concert Music

The programs played at these concerts were much more varied than we are accustomed to today. As the frequent appearance of the phrase "Concert [earlier spelled "Consort"] of Vocal and Instrumental Musick" indicates, songs were nearly always included. The instrumental pieces were overtures, symphonies (not usually performed in their entirety, as later audiences would come to expect), and concertos or solos for various instruments. Popular solo instruments were the violin, the guitar, the flute, the French horn, and the harp.

Programmatic pieces intended to depict momentous events began to appear toward the end of the eighteenth century. (Those events were usually battles but sometimes were travels by sea or land, which in those days were also momentous and could be equally hazardous.) *The Battle of Prague,* by the Bohemian-born Frantisek Koczwara (Franz Kotzwara, ca. 1750–1791), showed up on numerous programs for half a century and was a kind of prototype. American contributions to the genre were represented by *The Battle of Trenton,* a pastiche arranged from various sources by James Hewitt (when French titles became popular, this or a similarly inspired piece appeared on programs as *La Bataille de Trenton*), and after the French Revolution *The Demolition of the Bastille,* by John Berkenhead. These programmatic pieces persisted well into the nineteenth century.

The Audiences

What were the audiences for these concerts like? For one thing, they could be noisy—though not as noisy as theater audiences. Nevertheless, the admonition by the performer who "finds himself obliged to request that silence may be observed during his performance" was not unusual. Audiences could even be rowdy; one concert manager advertised that "every possible precaution will be used to prevent disorder and irregularity," and another promised that a "number of constables will attend to preserve order."

On another point, it is clear that audiences did not represent the broad spectrum of the populace at large—an advertisement in Charleston in 1799 makes it clear that "persons of color" will not be admitted, for example. And from the same city in 1782 we find an announcement to the effect that "gentlemen of the navy, army [referring to officers during the British occupation of the city] and the most respectable part of town" would be admitted. It is clear that concerts, at least in the early part of the period, were primarily for "gentlemen." "Ladies" typically were admitted on the "gentleman's" ticket, sometimes two for each.

BANDS AND MILITARY MUSIC

The functions of military music throughout history have been manifold: to dignify ceremonial functions, to lift morale, to enable soldiers to march in step together, and, of supreme practical importance, to convey signals and commands. The last two needs, essential but utilitarian, were met by the simplest means— that which has long been known as *field music.* For eighteenth-century foot soldiers this meant drums and fifes, which were incorporated into each company unit. The fifers were often young boys. Collections of music for the fife existed in print and manuscript in the eighteenth century, and the tunes were often those of songs or dances of the period. "Lady Hope's Reel" (CD 3/3) was one such tune. It was written down by a fifer in the Revolutionary War, Giles Gibbs, Jr., who was seventeen years old when he copied out a number of these tunes in the summer of 1777. He was captured and killed by a British raiding party in 1780.

Like a fiddle dance tune, "Lady Hope's Reel" is in binary form. Indeed, its two sections might be fairly described as a "low strain" and a "high strain," just as we heard in the fiddle tune "Soldier's Joy" (CD 1/4). The fiddle's role is assumed here by the more incisive, penetrating sound of the fife providing the melody. The steady, rapid-fire drumming adds an element that has become inseparable from our conception of martial music.

Listening Cue "Lady Hope's Reel" American Fife Ensemble (1:14)

Listen For ▪ fife ▪ martial drumming ▪ low and high strains

Visit http://www.music.wadsworth.com_3/Kingman for a full listening guide and other resources.

To fulfill more elaborate functions, larger ensembles, known as bands of music, were formed. The basic makeup was a pair of oboes, a pair of French horns, and one or two bassoons, often with a pair of clarinets either replacing or supplementing the oboes. "Washington's March" (one of many to bear this title) illustrates the sound (CD 3/4). The paired oboes, with their characteristically high, nasal quality, are the easiest to pick out here. The low, nasal bassoons are probably the most distinctive after that. Their shared "nasal" quality derives from the fact that both produce their sound by way of vibrating reeds that are set in motion by a focused stream of air blown in through the mouth. The French horns have a rounder, more mellow timbre that makes them a bit more difficult to pick out initially. But the French horn is a brass instrument well suited to the outdoors; it descends from a family of horns once used to sound calls and fanfares during mounted hunts.

Listening Cue "Washington's March" The Liberty Tree Wind Players (1:24)

Listen For ▪ oboes ▪ bassoons ▪ French horns

Visit http://www.music.wadsworth.com_3/Kingman for a full listening guide and other resources.

The kind of ensemble heard in "Washington's March" was well known in Europe, and masters such as Haydn and Mozart wrote a considerable amount of what was basically outdoor music for this collection of instruments, or augmented versions of it. "Bands of music" were usually employed by the regimental officers themselves and were used on social as well as military occasions. Made up of fairly skilled musicians, who often played stringed instruments as well, they came to play a rather prominent role in the musical life of the times, especially during the time of the Revolution, which in the cities (especially those occupied by the British) was not always marked by great austerity. These bands played for military ceremonies and parades, at which the public were often spectators. They also played for dances for the officers and their ladies, and even gave public concerts and, on occasion, played in the theaters.

MUSICAL THEATER

The musical theater, in its many varied forms, was the institution upon which most of the musical life in the cities centered in this period, especially after the Revolution. It was usually the theater that employed those professional musicians who were active in the United States, and that attracted performers, composers, and impresarios (organizers of public entertainments) from Europe, mostly from England.

In the eighteenth century, music was a nearly universal accompaniment to theatrical performances of all kinds. Even what we would regard today as straight drama (the plays of Shakespeare, for example) was usually presented with interpolated songs, dances, and incidental music. What is generally regarded as the first theater in the colonies was built in Williamsburg, Virginia, in 1716, and there is evidence that musicians were employed in this enterprise from the very beginning (Mates 40). Furthermore, it has been shown that the majority of stage works produced were actually "musicals"—belonging to one of the many various, confusing, and overlapping types that will be alluded to presently.

But if music was nearly always present in the theater, and its presence taken for granted, it was the most ephemeral ingredient of any production, and its providers were subordinate and often anonymous. The music for operas, or related musical genres, was often appropriated from other sources to begin with; it was also frequently changed from production to production, and from city to city, as the show traveled. The music was not usually published, and it was subsequently often lost altogether. From the truly impressive number of musical stage works presented in America in the century between 1730 and 1830, a disappointingly small amount of the actual music has survived.

Theatrical Genres

There existed in this period a vast array of entertainments in which music was a major ingredient. Until about 1800, the forms we would most recognize today as "musicals" were the famous ballad opera and its often less precisely defined successors, the pastiche opera and the comic opera. What they had in common was spoken dialogue, which was interspersed with songs, and sometimes with dances and choruses. The music was in a style familiar to its public. For the most part the characters and the situations were drawn from everyday life.

The original ballad opera was the famous *The Beggar's Opera*, on a libretto by John Gay (ca. 1685–1732), first performed in London in 1728. With its already popular tunes, its memorable low-life characters, and its satirizing of the conventions of the imported upper-class Italian opera of its day (which it nearly put out of business for a time), it was an instant success and was soon widely imitated. Though the initial intensity of its popularity, and the heyday of ballad opera in general, was over in London in a decade or so, a certain few operas of this genre proved to be amazingly long-lived, especially in America. *The Beggar's Opera* itself was performed in Providence, Rhode Island, by a "Sett of Inhabitants" (amateurs) at least as early as 1746, and by a professional company in

Illustrating the joyful "Chorus of Adventurers" that we hear on CD 3, track 5, Captain John Smith and his followers land in the New World in 1607 to found the Jamestown colony of Virginia (notice the watchful Indian on the right). *The Indian Princess,* the 1808 musical drama for which the "Chorus" was written, tells the romanticized story of Pocahontas, daughter of a Powhatan chief. Pocahontas played with the English children, brought much-needed food during the hard first year, and according to legend, prevented her father from executing John Smith.

New York by 1750 (McKay 140; Sonneck 15). Julian Mates has written that "it was *The Beggar's Opera,* in most places, which introduced the musical to America" (142). It was a staple of the repertory through the remainder of the eighteenth century and has been revived, in various forms, ever since.

By 1800 ballad operas and pastiches were no longer being written, and a new genre, the melodrama, appeared that coexisted with comic opera for the rest of the period with which this chapter deals. The melodrama introduced wordless instrumental music as an accompaniment to stage action. An American "Operatic Melo-Drame" that has survived is *The Indian Princess,* first performed in Philadelphia in 1808. It is based on an American subject—the story of Captain John Smith and Pocahontas.

The "Chorus of Adventurers" (CD 3/5) is an excerpt from *The Indian Princess.* It is a song of rejoicing sung by a band of English that, along with Capt. John Smith, has landed safely on the banks of the Powhatan River, in what is now Virginia. Fittingly enough, the music is generally light and gleeful, which is enough to make the point. But there are a couple of interesting details worth noting. First, notice how the singing in the chorus captures a sense of relieved, nervous laughter as the choristers reflect on having made it to shore. No bravado here—this is one of those "Phew, we made it!" moments. Second, notice how the strings take up the role of the storm (actually, the choristers' recollection of the storm) following "For the tempest's roar" and "heard no more." These are but two examples of how a resourceful composer can use music to suggest emotional states, and even memories, that are not being explicitly played out on the stage.

Listening Cue **"Chorus of Adventurers"** from *The Indian Princess*, The Federal Music Society Opera Company, John Baldon, conductor (2:03)

Listen For ▪ light, gleeful quality ▪ "relieved, nervous laughter" ▪ "memories of the storm"

Visit http://www.music.wadsworth.com_3/Kingman for a full listening guide and other resources.

Alice (wife of one of Smith's yeomen):
Jolly comrades, join the glee,
Chorus it right cheerily,
Jolly comrades, join the glee,
Chorus it right cheerily,

Chorus:
Jolly comrades, join the glee,
Chorus it right cheerily,
Jolly comrades, join the glee,
Chorus it right cheerily,

For the tempest's roar is heard no more,
But gaily we tread the wish'd-for shore:
We tread the wish'd-for shore.
Jolly comrades, join the glee,
Chorus it right cheerily,
For past are the perils of the blust'ring sea.
For past are the perils of the blust'ring sea.
Of the blust'ring sea.

From *The Indian Princess,* music by John Bray, lyrics by N. Barker, 1808.

In each of the three acts of *The Indian Princess* there is, as the defining feature of melodrama, music to accompany stage action, as for example "Smith brought in prisoner," "Smith is led to the block," "The Princess leads Smith to the throne," "She supplicates the King for his pardon," and "Smith is pardoned—general joy diffused." Also of interest is the inclusion of the Irishman, Larry, and his lament—an early appearance of the ethnic characters that were such a feature of the popular musical theater in the late nineteenth century (see Additional Listening).

Political independence of the colonies from England was declared in 1776, but cultural independence evolved much more slowly. For three-quarters of a century more, the legacy of English comic opera—with its comic characters, its homely but pungent satire, and its popular, folklike songs—was entertaining Americans, if not continuously in the large cities of the eastern seaboard, then in crude, sparsely documented, but keenly enjoyed performances in frontier towns and cities. The tenacity of the pieces themselves was amazing. An example is *The Poor Soldier* (a favorite of George Washington), written by an Irish playright, John O'Keeffe, and first performed in London in 1783. It reached the United States in 1785, and after a successful New York run of nineteen performances by the famous Old American Company, it was taken on the road by that company. Thereafter, until the end of the eighteenth century, hardly a year went by without a performance of *The Poor Soldier* somewhere, by some company. In 1801 it was done in Cincinnati—the first play performed in the Northwest Territory—and it continued to be played throughout the Ohio Valley for twenty years. *The Poor Soldier* was part of the American theatrical scene in one form or another almost until the Civil War (1861–1865).

In addition to the comic operas, there was a bewildering variety of theatrical entertainments, all of which employed music in some form. Theatrical presentations hardly ever consisted of just a single play, and could go on for four or five hours! There were shorter "afterpieces," sometimes known as *farces,* that followed the main play or opera. *Interludes* were even slighter pieces that went between the acts of longer works. In addition there were forms such as the *pantomime,* in which stage action and speech were accompanied by wordless music.

Theaters and Audiences

The first theatrical performances in the colonies were given in buildings made for other purposes—often in taverns or warehouses (though not, of course, in churches). The first musical in America, in 1735, was given in the courtroom in Charleston, South Carolina. By midcentury, theaters had been built in most cities. The space for the audience, according to a plan that remained basically unaltered to the twentieth century, was divided into three distinct parts: at the bottom level was the "pit" (now called the "orchestra"); above that, in a horseshoe shape around the walls, were one or more tiers of boxes; and above the boxes was the gallery. The distribution of the audience was rigidly defined: "ladies and gentlemen in the boxes, the pit occupied almost entirely by unattached gentlemen, and the gallery 'reserved for the rabble'" (Mates 64).

The behavior of audiences was, by our standards, notoriously bad. Thieves and pickpockets were common fixtures in the theaters. There was loud talking and often card playing in the boxes, and coming and going, with the slamming of doors. Prostitutes, who used the theater (in Sonneck's words) "as a kind of stock exchange," were by custom assigned the upper boxes. Liquor was served to the "unattached gentlemen" in the pit. It was not until the end of the century that the custom of allowing some of the audience to sit on the stage during the performance was abolished. But the greatest disturbances came from the gallery. It was customary for people in the gallery to interrupt the orchestra's performance by shouting down requests for popular tunes—requests that, if not complied with to their satisfaction, would result in loud demonstrations. A letter to a New York newspaper as late as 1802 describes the behavior of the gallery "gods": "The mode by which they issue their mandates is stamping, hissing, roaring, whistling; and, when the musicians are refractory, groaning in cadence." The habit of the gallery's throwing objects at the orchestra, and into the pit, was notorious. "As soon as the curtain was down, the gods in the galleries would throw apples, nuts, bottles and glasses on the stage and into the orchestra." Mates quotes a report of a performance in 1794 "when half the instruments in the orchestra were broken by missiles from the upper reaches of the theater" (73). Riots were all too common, often provoked by something as simple as the orchestra leader calling a tune that someone did not like.

POPULAR SONG

Popular song—enjoyed by the general populace and not associated with the stage or the concert hall—is at once the most widespread kind of music making and the most difficult to chronicle. Secular songs were not published complete with lyrics and music together until the last decade of the eighteenth century. Before that time, popular songs were disseminated in print for the most part by the publication of the words alone, either as single-sheet *broadsides,* or in collections called *songsters.* By the time of the Revolution, newspapers, of which there were a great many in the colonies, had become another medium for the publication of lyrics, especially topical verses dealing with the patriotic and political matters that were of so much concern at the time. As many as 1,500 such lyrics were printed in more than 120 newspaper between 1783 and 1793 (Anderson). It is not possible to determine now whether all these versifications (often crude by literary standards) were in fact meant to be sung, but the strength of the ballad tradition, the number of tunes known to be in wide circulation, and the fact that in many cases the names of the tunes were given, justify our including this vast output in our consideration of popular song. Many patriotic songs, including "Yankee Doodle" and the many sets of words associated with it, were first disseminated in this manner.

One very popular song that was parodied in broadsides of the time was "The Dusky Night" or "A-Hunting We Will Go." Here is the text of the original version of the song, as used in a revival of *The Beggar's Opera* in England:

The Dusky Night rides down the Sky,
When wakes the Rosey Morn,
The Hounds all join the Jovial cry,
The Huntsman winds his Horn.

Chorus:
Then a Hunting let us go.
Then a Hunting let us go.
Then a Hunting let us go.
Then a Hunting let us go.

This image, appearing in England in 1774, shows an evil-looking group of colonists pouring tea into a British tax collector, while (left) more colonists dump tea into Boston Harbor. The tax collector has been tarred and feathered (covered with hot, sticky tar and then showered with feathers), a frequent punishment in vigilante justice. (Notice also the noose hanging from the Liberty Tree.) On CD 3, track 6, the "Junto Song"—meaning a secret group that intrigues its way to power, in this case American patriots seeking the overthrow of British rule—reflects the anti-tax feeling of the Revolutionary War period.

The broadside parody, attacking the British desire to raise more revenue from the colonies, appeared in journals of the day in New York and Philadelphia. Known as the "Junto Song" (CD 3/6), it substitutes "A-taxing we will go" for the original words of the chorus. In short, this is a colonial example of the protest song studied in Chapter 6. Like the protest song (and political stump speech) of today, the substituted lyrics stay doggedly "on message." The performance style in this recording also does little to distract from that message. It is delivered in a clear, emphatic, and decisive tone. The song can (and should) entertain, but its message will not be ignored.

Listening Cue "Junto Song" (excerpt), Seth McCoy, tenor; James Richman, harpsichord (0:50)

Listen For ▪ message of the lyrics ▪ direct, emphatic performance style

Visit http://www.music.wadsworth.com_3/Kingman for a full listening guide and other resources.

Verse:
'Tis money makes the member vote,
And sanctifies our ways;
It makes the patriot turn his coat

It makes the patriot turn his coat
And money we must raise.
And money we must raise.

Chorus:
And a-taxing we will go,
A-taxing we will go,
A-taxing we will go,
A-taxing we will go.

One single thing untax'd at home,
Old England could not shew,
For money we abroad did roam,
For money we abroad did roam,
And thought to tax the new.
And thought to tax the new.
(Chorus)

There was no very clear dividing line between sacred and secular in this period, and religion was often invoked in political and military struggles. William Billings' "Chester" (CD 2/18), especially with the updated topical verses added for its second version of 1778, is said to have been the most popular song of the Revolutionary War (see p. 155).

The turn of the century saw the beginnings of change, gradual but significant, in American urban secular music. The publishing of songs individually, rather than in sets, marked the beginning of sheet music, which became, during the nineteenth century, the basis for the entire popular-music industry, known later as Tin Pan Alley. In the first quarter of the nineteenth century, nearly 10,000 titles appeared of secular music alone (Wolfe). The range of songs was broad—from topical songs on political or patriotic themes, crude but timely, to settings of the poetry of Shakespeare, Sir Walter Scott, or Thomas Moore. Its very breadth is a striking indicator of the variety of tastes (and topical concerns) that drove the musical culture of the period.

PROJECTS

1. As revealed in the chapter, audiences in the eighteenth century were often inconsiderate and ill behaved. From personal observation, write a paper on the behavior of present-day audiences for a variety of events in a variety of locations: a classical concert, a jazz concert, a rock concert, a concert of folk music, and so on. To what would you attribute the differences, both between the eighteenth and the twenty-first centuries, and between various kinds of contemporary events?
2. Sketch a plot and scenario for a modern-day "ballad opera," dealing in a comical and even satirical way with some current issue or event. Read the texts of several ballad operas in preparation for this; the scenes should be short and

the characters few, and allowance should be made for the inclusion of "airs," which can be parodies of existing popular songs.

3. Study the modern edition of *Disappointment: or, The Force of Credulity* (Madison, WI: A-R Editions, 1976), an eighteenth-century ballad opera that was not performed until 1937! Read the two articles on the subject by Carolyn Rabson in *American Music* (vol. 1, no. 1 [Spring 1983], pp. 12ff, and vol. 2, no. 1 [Spring 1984], pp. 1ff). Write an article, in a lively journalist style, describing the piece and its history.

ADDITIONAL LISTENING

The Birth of Liberty: Music of the American Revolution. New World 80276.

Come and Trip It: Instrumental Dance Music 1780s–1920s. New World 80293.

John Bray: The Indian Princess. New World 80232.

Music of the Federal Era. New World 80299.

POPULAR MUSICAL THEATER AND OPERA FROM THE JACKSONIAN ERA TO THE PRESENT

The age of Andrew Jackson (president 1829–1837) was characterized by westward expansion and a new degree of political populism and marked the beginning of a new era of cultural populism as well. One useful yardstick of this new populism was the music publishing industry, which was expanding rapidly and catering to a much broader segment of the population. New methods of lithography (a printing process first used around 1800) made possible the use of black-and-white illustrations in sheet music in the late 1820s, and colored illustrations in the 1840s—developments that were clearly linked to a growing popular market, as can be seen in the popular nature and appeal of illustrated sheet music published in the 1820s and 1830s. Thus the period from 1820 to 1840, which saw the admission of three new western states into the union (Missouri, Arkansas, and Michigan), the opening of the Erie Canal, and the construction of the Baltimore and Ohio Railroad to carry paying passengers as far west as Harpers Ferry, also saw the mass publication of sentimental popular favorites such as "Woodman! Spare That Tree!"—and also, for less genteel tastes, "My Long-Tail Blue," "Jim Crow," and "Zip Coon"—all illustrated with blackface figures with exaggerated features, dress, and poses (Nathan 35–58).

As the country was expanding westward, so were its cities growing rapidly, both on the more settled eastern seaboard and in the Ohio and Mississippi valleys. And as the cities grew, so did the number and size of the theaters and the audience for the vast array of theatrical entertainments noted in the previous chapter—comic operas, melodramas, farces, and pantomimes. Two forms in particular—the *olio*, a kind of variety show that predated vaudeville, and the *circus*, which had incorporated comic song-and-dance acts into its original format—prepared the way for the first of a succession of truly indigenous forms of popular musical entertainment.

MINSTRELSY AND MUSICAL ENTERTAINMENT BEFORE THE CIVIL WAR

The first of these indigenous forms, and one that swept the country by midcentury, was the blackface minstrel show. It was based on what had become by then a common source of entertainment among the broader masses, both in America and in England: the exaggerated portrayal of any exotic people—rural people, Irish people, German people, Jewish people, and, as early as the eighteenth century, African people.

The faculty of black people for spontaneous song and dance, and for unbridled comedy, was well known to observers such as Lewis Paine. A white man from Rhode Island, Paine went to the South for an extended stay on business and was sentenced to prison there for helping a slave to escape. In Georgia in the 1840s, he described the festivities after a corn shucking:

> The fiddler walks out, and strikes up a tune; and at it they go in a regular tear-down dance; for here they are at home. . . . I never saw a slave in my life but would stop as if he were shot at the sound of a fiddle; and if he has a load of two hundred pounds on his head, he will begin to dance. One would think they had steam engines inside of them, to jerk them about with so much power; for they go through more motions in a minute, than you could shake two sticks at in a month; and of all comic actions, ludicrous sights, and laughable jokes, and truly comic songs, there is no match for them. (Southern 91)

There was abundant material here for imitation by white entertainers, once they saw its potential. The original black minstrelsy was an informal, spontaneous, and exuberant affair of the plantation. But its reputation spread. Thus it came about that the native songs, dances, and comedy of the slaves first reached the general American public in the form of parodies by white entertainers.

The Beginnings of Minstrelsy

Impersonations on the stage of the black man by the white were already taking place in the eighteenth century, both here and in England. In the 1820s and 1830s, two American entertainers, George Washington Dixon (1808–1861) and Thomas Dartmouth "Daddy" Rice (1808–1860), were well known for blackface song and dance. Dixon introduced the songs "Long Tail Blue" (referring to the blue swallowtail coat associated with the black urban dandy) and "Coal Black Rose." Rice was famous for his song-and-dance routine "Jim Crow," which he introduced in 1832 and which, according to a well-known story, he adapted from the singing and movements of a black man he encountered in Cincinnati (Hamm 118–21).

Familiar and very popular as single acts in olios and circuses, the impersonation of blacks had, by the 1830s, evolved into two stage types. One, typified by Gumbo Chaff or Jim Crow, portrayed the ragged plantation or riverboat hand, joyous, reckless, uncouth. The other, typified by Zip Coon or Dandy Jim, was a citified northern dandy with exaggeratedly elegant clothes and manners. The extent to which some songs of the minstrel period have remained in use today is scarcely masked by the occasional change of title. For example, "Old Zip Coon" has been perpetuated since the Civil War (1861–1865) as "Turkey in the Straw."

The minstrel show itself was put together in the early 1840s, and consisted of songs, dances, jokes, satirical speeches, and skits. The performers, only four in number at first, seated themselves in a rough semicircle on the stage. In the middle were the banjo player and the fiddle player. The two "end-men" played the tambourine and the bones, and these, along with the inevitable foot tapping of the banjo player, provided a basic "rhythm section." It was the end-men who indulged in the most outrageous horseplay. The bones, which were in the beginning actually just that, were held one pair in each hand and rattled together. The fiddle played the tune more or less straight, while the banjo, instead of merely strumming chords, as it would in the later jazz band, played an ornamented version of the tune. Because the banjo music was eventually written down and published, we know not only that it presupposes a good deal of agility but also that the lively and syncopated rhythms were similar to those that would appear later in ragtime.

The coming to town of the touring minstrel show was as eagerly anticipated as the coming of the circus, with which it had a good deal in common. The troupe's arrival was signaled by the inevitable parade through town, winding up at the theater where the evening performance was to be given. At this performance the public's expectations of an evening of vivid and diverting entertainment were seldom disappointed; they laughed hard at the comic songs, repartee, and antics of the end-men, and at the skits and parodies that made up the second half of the show. But there also may have been some moist eyes in the crowd at the close of the sentimental songs, which included "Old Black Joe," "My Old Kentucky Home," and "Old Uncle Ned."

Dan Emmett

Daniel Decatur Emmett (1815–1904) was a pioneer performer in minstrelsy, and one of the most important composers and authors of its early folkish and rough-hewn material. Born in a small Ohio town just emerging from the backwoods, Emmett grew up in a frontier society similar to that in which Abraham Lincoln was raised, with all its virtues and vices—its examples of courage and fierce independence, its violence and prejudices, and, above all, its rough-and-ready humor. At eighteen he enlisted in the army, where he mastered the drum and the fife. In the late 1830s he began appearing in circuses, singing and playing the drums and, later, the banjo and the fiddle.

Blackface singing and dancing with banjo accompaniment was by that time common in the circus; of the four performers who formed the original Virginia Minstrels in New York City in 1843 (Dan Emmett, Frank Brower, William Whitlock, and Richard Pelham), at least three had had experience in touring circuses. The Virginia Minstrels, the first group to use the classic instrumentation described earlier (fiddle, banjo, tambourine, and bones) and the first to put together a whole evening of minstrel music, dancing, and skits, caught on with both public and press in New York and Boston. The popularity of this

State Historical Society of Missouri, Columbia

Before railroads, the nation's rivers connected the country. The flatboat—such as we see here in George Caleb Bingham's *The Jolly Flatboatmen* (1846)—carried goods and passengers up and down America's waterways. Despite the grueling labor—the large boats were rowed by hand (notice the long oars)—the boatmen earned a reputation for merrymaking that inspired such popular art as the minstrel tune "De Boatman's Dance" that we hear on CD 3, track 7.

entertainment in the United States was so great that many imitators and competitors soon appeared—E. P. Christy and his troupe among them. Emmett himself was active for more than twenty-five years as a performer, and as composer-author of songs and skits, especially for the shows' finales, the "walk-arounds." His song "De Boatman's Dance" (CD 3/7) became so well known as to achieve the status of a folk song. A lively tune, with its emphatic repetition of short motives, it is typical of the exuberant songs of early minstrelsy. Notice the clicking of the bones and the attempt to approximate dialect in the lyrics. The structure of the lyrics is such that contrasting verses are embedded between two parts of a refrain.

Listening Cue "De Boatman's Dance" attr. Daniel D. Emmett; Vincent Tufo, fiddle; Percy Danforth, bones; Matthew Heumann, tambourine; Robert Winans, banjo (2:40)

CD 3
7

Listen For ▪ use of dialect ▪ lively repetition of short motives ▪ clicking of bones

Visit http://www.music.wadsworth.com_3/Kingman for a full listening guide and other resources.

(Instrumental Introduction)
Refrain 1:
High row de boatmen row,
floatin' down de river de Ohio.
High row de boatmen row,
floatin' down de river de Ohio.

Verse:
De boatmen dance, de boatmen
sing,
de boatmen up to ebry ting,
An when de boatmen gets on
shore,
he spends his cash and works for
more.

Refrain 2:
Den dance de boatmen dance,
O dance de boatmen dance,
O dance all night till broad daylight,
an go home wid de gals in de morning.
(Refrain 1)

I went on board de odder day
To see what de boatmen had to say;
Dar I let my passion loose
An dey cram me in de callaboose.
(Refrain 2)
(Instrumental Break)
(Refrain 1)

When de boatman blows his horn,
Look out old man your hog is gone;
He cotch my sheep, he cotch my
shoat,
Den put em in a bag an tote em in de
boat.
(Refrain 2)
(Refrain 1)

De boatman is a thrifty man,
Dars none can do as de boatman
can;
I neber see a putty gal in my life
But dat she was a boatman's wife.
(Refrain 2)
(Instrumental Close)

From *Dan Emmett and the Rise of Early Negro Minstrelsy,* by Hans Nathan. Copyright © 1962 by the University of Oklahoma Press. Reprinted by permission.

The boatman's reputation for merrymaking in spite of a grueling occupation inspired not only this minstrel tune, but also popular secular art such as George Caleb Bingham's *The Jolly Flatboatmen* (1846).

Dan Emmett is probably best remembered for "Dixie" (full title, "I Wish I Was in Dixie's Land") which he wrote for Bryant's Minstrels in 1859. Perhaps the most phenomenally popular song of the nineteenth century, it was minstrelsy's greatest legacy to American music. It soon acquired a significance entirely unintended and even resented by its composer, when it was adopted by the Confederacy at the outbreak of the Civil War.

Stephen Foster and Minstrelsy

Stephen Collins Foster (1826–1864) was minstrelsy's best-known composer. He was not, as Emmett was, a minstrel performer himself, but in 1845 he began writing minstrel songs, at first for the enjoyment of a group of friends. In Cincinnati he met a member of a professional minstrel troupe (the Sable Harmonists) who introduced his "Old Uncle Ned" in one of their programs. In 1848 he wrote "Oh! Susanna," selling it outright to a Pittsburgh publisher for $100. It became enormously popular. The next year he signed a contract with the leading New York publisher, Firth, Pond & Co., and committed himself to a songwriting career. In 1852 he made a brief steamboat trip down the Ohio and the Mississippi to

New Orleans—his only visit to the South. Stephen Foster will be considered more fully in Chapter 15, in connection with American popular song.

Zenith and Decline

The minstrel show reached its zenith in the years just before the Civil War. After the war, minstrelsy lost much of its original flavor and character. In cities such as New York, it was increasingly overshadowed by other forms of theatrical entertainment (see below). But minstrelsy continued strong in smaller centers of population and in rural America. After the Civil War, African American musicians and entertainers themselves began to participate, and all-black minstrel companies, such as the Georgia Minstrels, the Original Black Diamonds (of Boston), Haverly's Genuine Colored Minstrels, and W. S. Cleveland's Colossal Colored Carnival Minstrels, toured for another half-century or so. Minstrelsy thus became both a training ground and a source of employment for many black musicians who later branched out in the direction of blues or jazz. W. C. Handy was one, as was "Ma" Rainey, who toured widely in the South with various minstrel shows and circuses in the first two decades of the twentieth century.

Despite the (nominally) free status of blacks and the drastically changed social and economic conditions in the South after the Civil War, the basic content and characterization of black people in postwar minstrel songs remained virtually the same as during slavery, with continued nostalgic references to idyllic plantation life. These were performed, and often also composed, by blacks themselves. The songs of James Bland (1854–1911), the best-known black songwriter for the minstrel stage, are typical in this regard. "Oh, Dem Golden Slippers," "In the Evening by the Moonlight," and "Carry Me Back to Old Virginny" were all composed about 1880; from their characterization of black people and depiction of conditions in the South, they could have been written thirty years earlier. But the nostalgically clothed stereotype was what audiences continued to want to hear.

Less than a generation later, there were the beginnings of change. About the turn of the century, performers such as the team of Bert Williams (1874–1922) and George Walker (c. 1872–1911), black singer-comedians who also wore blackface makeup, helped to bring new standards of integrity to the stage portrayal of the black man. As George Walker said in 1906:

> The one hope of the colored performer must be in making a radical departure from the old "darkie" style of singing and dancing. . . . There is an artistic side to the black race, and if it could be properly developed on the stage, I believe the theatergoing public would profit much by it. . . . My idea was always to impersonate my race just as they are. The colored man has never successfully taken off his own humorous characteristics, and the white impersonator often overdoes the matter. (Gilbert 284)

Playing eventually in shows such as *In Dahomey* (1902) and *In Bandana Land* (1907), Williams and Walker were part of the first wave of black shows with black performers at the turn of the century.

FROM THE CIVIL WAR THROUGH THE TURN OF THE CENTURY

Immediately after the searing and costly War Between the States, the popular musical stage entered a period of exuberant growth, characterized by foreign importation and native experimentation. With the great leaps in industry and transportation, and the enriching inflow of diverse immigrant groups, a new and energetic era was beginning. Above all, the cities grew, and with them the wealth and expectations of influential segments in society. In an era of affluence and expansion, that public was in the market for—and got—new theatrical diversions.

The New York Stage in the 1860s

New York City's dominance as America's entertainment capital was well established by the mid-nineteenth century. It was the first stop for touring artists and companies from Europe, and already the magnet toward which all native talent was drawn. Beginning in the 1860s, it became the fantasyland of that dream of every producer, the "Broadway hit." The first of these was *The Black Crook*. Produced in 1866 in Niblo's Garden, the best-appointed theater in New York, with its stage completely rebuilt for the occasion, the original production lasted five and a half hours and was a spectacle lavish beyond anything that had been seen previously. Its thin, derivative, melodramatic plot was overwhelmed by huge ensemble numbers, costumes, extremely elaborate scenic effects and changes, and, as a significant ingredient, the dancing of no fewer than 200 French ballet dancers in "immodest dress." *The Black Crook* actually looked more to the past than to the future. None of its ingredients was new; what was new was the prodigally lavish scale of the production (said to have cost more than $35,000, an astounding outlay for the time), and the fact that it ran for 474 performances and grossed more than $1 million.

Vaudeville

After the impetus of *The Black Crook,* the New York stage became the arena for continued experiment on a new scale. One form emerged that was to become a prominent and typically American entertainment for half a century—*vaudeville.* Its antecedents were to be found in the minstrel theater, the English music hall, and, more immediately, the entertainments offered in beer halls and saloons to which the name "burlesque" had come to be applied. But in the 1880s Antonio "Tony" Pastor (1837–1908), called the "father of vaudeville," successfully turned it into clean, family entertainment. Vaudeville typically was a succession of individual acts, including dancers, acrobats, jugglers, magicians, and animal acts, usually headlined by a well-known comedian or singer.

Importations from London, Paris, and Vienna

The American popular stage languished musically until the importation of comic opera of exceptionally high quality from London, Paris, and Vienna beginning in the last quarter of the century. W. S. Gilbert and Arthur Sullivan in London,

Jacques Offenbach in Paris, Johann Strauss, Jr., in Vienna—each of these represented a peak of achievement in English, French, and German comic opera, all coming at about the same time. It was an unprecedented era of concentrated brilliance that cast beams on this side of the Atlantic as well.

The London "invasion" came first; *H.M.S. Pinafore* was heard (in a stolen version) in Boston in 1878 and became prodigiously popular at once. After *Pinafore*, there followed in short order *The Pirates of Penzance* (premiered in New York, this time with Sullivan conducting) and then *Iolanthe, The Sorcerer,* and *Princess Ida,* climaxed by the phenomenal success of *The Mikado* in 1885.

The new popularity of English comic opera created a popular audience for other European light operas as well, and both French *opéra bouffe* and Viennese operetta (which had been given in the United States earlier in their original languages) were presented in English translations. After a lull in the 1890s, Viennese operetta again enjoyed a great period of popularity in the United States with the advent of *The Merry Widow,* by Franz Lehar, in 1907 and *The Chocolate Soldier,* by Oskar Straus, in 1909. A host of operettas more or less on the Viennese model were subsequently produced by immigrant composers.

In a still from *Yankee Doodle Dandy,* the 1942 film biography of George M. Cohan, actor James Cagney, in a classic performance, sings and tap dances to "The Yankee Doodle Boy"—a version of which we hear on CD 3, track 8. Suspected of a lack of patriotism at the time, Cagney chose to prove his loyalty by portraying this most patriotic of composers. Seeing the film shortly before his death, Cohan called the performance "a tough act to follow."

The Americanization of the Musical

While these foreign importations were enjoying their popularity, a more indigenous kind of musical show was gradually emerging. The Harrigan and Hart comedies of the period represented an important early step toward the Americanization of the musical. Portraying with humor the Irish, the Germans, and the African Americans in believable comic situations growing out of the everyday lives of everyday people, they were an immediate success. The first was *The Mulligan Guard Ball* (1879), and this was followed by many Mulligan Guard sequels with the same characters, much in the manner as a television situation comedy series. The songs, all by David Braham (1834–1905), a London-born musician who came to the United States at the age of fifteen, became popular at the time in their own right and were sometimes borrowed for other shows.

The movement toward the Americanization of the musical comedy of this period culminated in the shows and songs of George M. Cohan (1878–1942), an energetic and ambitious showman who came up from vaudeville to become an author, composer, stage director, and performer who dominated the musical stage in the first two decades of the twentieth century. The one word inevitably used by writers to describe Cohan is "brash." The directness of his style, his informality, and above all his fast pace brought new vitality to the theater. Cohan was right for his time, and fittingly marked the last stage in the adolescence of American popular musical theater, sounding a decisive note of independence from Europe. His three most important and characteristic shows came early in the century: *Little Johnny Jones* in 1904, *Forty-five Minutes from Broadway* in 1906, and *George Washington, Jr.*, also in 1906. Each has its American hero (a jockey, a reformed gambler, a young superpatriot), and the three shows together contain the best of Cohan's show tunes.

"The Yankee Doodle Boy" (CD 3/8) from *Little Johnny Jones* typifies the "American-ness" of Cohan's songs. Note its fast pace, brash style, and, not least, its snatches of popular tunes: "Yankee Doodle," "Dixie," "The Girl I Left Behind Me," and "The Star-Spangled Banner."

Listening Cue "The Yankee Doodle Boy" *Little Johnny Jones;* Richard Perry, vocal (1:12)

Listen For ▪ fast pace ▪ brash style ▪ snatches of popular American tunes

Visit http://www.music.wadsworth.com_3/Kingman for a full listening guide and other resources.

Verse:
I'm the kid that's all the candy,
I'm a Yankee Doodle Dandy;
I'm glad I am
(So's Uncle Sam).
I'm a real live Yankee Doodle,
Made my name and fame and boodle
Just like Mr. Doodle did,
By riding on a pony.
I love to listen to the Dixie strain,
"I long to see the girl I left behind me."
And that ain't a josh,
She's a Yankee, by gosh.
(Oh, say can you see
Anything about a Yankee that's a phoney?)

Chorus:
I'm a Yankee Doodle Dandy,
A Yankee Doodle do or die.
A real live nephew of my Uncle Sam,
Born on the Fourth of July.
I've got a Yankee Doodle sweetheart,
She is my Yankee Doodle joy,
Yankee Doodle came to London
Just to ride the ponies,
I am that Yankee Doodle Boy!

By this time the chorus, which has the "main tune," has assumed the importance it will hold from now on in American popular music. Indeed, few ever remember the verses to such standards as "The Yankee Doodle Boy" (or even realize the songs have any).

THE FIRST HALF OF THE TWENTIETH CENTURY

Black Musicians on Broadway: The Emergence from Minstrelsy

Late in the nineteenth century it began to be apparent that the contributions of black musicians to America's popular musical stage need not—in fact, *could not*—be forever limited to the caricatured renditions of the minstrel stage. Change, however, was painfully slow.

Two important landmarks came in 1898. Robert Cole produced the first full-length all-black musical show, *A Trip to Coontown*. But more successful and memorable that year was an all-black musical comedy sketch, *Clorindy, the Origin of the Cakewalk,* with music by the talented and classically trained musician Will Marion Cook (1869–1944). With its characteristic music, dancing, and choral singing, *Clorindy* created a sensation and opened the doors for black music and musicians on the Broadway stage, performing for predominantly white audiences. The first wave of black musicals followed. Will Marion Cook himself wrote a succession of shows including three notable hits: *In Dahomey* (1902), satirizing the scheme to colonize American blacks in Africa; *In Abyssinia* (1906), an extravaganza laid in Africa; and *In Bandana Land* (1908), set in the American South.

After a lull during the second decade of the century, a second wave of black musical shows was inaugurated in 1921 by the famous *Shuffle Along,* with lyrics by Noble Sissle and music by Eubie Blake. One of its best-known tunes to this day is "I'm Just Wild About Harry." *Shuffle Along* is credited with helping to initiate the Harlem Renaissance of the 1920s—a period of unprecedented cultural activity and rising intellectual and artistic self-esteem among American urban blacks. From that time until the Depression, many all-black shows played Broadway. Blake and Sissle wrote three more, and among others of note were *Keep Shuffling* (1928) and *Hot Chocolates* (1929), with music by Thomas "Fats" Waller (1904–1943). A more recent black idiom, rhythm and blues, was brought to Broadway in a lavishly staged black adaptation of a classic (*The Wizard of Oz*) called *The Wiz* (1975).

THE MUSICAL IN ITS MATURITY: *SHOW BOAT* TO *WEST SIDE STORY*

The musical show had its period of greatest achievement in the thirty years that began with *Show Boat* (1927) and ended with *West Side Story* (1957). During this time the musical set itself new musical-dramatic problems (the term "musical

Here, members of the Jets gang show the tension and verve of Jerome Robbins' choreography for *West Side Story*. On CD 3, track 9, we hear the Jets sing "Cool," the song that occurs after a fight between the two gang leaders has ended in their deaths. Introducing the song, the new Jets leader, Ice, says, "Man, you wanna get past the cops when they start askin' you about tonight? You wanna live in this lousy world? You play it cool."

comedy" was no longer appropriate) and solved them, without ceasing to captivate and entertain its audience. It was a period of sustained creation by major writers devoting their talents principally to the live musical stage, and it was, moreover, a period when the popular stage still had its audience. Broadway was in a clear position of leadership and supplied America with some of its best popular music.

A glance at the thirty years under consideration reveals the dominance of five superbly equipped and successful composers: Jerome Kern (1885–1945), Irving Berlin (1888–1989), George Gershwin (1898–1937), Richard Rodgers (1902–1979), and Cole Porter (1891–1964), each of whom wrote music for at least a dozen shows. Four others also made important contributions: Kurt Weill (1900–1950) and, near the end of the period, Frederick Loewe (1901–1988), Frank Loesser (1910–1969), and Leonard Bernstein (1918–1990). During those thirty years, only one year passed without the appearance of a new show by at least one of these nine composers; in most years there were two or three. We will briefly examine the two musicals that frame this period: *Show Boat* and *West Side Story*.

Show Boat (1927)

Show Boat (music by Jerome Kern, book and lyrics by Oscar Hammerstein II) was adapted from Edna Ferber's (1885–1968) novel of 1926. It is representative of a great widening and deepening of the dramatic dimensions of the musical—a gain in both range and verisimilitude, without compromising the musical's essential nature as entertainment. Subject matter, plot, characterization, and range of emotion were all broadened.

Show Boat put real characters in believable situations—Magnolia, the sheltered daughter of the Mississippi showboat's owner, who survives a broken marriage with a riverboat gambler to make her way to the top as a musical comedy star; the half-caste Julie, singing two love songs that shattered the conventional sentimental mold, "Can't Help Lovin' Dat Man" and "Bill" ("an ordinary boy"). Also worthy of note is the realistic and sympathetic portrayal of African Americans on the stage. Joe's song "Ol' Man River" is especially famous in its interpretation by Paul Robeson. A poignant but minor plot element in the novel, the story of Julie has been emphasized in our time as groundbreaking for a novel written eighty years ago, as is her song about her love for an anti-stereotypical man, "Can't Help Lovin' Dat Man," in which she candidly acknowledges "dere ain't no reason why I should love dat man." There are no "perfect men" in this story.

The musical during this period gradually came to assign a far greater role to music itself; there was more of it, and it was given more work to do. Instead of being called upon only when it was time for a song or a dance, it underscored dialogue, accomplished transitions, or arranged itself in a sequence of movements that became the equivalent of the operatic scene. Furthermore, in the best musicals, the entire score had a unity to it. Jerome Kern took a large step in this direction in the score of *Show Boat* when he employed a few key snippets of melodies, associated with certain characters, at appropriate moments in the background. This was a technique long known to opera but new to the musical.

West Side Story (1957)

West Side Story (music by Leonard Bernstein, lyrics by Stephen Sondheim, book by Arthur Laurents) presented a modernized, urban plot derived from William Shakespeare's (1564–1616) timeless story, *Romeo and Juliet*. Instead of the feuding Montagues and Capulets we have two New York street gangs, the Jets (white) and the Sharks (Puerto Rican). In place of Romeo and Juliet, the impossible and tragic romance takes place between Tony, a member of the Jets, and Maria, the sister of the Sharks' leader. One interesting feature of this musical is its use of two contrasting types of music (jazz-rock and Latin) in juxtaposition to represent the essential conflict that is the basis of the story. This "coded" use of music—jazz-rock for the white gang and Latin for the Puerto Ricans—is analogous to Jerome Kern's use of certain melodic snippets to represent characters.

West Side Story reflects two important developments in the musical during its golden age: the increased importance of the dance, and the use of more sophisticated musical resources.

Song and dance had always gone together on the entertainment stage. But a new era began when George Balanchine, a noted Russian-born choreographer and ballet master who had come to the United States in 1933, was called upon to create a special jazz ballet for the show *On Your Toes* (1933) by Richard Rodgers and Lorenz Hart. The result was the famous "Slaughter on Tenth Avenue," an extended "story" ballet sequence within the musical. From that time forward, choreography and dance, in whatever style is appropriate, have become integrated ingredients in the best musicals. In *West Side Story*, it was the American choreographer Jerome Robbins (1918–1999) who contrived the dance and movement that are of central importance to the unfolding of the action. (This is one of the few musicals conceived and directed by a choreographer.) The score itself is nearly a succession of dances, with dance rhythms underlying even the most sentimental numbers.

During the thirty years framed by *Show Boat* and *West Side Story*, the Broadway show utilized more fully and freely the musical means that had long been at the disposal of classical composers. There is perhaps no better example of this practice than the score for *West Side Story* by Leonard Bernstein (1918–1990). Bernstein, a classically trained musician with a special admiration for Ludwig van Beethoven (1770–1827), used as a model in crafting the music for the dance sequence "Cool" (CD 3/9) one of Beethoven's most ingenious works, the *Great Fugue* (Op. 133) for string quartet. The sequence is titled "Fugue" in Bernstein's score, and he borrowed not only the main "fugue theme" from Beethoven's work, but also the whole feeling of barely restrained tension. The interruption of silence with brief fragments of music, now loud and now soft, produces the very same feeling of uneasy anticipation that pervades the opening of Beethoven's composition. (The analogous fugue in "Cool" begins at about 1:00 on this recording.) The beginning of "Cool," sung by Riff, the leader of the Jets (the white gang), draws appropriately enough from the "cool jazz" idiom with its incorporation of the vibraphone (see Chapter 16, p. 273). The extended instrumental passages indicate the central role of dance in this number.

Listening Cue "Cool" *West Side Story*, Original Broadway Cast (3:58)

Listen For ▪ "cool jazz" ▪ "classical" fugue at 1:00 ▪ extended instrumental passages

Visit http://www.music.wadsworth.com_3/Kingman for a full listening guide and other resources.

Riff:
Boy, boy, crazy boy,
Get cool, boy!
Got a rocket in your pocket,
Keep coolly cool, boy!
Don't get hot,
'Cause man, you got

Some high times ahead.
Take it slow and Daddy-O,
You can live it up and die in bed!

Boy, boy, crazy boy,
Stay loose, boy!
Breeze it, buzz it, easy does it.
Turn off the juice, boy!
Go man, go,
But not like a yo-yo schoolboy.
Just play it cool, boy,
Real cool!

THE MUSICAL SINCE *WEST SIDE STORY*

In the second half of the twentieth century, the musical continued to mine the familiar sources of ore for subjects: books, plays, and even operas (Giacomo Puccini's *La Bohème* for *Rent*, 1996). But it also searched further and further afield for its stories and ideas, from the Bible to the comic strip and the fairy tale. In a reversal of the usual process of producing a film version of a musical, older films became the basis for new musicals. Two spectacle musicals, *Grand Hotel* (1989) and *Sunset Boulevard* (1993), were both based on classic American films decades old. Show business itself has been a favorite subject—often in portrayals of the more selfish, ruthless, insensitive, and pathetic side of what goes on behind the scenes. The 2001 Broadway hit *The Producers* is a curious combination of trends. It is a musical adapted from a comic film of 1968 which itself deals with staging a musical (called *Springtime for Hitler*) that is designed to flop in order to defraud investors.

The period since *West Side Story* has to some extent seen an elimination of plot as an ingredient in the musical; a show can now simply be based on a concept. The concept could be the tangled relationships of sex, love, and marriage (*Company*, 1970); it could be the trauma of dancers desperately trying to be hired for shows (*A Chorus Line*, 1975); it could be the painter and his painting, and hence the relationship of art to life (*Sunday in the Park with George*, 1984). Or it could simply be the elaborately costumed setting of a series of descriptive verses by a well-known poet about a well-known domestic animal (*Cats*, 1981). As in the literature of the past quarter century, themes and issues have also become prominent. There could be mentioned in passing the onstage horror and bloodthirstiness of *Sweeney Todd* (1979). Of deeper contemporary significance is the theme of homosexual love, which appeared in *La Cage aux Folles* (1983) and was central to William Finn's *Falsettos* (1992). Works of the 1990s, including *Falsettos* and the "rock musical" *Rent* (1996) by Jonathan Larson (1960–1996), have dealt with the tragedy of AIDS.

Broadly considered, among the new musicals today there is a cleavage between, on one hand, the self-proclaimed "sophisticated shows," with far-out subjects, treatments, and messages, high critical acclaim, and small audiences and, on the other hand, the more popular shows—mostly the spectacles such as *Les Misérables* and *Phantom of the Opera*. These two types of shows are epitomized by two of the most powerful figures in the business today. As John Lahr has put it, the musical today is "caught between the boulevard nihilism of Stephen Sondheim, which doesn't send in the crowds, and the boulevard bravado of Lloyd Webber, which does." Of course, modern audiences have a third choice as well—revivals of classic shows such as *Show Boat* and *West Side Story*, which remain fixtures on the stages of professional as well as college and community theaters throughout the country.

OPERA IN AMERICA

The fundamental distinctions between opera and musical theater are fine ones. They reside most notably in the venues of performance, the extent to which music is used (opera tends to use it continuously), the singing styles particular to each, and, not least, perceptions among audiences and observers that opera is "elite and sophisticated" while musical theater is "popular and lowbrow." Yet both utilize the same essential ingredients—singing, acting, dancing, and a stage—to advance a plot or treat some theme, issue, or concept. Furthermore, some of the most interesting examples of America's contribution to the fundamentally European genre of opera have been those that draw from native folk elements and idioms, factors that move American opera, in particular, decidedly closer to the popular side of things.

Before the 1930s, opera in the United States was largely an exotic import often performed in a foreign language. There were notable exceptions, however. *Rip Van Winkle*, by George Frederick Bristow (1825–1898) was an opera on a thoroughly American tale by one of America's most competent composers, but its successful run of seventeen performances in New York in 1855 hardly set a precedent for American opera in its day. Scott Joplin's (1868–1917) *Treemonisha*, a remarkable work based on African American life and musical idioms, had only a barely noticed performance with piano accompaniment in 1915. (It was lavishly staged and recorded in 1975, and was awarded the Pulitzer Prize in 1976.) At the Metropolitan Opera of New York, a brief but explosive period of American operatic

Ray Fisher/Time Life Pictures/Getty Images

Here, Avon Long portrays the character Sportin' Life in a stage production of *Porgy and Bess*, first performed in 1935. Sportin' Life is the local supplier of "happy dust" (cocaine) and bootleg alcohol. In the song "It Ain't Necessarily So"—which we hear on CD 3, track 10—he offers his skeptical views on Bible stories: "They tell all you chill'en the devil's a villain, but it ain't necessarily so."

productions took place under the Italian general manager Giulio Gatti-Casazza (1869–1940) between 1910 and 1935. In that quarter-century, he staged sixteen new operas by native composers; many of these marked by American Indian and African American subjects and musical elements. In the thirty-eight years following Gatti-Casazza, under the next three managers, the number of American operas produced fell to a mere nine!

Porgy and Bess (1935) by George Gershwin (1898–1937), was America's landmark opera of the 1930s. It received its premiere at the Colonial Theatre in Boston, followed by a run of performances at Broadway's Alvin Theater. *Porgy and Bess* is a good example of the sometimes blurry distinctions between opera and musical theater; it has never really set comfortably in either one. Whatever debates may continue over its "true" nature, however, the work has settled firmly in the standard operatic repertoire. Gershwin himself referred to it as a "folk opera."

The Story Behind *Porgy and Bess*

In Charleston, South Carolina, in the early part of the twentieth century, there was a crippled black beggar named Samuel Smalls who got himself around by means of a cart pulled by a goat, and thus acquired the name of Goat-Sammy. A white Charleston writer, Du Bose Heyward, wrote a short novel—his first—based on this character, whom he renamed Porgy. He set the story in Catfish Row (originally Cabbage Row), a large ancient mansion with a courtyard that had become a black tenement. Through his knowledge of his city and its black people, he surrounded Porgy with thoroughly believable characters and spun a tale of humor, foreboding, violence, brief joy, and desolation. The novel appeared in 1926. George Gershwin read it, liked it, and wrote to the author proposing that they collaborate in making an opera out of it. (Heyward was at the time working with his wife on a play adaptation, which was staged in 1927. The play, in turn, nearly became a musical produced by Al Jolson, with music by Jerome Kern.)

Gershwin had many commitments at that time; after many delays, there was a period of intensive effort. Gershwin went to Charleston during the winter of 1934, and spent the summer of that year on one of the Sea Islands off its coast—composing, observing, and absorbing all he could of the atmosphere and the black people's music, with which he felt a great affinity. "Sheep, Sheep, Don't You Know the Road" (CD 1/7) is an example of the type of music he heard, and it is interesting in that light to hear the call-and-response pattern worked into the opera's famous "It Ain't Necessarily So" (CD 3/10).

Listening Cue "**It Ain't Necessarily So**" (George Gershwin, Ira Gershwin, Dorothy Heyward) *Porgy and Bess;* Lawrence Tibbett, vocal (3:03)

Listen For ▪ call-and-response pattern ▪ realism and authenticity of the music

Visit http://www.music.wadsworth.com_3/Kingman for a full listening guide and other resources.

Chorus:
It ain't necessarily so
It ain't necessarily so
De things dat yo' liable to read in de Bible
It ain't necessarily so

Verse:
Li'l David was small but oh my
Li'l David was small but oh my
He fought big Goliath who lay down and dieth
Li'l David was small but oh my

Wadoo, zim bam boddle-oo,
Hoodle ah da wa da,
Scatty wah !
Oh yeah ! . . .

Oh Jonah he lived in de whale
Oh Jonah he lived in de whale
For he made his home in dat fish's abdomen
Oh Jonah he lived in de whale

Li'l Moses was found in a stream
Li'l Moses was found in a stream
He floated on water 'til ole Pharaoh's daughter
She fished him she says from that stream

It ain't necessarily so
It ain't necessarily so
Dey tell all you chillun de debble's a villain
But 'taint necessarily so

To get into Hebben don' snap for a sebben
Live clean, don' have no fault
Oh I takes dat gospel whenever it's pos'ble
But wid a grain of salt

Methus'lah lived nine hundred years
Methus'lah lived nine hundred years
But who calls dat livin' when no gal'll give in
To no man what's nine hundred years

I'm preachin' dis sermon to show
It ain't nessa, ain't nessa
Ain't nessa, ain't nessa
It ain't necessarily so

Although Gershwin and collaborators used no actual African American folk songs, there are touches of unmistakable realism and authenticity in the music.

This came from a thorough immersion in the musical ambience of blacks in South Carolina. Du Bose Heyward described how, on a visit to a meeting of the Gullah blacks on a remote Carolina Sea Island, Gershwin joined wholeheartedly in the "shouting." Of his whole South Carolina experience Heyward said, "To George it was more like a homecoming than an exploration."

American Opera in Relation to American Culture After the 1930s

By the 1930s, America was developing its own diverse musical voices. In the years that followed, a number of operas were composed that had a valid and palpable relation to the culture of the country. None fits this description better than Virgil Thomson's *The Mother of Us All* (1947), with libretto by Gertrude Stein, who, despite her self-exile, continued to feel a strong identification with her native land. Thomson explains in his preface to the score: "*The Mother of Us All* is a pageant. Its theme is the winning in the United States of political rights for women. Its story is the life and career of Susan B. Anthony (1820–1906). Some of the characters are historical, others imaginary. They include figures as widely separated in time as John Quincy Adams and Lillian Russell." The vocal writing is exceptionally true to the rhythms of speech; and the music, of a self-effacing simplicity, reinforces its relevance through the use of nineteenth-century-style waltzes, marches, and hymnlike tunes. After *The Mother of Us All*, the floodgates were opened for a multitude of works having to do with the culture of the country. Some took historical figures as their basis, such as Douglas Moore's *Ballad of Baby Doe* (1956) and *Carry Nation* (1966). Operas based on novels included *Regina* (1949), by Marc Blitzstein, on Lillian Hellman's *The Little Foxes*, and *Of Mice and Men* (1970), by Carlisle Floyd, on John Steinbeck's novel of the same name. A shorter work by Lukas Foss is *The Jumping Frog of Calaveras County* (1950), based on the Mark Twain story. Jack Beeson used a famous American murder as the basis for *Lizzie Borden* (1965).

Over the past quarter of a century, opera seems to have found its niche by focusing on current events and figures. *Nixon in China* (1987) was commissioned from John Adams (b. 1947) by the Houston Grand Opera. The first act fulfills all the expectations of "grand opera." President Nixon and Chairman Mao have bestowed on them, in late-twentieth-century musical and stage terms, all the operatic ceremony associated in eighteenth- and nineteenth-century operas with kings and pharaohs. The spectacle everyone remembers, the landing on stage of the *Spirit of 76* and the emergence of Nixon and his wife, Pat, is the equivalent, as Adams has wittily observed, of the onstage elephants in *Aida* or the burning of Valhalla in *Die Götterdämmerung*—"the things people pay big bucks to see." Repetitive music seems to work well in *Nixon in China*. Here the music, without notable climaxes, stays in the background (as in traditional Chinese opera), changing harmony and color at appropriate times, and letting the vocal lines, which fit the inflections of the text, stand out in relief. Other grand operas in recent years have also had as their subjects present-day people and events. Adams treated a notorious assassination in the Middle East in *The Death of Klinghoffer* (1991). Anthony Davis' opera *X: The Life and Times of Malcolm X*, on the assassinated black leader, was produced in 1986. Another opera having to do with assassination is *Harvey Milk* (1995), by Stewart Wallace, which deals with the fatal shooting of San Francisco Mayor George Moscone and Supervisor Harvey Milk, San Francisco's first openly gay elected official, in 1978.

In recent years, the most anticipated and hyped event in the opera world has been the premiere of *The First Emperor,* by the Chinese-born composer Tan Dun (b. 1957). Tan Dun's work is perhaps best known through his Oscar-winning film score for *Crouching Tiger, Hidden Dragon* (2000). In advance of the scheduled December 2006 premiere of *The First Emperor* at New York's Metropolitan Opera (the house that commissioned the work), the *New York Times* publicized the event with a long series of articles on the opera that might signal a new era for that particular art form in the United States. To some extent, it suggests a return to the foreign imports and influences that dominated opera in America prior to the 1930s. But if that period was marked heavily by imports and influences from Western Europe, the new age of American opera will likely take its cues from the East.

PROJECTS

1. Compare the text of an original play with the "book," or libretto, of a musical show based on that play. Note technical changes and changes of plot, emphasis, and characterization. What do you think were the reasons for the changes? (For example, compare *Oklahoma!* with *Green Grow the Lilacs.*)
2. If there is a producing opera company in a city near you, make a survey of the percentage of American operas produced in this season's programming.
3. Read a story or a play that has been made into an opera by an American composer, comparing the original with the opera. Note the changes that have been made, and try to determine if they were made to fulfill the requirements of opera. For example, you could compare Du Bose Heyward's novel *Porgy,* or the play adapted by the author and his wife, with the opera *Porgy and Bess.*
4. In a brief paper, assess the pros and cons from your point of view of producing operas on current "newsworthy" happenings, especially murders or assassinations. Include a consideration of both the motivations and the dangers involved.

ADDITIONAL LISTENING

Adams, John. *Nixon in China.* Orchestra of St. Luke's. Cond. Edo de Waart. WEA/Atlantic/Nonesuch 79177.

Bernstein, Leonard. *West Side Story* (original Broadway cast). Musical director, Max Goberman. Sony 60724.

Gershwin, George. *Porgy and Bess* (cast recording). Houston Grand Opera. Cond. John DeMain. RCA 2109.

Kern, Jerome. *Show Boat* (1988 studio cast). London Sinfonietta. Cond. John McGlinn. Angel Records 49108.

14 POPULAR SONG, DANCE, AND MARCH MUSIC FROM THE JACKSONIAN ERA TO THE ADVENT OF ROCK

J ust over a half-century ago, when little serious attention was given to the study of popular culture, a writer began his history of popular music with the assertion that it "is an index to the life and history of a nation" (Spaeth 3). The songs that are enjoyed and sung by a broad segment of the populace do indeed afford a vivid picture not only of the life and history but also of the attitudes, feelings, motivations, prejudices, mores—in fact, the dominant *worldview*—of an era. Popular songs fulfill this role even better than does the popular musical stage. Musical theater, for all its popularity, could not possibly reach and be enjoyed by the masses to the extent that popular song could. An age that numbered its theatergoers in the tens of thousands would number in the millions those who sang its songs.

POPULAR SONG FROM THE 1830S THROUGH THE CIVIL WAR

At the beginning of the preceding chapter, we noted the changes that were then under way in what has been called the Jacksonian era (1829–1837) in American social, political, and cultural life, and the developments in music printing that went hand in hand with the growth of a mass market for sheet music. The growth of this market, however, and with it the birth of distinctively American song, was related to far more than technology. Nicholas Tawa begins his book *A Music for the Millions* by observing:

> A turbulent era in American history opened with Andrew Jackson's election to the presidency and his passionate attack on privilege. It closed with Lincoln's election and the onset of the Civil War. From 1828 to 1861, new democratic beliefs and practices interspersed themselves aggressively among older aristocratic ways of thinking. . . . Inevitably, music reflected the social, economic, and political upheaval of these years. The once-dominant European-derived composition mirroring a narrow, leisured constituency was soon overwhelmed by a different type of musical work,

one imbued with ideas favored by the common citizenry and exposed in the simplest verbal and melodic terms—the American popular song. (1)

The Parlor Song

The most flourishing genre of the period was what has become known as the parlor song. Parlor songs were purchased by, and sung in the living rooms of, the rapidly expanding numbers of middle-class families in cities and towns—to the accompaniment (kept purposely simple) of the piano, the harmonium (reed organ), or the guitar. Indeed, simplicity and directness of expression were values that were prized in these songs, even when they were performed by professionals.

Melodies from Italian operas, principally those of Rossini (1792–1868), Donizetti (1797–1848), and Bellini (1801–1835), were in circulation with English words and were more popular in America in the antebellum period than is generally supposed (Hamm, Chapter 4). But the basic models for the new popular song are to be found much closer to oral tradition. Irish folk melodies, especially as adapted and given new words by the Irish poet Thomas Moore (1779–1852), were popular in the United States throughout the nineteenth century, beginning with the first printing of Moore's famous collection, *Irish Melodies,* in 1808. The unadorned attractiveness and accessibility of the melodies (some of which are clearly related to dance tunes) helped win them wide acceptance. Then, too, Moore's new words often struck a note of melancholy and nostalgia that somehow, paradoxically for a new country with ever-widening possibilities, seemed in accord with nineteenth-century sentiments. Much of Moore's large collection is unfamiliar today, but a few of the songs have entered permanently into the body of American song, including "The Minstrel Boy" and "The Last Rose of Summer." Other imports from the British Isles were popular and helped set the American parlor song on its course. Among the most popular of these were "Home, Sweet Home" (1823) and "Long, Long Ago" (1833).

Surveying native-born American songs, we find many that were sentimental or nostalgic in tone—often having to do with separation, usually by death. "Flow Gently, Sweet Afton" (1838), with music by the American J. E. Spilman on a poem by Robert Burns, was one. "The Ocean Burial" (1850), a "favorite and touching ballad" with music by George N. Allen to words by Rev. Edwin H. Chapin, was another. The words to "The Ocean Burial," which begin "O! bury me not in the deep, deep sea," were later brought ashore and transformed into the text for one of the most popular of all cowboy songs, "O Bury Me Not on the Lone Prairie."

George Frederick Root (1820–1895) wrote such songs on the subject of death as "The Hazel Dell" (1853) and "Rosalie, the Prairie Flower" (1855). The best known of the songs of love, separation, and death by Stephen Foster began to appear in the 1850s, including "The Village Maiden" (1855), "Gentle Annie" (1856), and, perhaps his most famous song in this vein, "Jeanie with the Light Brown Hair" (1854). Stephen Foster himself, and the breadth of his song output, will be dealt with in due course.

Touring Professionals: Henry Russell and the Hutchinson Family

Parlor songs were not confined to the parlor; in the period before the Civil War, professional singers were on the road giving concerts. These performers played an important role in shaping public taste, in acquainting the public with new songs, and in promoting them. That even songs for the "parlor" could profit by such promotion is shown by the sheet-music covers, which frequently advertised songs as having been "sung by," or even "sung with distinguished applause by," some popular singer.

One of the most successful and influential of these was the Englishman Henry Russell (1812–1900 or 1901), who visited the United States twice between 1836 and 1844. A most effective singer who also played his own piano accompaniments, he pioneered as a "one-man show" at a time when few other performers could hold the interest of an audience for an entire evening by themselves. His style and his material (he performed mostly his own songs) were designed to be spellbinding. His diction was such that every word was understood. Thus he was eminently fitted for popularity at a time when the main purpose of both singer and song was to arouse the emotions.

His songs tell us much about what was popular with antebellum audiences. Of his sentimental songs the best known are "The Old Arm Chair" (1840) and "Woodman! Spare That Tree!" (1837). Both have as their basis a special kind of sentimentality prevalent in the nineteenth century—sentimental attachment to a particular object. Incidentally, this kind of sentimentality has survived in American popular culture and is frequently found in country music, as shown in songs such as "Send Me the Pillow That You Dream On" (see p. 111).

> Woodman! spare that tree!
> Touch not a single bough;
> In youth it sheltered me,
> And I'll protect it now;
> 'Twas my forefather's hand
> That placed it near his cot,
> There, woodman, let it stand,
> Thy axe shall harm it not!

More overtly dramatic songs of Henry Russell were such extended scenic monologues as "The Ship on Fire" and "The Maniac." Real spellbinders that depended for their effect on acting ability as well as singing, these were almost like one-man operatic scenes. Though it is clear that in the case of "Woodman! Spare That Tree!" the plea to save the tree was on sentimental, not ecological, grounds, many of Russell's songs did espouse social causes. The emotions so effectively aroused in his hearers were meant to be directed toward the alleviation of some current evil. That accorded with a prevalent view of the time as to the moral function of art, and especially of song. "The Maniac" was not merely a melodramatic scene; it also called attention to the wretched conditions in the mental asylums of his day. "The Dream of the Reveller" (1843) dealt with the evils of alcohol abuse, and after his return to England Russell wrote many antislavery songs. Thus, what Russell's compatriot Charles Dickens was aiming to do by literary means Russell apparently aimed to do with song.

Among the foremost American performer-composers to follow Henry Russell's example were the Hutchinson Family Singers. From a rural New England background of strong convictions, they composed and sang songs supporting many of the causes in which they so firmly believed. The cause that most absorbed them during the 1840s, their period of greatest activity, was the abolition of slavery. They sang frequently at antislavery meetings and rallies, appearing with the most radical abolitionists of the time, Wendell Phillips and William Lloyd Garrison. They participated in street marches, and on their tours they refused to sing in halls that would not admit blacks. They were well acquainted with Frederick Douglass, the escaped slave who settled in Lynn, Massachusetts, and they traveled with him to England. Abolition was by no means a universally popular cause, even in the North, and the Hutchinsons were hissed on occasion when they sang songs deemed "political." Their most famous abolitionist song, "Get Off the Track" (CD 3/11), was often sung to mixed reactions; it inspired wild enthusiasm among abolitionist sympathizers, and abuse, vocal and sometimes physical, from others.

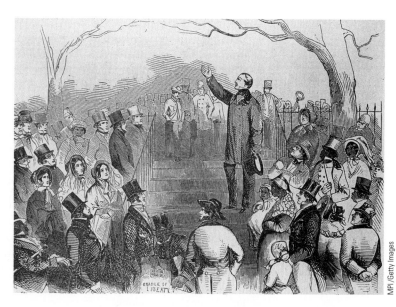

The Hutchinson Family Singers often appeared at antislavery rallies—such as we see here on Boston Common in 1835 (note the free blacks in the crowd)—in company with writer William Lloyd Garrison and Frederick Douglass, ex-slave and eloquent speaker. These contacts led Jesse Hutchinson to write the lyrics to "Get Off the Track," the abolitionist song that we hear on CD 3, track 11. The abolitionist movement, along with the era's other far-reaching reform movements (temperance and public schooling), grew out of America's Second Great Awakening, the religious revival that encouraged social activism in the early 1800s.

Listening Cue "Get Off the Track" The Hutchinson Family Singers;
George Berglund, Wayne Dalton, Bill Rollie, Judy Sjerven, solos; Linda Steen, piano (2:42)

CD 3
11

Listen For ▪ clear message ▪ train metaphors ▪ tune from a minstrel song

Visit http://www.music.wadsworth.com_3/Kingman for a full listening guide and other resources.

Ho! the car, Emancipation,
Rides majestic through our nation
Bearing on its train, the story
Liberty! a nation's glory.
Roll it along! Roll it along!
Roll it along! Thro' the nation
Freedom's car, Emancipation
Roll it along! Roll it along!
Roll it along! through the nation
Freedom's car, Emancipation.

Railroads to emancipation
Cannot rest on Clay foundation
And the tracks of 'The Magician'
Are but railroads to perdition.
Pull up the rails! Pull up the rails!
Pull up the rails! Emancipation
Cannot rest on such foundation.
Pull up the rails! Pull up the rails!
Pull up the rails! Emancipation
Cannot rest on such foundation.

First of all the train, and greater,
Speeds the dauntless Liberator
Onward cheered amid hosannas,
And the waving of free banners.
Roll it along! Roll it along!
Roll it along! spread your banners
While the people shout hosannas.
Roll it along! Roll it along!
Roll it along! spread your banners
While the people shout hosannas.

All true friends of emancipation,
Haste to freedom's rail road station;
Quick into the cars get seated,
All is ready, and completed.
Put on the steam! Put on the steam!
Put on the steam! All are crying,
And the liberty flags are flying.
Put on the steam! Put on the steam!
Put on the steam! All are crying,
And the liberty flags are flying.

Let the ministers and churches
Leave behind sectarian lurches;
Jump on board the car of freedom
Ere it be too late to need them.
Sound the alarm! Sound the alarm!
Sound the alarm! Pulpit's thunder!
Ere too late, you see your blunder.
Sound the alarm! Sound the alarm!
Sound the alarm! Pulpit's thunder!
Ere too late, you see your blunder.

Hear the mighty car wheels humming!
Now look out! the engine's coming!
Church and statesmen! hear the thunder!
Clear the track! or you'll fall under.
Get off the track! Get off the track!
Get off the track! all are singing,
While the liberty bell is ringing.
Get off the track! Get off the track!
Get off the track! all are singing,
While the liberty bell is ringing.

This early protest song is not folk music, but otherwise it certainly fits into the context of Chapter 6 as an "instrument of advocacy." The message is clear, and brought into sharper focus by the consistent use of train metaphors to drive it home. Like many protest songs, it uses an already existing tune. The irony in this particular case is that it is set to the tune of a blackface minstrel song, "Old Dan Tucker."

Stephen Foster

Without doubt the best-known composer of the entire century was Stephen Collins Foster (1826–1864). Although the popular Foster image is based on a good deal of misinformation and misinterpretation, the facts, insofar as modern scholarship can determine them, are more interesting than the fiction, and his accomplishments, his legacy, and his influence are undeniably impressive.

Foster was born as the ninth child into a fairly prosperous family in Pittsburgh. It was not to be expected, either of his family or of the mercantile environment of Pittsburgh in the 1830s, that his aptitude for music would be especially encouraged. Pursuing music in spite of that, Foster achieved enough success with some of his songs in the late 1840s (notably "Oh! Susanna") to induce him to sign contracts with publishers in New York and Baltimore. He actually became a professional songwriter in the 1850s and was able, for a time, to support himself in that way. His contracts provided for the payment of continuing royalties on sales—potentially a very favorable arrangement. But by the mid-1850s, serious problems began to surface, as manifested in his being persistently in debt (mostly to his brothers); in periodic, and ultimately prolonged, separations from his family; in a failure to manage prudently such resources

President Andrew Jackson—shown here holding the charter for the Second Bank of the United States—vetoed its renewal, on the grounds that fraud and corruption made it a tool of the rich, and redirected federal money to private banks. Ironically, the collapse of the Second Bank, combined with his demand for payments in gold or silver coin (over paper money), triggered the Panic of 1837, a severe economic depression (then called "hard times") that crushed middle-class Americans—as this cartoon vividly shows. Stephen Foster's "Hard Times Come Again No More," which we hear on CD 3 track 12, reflects the sorrow that the composer no doubt witnessed.

as he had; and finally, in the alcoholism that defeated him in his last years in New York.

Foster's output of songs can be divided roughly into two categories: parlor songs and songs for the minstrel stage. The songs he wrote for the minstrel stage (described variously on their covers—"plantation melody," "plantation song," "Ethiopian melody") are with few exceptions his most enduring. The comic songs, with their inherent rhythmic vitality and their simple but catchy melodic lines, show, of all his output, the closest relationship to the rough-hewn folk songs, sacred and secular, of the antebellum frontier. These exuberant, high-spirited songs for the minstrel stage include "Oh! Susanna" (1848), "Camptown Races" (1850), "Nelly Bly" (1850), "Way Down in Ca-i-ro" (1850, with its original piano part marked "a la banjo"), "Ring de Banjo" (1851), and "The Glendy Burk" (1860). The dialect so typical of minstrel material was used in Foster's early songs (such as "My Brudder Gum," and "Ring de Banjo"), but he dropped this mannerism in his later songs, rightly thinking that it would restrict the universality of their appeal.

The sentimental minstrel songs (Foster himself used the word "pathetic," in the sense of evoking pathos), unlike the comic songs, portray blacks with a profound sympathy, as human beings who felt the pain of separation and the unending weariness of a life of servitude—a weariness to be relieved only by an often welcome death. The grief of separation—whether from loved ones or from an irrevocable past—is uppermost in the four best-known "pathetic plantation" songs: "Old Folks at Home," "My Old Kentucky Home," "Old Black Joe," and "Old Uncle Ned."

The misery and hopelessness of poverty were not often dealt with in the parlor song, but one example, suffused with a degree of genuine sympathy, stands out: Stephen Foster's "Hard Times Come Again No More" (CD 3/12) from 1855. Though the lyrics do not mention blacks or imply slavery, the song was a hit on the minstrel stage.

Listening Cue "Hard Times Come Again No More" The Hutchinson Family Singers; Wayne Dalton, solo; Linda Steen, piano (3:05)

Listen For ▪ verse and chorus form ▪ quartet singing in the chorus ▪ melodeon

Visit http://www.music.wadsworth.com_3/Kingman for a full listening guide and other resources.

Let us pause in life's pleasures and count its many tears
While we all sup sorrow with the poor:
There's a song that will linger forever in our ears:
Oh! Hard Times, come again no more.

Chorus:
'Tis the song, the sigh of the weary;
Hard Times, Hard Times, come again no more:
Many days you have lingered around my cabin door,
Oh! Hard Times, come again no more.

While we seek mirth and beauty and music light and gay
There are frail forms fainting at the door:
Though their voices are silent, their pleading looks will say
Oh! Hard Times, come again no more.
(Chorus)

'Tis a sigh that is wanted across the troubled wave
'Tis a wail that is heard upon the shore
'Tis a dirge that is murmured around the lowly grave
Oh! Hard Times, come again no more.
(Chorus)

This song exhibits the typical nineteenth-century form of verse and chorus. It is an indication of the popularity of quartet singing by informal groups, in the home and other social gatherings. The chorus was frequently arranged and printed for four-part chorus of two sopranos, tenor, and bass, as it is sung on this recording. Though this convivial practice had declined by the 1890s, to judge from the printed music, the name "chorus," as applied to the more familiar part of the song, has survived into the present. The melodeon, also known as the harmonium, or reed organ, is a keyboard instrument operated by foot-powered bellows. It is heard prominently at the beginning of this recording. Developed in the first part of the nineteenth century, it was very popular as a parlor instrument until the 1920s.

A consideration of Foster's "pathetic plantation songs" would be incomplete without taking account of the appearance in 1852 of Harriet Beecher Stowe's novel *Uncle Tom's Cabin,* the central theme of which is slavery. The novel achieved instant popularity and was almost immediately adapted for the stage; William Austin writes that nine versions of it were produced in New York before the end of 1852. Foster originally conceived "My Old Kentucky Home" with the play in mind, though he changed his final version, deleting the name Uncle Tom. At one time or another, however, at least four of his plantation songs—"Old Folks at Home," "My Old Kentucky Home," "Massa's in de Cold Ground" (sung by chorus), and "Old Black Joe"—were sung in stage versions of *Uncle Tom's Cabin.*

Songs of the Civil War

Uncle Tom's Cabin was only one of many portents of the tragedy of epic proportions that America was to live through in the next decade. The Civil War (1861–1865), her greatest national trauma, left an indelible mark on all aspects of the culture. Popular song was quick to mirror the war's events, its ideals, its motivations, its slogans, and, of course, its anguish. By the time of the Civil War, the popular-music publishing industry was in place and functioning. It was able to get songs to the public with an immediacy that rivaled that of the newspapers. Within a few days of the Confederate bombardment of Fort Sumter, which began the war, George F. Root's "The First Gun Is Fired!" was in print. More than in any other period in our history, popular song was the journalism of the emotions.

To fill the immediate need for songs, both sides rushed to fit new words to existing tunes. New verses to "The Star-Spangled Banner" were attempted by both sides. "The Yellow Rose of Texas" became "The Song of the Texas Rangers," and Henry Russell's famous "Woodman! Spare That Tree! (touch not a single bough)" became "Traitor! Spare That Flag! (touch not a single star)." The ambivalence of Maryland as a border state was illustrated by the fact that both sides converted the German song "O Tannenbaum" into "Maryland, My Maryland," but with two sets of words urging diametrically opposed loyalties. At a time when secessionist feelings were running high, "Dixie" was used in a show in New Orleans (with no credit given to Dan Emmett as the composer); from there it spread rapidly throughout the South, becoming virtually the musical symbol of the Confederacy. It was not exclusively the property of the South, however; it could be found, with appropriate words, in virtually every state.

The other song most often associated with the Civil War is "The Battle Hymn of the Republic." It made its way, by gradual transformation, from a camp meeting song with the words "Say, brothers, will you meet us on Canaan's happy shore?" to a marching song used by Union regiments, growing out of that famous incident at Harpers Ferry in 1859, with the somewhat crude words "John Brown's body lies a-mouldering in the grave," to the loftier hymn, with words by Julia Ward Howe, that we know today. (For a capsule history see Heaps and Heaps 50–54.)

As rallying songs, the South had "The Bonnie Blue Flag" (1861), a "southern patriotic song" with an Irish lilt, by Harry Macarthy; the North had George F. Root's "The Battle Cry of Freedom" (CD 3/13) from 1862, an immensely popular song.

Listening Cue "The Battle Cry of Freedom" George Shirley, tenor; William Bolcom, piano (2:09)

Listen For ▪ verse and chorus form ▪ solo singing in the chorus ▪ rallying lyrics

Visit http://www.music.wadsworth.com_3/Kingman for a full listening guide and other resources.

Yes, we'll rally round the flag, boys, we'll rally once again,
Shouting the battle cry of Freedom,
We will rally from the hillside, we'll gather from the plain,
Shouting the battle cry of Freedom.

Chorus:
The Union forever, Hurrah boys, hurrah!
Down with the Traitor, Up with the Star;
While we rally round the flag, boys, Rally once again,
Shouting the battle cry of Freedom.

We will welcome to our numbers
The loyal, true and brave,
Shouting the Battle Cry of Freedom!
And although he may be poor
He shall never be a slave,
Shouting the Battle Cry of Freedom!
(*Chorus*)

So we're springing to the call
From the east and from the west
Shouting the Battle Cry of Freedom!
And we'll hurl the rabble crew
From the land we love the best,
Shouting the Battle Cry of Freedom!
(*Chorus*)

The importance of this song in the Union armies is attested by the fact that on the printed sheet music of another of Root's songs there appears this note: "In the Army of the Cumberland, the Soldiers sing the Battle-Cry when going into action, by order of the Commanding general." Once again, the song is in the popular verse and chorus form. Notice, however, that the "chorus" is performed by just one voice instead of a quartet as heard in "Hard Times Come Again No More" (CD 3/12). Although there is no contrast in the number of voices, the "chorus" music in "The Battle Cry of Freedom" is clearly distinguished from that of the verses by engaging the singer's higher vocal range.

POPULAR SONG FROM THE CIVIL WAR THROUGH THE RAGTIME ERA

The half-century between the Civil War and World War I (1914–1918) witnessed changes that mark the period as the beginning of the modern age. As such it presents contradictory images. Westward expansion, epitomized by the completion of the transcontinental railroad in 1869, a scant four years after Robert E. Lee's surrender at Appomattox, was perceived as progress; yet it was accomplished at the shameful cost of killing off many of the original inhabitants who had lived on the land for millennia, and destroying the survivors' way of life. Industry and invention flourished, manufacturing and selling goods undreamed of in any previous time, and raising the material standard of living (for most) far above what it had been; this was perceived as progress, and was celebrated in the many fairs and expositions that were held. Yet it was achieved only with a frightful waste of natural resources; and in many cases workers who produced the goods were exploited beyond the point of endurance, and strife between management ("the bosses") and the newly formed and struggling labor unions reached shockingly bloody proportions. Cities grew and prospered, as did the nation overall; yet corruption among those who governed was all too common. Immigrants poured into the country from both Europe and Asia; their hopes and prospects for a better life were on the whole justified, yet discrimination degraded many and worked against their entering the "mainstream" of American life.

The Gilded Age (to use Mark Twain's famous term) has been given many interpretations. For all its excesses—its "crass materialism" and flagrant examples of corruption and waste—the age of "rowdy adolescence" was also a time of solid accomplishments; schools, colleges, and libraries were built as well as bridges and railroads, and there was the Chautauqua Institution (founded in 1874 as an intellectual and artistic retreat) as well as the working-class burlesque.

Popular Song Before Tin Pan Alley

Popular song, which had itself become an industry by the end of the century, did not mirror the full range of the contradictory images just described. The most popular topical songs were those that presented the positive aspects of events; Henry Clay Work's enthusiastic tribute to progress, "Crossing the Great Sierra" (published in 1869 after the completion of the railroad), was more successful than his sympathetic and prophetic lament, "The Song of the Red Man" (1868), which has the following lines:

> Driven westward we came, but the paleface was here,
> With his sharp axe and death-flashing gun;
> And his great Iron Horse now is rumbling in the rear;
> O my brave men! your journey is done.

A few well-established songwriters wrote songs about social issues. Work, the composer of "The Song of the Red Man," also wrote one of the most popular temperance songs, "Come Home, Father" (1864). George Frederick Root wrote "The Hand That Holds the Bread" in 1874, in support of the Grange movement rallying farmers against middlemen and monopolists. Septimus Winner wrote "Out of Work" in 1877, reflecting one of the frequent depressions of the period. But except for a few of the temperance songs, songs of social comment were not big items in the general marketplace.

The Civil War left a legacy of bitterness, war-weariness, sorrow, and a general depletion of spirit. Songs of gentle sentiment were popular. "Whispering Hope (Oh how welcome thy voice)," by Septimus Winner (1868), speaks of comfort after sorrow. There was a preoccupation with growing old; three typical songs of love and remembrance in old age are all still well known: "When You and I Were Young, Maggie" (1866), "Sweet Genevieve" (1869), and "Silver Threads Among the Gold" (1873). Even the waltzing exuberance of "The Flying Trapeze" (1868), with its gracefully arching melody expressive of the swings of the aerialist and its ruefully comic final verses, is tinged with the sadness and hopelessness of lost love.

> Once I was happy, but now I'm forlorn,
> Like an old coat that is tattered and torn.

In many ways the popular song of the period was linked more to the past than to the future. There was (relatively) an innocence, a sincerity, and, above all, an artistic and business climate in which the individual, regardless of location or commercial connections, could still succeed. Thomas Westendorf, who wrote "I'll Take You Home Again, Kathleen" in Plainfield, Indiana, in 1876, was later sent a check for fifty dollars each month for many years "in gratitude" by the publisher, John Church & Co. (in Cincinnati), who, having bought the song outright, was under no contractual obligation to do so (Hamm 264). The whole story of this "hit" coming out of Plainfield, Indiana, would have been unthinkable (or at least highly unlikely) two decades later.

Tin Pan Alley: Popular Music Publishing Becomes an Industry

As American cities became larger, wealthier, and more sophisticated in the last two decades of the nineteenth century, two things happened that affected popular music. One was the increased vitality, and ultimately the Americanization, of the popular musical stage, as we saw in the last chapter. The other was the gradual emergence of a centralized industry for the publication and promotion of American popular songs. Both phenomena were centered in New York City.

Broadway and Tin Pan Alley were interrelated in complex ways but were never one and the same. They cohabited the same area in the beginning—what was then the theater district of East 14th Street in Manhattan, where Tony Pastor's famous Opera House, the home of vaudeville, was located. But the close relationship exemplified in this proximity grew looser over time, and as the musical theater developed, under the powerful influence of the great show composers of the new century, the stratification of American popular song took place. In craftsmanship and sophistication, Broadway show songs, from Victor Herbert to Jerome Kern, were at the top. George Gershwin discovered this early in his career. James Maher (in his introduction to Wilder's *American Popular Song*) describes Gershwin's "almost ecstatic sense of revelation when he first heard music by Jerome Kern"—music that made him conscious that most popular music was of inferior quality, and that musical comedy music was made of better material (xxxiv). Beginning in the 1890s, theater songs dominate the great canon of American popular song, which includes most of the "evergreens" such as "Smoke Gets in Your Eyes."

Slightly below the theater songs was a class of songs that began to appear in the 1930s, the movie songs. This category also includes a number of evergreens: "The Way You Look Tonight," "You'd Be So Nice to Come Home To," "Over the Rainbow," and "Laura" are among them.

Beyond theater songs and movie songs was that vast category of songs purveyed by what Maher has called "the marketplace-oriented music publishing companies known collectively as Tin Pan Alley." Its songs came forth in prodigious quantities, only the tiniest fraction of which attained "hit" status. Most of them were short-lived, manufactured to conform to the passing fashions of the year, the season, the month. Yet here too, as we shall see, were some "evergreens."

Painting by Victor Gilbert (1867–1935)/© Christie's Images/CORBIS

This painting, *The Ball*, captures a way of life that new fortunes created during America's Gilded Age. The post–Civil War economy generated wealth for many businessmen—including music publishers—but especially for the so-called robber barons (men who built immense wealth through ruthless business deals), such as Andrew Carnegie in steel, John D. Rockefeller in oil, and Cornelius Vanderbilt in railroads. As a journalist remarked after a theater opening, "The Vanderbilts and people of that ilk perfumed the air with the odor of crisp new greenbacks."

New York's dominance in publishing popular songs was not achieved at the hands of the old-line publishers—certainly not at the hands of publishers who would send monthly checks to songwriters out of sheer gratitude. As Sanjek has put it:

> [The] established arts- and parlor-music publishers failed to perceive the future. It was in the hands of music publishers specializing in new popular American music—first formed around 1885, whose founders . . . were, as one of them, Isidore Witmark, remembered, "youngsters who had caught on and had a fair notion of the direction in which they were headed. What they knew least about was music and words, what they cared about least might be answered in the same phrase. They discovered that there was money in popular song." (7–8)

The basic vehicle for the dissemination of the popular song, and therefore the basic commodity of the industry, continued, until the 1920s, to be sheet music. The money in popular song, it was realized by these new entrepreneurs, was in songs that sold not in thousands of copies but in millions. In the 1880s sales began to climb toward that goal, and in 1892 the song that perhaps more than any other symbolizes the era—"After the Ball," by Charles K. Harris—sold more than 2 million copies in its first few years, with sales eventually reaching more than 10 million.

For a song to reach anything even approaching that volume of sales (few did, and most barely paid for their printing costs), of course it had to be publicized, and that became a profession in itself, in which ingenuity and brashness paid off. The exploits of song "pluggers" included bribing performers across a wide spectrum, from established professionals, to hopefuls who sang on the popular amateur nights, to the Italian *padrone* who leased street organs to immigrant organ-grinders.

As to the form of the songs themselves, the earlier four-part chorus, typical of the Stephen Foster era, was replaced by the solo "chorus" (the older name stuck, though it was no longer literally accurate). In the conventional Tin Pan Alley song, it was the "chorus" that had the identifiable "tune"; the "verse," with its lead-in narration, was the part hardly anyone remembered, and it was frequently omitted, especially when the tunes were later used as jazz "standards." By this time, the squarer 4/4 meter of the typical antebellum song had given way to 3/4 and the "waltz song" dominated the field. Examples of waltz songs include "After the Ball" (1892, by Charles K. Harris); "Daisy Bell," better known as "A Bicycle Built for Two" (1892, by Harry Dacre); "The Band Played On" (1895, by Charles Ward); and "Meet Me in St. Louis" (1904, by Kerry Mills). The last of these was written as a promotional song for the 1904 world's fair.

A broad range of songs played quite deliberately on the sentiments. These were written out of sincere feelings or out of shrewd calculation as to what would sell. More likely, they were written as a combination of the two. The sentimental song was a big seller, possibly because it offered an opportunity for emotional release, even if vicarious, at a time when the outward display of emotion was not acceptable in Protestant middle-class society. Prominent in this genre were the songs about women either bought or betrayed—women not as objects of romance but as objects of pity. So much have these songs been associated with the period that their very titles have entered the language as phrases symbolic of the late Victorian age: "She May Have Seen Better Days" (1894), "Take Back Your Gold" (1897), "Only a Bird in a Gilded Cage" (1900). Songs about separation by death were numerous; familiar are "Dear Old Girl" (1903) and "My Gal Sal" (1905). Many a song that is actually about death reveals the fact only in the verse; the better-known chorus has more general sentiments. Examples are "When You Were Sweet Sixteen" (1898), "You Tell Me Your Dream, I'll Tell You Mine" (1899), and "In the Shade of the Old Apple Tree" (1905).

The Ragtime Song

The nature and origins of ragtime, whose brief but intense flowering began in the 1890s and was over before 1920, will be considered in the next chapter. Ragtime, in its revival, has come to be regarded as essentially music for solo piano. In its day, however, ragtime had a far broader meaning. We tend to see the ragtime or "coon" song as a vulgarized offshoot of pure ragtime, with its essential characteristics diluted. Both in the crudity of its words and in the grotesque caricatures of its sheet-music covers, the coon song appears today as grossly insulting to black people. In its day, however, the ragtime song was a popular manifestation of the "ragtime craze," and these songs were written and sung by black as well as white performers. With all its vulgarity, it brought a new dimension to American popular song. As Arnold Shaw has said, "Coon songs were an infusion into the pop music scene of high spirits, revelry, and rhythmic drive, much as Rhythm and Blues was later in the 1950s"; he also makes the point that, as in the case of rhythm and blues half a century later, the coon song was as much a style of singing as it was a type of song (42). The lineage of the female "coon shouter" starts perhaps with Mama Lou, in Babe Connors's St. Louis brothel, who, according to Shaw, may have been the writer of "Ta-Ra-Ra Boom-De-Ay" and "The Bully," songs that were later popularized on the New York stage by the white singer May Irwin (1862–1938).

The white composer Frederick Allen ("Kerry") Mills produced a memorable little "ragtime cakewalk" called "At a Georgia Camp Meeting," published in 1897 as a piano piece and in 1899 as a song. The tune, with its ragtime syncopations (accents that do not line up with the beats of a meter), became very popular and was much associated with a dance craze called the cakewalk, which swept America and even invaded Europe. (The cakewalk, originally a plantation slave dance, had appeared in exaggerated form as the minstrel show "walk-around" for years.)

So persistent, and evidently popular, was the "darky" (referring to black people) image in song that it was present even in songs whose well-known choruses gave little hint of it. "Ida! Sweet as Apple Cider" (1903) and "Coax Me" (1904) have faint traces of dialect, and references to a "dusky maid" and "dusky lovers" in their verses. Even the well-known "Mighty Lak' a Rose" (1901, by Ethelbert Nevin—a song that did not come out of Tin Pan Alley), in spite of the "eyes so shiny blue," has dialect (including the endearing term "Mammy") that shows a clear relationship to the long tradition of black dialect songs reaching back to the 1840s and before.

The Barbershop Quartet, Black and White

Flourishing about the same time as ragtime was another form of entertainment (popular at least as much for the performer as for the listener), the barbershop quartet. The relation of the barbershop itself to the quartet was mentioned in connection with the origin of the black gospel quartet, to which the black barbershop quartet is closely related (see pp. 181–182). James Weldon Johnson (who edited *The Book of American Negro Spirituals*) wrote in the preface:

> Pick up four colored boys or young men anywhere and the chances are ninety out of a hundred that you have a quartet. . . . In the days when such a thing as a white barber was unknown in the South, every barber shop had its quartet, and the men spent their leisure time playing on the guitar—not banjo, mind you—and "harmonizing." . . . When I was a very small boy

[about 1880] one of my greatest pleasures was going to concerts and hearing the crack quartets made up of the waiters in the Jacksonville hotels sing. . . . When I was fifteen and my brother was thirteen we were singing in a quartet which competed with other quartets. (35–36)

W. C. Handy, famous "father of the blues," as soon as he became a tenor, sang in the quartet that Florence, Alabama, had. (Nearly all Southern towns had such a quartet.) White barbershop quartets flourished somewhat later. (The formation of a clear picture regarding distinctions in repertoire, style, and history between black and white quartets awaits further investigation.) By the 1920s the growing popularity of jazz, radio, and sound films led to a decline in at least the professional quartets that had been formed. The recognition by 1938 that barbershop quartet singing had become in need of preserving resulted in the founding of the Society for the Preservation and Encouragement of Barber Shop Quartet Singing in America (SPEBSQSA), in the beginning an essentially white organization. The texture of the barbershop quartet is made up of a tenor, singing the melody, another tenor harmonizing above, a bass on the bottom, and a baritone supplying the other notes of the chords as needed. It is "close" harmony in that the voices sing in a tight texture, generally as close together as the chord will allow. The bass voice is excepted from the "close" harmony rule, and often stands out in a performance. The repertoire probably consisted mainly of the parlor songs and hymns popular in the late nineteenth century.

We have briefly sketched the rich mix that was popular song in the two decades surrounding the turn of the century—years when the "marvelous hit-machine" was being built. Before we follow popular song further into the twentieth century, let us look at another important ingredient in our popular musical culture: the American band.

THE BAND IN AMERICA AFTER THE JACKSONIAN ERA

Bands and Band Music to the Time of Sousa

As was noted in Chapter 12, the wind band was an important part of the American musical scene in the colonial and federal periods. Subsequent European experimentation and invention resulted in improvements in brass instruments, making them more flexible and capable of more notes. These improvements, as well as the greater durability and carrying power of brass instruments (important for outdoor functions), led to the gradual elimination of clarinets, oboes, and bassoons and the rise of the *brass band,* which dominated the scene until well after the Civil War. A sampling of the music played by these bands includes a fair reflection of the dances that were popular at the time—quicksteps, polkas, schottisches, and waltzes.

With the Civil War came the need for brass bands in ever greater numbers. The standard Civil War band was small by present-day standards, consisting of a dozen brass players and five drummers. But even before hostilities ceased, there was a portent of things to come. When Patrick Gilmore (1829–1892), then in New Orleans, was asked by General Nathaniel P. Banks to provide music for the inauguration of the new governor there, he assembled a band of 500 and a chorus of 6,000 and put on the first of his many mammoth concerts, climaxed by the firing of fifty cannon (electrically controlled from the podium) and the ringing of all the church bells in the city.

After the war, Gilmore expanded on the concept of the concert event of huge proportions. The ultimate came in 1872 as a World Peace Jubilee in Boston, for which he assembled 2,000 instrumentalists and choruses of 20,000 in a specially built, 100,000-seat coliseum. This jubilee lasted eighteen days, and to augment the entertainment, Gilmore invited bands from England, France, and Germany, as well as Johann Strauss and his orchestra from Vienna. Patrick Gilmore never again assembled anything on this scale (in its day the equivalent, in complexity and the sheer numbers involved, to the modern Olympic Games), but the "jubilee" concept—under the more modern designation "festival"—is still a cultural phenomenon worldwide, and the assembling of large instrumental forces survives in the "massed bands" heard today wherever school bands and band musicians gather.

Less spectacular but ultimately more significant was the work that Gilmore did beginning in 1873 in developing his Twenty-Second Regimental Band in New York into a combination concert and touring band. He was to establish a pattern for bands that lasted half a century. He played summer concerts at Manhattan Beach and winter concerts in Gilmore's Garden. In the spring and fall, Gilmore's band toured.

A typical band program of the late nineteenth century would show a judicious mixing of classical favorites, numbers by featured "headline" soloists, and popular songs and hymns. The classical ingredient consisted of transcriptions from the orchestral repertoire, mostly operatic overtures. Classical selections were always balanced by popular numbers; the soprano soloists who appeared with the bands might sing operatic excerpts but would be sure to include songs such as "Silver Threads Among the Gold," and even popular hymns such as "Nearer, My God, to Thee." Touring concert bands such as Gilmore's, and later Sousa's, played much the same role in the dissemination of popular songs as did the big dance bands of the 1930s and 1940s. Featured instrumental soloists were big attractions; these included accomplished performers on the saxophone, the baritone horn, and the trombone. But by far the most popular "stars" with the bands were the cornet soloists. The cornet had developed into an extremely facile virtuoso instrument that was to the band what the violin as a solo instrument was to the orchestra.

Gilmore tempered the sound of the brass band with the gradual reintroduction of woodwind instruments, which in time became numerically dominant, until by the end of the century the concert band consisted, in rough proportion, of one-third clarinets, one-third other woodwinds, and one-third brass; the percussion section was somewhat smaller in proportion than in the brass band days. Under Gilmore and Sousa, who were both very discriminating and demanding musicians, the professional concert touring band developed into an ensemble that in dynamic range, tone quality, blend, phrasing, and precision was comparable to the best orchestras of its day.

John Philip Sousa and the Band from the 1890s to the 1930s

John Philip Sousa (1854–1932) is the most important figure in the development of the American band and its music. Sousa began his independent professional career as an orchestral violinist (he played under the popular French composer and conductor Jacques Offenbach in Philadelphia in 1876) and a conductor with traveling musical shows. In 1880 he was invited to direct the U.S. Marine Band. By that time he had heard, and been impressed by, Gilmore's band, and he perceived the potential of the wind band. He thoroughly reorganized the Marine Band and its repertoire and raised it to a position of excellence and renown, even securing permission to take it on tour. In 1892 he formed his own independent band, which he conducted, except for an interval of training bands for the navy during World War I, until his death in 1932.

Sousa paid and treated his musicians well. At the same time, he made his band a profitable business, with stockholders. It was essentially a touring ensemble, and except for a very few regular engagements the band was on the road a great deal. He followed Gilmore's example in balancing his programs between popular and classical selections; furthermore, he kept up with developments in popular music. His solo trombonist, Arthur Pryor, was from Missouri, the cradle of ragtime, and he arranged and taught the band to play this new music. (Pryor's composition "Lassus Trombone," in this vein, was long a popular band number, especially with trombonists.) Sousa's band took ragtime to Europe in 1900, and his turn-of-the-century programs, with their "plantation songs and dances" and "coon songs," show that contemporary popular derivatives of black American music had a place on his programs. He later incorporated some form of jazz into his programs.

Considering his active public life, Sousa's creative output was phenomenal. He completed twelve operettas, eleven suites, seventy songs, nearly 100 other instrumental pieces of various kinds, and more than 200 arrangements and transcriptions, as well as three novels and an autobiography. But he is best known for his marches. "The Washington Post March" (CD 3/14), a march composed in 1889 for a ceremony honoring the student winners of an essay contest sponsored by that newspaper, attained instant and widespread popularity, and became indelibly associated with a new dance, the two-step.

Listening Cue "The Washington Post March" Advocate Brass Band, George Foreman, conductor (2:22)

Listen For ▪ independent strains ▪ repetition of strains ▪ short breakup strain (dog fight)

Visit http://www.music.wadsworth.com_3/Kingman for a full listening guide and other resources.

The form of the march is based (like fiddle tunes, and most other dance music) on a succession of musically independent "strains" (tunes) of equal length (sixteen bars of music), most of which are repeated. There is usually an introduction of some sort. After two strains in the main key (the first at 0:07 and the second at 0:36), there follows a contrasting strain in a related key (1:05). This latter strain is called the "Trio," a term applied since the seventeenth century to the second of two alternating dances. (It does not reflect the number of parts being performed.) The Trio includes a short "breakup" strain (1:34, sometimes called the "dog fight"), whose job is to add variety and set up the return of the main theme of the Trio, usually in a grand, pompous style (1:41).

Between 1877 and 1931, Sousa composed 136 marches. Like the songs of Stephen Foster, many of these have entered the domain of permanent national music. In addition to "The Washington Post," one can cite such standards as "Semper Fidelis," "The Thunderer," "The Liberty Bell," "King Cotton," "El Capitan," and "The Stars and Stripes Forever." Their popularity is not confined to the United States. Like the Foster songs and the waltzes of Viennese composer Johann Strauss, they have become part of a world music.

Sousa had a flourishing grassroots tradition on which to build. The 1890s, when his own band was touring and establishing its reputation, was the great era of American bands, especially in the towns and small cities of the Midwest. Town bands furnished music that was both functional and entertaining, and the bands themselves were a strong focus of community pride. Before the advent of movies and later of radio, it was town bands, along with singing and theatrical groups, that accounted for most of what local entertainment and culture existed. These attractions were augmented by such traveling entertainments as circuses, minstrel shows, and occasional visits by the bands of Gilmore and Sousa, among others.

The Band from the 1930s to the Present

The decline of the professional concert/touring band began about the time of Sousa's death in 1932. Subsequently there were two significant developments. The first was the passing of leadership to the academic band movement; college and university bands developed in size, in excellence, and in general esteem, especially in the Midwest. The second development, the creation of new works specifically for wind band, was related to this but was also the outgrowth of the work of Edwin Franko Goldman (1878–1956), whose professional band countered the general trend of decline. The Goldman Band performed continuously from 1918 to 1979, after Edwin Franko Goldman's death, under the leadership of his son Richard Franko Goldman (1910–1980). In the 1950s Richard Franko Goldman began to commission new works. Thus it was that works for the newly developed "symphonic band," or "symphonic wind ensemble," began to come from established composers. This flow of new works for band reached its peak in the 1950s and 1960s; there was hardly a major American composer of the time who did not contribute at least one work for band, including Virgil Thomson, William Schuman, Walter Piston, and Howard Hanson.

Popular Song from Ragtime to Rock

We now return to popular song where we last left it, at the close of the ragtime era, to describe the three decades between 1920 and 1950—decades that have generally been regarded as the "golden years" of Tin Pan Alley.

The Major Media Shift and the Role of the Big Bands

These "golden years" began with three technological developments that drastically changed the media by which popular song reached the public and thus brought fundamental changes to the entire industry. The phonograph recording became a significant factor after the turn of the century, radio in 1922, and the sound movie in 1929. What took place after 1920, then, was a gradual shift in the consuming public from an active to a passive role, as the phonograph and the radio replaced the parlor piano as a source of music in the home. Even that intermediate stage represented by the player piano ("canned" music produced by a "live" instrument) was edged out, sales of player pianos having reached their peak in 1923.

As the Depression arrived in the early 1930s, radio and the new talking pictures became the dominant media, dealing a severe blow to the phonograph (which did not really recover its position until the end of the decade) with recordings of the popular swing bands. Radio thus became a prime means for the dissemination and plugging of songs, as it has remained to this day (in changed form, and with a more specialized audience and material). Many of the prominent bands performed on weekly broadcasts in the 1930s, either from a permanent base or by remote hookup while on tour. Singers with the bands became increasingly important as purveyors of new popular songs. Some bandleaders were themselves composers, and a few of the best songs in this period came from the bands.

Stability and Pluralism in Popular Music Between the Wars

Although the big technological media shifts had profound effects on the popular music industry, the nature and style of popular song itself changed little in this period. But if popular song was essentially static during this period, it was also pluralistic. Russell Sanjek

Hulton Archive/Getty Images

On CD 3, track 15, we hear "Brother, Can You Spare a Dime?" a coin that doesn't buy a pack of gum today, but could feed a family in the 1930s. In this 1931 photo of the day's menu at the first ever Penny Restaurant operating in New York during the worldwide Great Depression (1929–1939), we see the food and drink that the desperate could buy for a penny at a time when one-quarter of the workforce was unemployed. Only the Hollywood film industry flourished—especially their productions of lavish movie musicals.

points out this pluralism by noting the cleavage in taste that determined the policies of Tin Pan Alley publishers in the 1930s:

> Well-written songs possessing any poetic qualities were rejected immediately, because it was the general Tin Pan Alley feeling that true sheet-music buyers had little or no interest in them and therefore they were "not commercial." Those "great" songs of the 1930s, beloved by cultural elitists and social historians, were well known only to a minority of Americans— those who were better educated and more affluent than the average radio "fan" and who had access to the Broadway stage and other sophisticated entertainment. (19)

This view does seem to be borne out by a few statistics. Hamm has compiled a list of the "top forty" songs between 1900 and 1950, in terms of those most often recorded. Of them, only twelve (30 percent) are from plotted Broadway shows, six (15 percent) are from revues (a form descended from vaudeville), and the other twenty-two (55 percent) are nonshow Tin Pan Alley songs (487–88).

The mainstay of Tin Pan Alley in this period was the love song. As a sample of the best the Alley had to offer in these three decades (again excluding show and movie tunes), we might turn to "I'll See You in My Dreams" (Isham Jones, 1924); "Blue Skies" (Irving Berlin, 1927); "Star Dust" (Hoagy Carmichael, 1929); and "Stormy Weather" (Harold Arlen, 1933). The popular singers of the period invariably sang with the bands, live, on the radio, and on recordings. Tin Pan Alley songs about the real life that surrounds us were a rarity. One famous example, however, is "Brother, Can You Spare a Dime?" (CD 3/15) from 1932. This song became popular in the Depression era, from a topical revue called *New Americana*. In this recording, it is performed by Bing (Harry Lillis) Crosby (1904–1977), one of the most popular entertainers in twentieth-century America, just about the time he was beginning his movie and radio career.

Listening Cue "Brother, Can You Spare a Dime?" Bing Crosby (3:10)

Listen For ▪ unusual lyrics dealing with realities of the Depression era

Visit http://www.music.wadsworth.com_3/Kingman for a full listening guide and other resources.

They used to tell me I was building a dream, and so I followed the mob,
When there was earth to plow, or guns to bear, I was always there, right on the job.
They used to tell me I was building a dream, with peace and glory ahead,
Why should I be standing in line, just waiting for bread?

Once I built a railroad, I made it run, made it race against time.
Once I built a railroad; now it's done. Brother, can you spare a dime?
Once I built a tower, up to the sun, brick, and rivet, and lime;
Once I built a tower, now it's done. Brother, can you spare a dime?

Once in khaki suits, gee we looked swell,
Full of that Yankee Doodley-dum,
Half a million boots went slogging through Hell,
And I was the kid with the drum!

Say, don't you remember, they called me Al;
It was Al all the time.
Why don't you remember, I'm your pal?
Say, Buddy, can you spare a dime?

"Brother Can You Spare a Dime?" by E. Y. "Yip" Harburg and Jay Gorney. Published by Glocca Morra
Music (ASCAP) and Gorney Music (ASCAP). Administered by Next Decade Entertainment, Inc. All
Rights Reserved. Used by permission.

TIN PAN ALLEY AND ITS RELATION TO JAZZ AND BLACK VERNACULAR MUSIC

Many of the leaders of the dance orchestras and big bands of the period composed and introduced songs. Duke Ellington contributed many, most of which
are decidedly instrumental in character. "I'm Beginning to See the Light" (1944),
a collaborative effort of Duke Ellington, Johnny Hodges, and Harry James, is a
typical song to come out of the stylistic milieu of the big band in that its melody
is made up of riffs—short melodic fragments repeated over changes of harmony.

Aside from these songs by bandleaders of the period, the typical popular song
between the wars (whether from Broadway, Hollywood, or Tin Pan Alley) had little relationship to jazz or other black vernacular music. The one exceptional bridge
was the blues. Harold Arlen was perhaps the closest to jazz and blues of any of the
major songwriters of this period. As Alec Wilder has written, "He, more than any
of his contemporaries, plunged himself into the heartbeat of the popular music of
his youth, the dance band." Wilder goes on to show how Arlen's "don't-worry-
about-the-mud-on-your-shoes attitude," characteristic of blues and jazz, is illustrated in songs such as "Sweet and Hot" (1930), "That Old Black Magic" (1942),
and especially the memorable "Blues in the Night" (1944) (Wilder 257–74).

Though they were distinct, one from the other, there was a symbiotic relationship between jazz and popular music in this period. Jazz was heavily indebted to Broadway, Hollywood, and Tin Pan Alley for its "standards"—songs
whose melodies and chord progressions became the basis for its arrangements
and improvisations. Consider jazz without the hundreds of renditions of "Star
Dust," without Coleman Hawkins's "Body and Soul," without Charlie Parker's
"Embraceable You," and without the score of bebop versions of "How High
the Moon."

For its part, popular music was indebted to jazz for a continuously revitalized
rhythmic basis and for the jazz arrangements by popular hot bands that contributed their flavor to, and helped promote, the songs. Performances by such
singers as Bing Crosby, Ethel Waters, Mildred Bailey, Jack Teagarden, Billie Holiday, Lena Horne, Sarah Vaughan, and Ella Fitzgerald, backed up by bands such
as those of Benny Goodman, Teddy Wilson, Artie Shaw, Harry James, and Duke

Ellington, impart, through interpretation, a jazz or blues flavor to songs that do not necessarily possess it inherently.

Finally, the relation of black vernacular dance to popular music in this period is crucial. Since the turn of the twentieth century, innumerable vernacular dances have entered the mainstream of popular dance. The Charleston, the shimmy, the Black Bottom, and various "animal dances," such as the turkey trot, the grizzly bear, and the bunny hug, began, despite opposition, to coexist with and gradually replace the older polkas, schottisches, and waltzes. (One animal dance—possibly made up by the popular and influential team of Vernon and Irene Castle before World War I—was the fox trot, which became "respectable" and survived well into the period under consideration.) The toddle was danced to Dixieland jazz. But the dance that became indelibly associated with swing jazz came out of places like the Savoy Ballroom in Harlem in the late 1920s (the home ground of many of the hottest bands). First known as the lindy hop (after Charles Lindbergh's famous flight), it became more broadly familiar as the jitterbug. Although most of the young could and did do it, when performed by accomplished jitterbuggers in its more flamboyant and elaborate form it was a dance to watch as well. It was the dance symbol of hot jazz, and the interaction and mutual stimulus between a hard-driving swing band and a group of equally hard-dancing, frenzied jitterbuggers on the dance floor were undeniable.

THE DECLINE OF TIN PAN ALLEY AND THE DISPERSION OF THE POPULAR MUSIC INDUSTRY

So what happened to Tin Pan Alley? In the 1950s, the Broadway–Hollywood axis was broken by an upheaval in the popular music industry that began in the far-removed "provinces." As we have seen in Part III, regional and ethnic musics began to account for significantly larger shares of the market. Coming out of the urban areas such as Chicago, Detroit, and Philadelphia was black "rhythm and blues"; from the South and the West came white hillbilly music, given the trade name "country and western." And as a commercial offspring of both came rock and roll. In essence, then, the centralization of popular music that had marked the golden age of Tin Pan Alley was shattered, appropriately enough, by rock. As we have seen in Chapter 9, its continued fragmentation has persisted to this day.

PROJECTS

1. Sigmund Spaeth restated a thought expressed many times when he wrote that our popular song "captures the civilization of each period far more accurately than do many of the supposedly more important arts." Taking any decade in our history, make a survey of its popular songs and assess the extent to which this statement applies, and how it applies.

2. If you come from a relatively small community in which a town or city band has been an important entity, assemble some recollections (either your own or those of relatives or acquaintances) of the band's activities and significance in the life of the community.

ADDITIONAL LISTENING

Brother, Can You Spare a Dime? American Song During the Great Depression. NW 80270.

"The Song of the Red Man." *The Hand That Holds the Bread: Progress and Protest in the Gilded Age.* NW 80267.

Songs of the Civil War. NW 80202.

Where Home Is: Life in Nineteenth-Century Cincinnati. NW 80251.

JAZZ AND ITS FORERUNNERS

Jazz, like blues and rap, came into being as the musical expression of African Americans. But jazz, to a greater extent than either of the others, has long since transcended exclusive racial identity. It occupies a position in the panorama of American music that is not easily classified by labels. It has never, except in the brief heyday of the swing bands, been what could be called broadly popular music. The terms "folk" and "classical" have been applied on occasion, but these don't really work either. Though jazz might be found to have points of contact with each tradition, it has never fit entirely under any of those umbrellas. Perhaps its "stand-alone" quality is part of what motivates people to think of jazz as the most distinctive American music. To some it represents *the* American music. The following chapters will contextualize that rich tradition.

Paul Thompson / War Department / National Archives / Time Life Pictures / Getty Images

*M*embers of the famed 369th Infantry Regiment—also called The Harlem Hellfighters and The Black Rattlers—wave from the deck of the ship bringing them home from World War I. The 369th, an all-black enlisted corps attached to the French Army to avoid American racism, became one of the war's most decorated combat units. One of its officers was Lt. James Reese Europe, who, in addition to his combat duty, also led the popular regimental band that introduced American ragtime to the French and British.

15 RAGTIME AND PRECURSORS OF JAZZ

THE CONTEXT OF RAGTIME FROM ITS ORIGINS TO ITS ZENITH

In the early years of the twentieth century, the terms *ragtime* and *jazz* both had broader and looser definitions than the more purist ones we find applied today. Our idea of ragtime as exclusively solo piano music is at variance with its contemporary perception. The dominant form of American popular music has always been the song, and as Edward Berlin has pointed out, it was the ragtime songs—songs such as "A Hot Time in the Old Town" (1896), "Mister Johnson, Turn Me Loose" (1896), and "Hello! My Baby" (1899)—that were more often recognized as "ragtime" in their day than the now familiar piano pieces. "Hello! My Baby" (CD 3/16), is an example of a ragtime song that continues to resonate in American culture today thanks to frequent revivals in various outlets for popular culture. The most famous is probably its performance by a singing and dancing cartoon frog that, until recently, was the mascot of the WB Network. Such modern revivals, however, tend to eclipse a part of the song that was very novel for its time—the lyrics based on the recent invention of the telephone.

CD 3

16

Listening Cue "Hello! My Baby" Don Meehan, vocal; Dave Corey, piano (1:14)

Listen For ▪ lyrics based on the recently invented telephone

Visit http://www.music.wadsworth.com_3/Kingman for a full listening guide and other resources.

Hello, my baby,
Hello, my honey,
Hello, my ragtime gal.
Send me a kiss by wire.
Baby, my heart's on fire.

If you refuse me,
Honey, you'll lose me,
Then you'll be left alone.
Oh baby, telephone,
Tell me I'm your own.
. . . Oh baby, telephone,
And I'll say,
Hello, my baby, hello, my honey, hello my ragtime gal!

The Origins of Ragtime

The roots of ragtime in our vernacular music are broad. Its most easily identifiable feature—a syncopated melody against a steady, marchlike bass in duple meter—can certainly be found in music published in the 1880s, not in the middle Mississippi Valley (generally considered to be the cradle of ragtime) but in New York. And the distinctive rhythms (including the syncopations) of the banjo tunes of the early minstrel show had appeared in print before the Civil War.

Both the ragtime songs and the dances of the period had their role in the development of ragtime. The earliest known ragtime instruction book, written in 1897 as the ragtime craze was just beginning, gives an alternative name for "rag time" as "Negro Dance time," and for the next two decades the names of specific dances were associated with published rags (Berlin 115). The *march* could be used as dance music; many early rags include "march" or "two-step" or both in their titles or subtitles. A specialty dance that also contributed to ragtime was the *cakewalk*. A march involving an exaggerated kind of strutting, it presumably originated on the plantations, with slave couples competing for the prize of a cake. It was taken over into the minstrel show and was on Broadway by the 1870s; by the 1890s it had become a popular, though strenuous and exacting, dance for the general public (Shaw 43–44). Many early rags also incorporated the term "cakewalk" in their titles.

Caribbean dance rhythms—rhythms of the danza, the habanera, or the *seguidilla*—have been cited as one of the sources of ragtime rhythms. Louis Moreau Gottschalk (1829–1869) incorporated these rhythms into most of his piano pieces with West Indian associations, including his "Danza" (1857), "La Gallina" (copyright 1869), and "Ojos Criollos" (no copyright date), the last two of which carry the subtitle "Danse cubaine." The earliest collections of Creole songs from Louisiana also contain syncopations identical to those found in ragtime (see "Miché Bainjo" in Allen, Ware, and Garrison). The actual extent to which this music could have influenced ragtime itself is debatable, however. The whole question of Latin American influence (principally rhythmic) on the origins of both ragtime and jazz is often overlooked and is in need of more investigation—investigation that might convince us, for example, that a piece like Scott Joplin's "Solace" (1909, subtitled "A Mexican Serenade"), an exquisite example of a rag with a habanera bass, is not the isolated anomaly that it may appear to be. (See Berlin 115–18.)

Ragtime as Piano Music and the Work of Scott Joplin

Despite the breadth of interpretations given the term *ragtime,* it was as music for solo piano that it ultimately achieved significance and endured. The dissemination of piano ragtime is widely thought to have been given considerable impetus by the gathering of ragtime pianists (before the term had been applied to the genre) at the World's Columbian Exposition in Chicago in 1893. There, according to Blesh and Janis, "hundreds of the itinerant piano clan had gathered" (including Scott Joplin, 1868–1917, and Ben Harney, 1871–1938), presumably to be heard on the "Midway" and in the red-light district; but more informative documentation as to what music was played will probably never come to light (Blesh and Janis 18, 41). Not long afterward—in the same year (1896) in which Ben Harney moved to New York from his native Louisville and began introducing ragtime through his highly successful playing and singing—Scott Joplin moved to Sedalia, Missouri, where for the next five years he composed, played, and published the first of the approximately three dozen piano pieces that he and his publisher referred to as "classic rags." Thus Ben Harney, the white Brooklynite Joseph Lamb (1877–1960), and others in New York, and Scott Joplin, Tom Turpin (1873–1922), Arthur Marshall (1881–1968), Scott Hayden (1882–1915), James Scott (1886–1938), and others in the Midwest, helped to launch ragtime as we know it into what became, in the next two decades, a national craze.

Frank Driggs Collection./Getty Images

As the formal dress in this portrait shows, ragtime composer Scott Joplin took care to promote his music by projecting an air of middle-class propriety appropriate to a serious composer. Playing piano at respectable black male social clubs, the Maple Leaf and the Black 400, in Sedalia, Missouri, Joplin sold "Maple Leaf Rag" to a local sheet-music publisher. Wildly popular, its royalties allowed Joplin to concentrate on composing. In 1916 he recorded six piano rolls, among them "Maple Leaf Rag," which we hear on CD 3, track 17.

Ragtime for the piano assumed in its initial stages three forms: piano renditions of ragtime songs; the "ragging" of unsyncopated music; and original compositions for the piano. The piano compositions began to be published in 1897—William Krell's "The Mississippi Rag" was possibly the first, with "Harlem Rag" by the St. Louis composer Tom Turpin coming out the same year. It is probable that at least 3,000 rags were published between 1897 and 1920; estimates have run as high as 10,000. As could be expected, most of these were mediocre musically, and were simplified in their published versions to be more suited to the modest pianistic abilities of the many who bought them and attempted to play them at home. What are today regarded as the masterpieces of piano ragtime were not necessarily best-sellers; Scott Joplin's most famous work, "Maple Leaf Rag" (1899), was virtually the only one of his works to become widely popular in his lifetime, and it was the work that justified his being heralded on sheet-music covers as "the king of ragtime writers."

Scott Joplin has emerged as the most important ragtime composer of the period. A versatile musician (he played the cornet and the piano and led a band) with high musical standards and determined ambition, he lavished a great deal of effort and resources on composing and producing large-scale works for the stage, none of which were successful in his lifetime. But his most enduring and influential works are his rags, whose musical inventiveness and craftsmanship set a standard against which others are measured and validate the term that he and his publisher applied to them—"classic."

The association of the piano with the ragtime era is no coincidence; figures show that the sales of pianos rose sharply after 1890, and declined just as steeply in the 1920s. But a modified form of the piano, the mechanical player piano, was also an important feature of the era; after 1900, player-piano sales also rose steeply, reaching a peak before the ragtime era was completely over (Hasse 15). Thus a great deal of ragtime (and its successor, "novelty" piano music) came into American homes in the form of piano rolls. These rolls could be either "hand-played," often by the composer himself, or "arranged" by the calculated punching of the paper rolls. In fact, many rags, including one by Joplin himself, appeared only in piano rolls, and were never published in sheet-music form (Hasse 90ff).

Those who bought the sheet music, however, intent on playing it at home, soon discovered that ragtime is not easy to play. To aid the learner and cash in on the boom, instruction books in ragtime began to appear—the earliest by Harney himself in 1897. One truly valuable document is an all-too-brief set of six exercises by Scott Joplin, published as *School of Ragtime* in 1908, with accompanying explanations and admonitions. (Joplin concentrates most on accurate rendering of the rhythm, and warns the performer, as he was to do over and over again in his published rags: "Never play ragtime fast at any time.") To provide personal instruction, studios were opened to accept pupils; the first advertisement for "Ragtime Taught in Ten Lessons" appeared in Chicago in 1903.

In its heyday the creation and publication of ragtime was not, like Tin Pan Alley and the popular-song industry, concentrated in New York City. The mid–Mississippi Valley and the Ohio Valley were strong areas for ragtime, and an examination of sheet music shows that rags were published not only in St. Louis, Kansas City, Columbia, and Sedalia, Missouri, but also in Indianapolis, Cincinnati, Memphis, Nashville, Chicago, Detroit, New Orleans, Dallas, and San Francisco, and even in such places as Temple, Texas (for early Joplin pieces); Moline, Illinois; New Albany, Indiana; Kiowa, Kansas; and Oskaloosa, Iowa. John Hasse, who has been both a researcher into and a performer of Indiana ragtime, has termed the ragtime era "the golden age of local and regional music publishing." Piano ragtime was also a genre to which female composers contributed significantly; May Aufderheide (1890–1972), of Indianapolis, was only the best known among many (Hasse 154ff, 368ff).

Ensemble Ragtime

The performance of ragtime was not limited either to the solo piano version or to the song; as soon as it became popular, this music began to be played by many kinds of ensembles, including brass bands, concert bands, dance bands and orchestras, and smaller groups that included mandolins, guitars, and banjos. "St. Louis Tickle," recorded in 1904 with a banjo, mandolin, and guitar trio, is illustrative. Publishers issued "stock" arrangements for bands and orchestras (mostly for dancing), and sheet-music publications of rags for piano often advertised versions of the same piece "published for band, orchestra, mandolin, guitar, etc." John Philip Sousa was quick to recognize the popularity of ragtime. He began to program it in the 1890s, and on his first tour of Europe in 1900 he gave most of his audiences there their first taste of ragtime with arrangements of such pieces as "Smoky Mokes" and "Bunch o' Blackberries" (Hasse 268). Sousa's band recorded in 1908 an instrumental version of Kerry Mills's well-known ragtime song "At a Georgia Camp Meeting."

THE MUSICAL CHARACTERISTICS OF RAGTIME

Ragtime Rhythm

"Syncopation" is basic to the rhythmic life of much American music. It has been defined briefly elsewhere in the book, but a closer look is warranted here as syncopation is a key feature of ragtime. Essentially, it entails the displacing of accents from their normal position in the musical measure, so that they contradict the underlying meter. Syncopation assumes a steady beat, stated or implied, and cannot be said to exist without it. This is normally supplied in ragtime by the steady "oom-pah" of the left hand, while the right hand has the melody, with its characteristically displaced accents. The displaced accents work against the prevailing background meter, infusing the work with an exciting tension and vitality.

Ragtime Form

It is in its standardized form that ragtime shows most clearly its relation to the march and the two-step; in fact, the name "march" or "two-step" is incorporated into the titles of many piano rags. Like the march (see p. 240), the form of the rag is based on a succession of musically independent strains of uniform length (sixteen bars), most of which are repeated. An introduction is optional; Joplin almost invariably uses one (his famous "Maple Leaf Rag" is one exception). There is another similarity to the march in the use of a trio section, here too in a related key. Unlike the march, which usually ends in the related key, the rag will often go back to the key in which it started. The rag also tends to restate the strain with which it started before moving on to the trio. To note one more difference, there is no section that compares with the "dog fight" of the march.

Ragtime rhythm and form are exemplified in Joplin's "Maple Leaf Rag" (CD 3/17). The first two strains are at 0:00 and 0:36. The trio strains are at 1:29 and 2:02. Notice that there is no introduction—very unusual for Joplin.

Listening Cue "Maple Leaf Rag" Scott Joplin, piano (2:38)

Listen For ▪ contrasting strains ▪ syncopation against steady, accented notes

Visit http://www.music.wadsworth.com_3/Kingman for a full listening guide and other resources.

THE DECLINE AND DISPERSION OF RAGTIME

Ragtime's original heyday was brief, in retrospect; scarcely a generation elapsed between its full-fledged appearance in the 1890s and its decline and metamorphosis into other styles. Recognizing the dual forms, vocal and instrumental, that ragtime assumed, Berlin has noted that by the mid-1910s vocal ragtime (as the ragtime song) "merged with the mainstream of popular music, while piano ragtime inclined toward what became known as jazz" (61). Piano ragtime, in its dispersion, assumed several forms and affected several distinct genres. Foremost, of course, was its merging with jazz. For a time, the two terms were used almost interchangeably.

Jelly Roll Morton

Ferdinand Joseph ("Jelly Roll") Morton (1890–1941), a New Orleans–born pianist and bandleader, was a key figure in this transition. His own works (variously and somewhat imprecisely titled "rags," "blues," and "stomps," among other designations) date mostly from the post-ragtime era. In these we can see that Morton's own style had superseded classic ragtime, while reinterpreting some of its elements. Morton's identity as a bandleader is also evident; not only did many of the pieces exist as band numbers, but also Morton often wanted his piano itself to "sound as much like a band as possible." Nevertheless, he drew a clear distinction between the new jazz and older ragtime, which he had grown up with and knew thoroughly. His historic recordings, with commentary, made for Alan Lomax at the Library of Congress in the late 1930s, illustrate these distinctions and are a valuable source of information about the transition from ragtime to jazz. Though Morton makes his first appearance in our panoramic survey in connection with ragtime, it is really for his work in the formative stages of jazz that he is most important. After extensive traveling from 1904 to 1922, he went to Chicago, where he recorded, both as piano soloist and as bandleader, the works by which he is known (Lomax; Hasse 257ff).

Two Offshoots of Ragtime: Stride Piano and Novelty Piano

As classic piano ragtime declined, two offshoots appeared—descendants of the parent form, but not to be confused with it. One was the largely New York phenomenon of "stride piano," also known as "Harlem piano." This genre, cultivated by James Price Johnson (1894–1955) and Fats Waller (1904–1943) in the 1920s and 1930s, retains some of ragtime's characteristics, most notably a steady left-hand rhythmic pulse with syncopated right-hand figuration. A distinctive feature, however, is that the steady pulses are created by wide, leaping "strides" between low bass notes and midrange offbeat chords. Basically a virtuoso form developed by pianists with phenomenal facility, stride piano is often faster than ragtime, with a driving beat and very elaborate melodic line. James P. Johnson's ebullient "If Dreams Come True," as recorded in 1939 (CD 3/18), is a fine example.

An originator of stride piano, James P. Johnson—
whom we hear on CD 3, track 18—wrote what many
consider the definitive song of the Roaring '20s,
"Charleston" (1923). After suffering several small
strokes in the 1930s, Johnson returned to lead
a small swing group, shown here in a 1943 jam
session: (l. to r.) Wilbur De Paris on trombone,
Franz Jackson on saxophone (behind De Paris),
Irving Fazola on clarinet, Al Mott on bass, and
(in the foreground) Eddie Condon on guitar and
Johnson at the piano.

Listening Cue "If Dreams Come True" James P. Johnson, piano (3:11)

Listen For ▪ quick, steady pulse ▪ "strides" ▪ elaborate, syncopated melody

Visit http://www.music.wadsworth.com_3/Kingman for a full listening guide and
other resources.

Another offshoot of ragtime was the "novelty piano" music of the early 1920s;
anyone familiar with such pieces as "Nola," "Canadian Capers," "Kitten on the
Keys," or "Dizzy Fingers" knows the style. A "show-off" kind of piano music
(carefully made to sound more difficult than it actually is), it has been described
by Ronald Riddle as "a refined, white suburban extension of ragtime" (Hasse
285). The "novelty" itself was an attraction in tune with the times; such words as
"tricky," "sparkling," and "scintillating" were used to describe and sell it. It was
ideal for the medium of the player piano during the last few years of that instrument's popularity; before being replaced by the phonograph and the radio, the

player piano made this novelty music accessible to people without the technical ability to play it themselves. But the sheet music also sold extremely well; Zez Confrey's "Kitten on the Keys" (which first appeared as a piano roll played by the composer) outsold "Maple Leaf Rag" when it was issued as sheet music in 1921. Musically, novelty piano shared the basic underlying features of ragtime but emphasized greater speed and an obviously exhibitionist kind of virtuosity.

The composer most closely associated with the genre was Edward E. "Zez" Confrey (1895–1971). Novelty piano, for all of its short-lived superficiality, had an unmistakable influence on certain piano music of the 1920s and 1930s, especially that of George Gershwin. Riddle has mentioned Confrey's influence, by way of the popular "Kitten on the Keys," on Gershwin's *Rhapsody in Blue*. He has also pointed out its influence on European composers such as Ravel and Martinu, when they wrote in an obviously "jazzy" style; in fact, some aspects of novelty piano were taken by outsiders to be synonymous with jazz at the time. Novelty piano was a hot item, indeed. But predictably, it would lose its "novelty" and, like many other fads, recede into the background.

THE RAGTIME REVIVAL

It was only in revival that ragtime regained its integrity and distinctiveness. This selective revival, focusing almost exclusively on piano rags, which began about midcentury, has now lasted far longer than did the ragtime era itself.

The revival of traditional jazz, under the umbrella name of "Dixieland," began in the 1940s. Working backward chronologically, the next step, given the obvious relationship of ragtime to early jazz, was the rediscovery and study of ragtime itself, which was then generally viewed as a quite dated and old-fashioned precursor of jazz. Writers Rudi Blesh and Harriet Janis and performer, entertainer, and scholar Max Morath were among the first to give ragtime serious attention. They discovered in the best of the piano rags musical excellences that had largely escaped the public in the ragtime era itself. Joshua Rifkin made studio-quality recordings, on a concert grand piano, of the rags of Scott Joplin in 1970; with his first best-selling record he separated ragtime from its association with the tinny, out-of-tune barroom piano and its accompanying stereotypical milieu and focused on its musical values. In 1972 Gunther Schuller reinstated instrumental ragtime when he refurbished old stock arrangements (notably those found in the famous "Red Back Book") and founded and rehearsed the New England Conservatory Ragtime Ensemble. William Bolcom and John Hasse are among those who not only have continued to perform and record piano ragtime but also have composed rags of their own. This renewed attention to the musical aspects of ragtime has made the works of some of the early composers of what has now become known as "classic" ragtime, especially Scott Joplin, James Scott, and Joseph Lamb, stand out in perspective against the mass of mediocrity perpetrated in the ragtime era itself. Thus a few dozen rags emerge as small gems, illustrative of the potential for investing miniature and highly circumscribed forms such as the rag with refinement, craftsmanship, and vitality.

PRECURSORS OF JAZZ

Minstrelsy, ragtime, and the blues were only the most public and audible forms of black (or black-derived) music that came before jazz. Behind them, mostly unheard and unheeded by white Americans, were all the varied musical manifestations of what has been called the "black experience." Where and when, from all this background, did actual jazz begin to emerge? This is a complex question, the first part of which cannot be adequately answered with the single place name New Orleans. It will be necessary to take a broader look geographically, for there were musical developments in all the cities and towns of the South and in the larger cities of the North (in other words, wherever there was a sizable population of African Americans) that set the stage for the emergence of jazz.

James Reese Europe and African American Bands at Home and Abroad

An important forerunner of jazz in New York was orchestral ragtime, which from the late 1890s until after the first World War was heard both in stage shows and as played by black dance orchestras. In many parts of the country it had long been the role of black musicians to furnish music for dancing. As Eileen Southern has said, "In many places the profession of dance musicians was reserved by custom for Negroes, just as was, for example, the occupation of barber. Consequently, black dance orchestras held widespread monopolies on jobs for a long period in the nation's history—even after World War I" (Southern, *Music* 338).

In the early 1900s New York's Black Bohemia (an area in West Manhattan around 53rd Street) furnished the "syncopated dance orchestras" that were much in demand for all occasions. Such an orchestra gave a public concert in 1905, and by 1910 James Reese Europe (1881–1919) had founded the famous Clef Club, whose orchestra gave public concerts, including a famous and highly successful one at Carnegie Hall in 1912. Europe, a pioneer in jazz orchestration, aimed at developing an orchestra that "is different and distinctive, and that lends itself to the playing of the peculiar compositions of our race." Two features distinguished this orchestra from the standard white orchestra of the time. One was the increased importance, and often dominance, of drums and other percussion; the other was the presence of proportionately large numbers of banjos and mandolins, which, as Europe explained, took the place of the second violins and gave "that peculiar steady strumming accompaniment to our music." James Weldon Johnson, the well-known black poet, wrote of the Carnegie Hall concert: "New York had not yet become accustomed to jazz; so when the Clef Club opened its concert with a syncopated march, playing it with a biting attack and an infectious rhythm, and on the finale bursting into singing, the effect can be imagined. The applause became a tumult!" Europe's 1914 recording of his "Castle House Rag" with his Society Orchestra is illustrative of what New Yorkers were hearing, especially the surprising and famous final strain, which Lawrence Gushee describes as "ferociously raggy" (Badger 51; for a recording of "Castle House Rag," see Additional Listening).

With the entry of the United States into World War I in 1917, African Americans joined the armed forces in large numbers, and bands were formed of black musicians whose services were much in demand. The most famous of these bands was formed and led by James Reese Europe himself. The band was enormously popular in France, not only with the American troops but with the French as well (Little, in Southern, *Readings*). Europe was commissioned as a line officer, and he and the members of his band fought as combat soldiers in the all-black 369th Infantry Regiment (the "Hellfighters"), one of the most highly decorated units of the war.

Was Europe's band playing jazz? Perhaps not in the strictest sense, since he laid great stress on the musicians' reading the music accurately. (Eubie Blake, who had played with Europe in 1916, described "that Europe gang" as "absolute reading sharks. They could read a moving snake, and if a fly lit on that paper he got played.") Europe's own description of the band's playing is illuminating:

> We accent strongly . . . the notes which originally would be without accent. It is natural for us to do this; it is, indeed, a racial musical characteristic. I have to call a daily rehearsal of my band to prevent the musicians from adding to their music more than I wish them to. Whenever possible they all embroider their parts in order to produce new, peculiar sounds. (Southern, *Music* 352)

James Reese Europe and the band had a triumphant return to the States in 1919 and almost immediately embarked on a world tour. Had he not been killed in May of that year (stabbed by a mentally ill band member during a concert in Boston), he surely would have played a still more prominent role in the art of nascent jazz. More formally educated and more commercially successful than most early jazz musicians, critics have tended to dismiss him as a mere popularizer. Yet, as J. Reid Badger has pointed out, "By recognizing the achievements of Jim Europe, we can better understand the musical and historical context that eventually produced such major jazz orchestrators as Fletcher Henderson and Duke Ellington" (60). (For a recording of "Memphis Blues" by Europe, see Additional Listening.)

Brass Bands

Better known as precursors of jazz were the smaller, more informal black brass bands that took part in the nationwide flourishing of bands noted in the preceding chapter. New Orleans, possibly owing to French influence, had an exceptional number of bands, as well as dance orchestras. The French interest in the military, or brass, band goes back to Napoleonic times. There were also trained musicians playing in the French Opera House who regularly taught the instruments.

The bands were not large by present standards, consisting of only ten or twelve pieces, including trumpets or cornets, alto and baritone horns, trombones, tuba, clarinets, and drums. They could furnish music for concerts as well as parades; in addition, there was often a smaller group affiliated with the band that played for dances, since many of the men doubled on stringed instruments.

© Philip Gould/CORBIS

Here, the jazz band Olympia plays in a funeral procession through the French Quarter of New Orleans, Louisiana. Building on the old tradition of military brass-band funerals, but with a twist that would produce so-called jazz funerals, the musicians of New Orleans play solemn music on the way to the cemetery and upbeat music on the way back. We hear examples of both processions on CD 3, the slow "Eternity" on track 19, and the jazzy, up-tempo "Just a Little While to Stay Here" on track 20.

The repertoire of both groups had of necessity to be broad; it by no means consisted entirely of the new ragtime but included quadrilles, polkas, waltzes, and mazurkas.

It was for their parade music that black bandsmen in the South ultimately became most famous, and not the least important job of these bands was playing for funerals. The lodge or secret society (often more than one) to which the deceased belonged would engage the band. In the legendary and often described scene, the band would march solemnly to the graveyard, playing hymns such as "Nearer, My God, to Thee" or "Come, Ye Disconsolate," or "any 4/4 played very slow." After the burial the band would re-form outside the cemetery and march away to the beat of the snare drum only. After it was a block or two away from the graveyard, it would burst into ragtime—"Didn't He Ramble," or a "ragged" version of a hymn or spiritual. It was then that the "second line" of fans and enthusiastic dancing bystanders would fall in behind the band (Stearns 50–51).

The Excelsior and the Onward were the most famous bands. No recordings exist of those bands. But recordings by the surviving Eureka Brass Band (an organization dating from the 1920s), which were made in the 1950s, give some idea of the sound. The juxtaposition of "Eternity," the kind of piece that would have been played in the solemn march to the graveyard, and "Just a Little While to Stay Here," the kind of upbeat jazzed version of a hymn tune that would have been played on the way back, furnish a kind of aural synthesis of this experience. (See CD 3/19 and 3/20.)

Listening Cue "Eternity" Eureka Brass Band, New Orleans (0:55)

    Listen For ▪ slow, solemn march (leading to the graveyard)

Listening Cue "Just a Little While to Stay Here" Eureka Brass Band, New Orleans (1:56)

    Listen For ▪ upbeat, jazzy tune (leading away from the graveyard)

Visit http://www.music.wadsworth.com_3/Kingman for a full listening guide and other resources.

There was keen competition among the bands, and "cutting" or "bucking" contests—in which one band would try to outplay another—were common. A few legendary names emerge from this period—none larger than that of Charles "Buddy" Bolden (1877–1931), the New Orleans trumpet player. He was a versatile musician, reading music when necessary but preferring to play by ear. Bolden played "sweet" music for the general public and "hot" music for the "district" and its patrons. It was for the latter that he became most famous, introducing his "hot blues" about 1894. Was Buddy playing jazz that far back? Earwitnesses like Bunk Johnson (1889–1949) say that he was. It is certain that he was heavily imbued with the blues. The New Orleans bass player "Pops" Foster has written of him, "He played nothing but blues, and all that stink music, and he played it very loud" (Cook 88). Here was ample evidence at an early date of the perennial and symbiotic relationship between blues and jazz.

PROJECTS

1. A broad and general sensitivity to the feelings of any group perceived as a minority (whether defined by race, color, religion, or any other basis) is fairly recent and still imperfect, as our jokes and our songs reveal. The study of popular art is a study not of what later periods may select but of what is actually popular in contemporary culture, and therefore revealing of its nature. This precept leads a scholar such as Vera Brodsky Lawrence to include sheet-music covers in her edition of the works of Scott Joplin, and Edward Berlin and Arnold Shaw, to discuss the "coon song" in their treatises. If you were doing an illustrated lecture on American popular culture since the Jacksonian era,

think about how you would treat the minstrel skit, the coon song, the Irish (or Jewish, or Chinese) song, the Polish (or Italian, or Catholic, or Mormon) joke. Discuss your views in a paper. Is censorship justifiable, and under what circumstances?

2. Write a paper comparing the role of women in ragtime with the role of women in jazz. To get started, you might consult Max Morath's article "May Aufderheide and the Ragtime Women" in John Hasse, ed., *Ragtime: Its History, Composers, and Music* (New York: Schirmer Books, 1985), along with Sally Placksin's *American Women in Jazz, 1900 to the Present: Their Words, Lives, and Music* (New York: Wideview Books, 1982) and Linda Dahl's *Stormy Weather: The Music and Lives of a Century of Jazz Women* (New York: Pantheon, 1984).

3. The musical relationship between blues and ragtime was, in the classic period of ragtime, somewhat noticeable but not great. Investigate the relationship between the texts of ragtime songs (such as those mentioned in the chapter) and those of early blues. For ragtime songs, consult Edward Berlin's chapter "Ragtime Songs" in Hasse, *Ragtime: Its History, Composers, and Music;* and Blesh and Janis's *They All Played Ragtime.* For blues lyrics, see Chapter 8 and such sources as the W. C. Handy anthology and Paul Oliver's *The Meaning of the Blues.*

ADDITIONAL LISTENING

"Castle House Rag," by James Reese Europe. *And the Beat Goes On.* CDI 38.

Come and Trip It: Instrumental Dance Music 1780s–1920s. New World 80293.

"Memphis Blues" (James Reese Europe). *Ken Burns Jazz: The Story of America's Music.* Sony 61432.

Ragtime I: The City. Smithsonian/Folkways RF017.

Ragtime II: The Country. Smithsonian/Folkways RF018.

"The Washington Post" (John Philip Sousa). *The Washington Post & Other American Newspaper Marches.* Advocate Brass Band Recordings 820.

JAZZ

THE NEW ORLEANS STYLE: THE TRADITIONAL JAZZ OF THE EARLY RECORDINGS

The most representative early jazz recordings date from about 1923. By that time the style known as "traditional" or New Orleans jazz was well established, though that city was no longer at the center of its development. Because those early recordings were so important in defining what jazz was and in laying the groundwork for what it was to become, we shall begin by examining an early recording in some detail, using it as a point of departure for a brief description of the basic nature and structure of jazz.

Traditional Jazz as Illustrative of Jazz Method and Structure

Our example is the famous "Dippermouth Blues." Though recorded by King Oliver's Creole Jazz Band in the North in 1923, it is representative of the New Orleans style in instrumentation, form, and manner of performance. The fact that this New Orleans group made recordings of this piece in Chicago and in Richmond, Indiana, shows the state of dissemination and transition that jazz had already entered by 1923.

The essence of jazz has been from the beginning, and remains, a *way* of playing and singing—a style of performance with many intangible features, but whose tangible aspects can be defined by accent, phrasing, tone color, the "bending" of pitch and rhythm, and the freedom of the individual player to improvise within well-understood limits. The basic *procedure* of jazz, from the traditional to much of the most recent, is to produce a series of variations on a standard formal harmonic plan, whether that of a popular song (a "standard"), or simply the "ground plan" of the blues, as outlined in Chapter 8.

A perception of *form* (whether they use the term or not) is something all jazz performers have; they always know at any given moment exactly where they are in the phrase, and in the chorus. Listeners can enrich their perception of jazz by developing this skill as well. Keeping track of the phrases gives the listener a feel for the blues form, and also where the boundaries are between the choruses. Not

Although Joe "King" Oliver's Creole Jazz Band stayed together for only four years, it recorded extensively and was one of the most influential early jazz bands. Here, in Chicago in 1923, we see its members: (back row, l. to r.) Honore Dutrey, trombone; Baby Dodds, drums; Joe "King" Oliver, cornet; Bill Johnson, banjo; Johnny Dodds, clarinet; (front) Louis Armstrong, slide trumpet (his main instrument, the trumpet, lies beside him on the floor); and Lil Hardin on piano. We hear the band play "Dippermouth Blues" on CD 3, track 21.

all jazz is in blues form, of course, but acquiring some sense of form serves well for most jazz listening, and it also makes it apparent when the standard form is deviated from, or abandoned entirely, as in modern or free jazz.

Listening Cue "Dippermouth Blues" King Oliver's Creole Jazz Band (2:18)

Listen For ▪ twelve-bar blues form ▪ varied instrumental grouping in each chorus

Visit http://www.music.wadsworth.com_3/Kingman for a full listening guide and other resources.

Form and Harmony

In its form, "Dippermouth Blues" (CD 3/21) is an apt illustration of the fundamental variation technique of jazz. After the short introduction (0:00 to 0:04), each of the nine sections (called "choruses") is an exposition of the twelve-bar blues form. A particularly clear example of the basic form is illustrated by King Oliver's chorus on the cornet between 1:16 and 1:29. For those keeping count, this is the sixth chorus.

Instrumentation The instrumentation of "Dippermouth Blues" is two cornets, one clarinet (0:32), one trombone (heard sliding into the first chorus 0:04), and a rhythm section of piano, banjo, and drums. Except for the addition of a second cornet, innovative for its time, this is a typical makeup for traditional jazz. The cornets, played by King Oliver and Louis Armstrong, were only later replaced by trumpets, which have a more incisive sound.

Texture In describing the texture, we can make an analogy with ragtime. The melody, or "front-line," instruments (in this case, the cornets, the clarinet, and the trombone) correspond to the right hand, to which is entrusted the melody, or the simultaneous overlayering of melodies. The rhythm section corresponds to the left hand, which has the job of keeping the beat going and of outlining the harmonies. If we grasp this division of function between front-line, or melody, and rhythm sections, it will serve us well in understanding jazz texture throughout the decades to follow. The front line will later increase, in the big band, to complete sections of saxophones, trumpets, trombones, and whatever additional melody instruments may be employed. The rhythm section, on the other hand, will remain to a remarkable degree the same as we hear it in these early recordings, only dropping the antiquated banjo and adding the string bass (in place of the tuba that was sometimes used in early jazz). The rhythm section is to remain the most stable and indispensable element of the jazz ensemble.

Ragtime, as a solo piano form, had a single melody (at most lightly harmonized) in the right hand. Traditional jazz, on the other hand, exhibits in its most typical choruses a complex layering of melodic lines, with the cornet (or cornets) in the middle, the trombone below, and the clarinet adding a more ornate and decorative line on top of it all. "Dippermouth Blues" shows this texture in all but the solo choruses, in which the clarinet and later the first cornet emerge as soloists.

Improvisation

Another vital ingredient of jazz is improvisation. Upon a formal and harmonic ground plan such as the one illustrated above, the musicians are free to invent, in an appropriate jazz style, their own melodic lines that fit with, and express, that harmony and that form. Ideally, as improvisation, it never sounds exactly the same twice. Depending upon the talent and the mood of the performer, the improvisation can be fresh, spontaneous, and loaded with new ideas, or it can follow patterns already established in previous performances or by other performers. But jazz improvisation is never a matter of "anything goes." It is a product of a fine balance between discipline and freedom—in the case of the jazz solo, between the discipline imposed by the preset form and harmony and the freedom to create within these limitations.

Frank Driggs Collection/Getty Images

In this publicity photo for Okeh Records in 1925 Chicago, the great jazz musician, Louis Armstrong, sits holding his trumpet at a piano while His Hot Five band stands around it: (l. to r.) Johnny St. Cyr, banjo; Johnny Dodds, saxophone; Kid Ory, trombone; and Armstrong's second wife, Lil Hardin, piano player and composer of "Hotter Than That," the selection we hear Louis Armstrong and His Hot Five play on CD 3, track 22.

Louis Armstrong (1898–1971) has been deemed the first great improvising soloist in jazz. He was one of the performers who defined the "hot" style of playing in the 1920s, and was an early master of "swing." Swing is not easily described, but all its elements amount to contradictions or dislocations, in one way or another, of a regular metric pattern—playing pairs of shorter notes unequally within a beat so as to give more length and stress to the first, displacing accents, or playing notes slightly behind or ahead of the beat. His solos, with their melodic inventiveness, rhythmic drive, and variety of tonal color, especially during the period from the 1920s through the late 1930s, were models that had a great influence on the course of jazz as it moved out of the traditional period. Also noteworthy was Armstrong's "scat" singing (at 1:18)—wordless improvising of complete choruses. All of this is well illustrated in "Hotter Than That" with Armstrong's Hot Five, recorded in Chicago in 1927 (CD 3/22). There is a clarinet solo (at 0:43) by Johnny Dodds, who was also the clarinetist in "Dippermouth Blues," and added to the "Five" is Lonnie Johnson on the guitar, with an interesting interplay with Armstrong's cornet near the end (Schuller, *Early Jazz* 111).

Listening Cue "Hotter Than That" Louis Armstrong and His Hot Five (2:58)

Listen For ▪ melodic inventiveness of cornet solos ▪ clarinet solo ▪ scat singing

Visit http://www.music.wadsworth.com_3/Kingman for a full listening guide and other resources.

DISSEMINATION AND CHANGE: BEFORE THE SWING ERA

Chicago

There were two jazz styles in Chicago in the 1920s, black and white, both played by musicians from New Orleans. There were the white bands such as the Original Dixieland Jazz Band, which had begun to record in Chicago in 1917, and the New Orleans Rhythm Kings. Young white musicians in Chicago who began to play jazz had heard the Original Dixieland Jazz Band, but not necessarily King Oliver's Creole Jazz Band, and it was the white bands that were their model. King Oliver, Louis Armstrong, and other black musicians were recording and playing on Chicago's South Side—but necessarily playing in places where the young white musicians weren't supposed to go. Mezz Mezzrow, a Jewish jazz player from Chicago who tried his best to *become* black, writes of the white Chicago jazz, "Chicago style is an innocent style. It's the playing of talented youngsters just learning their ABC's, and New Orleans was its source, but you can't expect any derivative to be as good as the source. New Orleans was simple, but not innocent" (Mezzrow and Wolfe 307).

One very talented Chicago youngster with a musical family background, who grew up knowing his musical ABCs, was Bix Beiderbecke (1903–1931). He listened to King Oliver and Louis Armstrong as well as the Original Dixieland Jazz Band, played cornet jobs around Chicago as early as 1921, and formed his own band (the Wolverines) in 1923. Bix's cornet solos are unique landmarks and attest to the talent of the "youngster" who was one of the greatest white jazz musicians of his time. An early recording by Beiderbecke's Wolverines is "Jazz Me Blues" of 1924 (see Additional Listening).

What was the milieu of jazz in the 1920s? Musicians played a great deal for and among themselves after hours, but for the paying public (a rapidly growing constituency) the home of jazz was the nightclub and its orbit of related establishments. This was to constitute its basic environment, physically and economically, for years to come. One effect of Prohibition was to relegate the public dispensing of liquor to the tough guy—the mobster who could either dictate to the law or take it into his own hands. Consequently, especially in Chicago and places like it, jazz came under the aegis of the gangster (Morris; Mezzrow and Wolfe). For a fuller understanding of jazz, one must keep in mind its environment—not only its effects on the lives of its musicians, but the whole set of prejudices that grew up around it. The nightclub and its milieu are still basic to the day-by-day support of a sizable core of players who earn wages playing jazz.

Two New York Developments

New York became the scene of intense jazz activity in the 1920s. But the stage had been set for this long before, as we saw in the preceding chapter. Two important developments began to emerge in New York before 1930. The first was the "Harlem piano" (or "stride piano") described in Chapter 15 (CD 3/18). The second was the evolution of the big band. This led directly into the period of jazz's greatest stability, popularity, and economic security—an era that lasted until the end of World War II, and that has been designated as the *swing era*. New York can claim no monopoly in the development of the big bands. But it did serve as a magnet to draw talented musicians from New Orleans (often by way of Chicago), from Chicago itself, from Kansas City, and elsewhere—musicians who helped forge the new ensemble that was to carry jazz to every part of the land and, ultimately, the world.

Early Steps Toward the Big Band

The term *big band* may be misleading. Compared with a full orchestra, the bands were still small—scarcely more than about fifteen musicians. But that was twice the size of a New Orleans–style band, and many players and jazz fans considered the "big" bands a betrayal of the very essence of jazz. We can see the big bands today as a pragmatic solution to the problem of balancing the demand for a fuller, larger, and more varied sound with the need to retain the key characteristic of jazz—improvisational freedom, and the elusive hot quality that goes with it.

We have examined "Dippermouth Blues" as recorded by King Oliver's Creole Jazz Band, with only seven musicians. Fletcher Henderson (1897–1952), a pianist and leader-arranger from Georgia, recorded the same piece, with slight additions, in New York in 1925, calling it "Sugar Foot Stomp." The differences constitute an interesting documentation of the beginnings of the big band. There are now eleven musicians, the most significant addition being two saxophones. The individual hot solos are still there, the most memorable being the choruses played by Louis Armstrong himself, who had come from Chicago to join Henderson's band and who plays essentially the same solos as in the earlier, King Oliver version. But the new trend toward *arranged* jazz is apparent in the way the instruments play predetermined figures together at the "breaks" (the fill-in passages at the ends of the phrases), in the tightly disciplined and rehearsed (if not written-down) clarinet ensemble playing, and especially in the almost choralelike presentation of the blues progression near the end. (This piece, important for a fuller appreciation of the development of the big band, is available from several sources; see Additional Listening.)

THE SWING ERA AND THE BIG BANDS

The big-band style in the East drew on the New Orleans archetypal style, either directly or by way of Chicago. The swing era, virtually synonymous with the heyday of the big bands, is usually thought to have begun in the early 1930s, to have come to full flower about 1935, and to have bloomed gloriously for nearly a decade. By that time, after the repeal of Prohibition and partial recovery from the Depression, the mob-controlled nightclubs no longer constituted the nearly exclusive support and environment for jazz. Dance halls, which by the mid-1930s had grown into large, well-appointed, and well-attended ballrooms, gave jazz a new forum and a broader popular base. The big "name" bands toured these and gave stage shows in theaters. Recordings sold extremely well by that time, and could be heard on phonographs at home, in the jukeboxes that provided background music at just about any establishment where you could eat or drink, and on the new popular mass medium of the day, radio. The disc jockey, with his enormous influence, came into being. There were also weekly broadcasts of live bands. Movies featured jazz bands. This was the period when jazz enjoyed its widest public.

Three Significant Bands

Duke Ellington Of all the jazz musicians who came into prominence with the big band, none had a more influential career than Edward Kennedy "Duke" Ellington (1899–1974), whose creative activity spanned half a century. He was a pianist, but his medium of expression was the band itself, and as leader, arranger, and composer he made music with a group that held together with exceptional consistency and continuity throughout the years. A famous early piece is "East St. Louis Toodle-oo," which shows already the smooth and disciplined playing and the use of instrumental effects and colors typical of Ellington's essentially orchestral approach to jazz (see Additional Listening).

The Ellington band's unique use of instrumental color is the product of two factors: the imagination of Ellington himself (joined, from 1938 on, by his arranger, Billy Strayhorn) and a succession of remarkable players that Ellington had in his band. Trumpet players Bubber Miley, Cootie Williams, and Ray Nance (who was also a violinist); trombonists Joe Nanton and Juan Tizol; clarinetist Barney Bigard; and saxophonists Johnny Hodges (soprano and alto), Ben Webster (tenor), and Harry Carney (baritone) are a few of the musicians whose expansion of the tonal possibilities of their instruments, together with Ellington's use of those new possibilities, contributed to the Ellington sound. From the crucial period of the 1940s is "Ko-ko" (CD 3/23).

Frank Driggs Collection/Getty Images

Duke Ellington sits at the piano in front of his band at the Cotton Club where, from 1927 to 1931, they played nightly for dancing and the extravagant floor shows that made the club famous. Located at Lenox Avenue and 142nd Street in New York City's Harlem, within an easy cab ride of Broadway, the Cotton Club offered its comfortable after-theater crowd the slightly illicit excitement of enjoying black entertainment in a black neighborhood while remaining part of an all-white audience. We hear Ellington and his orchestra perform "Ko-ko" on CD 3, track 23.

Listening Cue "Ko-ko" Duke Ellington and His Orchestra (2:40)

Listen For ▪ twelve-bar blues ▪ call-and-response pattern ▪ varied tone colors

Visit http://www.music.wadsworth.com_3/Kingman for a full listening guide and other resources.

In addition to being a noteworthy example of the varied tone colors (sounds and textures) for which the Ellington band was famous, "Ko-ko" is formally a twelve-bar blues in the less usual minor mode (actually E-flat minor). Much of its rhythmic structure is an expression of the familiar call-and-response pattern (for example, at 0:12, 1:25, and 1:43) found so often in African American music. The eerily human "ya-ya" first heard at 0:31 is a trombone played with a plunger mute. Duke Ellington is heard playing the piano solo at 1:08 accompanied by repeated figures ("riffs") in the saxophones.

As a composer, Duke Ellington had a broad range. He was primarily an instrumental composer, writing for his band, but he also was responsible for a fairly large output of songs. Some songs began as such, and some resulted from putting words to his band numbers; *Concerto for Cootie* of 1940, for example, later became the basis for the song "Do Nothing Till You Hear from Me." He pioneered in writing more extended works for jazz ensemble, beginning as early as 1931 with *Creole Rhapsody* (which filled two sides of a ten-inch 78-rpm record) and including *Black, Brown and Beige* (1943, a multimovement commentary on the history of black people in America) and many suites, from the *Deep South Suite* of 1946 to the *Togo Brava Suite* of 1971. He also wrote musicals, film scores, a ballet, incidental music to a Shakespeare play, and, in the late 1960s and early 1970s, a series of *Sacred Concerts*.

The Midwest and Count Basie There was another part of the country to be heard from in the 1930s. This was "the West" to easterners, but it was actually the heartland, and in particular Kansas City. In the days before mass media threatened to blanket the whole country and induce a homogenized culture suffocating to regional artistic identity, it was possible for different areas to develop artistic dialects as distinctive as their speech. It might seem like a fine distinction, but the hard-driving beat—"jump," it was called, or "four heavy beats to a bar, and no cheating" (to quote Count Basie)—of "Taxi War Dance" from 1939 is nonetheless a key factor (see Additional Listening). These steady, hard, and insistent four-beats are the Kansas City ingredient that went into big-band jazz after the arrival in the East of Bennie Moten (1894–1935), William "Count" Basie (1904–1984), Lester Young (1909–1959), and a host of other players from "the West." It was closely akin to the drive of boogie-woogie, which had come from the same part of the country.

Benny Goodman Anyone born before 1925 has lived through this most opulent period in the history of jazz and can call up a litany of the big bands and their star players. Duke Ellington, Count Basie, and Benny Goodman have been taken as representative, but there are many more. Benny Goodman (1909–1986), clarinetist and bandleader, was an important white musician of the swing era. His highly skilled band of fourteen to sixteen musicians played an essentially hot style closely derived from that of black jazz artists of the time. Goodman acknowledged this heritage, using arrangements written for him by Fletcher Henderson, some of which were based on traditional New Orleans originals by King Oliver or Jelly Roll Morton. In addition, Goodman was one of the first to incorporate black musicians into his ensembles, using them at first as featured performers in his trio, quartet, and sextet. The disciplined but driving swing of his band helped to bring jazz to a new plateau of popularity and acceptance as dance music. Typical of the Goodman swing style is the Fletcher Henderson arrangement of Oliver's "Sugar Foot Stomp," which may be compared with two earlier versions of that work: Fletcher Henderson's own 1925 New York recording and its original 1923 recording as "Dippermouth Blues" (CD 3/21).

Four More Aspects of the Swing Era

The Great Jazz Singers Though jazz is fundamentally instrumental music, the period of its greatest popularity—the era of the big bands, their tours, their live radio shows, their recordings, their movies—was also the period of the great jazz singers: Bing Crosby, Billie Holiday, Ella Fitzgerald, and Frank Sinatra, to name a few. Most of the songs they sang were tied to musicals, which flourished during the same period that jazz did. But there were some memorable nonshow tunes as well—"Star Dust" (1929, Hoagy Carmichael, with words by Mitchell Parish); "Sophisticated Lady" (1933, Duke Ellington); and "Stormy Weather" (Harold Arlen) among them.

Latin Influence Latin bands were very popular at the time. The rumba craze was no less intense than that of the tango earlier, or the mambo, samba, or chachachá later. What the purely Latin bands played was not jazz, but it illustrates and reminds us of the perennial Latin presence and influence in American music. Jazz was by no means unaffected by it, and Latin drummers were soon to be incorporated into jazz ensembles (as were those from Africa, which has quite a different tradition). An interesting example, from somewhat later, of this Latin assimilation is "Jahbero" (1948), with the celebrated Cuban drummer Chano Pozo.

The Small Combo Another aspect is the simultaneous cultivation of the small ensemble in the era of the big band. This was no longer the old-time jazz ensemble (which did indeed enjoy a revival) but the intimate group of three to seven players that was the vehicle for developing some of the newest ideas in jazz. Its commercial aspect was represented by the "cocktail combo" playing in small bars, but there were important artistic dimensions to the small combo as well. The Benny Goodman Sextet's recording of "I Found a New Baby" (1941) is a particularly good example because of the solo for electric guitar by Charlie Christian. Actually the small combo has been present at every turn in the history of jazz; it was not an invention of the post–World War II "cool" or "progressive" schools.

Louis Armstrong had recorded with from two to six musicians in the 1920s. The solo pianist also flourished; Earl Hines (1903–1983), Art Tatum (1909–1956), Bud Powell (1924–1966), and Erroll Garner (1921–1977) were leading figures.

The Traditional Revival The traditional, or New Orleans, style of jazz has shown a persistent vitality. An early copy of New Orleans style (mostly white and more or less New York–oriented), known generally as "Dixieland," was translated into big-band terms in the work of such white bandleaders as Bob Crosby ("South Rampart Street Parade," 1937) and Eddie Condon ("Somebody Loves Me," 1944). But a real revival of the older style was one of the landmarks of the 1940s as well. In an episode in American music replete with both nostalgia and human interest, players who had been active in the very early days of jazz (some of whom had never before been recorded) were located, sometimes with considerable difficulty, and reinstated with honors in the kingdom of jazz, for the purpose of re-creating the authentic traditions and music of the long-gone New Orleans beginnings. How authentic such re-creations can be in an art so basically improvisational, and so dependent upon the player's subjective impressions of a *total* environment, may be open to question. But the documents are there now, recorded a generation after the fact, for all time. For examples, listen to Bunk Johnson, legendary symbol of this revival, in "Down by the Riverside" (1942; see Additional Listening), or Kid Ory, in any number of revival recordings. Younger musicians, including Lu Watters and Turk Murphy, also became interested in the old style.

Wartime and the Seeds of Change

In turbulent times, people tend to find comfort in things that are familiar. Thus, with the entry of the United States into World War II in 1941, Americans flocked to ballrooms to hear the name bands and bought the latest records; and overseas soldiers, sailors, airmen, and marines heard the same bands and the same pieces. (Nonetheless wartime hardships, including shortages of gasoline for touring, took their toll among the bands, some of which disbanded even before the war was over.) Meanwhile, underneath the desperately needed continuity of the surface, changes were being wrought that would profoundly alter the jazz scene once the war was over.

THE EMERGENCE OF MODERN JAZZ: BOP AS A TURNING POINT

In the decades since the end of World War II in 1945, the whole fabric of Western music has frayed into so many different strands that it has become a daunting task to keep track of them. Jazz has been no exception. Beginning in the 1940s a combination of factors wrought changes in jazz that brought a whole new set of leaders to the fore and made significant alterations, not only in the music itself, but also in the function of jazz, in its audience, and in the way it was perceived. From the beginning of the 1930s through the end of World War II, there had been, for most fans, one kind of jazz—that of the big bands. The best-known names were Benny Goodman, Glenn Miller, Artie Shaw, Tommy Dorsey, Harry James, and the like. (White bandleaders all, to be sure. Even then, the bands of Duke Ellington, Count Basie, Billy Eckstine, Lionel Hampton, Jimmie Lunceford, and other black jazzmen, who were regarded by aficionados as playing "real jazz," had a smaller public.) Jazz, however attenuated by the popular bands in the minds of its devotees, came as close in this period to being synonymous with America's popular music as it has ever been or is ever likely to be again. After the war, all was different; the place of jazz in American culture changed. It lost its mass following, especially among the young, who have shown repeatedly that what they really like most is music with a strong beat that they can dance to (a need that was soon to be met by black rhythm and blues, and white rock and roll). At the same time, jazz began to be considered seriously as art music, not only by its fans and critics, but by some of its practitioners as well.

The trend began with bop (a shortening of "rebop" or "bebop"). The first outstanding exponents of the new style were the trumpeter John "Dizzy" Gillespie (1917–1993) and the alto saxophonist Charlie Parker (1920–1955), together with pianist Thelonious Monk (1917–1982) and drummer Kenny Clarke (1914–1985). Gillespie and Parker had keenly creative minds and extremely facile techniques on their respective instruments. Bop developed as the first jazz to demand an entire ensemble of virtuoso performers. (In this sense, bop bore the same relationship to swing jazz that bluegrass did to country music.) The ensemble was characteristically small—a quintet or a sextet made up of a rhythm section (piano, bass, and drums) and a front line of just two or three instrumentalists. In addition to an astounding virtuosity, there was an obscuring of the familiar melodies jazz fans had grown accustomed to hearing. Bop continued to use the harmonic basis (the "changes") of certain jazz standards (Gershwin's "I Got Rhythm" was a favorite), but free, elaborate, and very difficult new melodic variations were invented on the original harmonies, often overlapping phrase endings. Frequently the harmonic plan itself, the very basis of jazz, would be changed through the use of substitute chords. The speed (tempo) was usually very fast, and the supporting rhythm section became much lighter. The cymbal, with its bright, insinuating tone, and the string bass, now "walking" at a fast pace, together took over from the drums the job of keeping the beat, and the drums could now be used both less frequently and more effectively for accentuation, or for the superimposing of cross-rhythms that made the rhythmic texture more complex and tended at times to obscure the beat. From then on, the jazz rhythm section was permanently transformed—a development that would outlast bop itself. This lightening and obscuring of the beat, together with the fast tempos, discouraged dancing to bebop; it became instead a music for listeners, and this encouraged its being perceived as an art music.

Early bop was not well documented in commercial recordings, which began to pick it up after its influence among jazz players had spread to a considerable extent. There is no more typical or frequently cited example of early bop than Charlie Parker's "KoKo" of 1945 (not to be confused with Ellington's "Ko-ko"), a superb distillation of the essence of the style.

Frank Driggs Collection/Getty Images

Three great jazz musicians of the bebop era appear on stage at Charlie Parker's legendary nightclub, Birdland, in Manhattan, New York, in 1951. From the left, they are Tommy Potter on bass, Charlie Parker on alto saxophone, and Dizzy Gillespie on trumpet. On the right, briefly joining them, is tenor saxophonist John Coltrane, who will take jazz in a new direction. On CD 3, track 24, we hear Charlie Parker play "KoKo," and on track 15, John Coltrane performs an excerpt from "Out of This World."

CD 3

24

Listening Cue "KoKo" Charlie Parker (2:55)

Listen For ▪ very fast tempo ▪ small ensemble ▪ unison passages

Visit http://www.music.wadsworth.com_3/Kingman for a full listening guide and other resources.

There are only four performers: Charlie Parker, alto saxophone; Dizzy Gillespie, trumpet and piano; Curley Russell, bass; and Max Roach, drums. Note the unison passages (all players performing together) that open and close the number. (These passages possibly had their origins in the rigorous practice sessions Parker and Gillespie had in the early days, playing musical studies in unison in every key as fast as they could.) The unisons were new to jazz, and were a contradiction of the old spirit of individualistic performances and improvisations that underlay the traditional jazz of the 1920s and 1930s. The unison lines became in turn a tradition that stuck, reappearing in post-bop works.

In due course bop was translated into big-band terms, just as traditional jazz had been before it. In "Things to Come" (1946), Gillespie records with a band of seventeen pieces (large even for the big-band era) a work that transfers to the large ensemble the drive and virtuosity of bop. "Oop-Pap-a-Da" (1947) and "Lemon Drop" (1948) show another characteristic, vocalizing on nonsense syllables (which provided titles for many of these pieces). The singing exhibits the same fluidity and virtuosity that we hear in the instrumental solos. (Scat singing, as this is called, was not new to jazz; Louis Armstrong, as we heard in CD 3/22, was doing it in the 1920s.)

The Progeny of Bop

Cool Jazz What has become known as "cool" jazz followed so closely on the heels of bop that it can almost be regarded as the other side of the same coin. It presents a stark contrast to bop, exhibited in a music of understatement, of restraint, of leanness. However, many of the same musicians played both bop and cool, including Miles Davis, J. J. Johnson, and Kenny Clark. "Criss-Cross" (1951), by Thelonious Monk, reveals key characteristics of the cool trend. One of the most important is the use of the vibraphone, which produces a warm, undulating tone. The tone of the "vibes" made it almost a symbol of cool jazz. Cool jazz dominated what was *new* in jazz of the 1950s—not what was popular. Its adherents were to be found mostly in intellectual circles—on college campuses, among both students and professors.

Hard Bop and Funk In the 1950s and 1960s, there was a reaction to the restraint and contrived intellectualism of cool jazz in the form of *hard bop*. It represented a pull back toward the roots of jazz, especially its roots in black gospel music. Pianist and composer Horace Silver (b. 1928) and drummer Art Blakey (1919–1990) were prominent figures in hard bop. Many of the features of bop are present (the texture of the rhythm section, the unison openings and closings). But hard bop tended to relax the frenetic speed of bop, and the rhythmic basis of the newer *funky jazz*, as it was called, often showed a return to the characteristically black backbeat. There was a preference for darker, "earthier" tone colors; for that reason the huskier tenor saxophone was preferred over the lighter alto. This is illustrated in "Now's the Time," by a quartet that includes Sonny Rollins, tenor sax, and Herbie Hancock, piano.

Modal Jazz Another successor to bop in which many of the same musicians were involved has been called *modal jazz*. It represented a new venture for jazz both harmonically and structurally, in that it no longer used the chord progressions of standard tunes as the basis for improvisation; what replaced these was simply a succession of scales on which the performer improvised. A seminal set of pieces that set a precedent for jazz in this direction was the 1959 album *Kind of Blue*. The trumpeter Miles Davis (1926–1991), who had a hand in influencing new developments and indicating new trends in jazz for more than three decades, beginning in the late 1940s, was the leader and stimulator of the small combo that produced this album.

John Coltrane (1926–1967) was a crucially important voice in the jazz of the decade 1955–1965. A commanding player technically, he was also one of the most serious-minded composer-performers in jazz. "Out of This World" (CD 3/25), a fourteen-minute meditation on the tune by Harold Arlen, is a landmark work recorded in 1962. The harmony is virtually static for the whole piece, with a rocking back and forth between two chords. (No chord changes here as one can expect in traditional jazz.) But this static background is a perfect foil for Coltrane's contribution on the saxophone, which weaves an increasingly involved and tense commentary on the Arlen tune. Notice also the virtuosic display of the drummer throughout. A brief excerpt is given here.

Listening Cue "Out of This World" (excerpt), John Coltrane (4:00)

Listen For ▪ static harmony on piano ▪ saxophone's elaboration of tune ▪ virtuosic drumming

Visit http://www.music.wadsworth.com_3/Kingman for a full listening guide and other resources.

Free Jazz A small proportion of Coltrane's later work fell into the category of one of the most extreme, least understood, and least popular movements in jazz history—free jazz. Ornette Coleman's album *Free Jazz* of 1960 gave the concept its name and was a seminal recording. Free jazz exhibits one or more of the following characteristics: (1) collective improvisation; (2) freedom from preset chord progressions and/or established tonality; (3) extension of the sonorous range of instruments (especially the saxophone) by playing extremely high pitches, or making the instruments squeal, shriek, or groan; (4) playing deliberately "out of tune" in relation to conventional intonation; (5) expansion of form, by creating pieces in which the length of the sections, and hence the overall length, is not predetermined, and which may thus be quite extensive. ("Free Jazz" lasts thirty-six minutes, Coltrane's "Ascension" nearly forty, Cecil Taylor's "3 Phasis" nearly an hour.) The Art Ensemble of Chicago's "Certain Blacks" (early 1970s), with its spoken or chanted additions, is typical of the more theatrical, satirical, and racially specific aspects of the genre.

Some writers (Jones; Roberts; Kofsky) have emphasized the relationship of all the jazz of the 1960s, in which black musicians played a leading role (hard bop, modal jazz, free jazz, and so on), to the social turmoil of the times. Those writers also point out the identification of many of the young black jazz musicians, such as Albert Ayler (1936–1970) and Archie Shepp (b. 1937), with one aspect or another of the black nationalism movement.

A turning away from extremism and experimentalism, and a reaching out to a larger audience, began to occur in both jazz and classical music in the 1970s. The overtly and even militantly racial overtones that characterized some black jazz of the 1960s abated in the 1970s, and many of its proponents began to adopt (or readopt) more accessible and popular styles such as rhythm and blues.

Metronome/Getty Images

Here Miles Davis (in dark sunglasses) plays a trumpet solo while tenor saxophonist John Coltrane stands by in 1958, when Coltrane played in Davis' Sextet. We hear Coltrane on CD 3, track 25, and on track 16, an excerpt from Miles Davis' "Bitches Brew," the 1969 recording that introduced rock-and-roll rhythms and harmonies along with electronic keyboards to a jazz audience. After "Bitches Brew," Miles Davis became a popular draw at such rock venues as the famed Fillmore Auditoriums in New York and San Francisco.

The "Third Stream" and Other Developments Parallel to Bop

Parallel to the lineage of bop to cool to modal to free jazz was another set of related developments. What these developments had in common was the incorporation of musical elements, procedures, and actual instruments (violins, cellos, flutes, and French horns, for example) that had been considered foreign to jazz up to that point. Gunther Schuller (b. 1925) invented and applied the term "third stream" shortly after midcentury to the merging of elements from the jazz and "classical," or European, traditions to form a new "stream" in music.

Small combos playing a species of "cool" jazz began to incorporate materials derived from the European classical tradition. The so-called West Coast school of jazz (mostly white performers, including such musicians as Dave Brubeck, Paul Desmond, Gerry Mulligan, and Shorty Rogers) is illustrative of this development.

One aspect of these explorations was rhythmic innovations that took jazz out of the duple grouping of pulses that had characterized it since its earliest associations with the march and the two-step. The first change in this direction was the introduction of triple meter, typified by the waltz. Then followed so-called asymmetrical meters, in which groupings of two, three, and four pulses were mixed in recurring sequence. "Take Five," by Paul Desmond, is illustrative (see Additional Listening).

Gunther Schuller himself worked toward a synthesis of avant-garde European procedures and sounds with jazz styles and improvisation, over a considerable period of time between the late 1940s and the early 1960s; several of his resulting compositions were included in the album *Jazz Abstractions*.

THE PLURALISM OF THE LAST QUARTER-CENTURY

Rock Fusions and Electric Jazz in the 1970s and 1980s

The piece "Bitches Brew" (CD 4/1), from Miles Davis' landmark album of 1969 (also titled *Bitches Brew*), hints at a *jazz-rock fusion* that was to be further explored in the 1970s. The piano and the guitar have been completely replaced by their electric counterparts, and there is a change in the *rhythmic* basis of the music—always an indicator of major developments in jazz. The beat is now mostly the "square" beat of rock—that is, with evenly spaced subdivisions. To hold this extended piece together (it takes almost a half hour to play), "Bitches Brew" uses an older and more basic device—that of the *ground bass*. After a long introduction (nearly three minutes) featuring a collage of apparently random unmeasured sounds and electronically induced echo effects in Davis' trumpet playing sound, the bass lays down an insistent ostinato that, except for the return of the introductory material at the end, will underlie the rest of the piece. We have encountered the ostinato in boogie-woogie; "Bitches Brew" extends that device through hundreds of repetitions. The excerpt presented here is from about three minutes into the piece and highlights the ground bass as it makes its initial appearance. With close listening, it can be heard throughout.

Listening Cue **"Bitches Brew"** (excerpt), Miles Davis (2:32)

Listen For ▪ electric instruments ▪ square rock beat ▪ ground bass

Visit http://www.music.wadsworth.com_3/Kingman for a full listening guide and other resources.

Many of the players on these Davis recordings of the late 1960s became important in further developments in the jazz-rock fusion of the 1970s, including pianists Herbie Hancock, Chick Corea, and Joe Zawinul, guitarist John McLaughlin, and saxophonist Wayne Shorter. The group Weather Report, formed in 1971 by Josef Zawinul, reflected a broad range of trends and influences. Indeed, their work can serve as an index of the ingredients of much of what has been called *electric jazz*, or the fusion music of the 1970s. In 1983, pianist Herbie Hancock, an alumnus of the Miles Davis group of the 1960s, dispensed with horns entirely. With the aid of a very complex electronic technology, Hancock produced a piece titled "Rockit" that was number one on the pop charts and represented an extreme of "electrification" in jazz.

The New Virtuosity, the Return to Acoustic Jazz, and the Reconnection with Tradition

One of the most significant developments in the last two decades has been the post-fusion resumption of the acoustic jazz tradition. Like the bebop of fifty years before, this new resurgence has been led by a new generation of virtuosos—highly skilled performers who are also composers and who, in addition, have a thorough understanding of jazz traditions. A well-known example is the trumpet player Wynton Marsalis (b. 1961), who has demonstrated a remarkable fluency in both jazz and classical music—a flexibility that is increasingly common among today's musicians.

There has been a resurgence—a reinterpretation—of bebop, to the extent that the term "neo-bop" has, not surprisingly, been applied to this stage of jazz. The unison openings and closings are there, and as an occasional alternative to the prevailing small combo, "big bands" (big in sound, at least) have been formed, made up of virtuoso performers throughout, reminiscent of the Gillespie bands of the 1940s. Tempos that are fast even by the standards of bop in the 1940s and 1950s make the term "super-bop" appropriate; perhaps the stretching of the limits of human capacity, so pervasive in athletics, is a characteristic of our times.

The new post-fusion acoustic jazz is not revivalism; new aspects, new additions, new influences are evident. The palette of instrumental color has been expanded; Jaco Pastorius (1951–1987), for example, in addition to presenting the electric bass as a jazz solo instrument (a troublesome exception, perhaps, to labeling this development acoustic jazz), also introduced virtuoso harmonica (as played by "Toots" Thielemans) and virtuoso steel drum (as played by Othello Molineaux) with his band Word of Mouth, in "Invitation" (1983).

Accompanying the return to acoustic jazz has been the appearance of a number of albums that pay homage to the composers, performers, and songs of the past. This homage takes the form of reinterpretations of jazz standards by song and show composers such as Gershwin, Rodgers, Kern, Porter, and Arlen, and of instrumental compositions by jazz performers such as Charlie Parker, Thelonious Monk, and Ornette Coleman. Along with the *reinterpretation* on their own terms of jazz standards by present-day artists, there is also the actual *conservation* of jazz classics as live music. There are a growing number of *repertory bands*—bands whose function it is to re-create specific pieces. Since much of what is unique to jazz is often not written down in musical notation but improvised, these bands rely on what has been preserved on recordings. Repertory bands began to develop in the 1970s, as a result of the independent work of Gunther Schuller and of noted jazz critic Martin Williams. In the 1980s the American Jazz Orchestra and the Lincoln Center Jazz Orchestra began playing in New York, and in 1990 the Smithsonian Jazz Masterworks Orchestra was founded in the nation's capital. There are also the numerous school workshops and clinics, such as those established by Stan Kenton and Maynard Ferguson, which have helped to make jazz programs in schools and colleges effective conservators of the big-band tradition.

PROJECTS

1. Make an assessment of jazz in your local area. Where is it being played, and for whom? What styles can one hear? Are there bands playing in a revival of the big-band style? of traditional (Dixieland) jazz? of cool?

2. If the calendar of musical events in your area allows, or your travel capabilities permit, attend three live jazz performances. Try for a variety of experiences. Write a commentary on the music of each, placing it in the general framework of contemporary jazz as outlined in this chapter.

3. If your area has a radio show devoted to jazz (on a public radio station, for example), interview the commentator or disc jockey on one of the following topics: (a) his or her assessment of the current trends in jazz; (b) what mail or telephone responses tell about local tastes in jazz; (c) his or her own list of the five best new releases of the past year or so, with reasons for the choice; (d) a topic of your own invention.

4. If there is a retired jazz musician in your community, interview him/her about his/her experiences, recollections of noted jazz figures, working conditions, comparisons of jazz *now* with jazz *then,* and so on.

ADDITIONAL LISTENING

Ken Burns Jazz: The Story of America's Music. Sony 61432.

"Down by the Riverside." Bunk Johnson, *Bunk and the New Orleans Revival, 1942–1947.* Jasmine Music 635.

"East St. Louis Toodle-oo." Duke Ellington, *The Very Best of Duke Ellington.* RCA 63729.

"Jazz Me Blues (with the Wolverines)." Bix Beiderbecke, *Bix Beiderbecke & The Chicago Cornets.* Milestone 47019.

"Sugar Foot Stomp." Fletcher Henderson, *New York to Chicago: 1924–1936.* Fremeaux & Assoc. 219.

"Take Five." Paul Desmond, *The Paul Desmond Quartet Live.* Polygram Records 543501.

"Taxi War Dance." Count Basie, *The Essential Count Basie, Vol. 1.* Sony 40608.

CLASSICAL MUSIC

VI

Considered against an expansive background dominated by vernacular traditions including jazz, blues, rock, and country music, classical music would seem to occupy only a small corner of the American musical panorama. Yet no consideration of American music would be complete without it. Americans have cultivated classical music (known variously as concert music, art music, or fine-art music) with an intense fervor, and from many different perspectives. Certain composers, performers, writers, and critics, for example, have chosen to treat classical music as an elevated, even esoteric, art form, while others have sought to make it more accessible and meaningful to a broader audience. Some have used it to assert a cultural authority abroad, others to project a cultural identity at home. Although the corner occupied by classical music in America might seem small, its history is rich and complex, and only recently has it begun to be told. (An excellent step in that direction is *Classical Music in America: A History of Its Rise and Fall*, by Joseph Horowitz.) In the three chapters that follow, classical music is examined according to three different ways in which it has been produced (there are many more): first, as a means of projecting an American identity on the national and world stages; second, as a site for exploring innovative approaches to experiencing music as art; and finally, as a mainstream currency of American popular culture within the film industry—a largely unrecognized context in which a significant part of the U.S. population consumes classical music on a regular basis.

Here, young musicians tune up for orchestra class at the Knowledge Is Power Program Academy in the South Bronx, New York. Part of a network of public middle schools, the KIPP Orchestra regularly tours in the summer and has played at Carnegie Hall and Harlem's Apollo Theater. Strong programs such as the KIPP Academy embrace the value of classical music in education as part of the rigorous training and preparation they give their students.

THE SEARCH FOR AN AMERICAN IDENTITY

If jazz is viewed by many as the most representative form of American music, it would be fair to say that classical music is perceived to be the least. There are two reasons for this. First, classical music is rooted in the elite, aristocratic traditions of Western Europe, which are distinctly at odds with the values of egalitarianism upon which the United States was founded. To this day, classical music is tinged with an air of "elitism" that has contributed to its marginalization in America. Second, the core repertories performed by American orchestras have historically favored the music of Western European composers. A dramatic illustration of the latter was the main concert event of the American Centennial Exposition held in Philadelphia in 1876.

On May 10, 1876, an orchestra of about 150 instrumentalists assembled to mark the 100th anniversary of the American Declaration of Independence. With President Ulysses S. Grant in attendance, the most celebrated conductor in America at the time, Theodore Thomas (of German extraction), raised his baton to begin the centerpiece of the concert, a special work that had been commissioned specifically for the occasion: the *Grosser Festmarsch* (also known as the *Centennial March*) by the German composer Richard Wagner (1813–1883).

The value of Wagner's contribution to the American Centennial concert can be measured by the $5,000 price tag that went along with it—a large amount now, even more so then. More important, the value of European music in general was reflected in the fact that other works performed on that most American occasion were by such European luminaries as Beethoven, Mozart, Handel, Strauss, and Schubert. Only two American composers were programmed: John Knowles Paine (1839–1906) and Dudley Buck (1839–1909).

The Centennial concert program of 1876 reveals a fundamental issue faced by American composers of classical music at the end of the nineteenth century: they simply could not escape the long shadows cast by the Europeans. Furthermore, the sound of music by American composers at the time was largely indistinct from that of their European counterparts. The cool reception of works on concerts dedicated wholly to the music of American composers at the Exposition

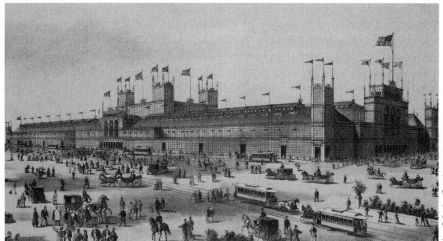

On opening day of the 1876 American Centennial Exposition in Philadelphia, conductor Theodore Thomas led an ensemble of 800 singers and 150 instrumentalists assembled on an enormous wooden platform stretching along the length of the Main Building (shown here) and out onto the fairgrounds. The concert, which performed only two American works, pointed to the need for an authentic classical sound that captured the American identity—a need that is answered by the selections we hear in these final chapters.

Universelle of 1889 in Paris points up this fact. As one reviewer said of the works, "There does not exist in America a compositional school, properly speaking. . . . Like the race that produced them [that is, the works], [their music is] formed of a mélange of German, English, and French elements." Another remarked, "American music is not yet born; it is still searching. In the country of [Thomas] Edison, all discoveries are possible, and as everything there goes at great speed, we may expect, one of these days, to see the music of the New World arise, fully formed, dazzling, and original to enchant us at the first note. Meanwhile, it has not found itself" (Bomberger 54).

The lack of an "American Mozart," an "American Beethoven," or an "American Wagner," and the perceived absence of an authentic, native sound that was characteristic of the United States at the end of the nineteenth century galvanized the search for an American identity in the decades that ensued. That search, oddly enough, would be sparked in some circles by a European composer who visited the United States between 1892 and 1895, the Czech composer Antonin Dvořák.

This chapter focuses on American attitudes toward classical music in the nineteenth century and the first half of the twentieth. In particular, it looks at various ways in which America attempted to stake out its own identity in a cultivated art form that is fundamentally European. Is there a distinctly American contribution to classical music? No less important to staking out an American identity in classical music is the issue of having Americans identify with the result. Thus, an issue that continually arises is that of accessibility: how to make an art form that is historically grounded in the elite, aristocratic circles of Europe accessible to a broad American audience.

MUSIC EDUCATION BEFORE THE CIVIL WAR

The most significant endeavors of the decades preceding the Civil War (1861–1865) had to do with the teaching of music to the broad masses of people, and especially to children. Three men were representative of this movement: Lowell Mason (1792–1872), Artemas Nixon Johnson (1817–1892), and George Frederick Root (1820–1895). We have already encountered Root in Chapter 14, incidentally, as the composer of some enormously popular Civil War songs, including the "The Battle Cry of Freedom" (CD 3/13).

What is most important to note is that the teaching of music, the establishment of music schools, the publication of numerous graded collections of music, and the founding of choral societies (all in a way outgrowths of the singing-school movement described in Chapter 10) did not cater to a musical elite but, on the contrary, sought to bring what were seen as the benefits of music to the broadest possible public. Neither Mason nor Root had exaggerated pretensions as composers, but they wrote songs, hymns, anthems, and cantatas that were accessible to singers of modest abilities. Both became shrewd businessmen, and by successfully reaching this broad public, they became wealthy (both were connected with their own publishing firms). But they never abandoned the ideal of supplying what Root called the "people's song." As Root explained, "I respected myself, and was thankful when I could write something that all the people would sing" (83).

George Frederick Root composed many works in the then popular genre of the cantata (music for a choral group). *The Haymakers* (1857), a large-scale secular work, deals in an idyllic way with one episode of farm life—a life that Root knew well from his personal background. Unjustly forgotten, *The Haymakers* shows Root to have been a more accomplished composer than would be evident from his popular songs. His music is expressive, even on occasion dramatic, while remaining well within the capabilities of the amateur singers for whom it was intended. It is an extremely rare example of attention paid in the arts to the life and work of the American farmer.

Outspoken Nativists of the Mid-Nineteenth Century

Given the cultural background of the adolescent nation, it was understandable, even inevitable, that most of those concerned with improvement, education, and reform in music should turn to Europe for models. There was, especially in the intellectual and culturally elite circles in Boston, New York, and Philadelphia, an increased regard for Europe as the fount of all art, including music. However, a few voices of the time were heard in support of the ideal of self-reliance in American music. Anthony Philip Heinrich (1781–1861, dubbed "The Loghouse Composer of Kentucky"), William Henry Fry (1813–1864, practicing journalist and opera composer), and George Frederick Bristow (1825–1898, a competent, versatile professional who spent his entire life in and around New York City) had this in common as composers: they were among America's most outspoken "nativists." They wanted to see flourish a distinctive American music, written by American composers, and, equally important, actually *performed* for American audiences. Bristow, who composed four symphonies and a full-length opera, *Rip Van Winkle*, complained in a letter published in 1853:

> During the eleven years the Philharmonic Society [of which Bristow was a member] has been in operation in this city, it played once, either by mistake or accident, one single American composition, an overture of mine. As one exception makes a rule stronger, so this single stray fact shows that the Philharmonic Society has been as anti-American as if it had been located in London during the Revolutionary War, and composed of native-born British Tories. (Chase 308)

The Debate over Nationality

These three composers, different as they were, all espoused a nativist view—that there should evolve a distinctively American music, developing a life of its own not in the shadow of European tradition, together with an audience to appreciate and support such music. There were critics, however, who took an opposite view—a view that has been called "expatriate." These critics were imbued with a reverential attitude toward those European masters—mainly Germanic—whose music was just beginning to be performed in the culturally adolescent republic. Theirs was an idealistic dedication to the *cosmopolitan*, the *universal*, the expression that seeks to transcend place and time. This competed with an equally idealistic desire to express the *national*, the *specific*, the unique sense of *this* place and *this* time. This is a debate that takes place in all eras, but at this time it was played out against the background of the country's greatest national expansion, between the Louisiana Purchase and the Civil War. It was a time of fierce national pride; "Manifest Destiny" was its appropriate motto.

MUSIC EDUCATION AND CULTURE AFTER THE MID-NINETEENTH CENTURY

After the trauma of the Civil War, the patterns of American life changed. The changes were wrought by the westward movement of a substantial portion of the population, by settlement and cultivation of the land, by the building of towns and cities, by the exploitation of natural resources, and by industrialization. The telegraph was quickly followed by the railroad in linking east and west. Great wealth began to accrue to a new class of people—the builders of a new industrial society, entrepreneurs in growing new enterprises: coal and iron mining, steel-making, railroad building, engineering, construction, manufacturing, and the extracting and refining of petroleum.

With this new wealth came the desire to advance education and culture. Educational and cultural enterprises conceived in the earlier part of the century prospered on a scale impossible before the industrial age. Colleges and universities were founded and endowed, as were libraries and art museums. In the larger cities, the two most expensive forms of music-making—opera and the symphony orchestra—began to flourish conspicuously.

The symphony orchestra flourished much sooner than did opera. Not just New York and Boston, but Philadelphia, Pittsburgh, Cincinnati, St. Louis, and even Los Angeles had established symphony orchestras by 1900. A reasonably complete account of the growth of the symphony orchestra in America would have to consider the seminal work of an immigrant boy from a small town in north Germany, who arrived in the United States as an accomplished violinist at the age of ten and went on to become the leading founder and conductor of American symphony orchestras. The influence of Theodore Thomas (1835–1905) is encountered again and again in the story of American music, in his era and beyond. The 1,000-plus professional, semiprofessional, community, and college orchestras that once flourished in cities throughout the United States owe a debt of gratitude to his unremitting, pioneering work.

Thomas championed an elite music while coming from a humble background himself. In no small measure, he ingrained in the American consciousness an orchestra that was "a model of Germanic discipline and polish" and orchestral programs in which composers such as Schubert, Mendelssohn, and Schumann were showcased between the cultural pillars of Beethoven and Wagner. In a fitting tribute, Joseph Horowitz has noted of Thomas: "His self-reliance, self-education, and self-definition were American traits; he treasured high culture as one who had not acquired it by birthright or pedigree, who expected others similarly unprivileged to acquire it with similar gratitude and alacrity" (Horowitz 35).

The Second New England School

Boston, the hub of New England life, has always been an important cultural center, but it occupied an especially commanding position of leadership from the mid-nineteenth century to World War I. With Cambridge and nearby Concord included in its orbit, Boston's intellectual life, by the time of the Civil War, had already been marked by the great literary and philosophical tradition that included Emerson, Hawthorne, Longfellow, Whittier, and Thoreau.

Musically the ground had been cultivated by the First New England School: the eighteenth-century singing-school composers that included William Billings among others (see Chapter 10). In 1815 the Handel and Haydn Society was formed, followed by the Boston Academy of Music, founded under the aegis of Lowell Mason in 1833. In 1867 the New England Conservatory, one of America's leading music schools, was founded; and in 1881 the Boston Symphony Orchestra was formed. It was a time of great patrons and patronesses. One of the most notable was Henry Lee Higginson (1834–1918), who founded and supported (for a long time almost single-handedly) the Boston Symphony and built Symphony Hall for it in 1900.

It is not surprising, then, that Boston should have nurtured a tradition of musical composition and a group of composers who are often (conveniently, though inaccurately) considered together as a "school." What these composers had in common was a dedication to excellence of musical craftsmanship and to the highest ideals of serious composition as they saw them. The musicians of the Second New England School broke ground for the American composer, helped to establish the place of music in American colleges and universities, and left behind an impressive body of music.

Because he came earliest and was gifted with tenacity and a sense of purpose, to John Knowles Paine (1839–1906), competent and dedicated, fell the role of pioneer. At nineteen, already an accomplished organist, Paine was giving subscription organ concerts to raise money for study in Europe. Important ground was broken for the place of American music in her colleges when Paine received the first full professorship of music at Harvard—and the first in the United States—in 1875. A good introduction to the works of John Knowles Paine is his ten-minute Overture to Shakespeare's *As You Like It,* Op. 28 (see Additional Listening).

Another New England pioneer, George Whitefield Chadwick (1854–1931), was brought up in a typical Yankee musical atmosphere: his father, in his spare time from his varied pursuits, taught singing schools and organized a community chorus and orchestra. George, after some study at the New England Conservatory, went to Germany at the age of twenty-three for three years of study. In 1897 he became director of the New England Conservatory, a post he occupied until his death. The range of Chadwick's compositions was broad. He wrote a comic opera, *Tabasco,* and a serious opera, *The Padrone,* which invites comparison with the modern film *The Godfather.* Perhaps his best-known work is a suite for orchestra titled *Symphonic Sketches,* written between 1895 and 1904, a work marked by flashes of satire and humorous incongruities (see Additional Listening).

One of the most precocious, talented, and energetic composers of this time and place was also America's first prominent female composer, Amy Marcy Cheney Beach (1867–1944). She was composing piano pieces at the age of four, playing public recitals at seven, and performing as soloist with the Boston Symphony Orchestra before she was eighteen. Unlike Paine and Chadwick, who went to Europe to study, Amy Beach acquired her musical training entirely in Boston. She composed many songs and piano pieces, as well as chamber music, choral music, and larger works that included a piano concerto, an opera, and the splendid thirty-minute *Gaelic Symphony* (1894, see Additional Listening). Persistent and resourceful in securing performances of her own works, she was also generous in helping young musicians, and assumed leadership in many musical organizations, including the co-founding of the American Association of Women Composers in 1926.

Three Individualists Around the Turn of the Century

Roughly contemporaneous with the Second New England School were three composers—Edward MacDowell, Henry F. Gilbert, and Arthur Farwell—who had little in common except that each had a highly individual background and artistic stance.

America's first success story in producing a composer of truly international recognition was the career of Edward MacDowell (1860–1908). MacDowell had gone to Europe to study at the age of fifteen. While still in his twenties he had become a successful pianist, teacher, and composer there, and had virtually settled in Germany when he was persuaded to return to the United States and take an active part in its rapidly developing musical life. In 1888 he came back and settled in Boston, then a center of intense cultural activity. For the next eight years he concertized, composed, and had his works widely performed. From that period come many songs; many solo piano pieces, including the famous *Woodland Sketches;* and some of his most important orchestral compositions, including the *Indian Suite,* published in 1897, which incorporates genuine Indian themes (see Additional Listening). But MacDowell was no nativist. The *Indian Suite* was untypical of his work in that he otherwise seldom used indigenous melodies and generally took a skeptical view of using such material to create a national music.

In contrast to MacDowell, Henry F. Gilbert (1868–1928) had distinct nativist leanings. He incorporated African American melodies, Indian melodies, and ragtime into his compositions. Impressed with the work of the photographer Edward S. Curtis and his pioneering studies of American Indians, Gilbert transcribed phonograph recordings Curtis had collected in the field and wrote a score, performed by an orchestra of twenty-two musicians, to accompany Curtis's photographic presentation "The Story of a Vanishing Race," which opened at Carnegie Hall in 1911. Gilbert gave full rein to his impulsive curiosity, traveling to Chicago to hear exotic music at the Columbian Exposition of 1893. Illustrative of Gilbert's interest in America's vernacular musical sources is his eleven-minute symphonic poem *The Dance in Place Congo,* composed in 1906–1908 (see Additional Listening). The setting, the tunes, and the title are taken from George Washington Cable's 1886 articles on African American music-making in New Orleans during the Reconstruction era.

Arthur Farwell was arguably without parallel in his idealistic vision of promoting a native music. He is considered separately following, after a brief orientation on the context that helped fire his imagination.

Idealistic Promoters of a Native Music

At the same time that MacDowell and the Boston classicists were at work cultivating America's taste for a music that was basically European in its musical forms and modes of expression, there were other musical winds stirring in the land. To understand these, it is necessary to recall a few things that had happened meanwhile on the broad musical scene. In the 1870s the Fisk Jubilee Singers (followed soon by other groups) had begun to open up a reservoir of African American musical culture vastly different from the popular caricatures of the minstrel stage. In the 1880s American Indian music was beginning to be seriously collected and studied. On the popular musical stage about the same time, Harrigan and Hart were presenting plays with music that dealt with a cross-section of the everyday life of the people of New York. Ragtime arrived from the Midwest in the 1890s.

One of the most influential events, however, was the arrival in America of the Czech composer Antonín Dvořák (1841–1904) in 1892. Dvořák assumed the directorship of the National Conservatory in New York City from 1892 to 1895 at the invitation of Jeannette Thurber (d. 1946), who had founded the conservatory in 1885 as part of her aim to nurture a distinctly American school of music. Dvořák was a natural choice for Thurber since he had earned an international reputation for his art compositions based on native Czech music. The composer, in turn, was well aware of his charge:

> The Americans expect great things of me and the main thing is, so they say, to show them to the promised land and kingdom of a new and independent art, in short, to create a national music. If the small Czech nation can have such musicians, they say, why could not they too, when their country and people is so immense. . . . It is certainly both a great and a splendid task for me and I hope that with God's help I shall accomplish it. There is more than enough material here and plenty of talent. (Horowitz 224)

Dvořák set about his task in a variety of ways. His African American student Harry Thacker Burleigh (1866–1949), later to become a prominent composer, arranger, and concert singer, was a frequent visitor to his New York apartment and repeatedly sang spirituals for him. Dvořák heard the songs of Stephen Foster, and he spent summers in Iowa where he heard Indian music. Impressed by the wealth of material, Dvořák issued what was in effect a challenge to American composers: to look to their own native music as a foundation on which to establish in America what he termed "a great and noble school of music." Dvořák set the example by incorporating the sounds of the African American spiritual in his *Symphony "From the New World"* (1893) and String Quartet in F (1894), popularly known as "The American" quartet.

Arthur Farwell

Among those ready to accept the challenge that the nativists had set forth was Arthur Farwell (1872–1952), an individual whose initiative, enterprise, and integrity of ideals made him a leader and a mover. In 1903 Farwell addressed himself to "all composers who feel the pulse of new life that marks the beginning of an era in American music," inviting them to join those workers who had been striving

> to draw out of the dawning, through widely distributed realities and possibilities of American musical life, the elements and forces necessary to form a definite movement which shall make for the untrammeled growth of a genuine Art of Music. Such an art will not be a mere echo of other lands and times, but shall have a vital meaning for us, in our circumstances, here and now. While it will take the worthier traditions of the past for its point

of departure, it will derive its convincing qualities of color, form, and spirit from our nature-world and our humanity. (Farwell, "Letter" xvii)

A native of the Midwest, Farwell settled in Newton Center, Massachusetts, after a period of study that included the study of American Indian music, and entered upon a significant venture for American music. Having tried unsuccessfully to get his *American Indian Melodies* published, and having met other American composers who had suffered similar rejections, he resolved to try to overcome the resistance to American music by founding a composers' press. The result was the Wa-Wan Press, which came into being late in 1901. (The name "Wa-Wan" is that of an Omaha Indian ceremony of peace and brotherhood.) The emphasis of its publications was on quality—quality not only of the music chosen but of design and typography as well. The press was in existence for ten years, and in that time it published the work of thirty-six American composers, including nine women.

One of the works published was Farwell's "Pawnee Horses" (CD 4/2), a concert work for solo piano inspired by an Omaha Indian melody. It appeared in a collection titled *From Mesa and Plain* (Wa-Wan Press, 1905), which also included his "Navajo War Dance." The title page bears the inscription "There go the Pawnee horses. I do not want them,—I have taken enough." In 1937, Farwell arranged it for unaccompanied chorus. A notable feature of this piece is the rhythmic complexity of the main melody (0:07 and 0:40), its syncopations set in relief against steady repeated figures (essentially an ostinato) in the background. (In principle, this is not fundamentally different from the rhythmic interest we find in ragtime.) The melody's narrow range and its general placement in the middle register of the piano evoke the overall sound of an Indian chant. The gradual descent of the melodic line is also typical of American Indian melodies (see Chapter 3).

Listening Cue "Pawnee Horses" by Arthur Farwell; Dario Müller, piano (1:19)

Listen For ▪ syncopations ▪ descending melodic line ▪ narrow melodic range

Visit http://www.music.wadsworth.com_3/Kingman for a full listening guide and other resources.

A second aim of the Wa-Wan Press, and of Farwell himself, is less easily stated, but it had to do with developing an American music more in touch with American life. "It must have an American flavor," he wrote. "It must be recognizably American, as Russian music is Russian, and French music, French" (Farwell, "Affirmation"). Arthur Farwell sounded for American music the same note that Ralph Waldo Emerson, two generations earlier, had sounded for American literature: first, find your own voice, cultivate your own field; second, do not divorce art from life. Farwell's concern with making music an active part of the lives of the great mass of the people expressed itself in many novel ideas, which his abilities as a leader and organizer enabled him to bring to fruition.

AMERICAN MUSIC AND AMERICAN LIFE

An attractive idea that emerged from Dvořák, Farwell, and other promoters of a native music in America was the notion that American classical music must be more in touch with American life and, furthermore, that it must be, in Farwell's words, "recognizably American." This section looks briefly at three works by composers who produced what is arguably the most quintessentially "American-sounding" classical music. Like Dvořák, whose American compositions were influenced by the African American spiritual, and Farwell, who drew heavily from the music of the American Indian, the following works turned for inspiration to native traditions from various segments of the broad American panorama: the blues, the Shaker hymn, and, of course, jazz.

George Gershwin, *Rhapsody in Blue* (1924)

George Gershwin (1898–1937), born to Russian immigrant parents in Brooklyn, New York, would become one of the most famous composers of classical music in America before reaching the age of thirty. He began his musical training as a classical pianist shortly after his family bought a piano in 1910, but his attention soon turned to opportunities in the popular music industry. In 1914, Gershwin dropped out of high school to work as a "song plugger" on Tin Pan Alley. This required long days of playing a publishing house's songs on the piano for prospective buyers; from 1917, he wrote for Broadway. As a composer and performer of popular music, Gershwin was in touch with the music that was a well-known and active part of life for large segments of the American population. In 1924, he drew on the increasingly popular jazz idiom to compose the concert piece that would establish him as a fixture in American classical music, *Rhapsody in Blue*.

Rhapsody in Blue (CD 4/3) is a jazz concerto for piano that was premiered at Aeolian Hall in New York on February 12, 1924. It was commissioned expressly for a concert mounted by jazz-band leader Paul Whiteman (1890–1967). The concert featured Gershwin as soloist with Whiteman's Palais Royal Orchestra at an evening billed as "An Experiment in Modern Music." *Rhapsody in Blue* was enthusiastically received, and although the experiment was really more about "the many faces of a new modern music called jazz," Gershwin's jazz concerto became a standard of the American classical repertory (Crawford 571).

Listening Cue *Rhapsody in Blue* (excerpt) by George Gershwin; Philadelphia Orchestra, Eugene Ormandy, conductor; Oscar Levant, piano (4:37)

> Listen For ▪ jazzy solos (clarinet, trumpet, piano) ▪ improvisatory feel

Visit http://www.music.wadsworth.com_3/Kingman for a full listening guide and other resources.

CD 4
3

With the lazy clarinet smear that starts the piece, the call-and-response pattern at about 0:16, and the muted trumpet solo at 0:48, Gershwin makes it abundantly clear to his audience from the very outset: "This is jazz, baby." The improvisatory feel of the piano part (it is actually all written out) also contributes to the jazz character that permeates this piece from start to finish. The extended passage for piano solo from about 1:10 (called a *cadenza* in classical music) is a good example.

William Grant Still, *Afro-American Symphony* (1930)

William Grant Still (1895–1978) was the most prominent African American composer of his time. Like Gershwin, Still had a substantial career in the popular music industry, and worked at one time with such individuals as W. C. Handy and Paul Whiteman. Unlike Gershwin, however, Still had extensive formal training in classical music. He studied in Ohio between 1911 and 1919, first at Wilberforce University and then at Oberlin College. Later he continued his studies with George W. Chadwick and Edgard Varèse (on Varèse, see the next chapter). His signal accomplishments include being the first African American composer to have a work performed by a major symphony orchestra (*Afro-American Symphony*, performed by the Rochester Philharmonic Orchestra in 1931) and the first black composer to have an opera staged by a major company (*Troubled Island*, on a libretto by Langston Hughes, staged by the New York City Opera in 1949).

In *Afro-American Symphony*, Still drew on African American musical idioms such as the blues, the spiritual, and ragtime to create a distinctly American sound within a fundamentally European form—the standard four-movement symphony. As Still wrote of the piece: "I knew I wanted to write a symphony; I knew that it had to be an American work; and I wanted to demonstrate how the blues, so often considered a lowly expression, could be elevated to the highest musical level" (Ciucevich). While the work sought to "elevate" the blues, in an ironic twist on the composer's intentions, it is in fact the blues and its peer forms of African American folk expression that elevate this symphony to a prominent position in the repertory of American classical music. The blues feel is most prominent in the first movement (titled "Longing"), where the principal melody is built on a twelve-bar blues pattern, breaks and all.

The third movement of the *Afro-American Symphony*, titled "Humor" (CD 4/4), makes reference to the more lighthearted genre of ragtime (at 0:12) with a syncopated melody in the strings over a steady oom-pa beat. Notice here that the offbeat is played on the banjo!

William Grant Still, shown here in 1936, brought blues and ragtime into the concert hall with his *Afro-American Symphony*—from which we hear the third (ragtime) movement on CD 4, track 4. His other notable works include the symphonic poem *Darker America* (1924), the choral protest ballad *And They Lynched Him on a Tree* (1940), and the orchestral work *In Memoriam: The Colored Soldiers Who Died for Democracy* (1943). Like George Gershwin and Aaron Copland, Still wrote American music that arose out of American life.

(Compare this with the rag "Hello! My Baby," CD 3/16, paying close attention to the emphasis given the offbeat.) Furthermore, note that the horns play a melody that sounds quite similar to Gershwin's famous "I Got Rhythm," published in 1930. Other passages throughout the movement are marked by bluesy inflections (for example, between 0:35 and 0:38; also between 2:45 and 2:58).

Listening Cue *Afro-American Symphony* (3rd movement, "Humor") by William Grant Still; Fort Smith Symphony, John Jeter, conductor (3:16)

Listen For ▪ ragtime idiom ▪ banjo ▪ bluesy inflections

Visit http://www.music.wadsworth.com_3/Kingman for a full listening guide and other resources.

Aaron Copland, Appalachian Spring (1944)

Aaron Copland (1900–1990) and Gershwin share a similar background in that both were born in Brooklyn, New York, to Russian-Jewish immigrants. After learning the basics of piano technique from his sister, Copland took up formal study on the instrument in 1913. After graduating from high school, he continued studying piano and composition with private mentors before going off to complete his musical studies in Europe during the 1920s, most notably under Nadia Boulanger in Paris. Though well versed in every modern style of musical composition (see the following chapter), Copland ultimately settled on a manner of writing that was clear and accessible to the average American. As he reflected in 1941:

> During the mid-'30s I began to feel an increasing dissatisfaction with the relations of the music-loving public and the living composer. The old "special" public of the modern-music concerts had fallen away, and the conventional concert public continued apathetic or indifferent to anything but the established classics. It seemed to me that we composers were in danger of working in a vacuum. Moreover, an entirely new public for music had grown up around the radio and phonograph. It made no sense to ignore them and to continue writing as if they did not exist. I felt that it was worth the effort to see if I couldn't say what I had to say in the simplest possible terms. (Copland 160)

To communicate more effectively with his public, Copland drew early on from the jazz idiom (*Piano Concerto*, 1927), and later from cowboy tunes (*Billy the Kid*, 1938; *Rodeo*, 1942) and even the modest Shaker hymn. "'Tis the Gift to Be Simple" (CD 2/21) appears as a main theme in a section of his ballet *Appalachian Spring* (1944), subsequently arranged for orchestra. *Appalachian Spring,* composed for the choreographer and dancer Martha Graham (1894–1991), is set in nineteenth-century rural Pennsylvania. Those attending its premiere at the Library of Congress in Washington, D.C., on October 30, 1944, read Graham's short synopsis of the story:

> Part and parcel of our lives is that moment of Pennsylvania spring when there was 'a garden eastward in Eden.'

Spring was celebrated by a man and woman building a house with joy and love and prayer; by a revivalist and his followers in their shouts of exaltation; by a pioneering woman with her dreams of the Promised Land. (Crawford 401)

Formally, the ballet is divided into eight sections; "'Tis the Gift to Be Simple" appears in the seventh (CD 4/5), which Copland described as follows: "Calm and flowing. Scenes of daily activity for the Bride and her Farmer-husband." After its initial statement by the clarinet, there are five presentations of the Shaker hymn by different instruments of the orchestra. These vary dramatically in mood and color, demonstrating Copland's ability to use the orchestra as an artist would his palette to "paint" different scenes for the audience.

Listening Cue. *Appalachian Spring* (Section 7) by Aaron Copland; New York Philharmonic, Leonard Bernstein, conductor (3:00)

Listen For ▪ Shaker hymn ▪ different moods and colors

Visit http://www.music.wadsworth.com_3/Kingman for a full listening guide and other resources.

AMERICA'S VIRTUOSO CULT

The works of Dvořák, Farwell, Gershwin, Still, and Copland demonstrate one way in which composers successfully staked out an authentic American voice in the classical world. Their lesson was that the seeds for a distinctly American sound lay in musical traditions of the United States that were native, folk, popular, and—in the case of jazz—new and contemporary. There were, of course, other styles of musical composition that were being explored in the United States. Although those styles are often less easily identifiable as "American" by their sound alone, they are no less a part of the American musical panorama and will be examined in the next chapter. If one approach was characterized by a mining of the past and popular, the other was an exploration of a new music for the future.

There was yet another avenue taken in the search for an American identity that has only recently begun to receive much attention: the act of performance. As Joseph Horowitz points out in his thought-provoking *Classical Music in America: A History of Its Rise and Fall*:

American classical music after World War I was mainly about the act of performance: not composers, but world-famous symphonic and operatic institutions, and celebrated conductors and instrumentalists, were its validating signatures. These, to be sure, were amazing in their way. But absent a vital national repertoire, they were irredeemably Eurocentric. (xiii)

The subject of classical music performance in America is vast and complex. Here, we will consider only a handful of performers whose extraordinary skills and musical talents drove what Horowitz has described as a "culture of performance" that is a "fundamental aspect of American classical music" (xiv).

Louis Moreau Gottschalk and "Blind Tom": Two Virtuosos in Nineteenth-Century America

Louis Moreau Gottschalk (1829–1869) was an exceptionally gifted American pianist. He was thoroughly familiar with the European classics of his time but knew that American audiences were not attuned to them in sufficient numbers to constitute the audiences that he needed to attract. Thus, he walked a careful line between popular and classical music, both as a composer and as a virtuoso performer.

Born in New Orleans, Gottschalk had learned all that he could from any musician there by the time he was eleven; when he was thirteen, his parents sent him to study in Paris. The director of piano classes at the Paris Conservatory in 1842 rejected him without even hearing him play. In his opinion, "America was nothing but a country of steam engines." Nonetheless, Gottschalk rapidly took his place among the leading young pianists of the day, and, in a fitting turn of events, was invited to judge examinations at that very conservatory seven years later, at the age of twenty. His remarkable appearance, stage presence, and charm were universally commented upon throughout his life.

By the time Gottschalk returned to the United States in 1853, he had already established himself as a composer. His works, in accord with his needs as a concert artist in the nineteenth century, included virtuoso concert pieces, or "paraphrases," consisting of medleys of operatic arias. Gottschalk also wrote "salon pieces," sentimental creations, which often bore gushy titles such as "The Dying Poet." Though he did not particularly care for salon pieces, as a popular artist he was expected to write, perform, and publish them. The most famous is "The Last Hope: Religious Meditation." It became almost an obligatory ritual for him to end his concerts with it, head bowed and eyes closed. Yet another type of composition was the work based on an American vernacular tune.

"The Banjo" (CD 4/6) is one of Gottschalk's concert works on an American vernacular tune—in this case, the music of the minstrel show. The piano here not only imitates the rhythmic drive and repeated-note figurations of the banjo but also invokes one of the most popular minstrel tunes, "Camptown Races" by Stephen Foster. The introduction hints at the verse, "The Camptown ladies sing this song, Doodah! Doodah!" and near the end of the piece is invoked the chorus: "Goin' to run all night! Goin' to run all day!" In spite of the flurry of virtuosic playing that brings "The Banjo" to a close, the melody of "Camptown Races" shines through clearly.

Listening Cue "The Banjo" by Louis Gottschalk; Eugene List, piano (3:53)

Listen For ▪ imitation of the banjo ▪ quotes from "Camptown Races" ▪ virtuosic style

Visit http://www.music.wadsworth.com_3/Kingman for a full listening guide and other resources.

Of this same type were three piano pieces Gottschalk wrote when still in his teens in Paris, based on folk tunes of the Louisiana blacks that he remembered from his childhood: "Le Bananier: Chanson nègre," "La Savane: Ballade créole," and "Bamboula: Danse des Nègres."

Another notable virtuoso of nineteenth-century America was the phenomenal Thomas Wiggins (1849–1908), an African American musician known universally in his lifetime as "Blind Tom." Tom was born into slavery on a plantation near Columbus, in Harris County, Georgia; his extraordinary musical abilities were recognized when he was four by the Columbus journalist-politician James Bethune, who had purchased him in 1850. Wiggins was subsequently taken on tours and "exhibited" as early as 1857. After the Civil War the Bethune family continued to manage and control Tom's professional career, both in America and in Europe. He appeared last on the Keith Circuit, as a vaudeville attraction, in 1905.

Judging from contemporary accounts, Wiggins was not only blind, but an autistic savant. He had a phenomenal memory for music, and could play long and difficult pieces after a single hearing. He also composed and played his own works, which numbered at least 100, including *The Battle of Manassas* (CD 4/7), reportedly composed after hearing one of Bethune's sons describe a Confederate victory. *The Battle of Manassas,* simply put, is a masterpiece of *program music* (music that illustrates a story) by any standard. It includes melodies to represent the opposing armies and, quite remarkably, pianistic effects that mimic the sounds of battle. The opposing generals trade trumpet calls on the field of battle at 3:31; from 4:00 on, cannon fire and bombs explode over popular tunes such as "Yankee Doodle," "The Marseillaise," and "The Star-Spangled Banner" (compare this with the account of Jimi Hendrix's performance at Woodstock in Chapter 9). At 5:47 the pianist makes train sounds with his mouth while playing "The Marseillaise" and continuing to imitate the explosions of bombs—all at the same time.

Listening Cue *The Battle of Manassas* by Thomas ("Blind Tom") Wiggins; John Davis, piano (7:46)

Listen For ▪ sounds of battle ▪ quotations from popular tunes ▪ virtuosic style

Visit http://www.music.wadsworth.com_3/Kingman for a full listening guide and other resources.

Toscanini and Van Cliburn: Two Virtuosos of the Twentieth Century

No conductor enjoyed greater fame or prestige in twentieth-century America than the Italian-born Arturo Toscanini (1867–1957). Following an illustrious European career, Toscanini was hired as conductor of the New York Philharmonic Orchestra (1926–1936) and, shortly thereafter, as conductor of the NBC Symphony Orchestra, a group created specifically for him. Toscanini remains one of the most formidable conductors ever to mount the podium of an American orchestra, a perfectionist with a dictatorial approach to art and a fiery temperament to back it up. In 1940, he led the New York Philharmonic on a European tour that reaped unprecedented success for his American orchestra. The New York Philharmonic won critical acclaim for its precise, virtuosic performances and set new standards for orchestras in the United States and abroad. Horowitz notes: "Never before had American classical music so set standards for the world. Significantly, the vehicle was not a composer (and Toscanini's tour repertoire included no American works), but an orchestra under a foreign conductor" (277). Another successful tour came in 1950, this time with the NBC Symphony Orchestra, which performed twenty-one concerts in twenty states across America. Throughout that tour, audiences were treated to stunning performances of Beethoven, Brahms, and Tchaikovsky but, here again (with the exception of encores that included "Dixie" and "The Stars and Stripes Forever"), no works by American composers. Toscanini had shown that American orchestras were capable of beating the Europeans at their own game. In essence, observes Horowitz, Toscanini with his American orchestra "fostered a new musical priority: performance as an end in itself" (277). For an introduction to Toscanini's legendary style, sample his recordings of Beethoven's nine symphonies with the NBC Symphony Orchestra (see Additional Listening).

Piano virtuoso Harvey Lavan ("Van") Cliburn presents almost the polar opposite of Toscanini in terms of his temperament and background. Van Cliburn was born in 1934 in Shreveport, Louisiana, but soon moved to the small town of Kilgore, Texas, where he studied piano with his mother until the age of seventeen. From that point, he continued his studies at the Julliard School under Rosina Lhévinne, and shortly thereafter made his debut at Carnegie Hall in New York in 1954. A major accomplishment, to be sure, it would pale in comparison with his monumental win at the first International Tchaikovsky Competition held in Moscow in April 1958. The cultural importance that Americans placed on that win was unprecedented and may never be seen again. It occurred during the Cold War, at the height of the "space race" (the Soviets had recently launched *Sputnik*), at a competition designed to showcase Russia's cultural strengths, and, not least, on Russia's own "turf." Van Cliburn—a shy and

New York Times Co./Getty Images

Loved by audiences, and feared by musicians, Italian-born Arturo Toscanini— shown here in 1945 and acknowledged then as the greatest living conductor— raised the artistic level of orchestral performances in America to unprecedented heights. His core repertory did not include any American composers, however. Instead, Toscanini exposed American audiences to a steady diet of music by European composers performed in a disciplined and polished manner that America was eager to claim as its own.

somewhat awkward six-foot, four-inch tall American from the South—claimed the top prize with a masterful performance of Tchaikovsky's *Piano Concerto No. 1*. Upon his return, Van Cliburn's accomplishments were recognized with a ticker-tape parade in New York; a month later *Time* magazine featured his likeness on the cover with the caption "The Texan Who Conquered Russia" (May 19, 1958). His recording of Tchaikovsky's first piano concerto (on the RCA label; see Additional Listening) would become the first classical recording to sell more than a million copies, and in 1962 the Van Cliburn International Piano Competition, held every four years in Fort Worth, Texas, was named in his honor. Through the pianistic virtuosity of Van Cliburn, America had once again asserted its cultural identity in the classical world, not through the art of composition but, rather, through the act of performance.

PROJECTS

1. Investigate what the classical music organizations in your town have done to reach out to a broader audience and write a paper on it. Include your own thoughts on how successful (or unsuccessful) those efforts have been. Propose some "outreach" activities or strategies of your own.
2. Sample the coverage given the arts in a local newspaper for a period of several weeks. Observe the proportion of space given to local artists and local live performances, as compared with space devoted to "name" artists or stars whose work is accessible mostly through the media of recordings, films, or television. Write a paper on how your findings relate to the "nativist" versus "expatriate" controversy dealt with in this chapter.
3. Interview a composer in your community. In addition to whatever questions you may wish to formulate on your own, ask how he or she goes about writing music for the public. Is there any concern for trying to make it accessible and meaningful to the average American? If so, how is it done?

ADDITIONAL LISTENING

Beach, Amy Marcy Cheney. Symphony in E minor (*Gaelic*), Op. 32. Detroit Symphony Orchestra. Cond. Neeme Jarvi. Chandos 8958.

Chadwick, George Whitefield. *Symphonic Sketches*. Detroit Symphony Orchestra. Cond. Neeme Jarvi. Chandos 10032.

Cliburn, Van, pianist. Tchaikovsky: Piano Concerto No. 1, for piano and orchestra in B-flat minor, Op. 23. RCA Victor Symphony Orchestra. Cond. Kiril Kondrashin. RCA 55912.

Gilbert, Henry F. Symphonic poem, *The Dance in Place Congo*, Op. 15. Los Angeles Philharmonic Orchestra with Zita Carno. Cond. Calvin Simmons. New World Records 80228.

MacDowell, Edward. Suite No. 2 (*Indian*), Op. 48, for orchestra. *American Orchestral Music. American Composers Series.* Vox (Box 2 Classical) 5092.

Paine, John Knowles. Overture to Shakespeare's *As You Like It,* Op. 28/Symphony No. 1 in C Minor. New York Philharmonic. Cond. Zubin Mehta. New World Records 80374.

Toscanini, Arturo, conducting. *Beethoven: The 9 Symphonies* (5-disc set). NBC Symphony Orchestra. RCA 55702.

18 TWENTIETH-CENTURY INNOVATION AND THE CONTEMPORARY WORLD

The last chapter addressed American classical music as it pertained to the issue of staking out a national identity in a tradition that is fundamentally European. Limiting our consideration to that issue alone, however, eclipses the rich variety of approaches to classical music in America, and particularly the approaches taken during the twentieth century—a century marked by musical innovation and experimentation. This chapter provides a mere sampling of innovative trends over the past 100 years or so. There is no attempt here to cobble together a fictive "evolutionary" narrative in which one trend "improves" upon another. Rather, the point is to visit select examples from the vast American musical landscape that, unlike those in Chapter 17, challenge us to stretch our ears, our imagination, and sometimes even our very notion of what music is. We begin with Charles Ives, the most important early innovator in American music.

CHARLES IVES: AMERICAN INNOVATOR IN MUSIC

Charles Ives (1874–1954) grew up in Danbury, Connecticut, a manufacturing town in the southwestern corner of the state that was of exceptional significance in his work; he drew upon its impressions throughout the whole of his fairly short creative life. There were two complementary sides to Charles Ives' early musical background. One was the curiosity and the open-mindedness toward experimentation that would later characterize his music; the other was the solid grounding in musical rudiments that the boy received from his father, a well-trained musician of broad practical experience, and from others. Ives, in common with many other New England composers, was a church organist. He got his first permanent job at fourteen, and worked steadily at it for the next fourteen years in Danbury, New Haven, and New York City. At twenty, Ives entered Yale, where he studied with the renowned composer Horatio Parker (1863–1919), a strict taskmaster and academician.

It is unlikely that Ives ever considered becoming a professional musician. As a product of the Yale of his time, he went into business when he graduated in 1898.

From that point until the distractions of the United States' entry into World War I in 1917, he was to pursue under full steam two careers at once: that of life insurance executive and that of composer. By the time he stopped composing altogether around 1927, Ives had written more than 150 songs, 75 works for piano solo or small instrumental groups, 41 pieces for chorus, and 43 works for symphony or band. After retiring from an extraordinarily successful career in the insurance business on New Year's Day 1930, Ives turned his attention toward getting his work, and that of other composers of new music, before the public. As an advocate of new music, Ives was an idealist. He disdained the copyrighting of his music, insisting that it was fine for anybody to copy or reprint it: "This music," said Ives "is not to make money but to be known and heard" (Cowell and Cowell 121). When he received the Pulitzer Prize for his Third Symphony (written mostly in 1904, but not performed until 1946), he reportedly told the committee that prizes were for boys, then gave the money away.

Charles Ives was a successful insurance executive who, in his spare time, wrote some of the most influential American music of the twentieth century. In "The Fourth of July" from his *Four New England Holidays*—which we hear on CD 4, track 8—Ives creates a dissonant collage of sound with familiar American tunes that have been twisted, distorted, and combined by the force of his imagination. As he reportedly told an autographer notating his music: "Please don't try to make things nice. All the wrong notes are right!"

Ives was fundamentally a composer of program music. Much of his music is "about" something, often with its roots in a vivid impression of a scene. Two sets of orchestral compositions illustrate this particularly well: *Three Places in New England* and *Four New England Holidays*. In the latter, each of the holidays is associated with one of the seasons. For "The Fourth of July" (CD 4/8)—in summer, of course—we have Ives' own description:

> It's a boy's 4th. . . . His festivities start in the quiet of midnight before, and grow raucous with the sun. Everybody knows what it's like—if everybody doesn't—Cannon on the Green, Village Band on Main Street, fire crackers, shanks mixed on cornets, strings around big toes, torpedoes, Church bells, lost finger, fifes, clam-chowder, a prize-fight, drum-corps, burnt shins, parades (in and out of step), saloons all closed (more drunks than usual), baseball game (Danbury All-Stars vs Beaver Brook Boys), pistols, mobbed umpire, Red, White and Blue, runaway horse—and the day ends with the sky-rocket over the Church-steeple, just after the annual explosion sets the Town-Hall on fire. (*Memos* 104n)

The multitude of impressions, seemingly random, crowding one another, superimposing themselves—all this finds a parallel in the collage that is Ives' musical composition. Everywhere he looks, there is something to record; he cannot get it all down. There is a quiet opening in which the violins and the string basses begin "Columbia, the Gem of the Ocean," the tune that is to be the mainstay of the movement. There is a gradual gain of momentum, as bits and pieces of a dozen other tunes are heard; there is an explosion of fireworks; the band finally comes on with a great tumultuous rendition of the main theme, wrong notes, missed beats, and all; there is a final explosion—and again quietness. The sound of the band in full swing in this movement is one of the most vividly realized moments in all of Ives' music: the tunes ("Columbia, the Gem of the Ocean," "The Battle Hymn of the Republic," "Yankee Doodle," and "Dixie" all heard simultaneously at about 4:54), recklessly off-key, are heard through the buzz and roar of the crowd noises.

Although Ives used familiar tunes, and the program is certainly one to which the average American can relate, it is clear that this is not music in the popular vein. Rather, Ives challenges us to make sense of its twisted melodies and distorted harmonies, which remain familiar enough only to make us uncomfortable. All of this is quite intentional. As he reportedly instructed one individual tasked with making a handwritten copy of the music: "Please don't try to make things nice. All the wrong notes are right!" Originally thought unplayable, even by Ives himself, these are some of his grandest and most successful pages.

Listening Cue *Four New England Holidays* ("The Fourth of July" III) by Charles Ives; Chicago Symphony Orchestra, Michael Tilson Thomas, conductor (6:04)

CD 4

8

Listen For ▪ distortion of familiar tunes ▪ collage of sound

Visit http://www.music.wadsworth.com_3/Kingman for a full listening guide and other resources.

For Ives the man there is no lack of admiration; his idealism, his grit, his humor, and his generosity fired the imagination of succeeding generations. Virgil Thomson (1896–1989), speaking for all subsequent composers, hailed Charles Ives as "whether we knew it or not, the father of us all."

NEW YORK AND EUROPE-RELATED "MODERNISM"

Much of the excitement and activity connected with innovation in America between the two World Wars was to be found in and around New York City—always more closely in touch with Europe than any other part of the country. New York, long established as a trend-setting capital, attracted composers and other artists from all parts of the United States, and eventually from Europe as well. One of the European trends that New York helped set in the United States was "modernism." In music, modernism was generally characterized by a rejection of norms in composition and performance that history and tradition had codified as "correct," "standard," or "beautiful." The modernist approach to musical composition was more subjective, and thus unhindered by what audiences might think is an appropriate instrument for a classical piece, or even by what the typical concert-goer might think sounds "in tune." In this respect, Charles Ives was an early trail-blazer in America, but others, including Edgard Varèse, would subsequently take modernism to a new level.

Edgard Varèse

Edgard Varèse (1883–1965) quickly became one of the most influential of the modernist immigrants. Though he had already begun to establish his career in Europe, he started it afresh when he arrived in the United States at the age of thirty-two. Though he is almost universally considered an American composer, he always perceived himself as European, and was so perceived in his time by others as well. This is but another potent reminder of the close ties of New York to Europe, and especially to France in the period between the wars.

At that time technology, especially machines, were a preoccupation of artists, including composers. The "Machine Age" manifested itself in many ways, not least in the use of everyday sounds in music, which meant an enlargement of and a new emphasis on the percussion section in ensembles and the introduction of noisemakers such as typewriters, electric bells, sirens, anvils, and propellers. Varèse's *Hyperprism* (CD 4/9), first performed in 1923, is an early example of Machine Age music. There are ten wind instruments that one would expect to find in any modern orchestra (a flute, a piccolo, a clarinet, three horns, two trumpets, and two trombones) and a large percussion section, consisting of three drums, a tambourine, a pair of crash cymbals, two suspended cymbals, a tam-tam (a large unpitched gong), and a triangle. But in addition to these are some highly unconventional instruments: an anvil, a slapstick, two Chinese blocks, a big and small rattle, sleigh bells, a siren, and a "lion roar" (a cord attached to the membrane of a large drum, which when grasped between pieces of leather and pulled produces an imitation of the real thing).

Listening Cue *Hyperprism* by Edgard Varèse; Columbia Symphony Orchestra, Robert Craft, conductor (4:10)

CD 4
9

Listen For ▪ siren ▪ lion roar ▪ diverse sound masses

Visit http://www.music.wadsworth.com_3/Kingman for a full listening guide and other resources.

Varèse conceived of music as spatial, and of musical sounds as analogous to masses in space, with quasi-geometrical characteristics. In a lecture given in 1936 he described his ideal music in an illustrative paragraph.

When new instruments will allow me to write music as I conceive it, the movement of sound-masses, of shifting planes, will be clearly perceived in my work. . . . When these sound-masses collide, the phenomena of penetration or repulsion will seem to occur. Certain transmutations taking place on certain planes will seem to be projected onto other planes, moving at different speeds and at different angles. There will no longer be the old conception of melody or interplay of melodies. The entire work will be a melodic totality. The entire work will flow as a river flows. (197)

MIDCENTURY MODERNISM

At the conclusion of World War II, the modernism that emerged, both in the United States and in Europe, took on new dimensions. For one thing, the new technologies that resulted inevitably from the fruits of wartime research became available to composers. The visible machines—the typewriters, electric bells, sewing-machine motors, sirens, metal "thunder sheets," wind machines, airplane propellers—were no longer there as interesting visual objects enhancing the percussion section. They were replaced by the invisible machinery of electronics, the only visible components of which were loudspeakers. Indeed, the search for new sounds, following up on the music of the Machine Age, continued to be a concern in most progressive classical music after midcentury, and this search added to the tonal palette sounds that included extended possibilities with traditional instruments (including the human voice), as well as electronically generated and/or processed sound. After midcentury, advanced amplifying and recording techniques made accessible previously unheard sounds—human brain waves, for example. Alvin Lucier based his *Music for Solo Performer* (Davis, California, 1965) on the amplification of the alpha current, a low-voltage brain signal. (See "New Technology and the New Music" on page 308.)

But there were also new aesthetic concepts that challenged the very definition of what constituted music. In the broadest sense, there were two major schools of thought: one that advocated the composer's maximum rational control over a work, and one that favored the composer's minimum rational control.

Maximum Rational Control by the Composer

The trend toward ever greater control over the end result of musical composition was manifested in two distinct but related areas. The first was control over every aspect of performance, going beyond the historically basic specifications of pitch, rhythm, and tempo to include the most detailed instructions regarding tone color and dynamic nuance. The ultimate realization of control, of course, is the composition directly on tape (electronic music), which eliminates the performer entirely.

A second, and more fundamentally crucial, area of increased control was that governing the myriad choices the composer makes in writing a piece to begin with. In the twentieth century the greatest degree of predetermined control of choices was represented by the technique of serial organization. Classical serial technique, derived from the work of German-Austrian composers beginning in the 1920s, consists of organizing music according to a series of twelve different and unrepeated pitches arranged in a certain invariable order that persists throughout the work. Serial technique applied to pitches alone has been used by many American composers, including Milton Babbitt, George Perle, and, in some works, Aaron Copland.

Ultimately, on both sides of the Atlantic, the move was taken toward subjecting the total aural result of a composition to the intellectual predetermination of serial procedures. What has become popularly known as total serialization involves a procedure by which the ordering not just of pitches, but of all measurable dimensions of sound—duration, intensity, timbre, and register—is serially determined. The idea itself has become well known, although actual pieces in which all the parameters of music have been serially predetermined are relatively rare. One such piece is Milton Babbitt's *Three Compositions for Piano* (1947), in which dynamics, rhythm, and pitch are serialized.

Minimum Rational Control by the Composer

The second path of the new music after midcentury was that of progressive relinquishment of rational control by the composer. In this opposite extreme to serialism, the musical result cannot be envisioned in full. The composer prescribes only certain parameters, leaving other aspects of the whole result to the performer or to the operation of chance, in some form or other. Music that makes deliberate use of indeterminacy, or chance, is called *aleatory music* ("aleatory" literally means to be dependent on a roll of the dice). One of its most fervent champions was the experimental music composer John Cage (1912–1992), of Los Angeles, California.

With Cage's dictum "my purpose is to remove purpose," we encounter at once a fundamentally different attitude and aesthetic. If the traditional role of the composer is eliminated, there is no alternative but to leave the artistic results, literally, to *chance*. John Cage's *Music of Changes*, a lengthy piano piece written in 1951, is an early example. It was composed through an elaborate process of using charts and coin tosses in accord with the Chinese oracular book of wisdom, *I-Ching* ("Book of Changes").

One of Cage's most interesting works is also one of his most controversial: *4'33"* ("Four Minutes and Thirty-Three Seconds," 1952). In *4'33"*, a performer or group of performers steps out on stage and, for the amount of time specified in the

New York Times Co./Getty Images

In this photo, taken at Gaveau Auditorium in Paris, France, in 1949, experimental composer John Cage alters the sound of his piano by placing screws and coins between the strings. In the 1950s, Cage challenged our accepted notions of music by exploring the worlds of chance and silence in works such as *Music of Changes* and *4'33"*.

title, sits or stands (or lies down for that matter) in "silence." Part of the point of this piece is that there is never real silence; the music in this aleatory composition is created by the humming of fluorescent lights, the creaking of floors, sniffling, sighing, a gurgling stomach—any sound that happens within the specified amount of time. Cage's role as composer was to set up the parameter of time, validating whatever random sounds occur as music. But is this music or just noise? Does merely specifying the amount of time for random sounds to happen make one a composer? There are bigger questions too: If this is not art, then what *is* art? The value of *4"33"* resides not so much in the piece itself but, rather, in the important questions it raises.

THE WEST COAST: COWELL, HARRISON, AND PARTCH

Henry Cowell (1897–1965) came into the world gifted with the kind of observant, eagerly absorbing mentality that was able to reap the full benefit of growing up in the richly polyglot atmosphere of the San Francisco Bay area just after the turn of the century—the same milieu that a generation earlier had nurtured Jack London and Gertrude Stein.

When he got hold of a battered old upright piano, he soon found he had an instrument that would open up new possibilities, and he began experimenting. In 1912, at the age of fifteen, he played in public in San Francisco a piece called *The Tides of Manaunaun;* it was a prelude to an opera he was writing based on Irish mythology. Manaunaun was the maker of great tides that swept through the universe. To convey the sense of this vast motion, Cowell hit upon the device of using huge groups of tones sounded together that could be played on the piano only with the entire forearm. These became known as tone clusters. Cowell used them in many of his piano works—became notorious for them, in fact—but nowhere more effectively than in this very early piece (see Additional Listening).

About 1923 Cowell began to produce works calling for the performer to play directly on the strings of the piano. In "The Banshee" (CD 4/10) from 1925, the performer does not sit at the keyboard of the piano, but instead sweeps his or her hands across the strings in various ways, glides them lengthwise on one or more strings, and occasionally plucks them. The music, bone-chilling in effect, is written down in a very rudimentary fashion. A few notes are indicated, and, between them, wavy lines to let the performer know the general direction and relative length of the hand sweeps across the piano strings.

Listening Cue **"The Banshee"** by Henry Cowell; performed by Henry Cowell (2:33)

CD 4

10

Listen For ▪ various effects produced by playing directly on the piano strings

Visit http://www.music.wadsworth.com_3/Kingman for a full listening guide and other resources.

An inventive, resourceful, and—above all—curious individual, Cowell was also the first American composer to remind us that the West Coast of the United States is, culturally as well as geographically, farther from Europe, and closer to Asia, than is New York. Growing up in San Francisco, he heard a great deal of Asian music. His works subsequently bore witness to his detailed study of musical cultures as widely separated as those of Japan, Persia, and Iceland. In 1956–1957 he went on a world tour, sponsored in part by the Rockefeller Foundation and the U.S. government, spending a considerable amount of time in Iran and in Japan. There he studied their music and, in turn, brought knowledge of American music to them. This marked the beginning of a series of works based on Persian music (*Persian Set*, 1957, and *Homage to Iran*, 1959) and Japanese music (*Ongaku* for orchestra, 1957). Later his interest expanded to include the music of Iceland; his Symphony No. 16 (1962) is subtitled *Icelandic*. In these works, Cowell only rarely uses traditional tunes but writes his *own* Persian, Japanese, or Icelandic music. Cowell's openness to a large vocabulary of sounds was carried further by two students of his: John Cage, who took it to an extreme in 4'33", and Lou Harrison.

Lou Harrison

Lou Harrison (1917–2003), born in Portland, Oregon, went east in the 1940s to become, for a time, an important part of the New York musical scene. But he always remained a son of the West Coast in his independence of "establishment" music and thinking. An American "Renaissance man" of the twentieth century, Harrison was a dancer, painter, playwright, conductor, and maker of musical instruments.

Two important focal points in Lou Harrison's work are interrelated. The first is his cultivation of percussion instruments, showing up as early as 1941 in his *Fugue for Percussion,* and through the years in a variety of ensemble pieces and concertos. The second is his knowledge of and love for the music of the Pacific Basin, particularly that of the Indonesian gamelan, an ensemble of percussion instruments. Lou Harrison and his partner William Colvig (1917–2000) built and performed on their own gamelans, each with its own unique name and tuning. Harrison often combined in his works Asian and Western instruments, as in his *Pacifika Rondo* of 1963, and in many smaller pieces.

Harry Partch

Harry Partch (1901–1974), the son of apostate former missionaries to China, was born in Oakland, California, but soon moved with his family into the southwestern desert area of Arizona and New Mexico. His father, who understood Mandarin Chinese, worked for the immigration service, moving frequently from one small railroad-junction town near the Mexican border to another. Thus the boy grew up, lonely and largely self-educated, among the diverse people of "the declining years of the Old West," as he put it—including the Yaqui Indians, the Chinese, and the hoboes and prostitutes his father and mother occasionally brought home. At fourteen Partch began to compose seriously. But at twenty-eight

Grey Villet / Time Life Pictures /Getty Images

In this photo from 1957, we see musicians playing a set of attractive percussion instruments built by composer and inventor Harry Partch.

he burned, in a big iron stove, all the music he had written up to that time and set out with determination and (as he described it) "exhilaration" on new paths. Hardly satisfied that conventional instruments would meet his creative ideals, Partch started building his own.

His first instruments included a Chromelodeon (an adapted reed organ) and a Kithara (a lyre-shaped plucked-string instrument with movable bridges that allowed for a sliding tone). With these, along with an adapted viola and an adapted guitar, Partch wrote his first major work, *U.S. Highball* (see Additional Listening). Described as "a hobo's account of a trip from San Francisco to Chicago," it is to a great extent autobiographical, for Partch's life between 1935 and 1943 consisted in large measure of hoboing, dishwashing, and wandering. *U.S. Highball* has a Subjective Voice (the protagonist) and several Objective Voices, whose words consist of "fragments of conversations, writings on the sides of boxcars, signs in havens for derelicts, hitchhikers' inscriptions"—all of which Partch had recorded in a notebook he always carried during his wanderings.

In succeeding years Partch built many new instruments, and rebuilt many earlier ones. The percussion instruments feature various marimbas. The Marimba Eroica is the largest; its lowest tone, below any of the notes on the piano, is produced by a Sitka spruce plank more than seven feet long suspended over a resonator eight feet long and four feet high. The smallest and softest is the Mazda Marimba, made of twenty-four lightbulbs "with their viscera removed," yielding a sound, according to Partch, like the "bubbling of a coffee percolator." Other percussion instruments include a Gourd Tree, Cone Gongs, and the bell-like Cloud-Chamber Bowls—the tops and bottoms of twelve-gallon glass carboys suspended. Appealing in sound, his instruments, especially as he redesigned them, came to have great visual appeal as well; they are very much "part of the set" of a Partch performance.

NEW TECHNOLOGY AND THE NEW MUSIC

The present sophisticated state of electroacoustic (and now digital) music can be understood as a composite of the following capabilities: the ability to record any sound or succession of sounds, the ability to create any imaginable sound or succession of sounds, and the ability to manipulate sounds obtained from either of these two processes in various ways, including slowing them down or speeding them up, raising or lowering their pitch, reversing their direction in time, changing their timbre by filtering out certain frequencies, combining any number of them simultaneously, introducing echo effects, making them endlessly repeat, and juxtaposing them in any way. *Sampling* constitutes a synthesis of all three of these capabilities, in that a sound from *any* source can be listened to, analyzed, synthesized, and subjected to any of the aforementioned manipulations.

In its first stages (roughly the 1950s), nearly all efforts were directed toward the production of sound on tape as the sole end product. To attend a performance, all you had to do was be in the presence of loudspeakers and listen. The first program of such music in the United States, at the Museum of Modern Art in New York in 1952, was the work of two of the pioneers of electroacoustic music, Otto Luening and Vladimir Ussachevsky. Because of the amount and cost of the equipment involved, universities were both the centers and the patrons of the development of electronic music—at first Columbia and Princeton, later joined by the Universities of Michigan and Illinois, and Stanford University. With the affordability of modern computers and digital technology, various techniques of sound manipulation, including sampling, have become commonplace not only in experimental music but in popular music as well.

MINIMALISM

Minimalism has as its "underlying impulse the radical reduction of compositional materials" (Dreier). This is so in both the visual arts (the works of Frank Stella, b. 1936, for example) and in music. In the latter, its most familiar manifestation is a musical texture in which short, simple patterns are repeated for long periods of time, either without variation or with subtle changes that gradually alter the melodic, rhythmic, or timbral content. As a form of musical composition, it began to appear prominently in the 1960s and was associated with two trends of the times. One was an increased interest in Asian and African music, in which repetition plays a very significant role. The other trend was a reaction, on the part of some composers born in the 1930s, to midcentury modernism itself, especially the serialism of the dominant academic East Coast/European "establishment."

Steve Reich (b. 1936), of New York City, was an influential composer of minimalist music in the mid-1960s. His approach was to treat music as a gradual, perceptible process, one that the listener can hear happening throughout the music. As he explains it:

> Performing and listening to a gradual musical process resembles: pulling back a swing, releasing it, and observing it gradually come to rest; turning over an hour glass and watching the sand slowly run through to the bottom: placing your feet in the sand by the ocean's edge and watching, feeling, and listening to the waves gradually bury them. (9)

The technology of tape recording suggested one means of treating music as a process: splicing tapes into loops so that fragments of speech or music could be recycled in a repeated pattern that could be played endlessly or combined with other loops in various ways. Many of the ideas and possibilities of sound manipulation and musical structure were originally suggested by experimentation with tape. Steve Reich tells of an accidental discovery that was to have far-reaching consequences for minimalism. This happened as he was working with the recording he had made of a young black Pentecostal preacher, Brother Walter, in Union Square, San Francisco, which eventually became the basis for Reich's composition *It's Gonna Rain* (1965).

> In the process of trying to line up two identical tape loops in some particular relationship, I discovered that the most interesting music of all was made by simply lining the loops up in unison, and letting them slowly shift out of phase with each other. As I listened to this gradual phase shifting process I began to realize that it was an extraordinary form of musical structure. . . . It was a seamless, continuous, uninterrupted musical process. (50)

Thus *phase shifting* came into being. Born of tape technology, the process was soon applied to pieces for human performers, as in Reich's *Piano Phase* (1967) for two pianos and *Clapping Music* (1972) for performers clapping hands. Although the music requires only the most basic material, the concentration, stamina, and endurance demanded of the musicians in order to effect the gradual process of phase shifting make pieces such as *Piano Phase* (CD 4/11) very difficult to perform.

Listening Cue *Piano Phase* (excerpt) by Steve Reich; Nurit Tilles and Edmund Niemann (3:00)

CD 4

11

Listen For ▪ phase shifting of two pianos

Visit http://www.music.wadsworth.com_3/Kingman for a full listening guide and other resources.

Other prominent composers of minimalist music include Philip Glass (b. 1937) and, more recently, John Adams (b. 1947). With Steve Reich, these three composers have been most successful at making minimalist music accessible to a broad audience.

MULTIMEDIA ART AND CONCEPT MUSIC

Very elaborate attempts were made in the late 1960s and early 1970s to create whole artistic "environments" that would actively involve the audience. A short environmental piece, *Souvenir* (1970) by Donald Erb, presented close coordination of aural, visual, and tactile components in a "happy" and "non-neurotic" (in the composer's words) piece for dancers, instrumental ensemble of winds and percussion, electronic tape, projections, and "props" that included weather balloons (bounced around in the hall by the audience) and Ping-Pong balls, which the audience afterward carried away as "souvenirs" (Cope 232–235). Once the traditional concert situation was superseded, the temptation to expand multimedia works to gargantuan proportions proved irresistible to some. Robert Moran's *39 Minutes for 39 Autos*, done in San Francisco in 1969, involved a "potential of 100,000 performers, using auto horns, auto lights, skyscrapers, a TV station, dancers, theater groups, spotlights, and airplanes, besides a small synthesizer ensemble." A more recent theatricalism, using a mixture of media, is the "performance art" of the 1980s and

1990s, centered on a solo performer who may play, sing, speak, act, and/or dance, in any combination, aided by a battery of visual displays and props. Laurie Anderson is perhaps the best-known performer in this vein.

"Concept music" consists of *ideas* for pieces, the actual realization of which would be either impossible or, as expressions of the philosophy motivating them, ambiguous at best. Of the first type, for example, would be pieces that would take several hundred years to perform. Representative of the second type would be La Monte Young's *Composition 1960 No. 9*, which, in his words, "consists of a straight line drawn on a piece of paper. It is to be performed and comes with no instructions." The pieces often contain no musical notes, but a set of instructions ("word-scores"), some of which are gentle invitations to become aware of the beauties of the environment or to relinquish some of the egotism of the "performer." Pauline Oliveros's *Sonic Meditations* includes instructions to "Take a walk at night. Walk so silently that the bottoms of your feet become ears" and "Become performers by not performing."

CLASSICAL MUSIC AND THE CONTEMPORARY WORLD

In the final years of the twentieth century, the American Composers Forum, a leading and innovative composers' organization (based, significantly, not in New York City but in St. Paul, Minnesota, in the "grassroots" heartland of the country), conceived the idea of having each of the fifty states produce a new work to celebrate the opening of the new millennium. The project was called, appropriately, Continental Harmony, a play on the title of one of William Billings' tunebooks, published a little more than 200 years earlier (see Chapter 10).

The Continental Harmony project stipulated that each work relate in specific ways to the history and the culture of the community for which it was written and in which it was performed. Thus the project as a whole illustrates the diversity of American music, and each individual work in itself bears witness to the *sense of place* that, though certainly recognized as vital to the legitimacy of a novel or a drama, is also vital to certain kinds of music, regardless of style or medium. What is interesting is that most of the composers did not live in the communities they composed for; they did, however, spend a considerable amount of time in residence in those communities. The works, then, represent the careful observation and commentary of a thoughtful "outsider" on the culture and history of the community. In a broader sense, each attempts to illustrate a different aspect of the relevance of classical music to the contemporary world. This chapter concludes by looking at a piece written for St. Louis, Missouri.

The Bushy Wushy Rag (CD 4/12), by composer Philip Bimstein (also then mayor of a small town in Utah), celebrates two cultural icons of St. Louis and the mid–Mississippi Valley: baseball and, in a subtler musical way, ragtime. After the initial sports announcer speaking over the crowd, the "narrator" is Robert Logan, a longtime vendor at the games of the St. Louis Cardinals. The music begins with a slowed-down version (in music this is called augmentation) of the first five notes of Scott Joplin's "Maple Leaf Rag" (review CD 3/17) played by the Equinox Chamber Players, a woodwind quintet comprising flute, oboe, clarinet, bassoon, and French horn. Toward the end of the excerpt it is not hard to recognize part of the "St. Louis Blues" (2:52). The piece also illustrates the modern techniques of the electronic manipulation of sounds used today in all styles of music. In this case, it is obvious in the collage of live crowd sounds and in the tape-loops of Robert Logan's voice. Less obvious is that the rhythmic punctuations heard between the phrases of the "Maple Leaf Rag" are actually the sounds, captured and manipulated to suit the composer's purpose, of a baseball hitting a catcher's glove.

Listening Cue *The Bushy Wushy Rag* by Philip Bimstein, 2000; Equinox Chamber Players and tape (3:10)

CD 4

12

Listen For ▪ sounds of a baseball game ▪ "Maple Leaf Rag" and "St. Louis Blues" ▪ electronic manipulation of sound

Visit http://www.music.wadsworth.com_3/Kingman for a full listening guide and other resources.

This work for the new millennium reveals the flexibility and technical resources of American classical music in our time. Whether it is relevant to modern audiences or not remains an open question that is ripe for debate. It does reflect, however, a sincere desire on the part of the composer to connect at the grassroots level in a way that is neither elitist (he uses the accessible materials of baseball, blues, and ragtime) nor condescending (the compositional techniques are unflinchingly avant-garde). Interestingly enough, technology aside, the compositional approach to *The Bushy Wushy Rag* is not fundamentally different from that taken by Charles Ives in "The Fourth of July" (CD 4/8), adding credence to composer Virgil Thomson's assertion that Ives was indeed "the father of us all."

PROJECTS

1. The music departments of many colleges and universities stage performances by "contemporary music ensembles" or "new music ensembles." Go to a concert and write a review. It is perfectly fine not to like the music, or even to find it uncomfortable or boring (remember, sometimes that's the point). Just be sure to explain exactly what motivates your impressions.

ADDITIONAL LISTENING

The Tides of Manaunaun. Henry Cowell, piano and vocals. *Henry Cowell: Piano Music.* Smithsonian/Folkways 40801.

U.S. Highball. Harry Partch. *Enclosure II.* Innova Records 401.

FILM MUSIC

The movie theater is a venue in which classical music continues to thrive in American culture. Audiences have become so accustomed to hearing classical music on film that it often goes without remark or notice. Yet, if it were taken away, one would definitely get the sense that something was missing. Imagine, for example, *Gone With the Wind* (1939) without the sweeping score by Max Steiner (1888–1971), *The Magnificent Seven* (1960) without the music of Elmer Bernstein (1922–2004), or any movie from the popular *Star Wars* saga (1977–2005) without the classical music of composer John Williams (b. 1932). Those might seem obvious examples. Less so, however, is the Sylvester Stallone action movie *First Blood* (1982), with its classical score by Jerry Goldsmith (1929–2004).

When we take the movie theater into consideration as a venue for experiencing classical music, we realize that a significant portion of the American population is, in fact, a regular consumer of classical music. Expand that consideration to include films enjoyed at home via television broadcast or DVD, and the portion becomes even larger, the frequency even more regular.

The 1930s saw the rise of the symphonic film score, with lush orchestral music mostly by European composers brought up in the European symphonic/operatic tradition. Film scoring rapidly became a very specialized job. Not until 1936 did a major American composer of concert music write for film, and then it was in the field of the documentary, a genre that, to a degree, is independent of the pressures of the entertainment industry.

A REALISTIC FILM OF THE AMERICAN WEST

In the mid-1930s the Resettlement Administration, a U.S. government agency, wanted a documentary film to propagandize on behalf of its program to aid farm families driven out of drought-stricken areas—mainly the Dust Bowl of the Southwest. Pare Lorentz (Leonard MacTaggart Lorentz, 1905–1992), a film reviewer turned filmmaker, was engaged to make this, his first movie. The result was a powerful documentary called *The Plow That Broke the Plains* (1936). The film still makes a stunning visual impact today, with its expressive footage of prairie grasslands; devastated, dust-blown farms; hard-hit, long-suffering farm families; and its visual analogies, as for example between military tanks and mammoth harvesters, or between a collapsed ticker-tape machine and bleached bones on the plowed-over, denuded land.

Virgil Thomson (1896–1989), composer, and a highly influential writer and critic, was engaged to write music for the film. Both Thomson and Lorentz felt the rightness of "rendering landscape through the music of its people," as the composer put it. The music therefore integrates material representative of the vastness and variety of American vernacular music, including a Calvinist psalm tune, cowboy songs, African American blues, and World War I songs. The music is available in the form of a thirteen-minute suite for orchestra in six movements fashioned by the composer himself, and is quite effective apart from the film, in which it is actually covered at times by the narration.

Of the six movements of the suite, the third, labeled "Cattle," is the one in which the landscape is most clearly rendered through the music of its people. In it we hear versions of three authentic cowboy tunes: "I Ride an Old Paint," "The Cowboy's Lament" (also known as "The Streets of Laredo"), and "Whoopie Ti Yi Yo, Git Along, Little Dogies." The fourth movement of the suite is "Blues," appropriately conventionalized and urbanized in the style of 1920s commercial jazz, to underscore the brash and ruinous exploitation of the land. Toward the end the music becomes progressively more dissonant (it is marked "Rough and violent"), and the themes more and more incoherent, climaxed by a final jangling chord that has as its underpinning, appropriately, the diminished triad. The sixth and last movement, "Devastation," brings back the material of the first, to complete the archlike structure. It goes on to include a fugue exposition, and ends this documentation of "the most tragic chapter in American agriculture" with a gigantic tango on a stretched-out version of the fugue theme (see Additional Listening).

TWO FILMS ABOUT THE SMALL TOWN AND THE BIG CITY

Aaron Copland (1900–1990) began his career, as did many other composers of his generation, with a period of study in France in the 1920s with Nadia Boulanger (1887–1979). As we saw in Chapter 17, he returned to become a potent force working on behalf of American music and its composers. A composer in virtually every public medium, including the concert hall, stage, screen, radio, and television, Copland wrote eight film scores between 1939 and 1961 (six feature films and two documentaries). One score was for the film *Our Town* (1940), based on Thornton Wilder's play about life and death, the commonplace and the universal, dramatized through episodes in the lives of two families in a small New England town. Much of the music is available in an orchestral piece called simply *Our Town: Music from the Film Score* (see Additional Listening).

Quite different from the music for *Our Town* is the score Leonard Bernstein (1918–1990) created for the Elia Kazan film *On the Waterfront* (1954). This film is about a longshoreman who possesses a degree of sensitivity and moral integrity that seems irreconcilably at odds with the harsh, brutal world of the waterfront in which he has always lived. The quiet opening melody, with its spare texture and references to jazz, is most appropriate to the urban setting and the theme of alienation. The film score was subsequently adapted into a twenty-three-minute symphonic suite (see Additional Listening).

THREE CAREER FILM COMPOSERS

Thomson, Copland, and (Leonard) Bernstein wrote film scores in addition to their various activities as composers of concert music, as conductors, and as critics. This section briefly surveys the artistic lives of three individuals who distinguished themselves almost exclusively as film composers who wrote in the classical style: Max Steiner, Bernard Herrmann, and John Williams.

Max Steiner

Maximilian Raoul Walter ("Max") Steiner (1888–1971) was born in Vienna, Austria. In his youth, he was thoroughly schooled in the European musical tradition at the Vienna Conservatory; from 1904 to 1914, he worked in Europe as a musical director and conductor for the theater, frequently in the cultural capitals of Paris and London. Following a move to the United States at the outbreak of World War I, he would become one of the most prolific composers for the American film industry.

A seasoned professional in European musical theater, Steiner's early career in the United States began quite naturally in New York, both on and off Broadway. There he found steady work in a variety of tasks that ranged from copying musical parts by hand to arranging and orchestrating scores to conducting shows. In 1924, he worked on George Gershwin's *Lady Be Good!* and Jerome Kern's *Sitting Pretty.*

Steiner's Hollywood career began in 1929 with *Rio Rita,* a Broadway musical that was being turned into a film for RKO Radio Pictures. With this move, note William Darby and Jack Du Bois, "Steiner became part of the music department at RKO when the advent of sound led to a plethora of large musicals designed to illustrate Hollywood's capacities for handling the new technology" (16). From 1929 to 1936 he would compose music for more than 130 films at RKO. His first celebrated full-length film score was for *King Kong* in 1933. From 1936 to the 1950s he worked mostly for Warner Brothers, but he wrote some of his most memorable works for producer David O. Selznick. One of those works was the famous score for *Gone With the Wind* (1939).

Although Steiner's earliest experiences in writing for film focused on adapting musicals for the big screen, his subsequent approach to film scoring would be rooted firmly in classical principles. His "melodies and orchestrations derive from nineteenth-century, central European models" and "his sense of music's dramatic functions accords with that of Richard Wagner, whom Steiner praised as the embryonic model for movie composers," note Darby and Du Bois (15). The connection with Wagner's late dramatic works is seen most readily in Steiner's use of melodies that are tied to specific characters. In *King Kong* separate melodies become specifically associated with Kong and Ann (played by Fay Wray), for example. In *Gone With the Wind*, Rhett and Mammie have their own melodies; Steiner's grand, soaring theme for Tara (the southern plantation owned by Scarlett O'Hara's family) has become emblematic of the movie itself.

Bernard Herrmann

Bernard Herrmann (1911–1975), a New Yorker by birth, studied the violin as a child and, later, conducting and composition at New York University and the Juilliard School. In 1933 he formed a small orchestra, the New Chamber Ensemble, which he led in performances of his own concert works and those of American contemporaries, including Charles Ives (1874–1954), with whom he developed a lasting friendship. From 1934 to 1940, Herrmann worked as an arranger and composer for CBS Radio which, according to his own testimony, prepared him for his subsequent career as a film composer. As he put it: "I learned to become a film composer by doing two or three thousand radio dramas" (Darby and Du Bois 345).

The radio industry provided Herrmann with important contacts that helped launch his career in film. While at CBS, he became associated with Orson Welles (1915–1985); the two collaborated in the famous *War of the Worlds* broadcast of 1938, among other projects. When Welles began developing *Citizen Kane* (1941) for Hollywood, he called on Herrmann to provide original music. The music for *Citizen Kane* was nominated for an Academy Award but was edged out by another of Herrmann's own scores, the one for the film *All That Money Can Buy*.

Herrmann's music is perhaps best known to audiences through his collaborations with filmmaker Alfred Hitchcock (1899–1980). Herrmann's work with Hitchcock stretches from *The Trouble with Harry* (1955) to *Marnie* (1964). A projected collaboration with Hitchcock on *Torn Curtain* (1966) never materialized, reportedly because of Herrmann's refusal to provide a score in the popular vein. Indeed, Herrmann's creative output reflects the fact that he held fast to the idea of composing for films in the "classical style" during the 1960s and 1970s, a time when pop, folk, and rock soundtracks were becoming more prevalent (in movies such as *The Graduate,* for example, with its soundtrack by the folk rock musicians Simon and Garfunkel).

The most recognizable Bernard Herrmann moment in film is undoubtedly the famous shower scene in Hitchcock's 1960 thriller, *Psycho* (CD 4/13). The score for *Psycho* was composed strictly for a string orchestra. There are no horns, woodwinds, or percussion instruments here. In this short "cue" (a passage of music that is written for a specific moment in a film), "screaming strings" produce the bone-chilling effect. Drawing on his practical knowledge of the violin, Herrmann achieved this effect by having each musician glide his or her fingers very quickly along the string (this is called a *glissando*), moving quickly from a lower pitch to a higher one. Furthermore, the string is played with short, agitated bow strokes. All the while, one instrumental group is layered upon another to create dissonant tone clusters. Unlike Steiner's broad, sweeping melodies, Herrmann tends to use short melodic fragments that are repeated over and over in an obsessive fashion

In the famous shower scene from Alfred Hitchcock's film *Psycho,* Marion Crane (played by Janet Leigh) screams in terror as Norman Bates tears open her shower curtain. Bernard Hermann's score for this scene—which we hear on CD 4, track 13—amplifies the terror and disorientation we feel at the murder of the film's star. A string orchestra, which we generally associate with lush, romantic sounds, suddenly transforms itself into violent and percussive "screaming strings." Film and music work together here to defy conventions and thwart audience expectations.

© Bettmann /CORBIS

(for example, beginning at 0:24). If Steiner's scores fall into the nineteenth-century "romantic" style of composition, Herrmann's lean heavily toward a "modernist" aesthetic.

Listening Cue **"The Murder"** *Psycho*, score by Bernard Herrmann; Los Angeles Philharmonic, Esa-Pekka Salonen, conductor (1:01)

CD 4

13

> Listen For ▪ use of *glissando* in the "screaming strings" ▪ short, repeated melodic fragments

Visit http://www.music.wadsworth.com_3/Kingman for a full listening guide and other resources.

John Williams

Like Herrmann, John Williams (b. 1932) was born in New York. He began studying the piano at the age of eight; when his family moved to Los Angeles in 1948, he continued his lessons there under jazz pianist and arranger Bobby Van Eps. From 1951 to 1954, Williams served in the U.S. Air Force, where he conducted and wrote music for the Air Force band; afterward he resumed his piano studies for a year at the Juilliard School under Rosina Lhévinne (whom we encountered in Chapter 17 as Van Cliburn's teacher). Williams returned to the West Coast and enrolled at the University of California, Los Angeles, supplementing his formal work with lessons from the Italian-born Mario Castelnuovo-Tedesco (1895–1968), a highly sought-after teacher of film music composition.

Whereas Steiner's career began in musical theater, and Herrmann's in radio, Williams got his start arranging and composing for television during the 1950s. By the 1960s he was writing for comedy films, and in the 1970s for a string of "disaster films" that included *The Poseidon Adventure* (1972), *Earthquake* (1974), and *The Towering Inferno* (1974). The first of his memorable collaborations with director Steven Spielberg was *The Sugarland Express* (1974), followed by *Jaws* (1975), *Close Encounters of the Third Kind* (1977), *Raiders of the Lost Ark* (1981), and *E.T. the Extra-Terrestrial* (1982). More recent examples of their many films together include *Schindler's List* (1993) and *War of the Worlds* (2005).

The musical style of John Williams takes us right back to the broad, lush, nineteenth-century approach of Max Steiner. His music for George Lucas's *Star Wars* (1977) has been credited with bringing back the symphonic film score at a time when (with the notable exception of Bernard Herrmann) film composers had begun to turn more and more frequently to popular music as the basis for their scores. Music for the *Star Wars* saga, which extends over six related films from *Star Wars: A New Hope* in 1977 to *Star Wars: Revenge of the Sith* in 2005, has followed the classical technique of Richard Wagner (and the classic film technique of Max Steiner) in using specific melodies to identify specific characters. These melodies often change to reflect character development (or deterioration) as well. Once we focus on this technique, it becomes impossible to disassociate the theme from its character in many cases. Consider, for example, "The Imperial March"—the theme that typically accompanies Darth Vader.

"The Imperial March" (CD 4/14) is not merely an "aural stamp" for Darth Vader, it adds gravity to his character. The musical style and pacing, with its forward (but unhurried) momentum, evoke a very serious, sure-footed march. The minor key provides a dark musical soundscape. The use of blaring brass instruments over "shuddering" strings projects a semblance of overwhelming power. All of these musical elements—style, tempo, key, dynamics, and instrumentation—are as much a part of Darth Vader's character as the black mask and helmet, the flowing cape, and body armor that make him such an ominous villain on the big screen.

© Roger Ressmeyer/CORBIS

In the popular *Star Wars* saga, Darth Vader, Dark Lord of the Sith, was the sum of many parts. The actor David Prowse played his dramatic scenes; fencer Bob Anderson performed his dueling scenes; and actor James Earl Jones supplied his voice. American composer John Williams added yet another dimension to this complex character with "The Imperial March," which we hear on CD 4, track 14.

Listening Cue "The Imperial March (Darth Vader's Theme)" *Star Wars: Episode V—The Empire Strikes Back,* score by John Williams; London Symphony Orchestra, John Williams, conductor (3:02)

CD 4

14

> Listen For ▪ march style ▪ dark musical key (minor) ▪ blaring brass instruments

Visit http://www.music.wadsworth.com_3/Kingman for a full listening guide and other resources.

EPILOGUE

Of course, music in film has not relied exclusively on the classical genre. Although the classical style has been a mainstay historically, notable film soundtracks have also drawn from jazz (*A Streetcar Named Desire,* 1951), the Broadway musical (*Oklahoma!* 1955), folk rock (*The Graduate,* 1967), rock and roll (*American Graffiti,* 1973), ragtime (*The Sting,* 1973), modern country (*Urban Cowboy,* 1980), and "old-time" country and blues (*O Brother, Where Art Thou?* 2000), to name just a few. What this chapter has demonstrated, however, is that classical music does indeed occupy a prominent role in modern American life. More than the concert stage and the opera house, films of the popular entertainment industry have brought classical music to the very heart of the American experience.

PROJECTS

1. See a movie and pay special attention to the role of music. What style of music is used in the film? Does the film use different styles? If so, why, and at what moments?
2. In any movie you see, discuss the role of the music. Does it enhance the action? Comment on the action? Prepare for upcoming events? Dominate or support?

ADDITIONAL LISTENING

Our Town, music from the film score. *Copland Conducts Copland.* London Symphony Orchestra. Sony 42429.

On the Waterfront, symphonic suite. *Candide/West Side Story/On the Waterfront/Fancy Free.* New York Philharmonic. Cond. Leonard Bernstein. Sony 63085.

The Plow That Broke the Plains, film score and suite for orchestra. Symphony of the Air. Cond. Leopold Stokowski. Vanguard Classics 1.

MUSIC IN YOUR OWN BACKYARD

The following chapter is devoted to issues in American music as they pertain to two specific places in the United States. The places themselves are beside the point; they just happen to be where Daniel Kingman and I have lived, worked, and experienced American music on a daily basis. Any other place would do as well; in fact, the whole idea of this chapter is to encourage you to look around, wherever you may be, and become aware of how many different kinds of music, made by people of many different backgrounds and places of origin, can be found in your own backyard. No less important, we encourage you to look into the histories of your local music traditions and the organizations that have sustained them.

20

TALES OF TWO CITIES: AUSTIN, TEXAS, AND SACRAMENTO, CALIFORNIA

This closing chapter illustrates how broader topics engaged throughout this book might be applied at the local level—literally, in the place where you live. It consists of two case studies. The first focuses on Austin, Texas, and relates to issues covered in Chapter 17, the search for an American identity in classical music. The source materials rely extensively on old newspapers that were archived on microfilm in local public libraries. The second case study is a broad consideration of regional diversity in the Sacramento Valley, California, and relates to chapters covered in the first part of the book. This required doing some background research on the area to provide context, but, more important, talking to many different people (those who make music, and those who consume it) and taking in a variety of concerts—all the while keeping careful notes about impressions and experiences.

Whether you are a quiet library type or gregarious, whether you prefer short stories on focused topics or long views of broader issues, there is a project for you in helping to tell the story of America's music. The following "tales of two cities" advances that cause while providing models for your own contribution.

CLASSICAL MUSIC IN AUSTIN, TEXAS: ASPECTS FROM THE 1830S TO WORLD WAR I

German Roots

The earliest immigrants from modern-day Germany settled into the area that would become the state of Texas during the 1830s. In 1836, the newly declared Republic of Texas opened its borders to immigrants, offering large grants of inexpensive land to those willing to transform wilderness into viable communities. Nearly 7,500 Germans arrived in Texas between 1844 and 1846. The first major settlement was New Braunfels, about forty-five miles southwest of Austin, in 1845. That same year, Texas entered the Union to become the twenty-eighth state. Fredericksburg, just over eighty-five miles west of Austin, was settled one year later.

German Singing Societies

The Germans who arrived in Texas during the 1830s, 1840s, and 1850s, brought with them many of the cultural traditions they had come to know and love in Europe. One of the most cherished traditions was active participation in German "singing societies," organizations that can be largely credited for major advances in music performance and education in Texas during the second half of the nineteenth century. The benchmarks against which German singing societies throughout the state measured themselves were performances at the popular and highly competitive State Singers' Festivals held annually in Houston, San Antonio, Dallas, Austin, and the surrounding Hill Country.

A look at the Singers' Festival that Austin hosted in 1889 reveals that these were major events, admitting both mixed choruses and purely orchestral works.

State Singers' Festival. Closing concert. Austin, Texas. April 24, 1889

Work	Composer
Trompeten Ouverture, op. 101 Orchestra	Felix Mendelssohn (1809–1847)
When the Larks Return Massed Choruses	Weinziger [?]
Twilight at Eve Austin Saengerrunde	Franz Abt (1819–1885)
The Return Houston Saengerbund and Liederkranz	[no composer indicated]
Forest Dreams San Antonio Frohsinn	Franz Abt (1819–1885)
The Chase Orchestra	Zickoff [?]
The German Muse	Johann Wenzel Kalliwoda (1801–1866)
Die Stiftungsfeier Massed Choruses	Felix Mendelssohn (1809–1847)
Serenade [in F major, op. 63] String Quintet	Robert Volkmann (1815–1883)
Wie kam die Liebe? San Antonio Beethoven Maennerchor	Martin Frey (1872–1946)
Prayer from *Lohengrin* Quintet, Mixed Chorus and Orchestra	Richard Wagner (1813–1883)
Morning [Morgenlied?] Austin Musical Union	Ries [Julius Rietz (1812–1877)?]
The Crown in the Rhein Massed Choruses and Orchestra	Carl Hirsch (1858–1918)
Overture to *The Beautiful Galatea* Orchestra	Franz von Suppé (1819–1895)

The program is impressive in its broad scope and variety, featuring the works of well-known composers such as Mendelssohn, Wagner, Abt, and von Suppé, alongside those of lesser-known composers including Robert Volkmann, Martin Frey, and Carl Hirsch. Weinziger and Zickoff were possibly local composers. The largely (indeed, almost entirely) Teutonic program was typical of repertories favored by German singing societies throughout the state. This, in short, was representative of the classical music scene in Texas during much of the nineteenth century and for nearly the first two decades of the twentieth.

Cultural Consequences of World War I

German immigrants and German music were cornerstones of Texas music culture, and would remain so until April 1917, when the United States declared war on Germany. At that point, all things German suddenly became unpatriotic to the "true American." The suspect German language was virtually banned in all public areas, even in parts of Texas where the population was predominantly German. So, too, there was a renaming campaign. Streets with German names were promptly given new "patriotic" names such as "Freedom Avenue." Even foods were renamed; sauerkraut became "Liberty cabbage." Defenders of German music, of course, were not exempt from suspicion, and in a state that had placed so many of its musical eggs in the German basket, the utter rejection of all things German posed a crisis.

Austin's Search for an American Musical Identity

The first sustained efforts at establishing a symphony orchestra in Austin, between 1916 and 1918, occurred immediately after the demise of the State Singers' Festivals, the last of which was held in San Antonio in May 1916. Contemporary newspapers reflect a clear shift away from music of the German tradition and toward a concerted effort to stake out a distinct American identity in classical music.

The early seasons of the Austin Symphony Orchestra under director Frank L. Reed (1871–1938), a music professor at the University of Texas, suggest not only that the group aimed to fill a void left by the discontinued German singing festivals, but that it was dedicated to projecting an American identity and nationalistic spirit as the United States entered the Great War. Here, for example, is the program for Reed's Austin Symphony Orchestra concert of December 16, 1917.

Austin Symphony Orchestra. Program for December 16, 1917
The Star-Spangled Banner
Military Symphony [no. 100 in G]	Joseph Haydn (1732–1809)
The Hymn of Free Russia	Alexander T. Gretchaninoff (1864–1956)
America [with a new verse]	[Audience and Orchestra]
Finlandia, op. 26	Jean Sibelius (1865–1957)
Military Polonaise in A, op. 40, no. 1	Frédéric Chopin (1810–1849)
Patrol of the Scouts	E. Boccalari (dates unknown)

Reports in local newspapers help fill in the picture. The program was touted as a "military concert," and justified the works by Haydn, Chopin, and Boccalari by virtue of their "military character." Gretchaninoff's "Hymn of Free Russia" was referred to in the press as "The first musical manifestation of the Russian revolution." Sibelius was touted as "one of the living composers who feels the titanic struggle of his own nationality." According to newspaper reviews, the highlights of this patriotic program were a performance of "The Star-Spangled Banner" (which did not become the American national anthem until 1931) and an audience-participation rendition of Samuel Francis Smith's "America" ("My Country 'Tis of Thee") with a verse that was newly written for the occasion, tailored to suit the war effort.

> God save our splendid men
> Bring them safe home again
> God save our men.
> Keep them victorious
> Patient and chivalrous
> They are so dear to us
> God save our men.

The patriotic event was a major success, and not long after Frank Reed began discussing the future plans of the Austin Symphony Orchestra. In January 1918, the *Austin American,* the city's daily morning paper, noted the following:

> The success of the concert given on Dec. 16, has encouraged the promoters of the orchestra to continue the admirable civic activity. The conductor [Frank Reed] has arranged two most suitable programs for the next two concerts: the first to be devoted exclusively to musics of the five allied nations, Great Britain, France, Italy, Russia, and America; and the second, to be devoted exclusively to the compositions of American composers. Orchestral compositions based upon the native music of the American Indian and the characteristic music of the negro will be featured.

Reed obviously took his cue from the "nativist" point of view (see pp. 288–290) and worked feverishly on this project. He contacted American composers for music and promised the Austin public that much of what would be performed had not been published and would have to be played from the composers' manuscripts. Unfortunately, there is no record of who the composers were, and ultimately Austin's "all-American" extravaganza would not come to pass. But the planned concert of allied nations did, in fact, occur on March 24, 1918. The program was advertised as follows:

Austin Symphony Orchestra. Concert of Allied Nations. March 24, 1918

The Star-Spangled Banner	[United States]
Overture to Shamus O'Brien	Sir Charles V. Stanford (1864–1956) [Great Britain]
L'Arlésienne, Suite No. 1	Georges Bizet (1838–1875) [France]
Prelude	
Minuetto	
Adagietto	
Carillon	

Symphony no. 6, Pathétique	Pyotr Ilyich Tchaikovsky (1840–1893) [Russia]
Allegro con grazia	
Adagio lamentoso	
Polonaise from Eugene Onegin	Pyotr Ilyich Tchaikovsky (1840–1893) [Russia]
Negro Episode	Henry F. Gilbert (1868–1928) [United States]
Overture to Italian in Algiers	Gioachino Rossini (1792–1868) [Italy]

Most interesting here is the fact that American concert music was represented by the "Negro Episode" of Henry F. Gilbert (1868–1928), a nativist who collected and studied the musics of African Americans and American Indians. As part of the "Americanist" fervor taking place in Austin around this time, the newspapers also report that a local quartet had recently performed Antonin Dvořák's String Quartet in F, popularly known as "The American" quartet (1894). The *Austin American*, however, referred to it as Dvořák's "Negro Quartet," a clear reference to its incorporation of the sounds of the African American spiritual.

As the United States entered the Great War, Austin's classical music scene projected its patriotic stance, in part, by rejecting German repertories and Germanic performance venues such as the formerly popular State Singers' Festivals. This was unfortunate in its own way; even more so when we realize that it was just a small part of the widespread alienation and discrimination that German immigrants faced at the time. It is instructive to see, however, that in their search for an American identity—an authentic voice—in classical music, concert organizers in Austin, Texas, were greatly affected by the lessons of nativists such as Dvořák, Gilbert, and Farwell. While the current Austin Symphony Orchestra is at a far remove from these signal events in the early twentieth century, the search for an American identity is an inextricable part of the city's musical heritage.

THE SACRAMENTO VALLEY: A RICH MIX OF CULTURES

The Sacramento Valley of California is a broad alluvial valley between two mountain ranges—a low coastal range to the west, and the Sierra Nevada to the east. From the high, snow-trapping barrier range of the Sierra flow down into the valley a series of tumultuous rivers that, until barely a century ago, spread wide out of their banks in the spring, flooding the valley, depositing rich alluvial soils and clays, and filling the huge old basins with half a million acres of water from January to May. Tamed now by scores of dams and hundreds of miles of levees and canals, they furnish the water that allows a multitude of crops to grow through the long hot season from May to October, when no rain falls.

Unlike Louisiana and the upper Midwest (two places studied in Chapter 5)—which are longer-settled regions whose cultural identity, bearing the characteristics of one or two dominant immigrant groups, has been established for well over a century—the Sacramento Valley presents a picture of a complex "cross-bedding" of successive migrations from many directions. This has left a rich mix of cultures, many of them still distinct and unassimilated. The phase of greatest influx is so recent that the sense of transiency has still not been replaced by one of settled permanency, and there is nothing that can be identified as a single distinctive regional culture. Each wave of newcomers has come with its own culture, in its own time, and for its own reasons. Trappers, mission founders, would-be empire builders, gold seekers, agricultural barons, land speculators, laborers imported en masse for railroad building or harvesting, networks of immigrants bringing relatives from foreign countries, military, defense, and government workers, wealthy entrepreneurs, and refugee populations—all have formed part of the picture.

A Brief Cultural Timeline

A peaceful Indian population with a culture singularly well adapted to the unique region were the original inhabitants; they and their way of life have been all but gone for a century. The Spaniards scarcely penetrated the valley to any extent, and the Mexican government, heir to Spain's territorial claim in 1822, could exercise only a tenuous hold on an area where American trappers and adventurers roamed freely. (The significant Mexican influence and presence was destined to come much later.) The discovery of gold in the Sierra foothills in 1848 brought sudden, irreversible, and drastic change. With the rapid influx of easterners (accompanied by significant immigration from Europe, Central and South America, and Asia), acquisition by the United States and statehood (in 1850) were inevitable. The population soared, and when the easily obtainable placer gold ran out (about 1853), large corporations took over the mining, and individual miners left or went into farming, which was destined to become the fertile valley's major industry. Railroad building in the 1860s brought in the first of the great laborer populations, the Chinese; as an immigrant labor population the Chinese were replaced by the Japanese beginning about 1900.

From 1900 to 1920 was the time of the great land boom, and the period saw further diversification of the valley's population. Land companies bought up large tracts (many upon the dissolution of the huge holdings that had originally been Mexican land grants) and advertised heavily in the East. Colonization projects brought more immigrants.

As agriculture in the valley changed from the growing of wheat, which could easily be harvested mechanically, to fruit and vegetable crops, which required handpicking, the need for seasonal labor grew; this has made a large transient population of farmworkers, with the social problems attendant on it, a part of the Sacramento Valley scene since very early in the twentieth century. Since as early as 1919, Mexicans have been coming to do this work.

The Depression and drought of the 1930s brought many from the Dust Bowl areas of Texas, Oklahoma, and Kansas (thus adding to the constituency for country music, which became especially strong in the adjoining San Joaquin Valley to the south). World War II brought further shifts in population throughout the nation; many who came to the valley during the war stayed or returned to it, thus beginning another period of population growth, which is still going on. Significant recent additions are large refugee populations from Southeast Asia.

Toward a Cultural and Musical Inventory of the Sacramento Valley

Among the American Indians there is, as described in Chapter 3, a new movement under way to restore and revitalize their native dance, music, crafts, and culture. This movement is strong in the Sacramento Valley, even though few of the Indians there may be descended from the original tribes. There are frequent intertribal powwows, often under the auspices of a college or university. There is considerable mutual cooperation and support between the American Indian and the Latino movements.

Many Chinese came to the valley and worked as miners during the gold rush, until driven out of this occupation by the Americans. Many more were brought in during the ensuing decade to build the railroad. Hardworking, canny, thrifty, keeping to themselves and to their own traditions, they were the object of scorn and persecution. Their numbers in the valley declined after 1890. In the decades since World War II, many Chinese have become fully integrated into the social, economic, and cultural life of the valley, but small groups cultivate Chinese culture, language, and music. Beginning in the 1960s the influx of Chinese as refugees from Vietnam and other parts of Southeast Asia increased dramatically.

Another early immigrant group was the Portuguese, who were among the first Europeans to settle in the Sacramento area, some arriving with the gold rush. Coming mostly from the Azores, they established small family farms. Following a familiar pattern, the immigrants, once established, encouraged others from the same areas to come, and provided for them upon their arrival. The Portuguese tended to form tightly knit communities, their social activities centering on the church (St. Elizabeth's in Sacramento still celebrates a Portuguese Mass) and its holy days. The festas are colorful celebrations, including a procession with music, followed by a feast. For years there were radio programs with a live band playing Portuguese music. Portuguese dances and songs are performed in the social halls in the community, accompanied by traditional violas de arames, violãos, and guitarras. A popular folk song from the Azores known and sung by the Portuguese in Sacramento is "Lira."

The Japanese began immigrating in significant numbers around the turn of the century, many coming from Hawaii after its annexation by the United States. Replacing the Chinese as a source of labor, they too were targets of persecution and mistrust until after World War II. Members today of a highly visible and well-integrated component of valley population, a few Americans of Japanese descent are now making conscious efforts to keep alive their own rich traditions of music, dance, and drama. Of special interest is the cultivation of minyo, or folk music and dance (as distinct from buyo, the highly cultivated classical dance). This costumed dance for multiple dancers is accompanied by a solo singer (either man or woman), one or several shamisens (a plucked stringed instrument of three strings), a yokobue (transverse flute), a kane (small bell), and a taiko (drum). Also accompanying the performance is the hayashi, a chorus of women's voices that "responds" to the solo singer's phrases with high-pitched rhythmic vocables that have no literal meaning. Their refrains have been referred to as "cheering calls." The dance movements of minyo odori consist largely of stylized interpretations of the body motions of work performed in the various localities from which the songs come—for example, work in the rice fields, coal mining, fishing, rice pounding, and cattle driving.

The major influx of Mexicans, and their considerable contribution to the cultural mix, is fairly recent, beginning with the harvests of the early 1920s. Their music today is mainly of the musica norteña tradition described in Chapter 4.

Immigrants from Greece, primarily from Peloponnesus, began arriving in the early 1900s and built their first church in Sacramento in 1921. Though the Greeks are thoroughly integrated into the community, they have preserved a good deal of their culture, focused on the Greek Orthodox Church. Since the 1950s and 1960s there has been a renaissance of Byzantine liturgical music in California. This was followed in the 1970s and 1980s by a renewed interest in Greek folk dance and costumes, and consequently in authentic Greek folk music, with regional distinctions preserved. Folk dance festivals, in which many young people take part, are frequent events. Several Greek bands are active, playing popular American as well as traditional Greek music. The traditional klarino (a type of clarinet) is no longer much used in the bands in Sacramento, but the bouzóuki, a fretted lutelike instrument with a long neck, has appeared in ensembles with greater frequency since the popularity of the film *Zorba the Greek*. It keeps company in the bands with electric guitars, drums, and electric keyboards. Greek music is flourishing but adapting—or, rather, flourishing by adapting.

Immigration from the Ukraine to the United States has occurred in five waves, beginning in the 1870s. The latest wave, in the late 1980s and 1990s, followed glasnost and the breakup of the Soviet Union, and consisted mostly of Ukrainian Baptists and Pentecostals who were escaping religious persecution. This wave added substantially to the 120 families that previously constituted the population of Ukrainian descent in Sacramento. Today there are in the Sacramento area Ukrainian Catholic, Baptist, Evangelical, and Pentecostal churches, each with a choir and a cantor, and some with a small orchestra. The Ukrainian Heritage Club of Northern California promotes Ukrainian culture, including music, as does the School of Ukrainian Studies, which has a children's choir.

Of special interest is the cultivation of the Ukrainian bandura, a plucked stringed instrument that was originally used to accompany the singing of epic folk ballads as early as the seventh century. Enlarged and perfected, it has become, in the hands of accomplished bandurists such as Ola Herasymenko Oliynyk of Sacramento, a concert instrument. She performs numerous solo and ensemble works for bandura, and has formed and leads the Bandura Ensemble of Northern California.

To be complete, this inventory of ethnic cultures of the Sacramento Valley and their musics would have to include many other communities as well. Among those that have active organizations devoted to preserving and celebrating their customs and their cultures, in addition to those treated previously, are Filipinos,

Laotians, Vietnamese, Koreans, Sikhs, Pacific Islanders, Armenians, Serbs, Croats, Norwegians, Poles, and Italians. The sheer number of traditions mentioned here in relation to the Sacramento Valley alone serves to underscore the vastness, complexity, and diversity that are the most outstanding characteristics of American music. That would seem a fitting close for this book, but it is no less a clarion call for the work that lies ahead. The projects that follow might stimulate some ideas.

PROJECTS

1. Look around in your own community and make an inventory of the various cultures, not in the "mainstream," that have retained their culture and perhaps their language as well, and that have their own distinctive and identifiable music and musical tradition.
2. Pick one culture in your own community that fits the description in project 1, and make a study (through interviews, attendance at social and religious events, etc.) of their music and the way it functions in their culture.
3. Find out about any national holidays that are celebrated by ethnic groups in your community, and attend and report on them. These are usually celebrations of national independence like the American Fourth of July; Mexicans, for example, celebrate Cinco de Mayo (May 5) and Norwegians, Syttende Mai (May 17).
4. Find out about and report on the support your state government gives to folk, ethnic, or regional arts, through a state folklorist or a state arts board or arts council.
5. Investigate and report on the history of one or more of your local fine arts organizations (the symphony, the opera, a quartet, for example). The narrative may be broad, or, you may choose to focus on a more specific period of its development.

REFERENCES

1. The Anglo-Celtic-American Tradition

Child, Francis James. *The English and Scottish Popular Ballads.* 5 vols. Boston, 1882–98. New York: Dover, 1965.

Christeson, R. P. *The Old-Time Fiddler's Repertory.* Columbia: Univ. of Missouri Press, 1973.

Cohen, John, and Mike Seeger. *Old-Time String Band Song Book.* New York: Oak, 1976.

Laws, G. Malcolm, Jr. *Native American Balladry.* Philadelphia: American Folklore Society, 1964.

Lomax, Alan. *The Folksongs of North America.* Garden City, NY: Doubleday, 1960.

Nathan, Hans. *Dan Emmett and the Rise of Early Negro Minstrelsy.* Norman: Univ. of Oklahoma Press, 1962.

Owens, William A. *Texas Folk Songs.* Dallas: SMU Press, 1976.

Randolph, Vance. *Ozark Folksongs.* Ed. and abr. Norm Cohen. Urbana: Univ. of Illinois Press, 1982.

Seeger, Charles. "Versions and Variants of the Tunes of Barbara Allen." *Selected Reports,* no. 1, Institute of Ethnomusicology, Univ. of California, Los Angeles, 1966.

Sharp, Cecil. *English Folk-Songs from the Southern Appalachians.* Ed. Maud Karpeles. London: Oxford Univ. Press, 1932. 2 vols. reprinted in 1, 1966.

Thede, Marion. *The Fiddle Book.* New York: Oak, 1967.

Thomas, Jean. *Ballad Makin' in the Mountains of Kentucky.* New York: Oak, 1964.

Wimberly, Charles. *Folklore in the English and Scottish Ballads.* New York: Dover, 1965.

2. The African American Tradition

Allen, William Francis, Charles Pickard Ware, and Lucy McKim Garrison, eds. *Slave Songs of the United States.* New York, 1867.

Courlander, Harold. *Negro Folk Music, U.S.A.* New York: Columbia Univ. Press, 1963.

Epstein, Dena J. *Sinful Tunes and Spirituals: Black Folk Music to the Civil War.* Urbana: Univ. of Illinois Press, 1977.

Jackson, George Pullen. *White and Negro Spirituals.* New York: Da Capo, 1975.

Johnson, James Weldon, and J. Rosamund Johnson, eds. *The Books of American Negro Spirituals.* 2 vols. in 1. New York: Viking, 1940.

Katz, Bernard, ed. *The Social Implications of Early Negro Music in the United States.* New York: Arno, 1969.

Laws, G. Malcolm, Jr. *Native American Balladry.* Philadelphia: American Folklore Society, 1964.

Lomax, John A., and Alan Lomax. *Our Singing Country.* New York: Macmillan, 1941.

Maultsby, Portia K. "West African Influences and Retentions in U.S. Black Music." *More Than Dancing: Essays on Afro-American Music and Musicians.* Ed. Irene Jackson. Westport, CT: Greenwood, 1985.

Murphy, Jeannette Robinson. "The Survival of African Music in America." *Appleton's Popular Science Monthly,* Sept. 1899.

Sandburg, Carl. *The American Songbag.* New York: Harcourt Brace & World, 1927.

Southern, Eileen. *The Music of Black Americans.* 2nd ed. New York: Norton, 1983.

———, ed. *Readings in Black American Music.* 2nd ed. New York: Norton, 1983.

3. The American Indian Tradition

Densmore, Frances. *The American Indians and Their Music.* New York: Women's Press, 1926.

Heth, Charlotte. "Notes." *Music of the Yurok and Tolowa Indians.* NW 80297.

Levine, Victoria Lindsay. "Musical Revitalization among the Choctaw." *American Music* 11.4 (Winter 1993).

Lornell, Kip, and Anne K. Rasmussen, eds. *Musics of Multicultural America.* New York: Schirmer Books, 1997.

McAllester, David P. *Peyote Music.* Viking Fund Publications in Anthropology, no. 13. New York: Viking, 1949. 85.

Nettl, Bruno. "Indians, American/Music/Styles." *The New Grove Dictionary of American Music.* Vol. 2. London: Macmillan, 1986. 464–68.

———. *North American Indian Musical Styles.* Philadelphia: American Folklore Society, 1954.

O'Kane, Walter Collins. *Sun in the Sky.* Norman: Univ. of Oklahoma Press, 1950.

Rhodes, Willard. "Acculturation in North American Indian Music." *Acculturation in the Americas.* Chicago: Univ. of Chicago Press, 1952.

Robb, J. Donald. *Hispanic Folk Music of New Mexico and the Southwest.* Norman: Univ. of Oklahoma Press, 1980.

4. Latino Traditions

Aparicio, Frances R. *Listening to Salsa: Gender, Latin Popular Music, and Puerto Rican Cultures.* Hanover, NH: Wesleyan Univ. Press, 1998.

Contreras, Maximiliano. *Crossing: A Comparative Analysis of the Mexicano, Mexican-American and Chicano.* San Pedro, CA: International Universities Press, 1983.

Fernández, Joaquin. Note to Daniel Kingman.

Geijerstam, Claes af. *Popular Music in Mexico.* Albuquerque: Univ. of New Mexico Press, 1976.

Koegel, John. *Inter-American Music Review* 13.2 (Spring–Summer 1993). Includes "Mexican and Mexican-American Musical Life in Southern California, 1850–1900" and "Calendar of Southern California Amusements 1852–1897; Designed for Spanish-Speaking Public."

———. "Spanish and Mexican Dance Music in Early California." *Ars Musica.* Lamont School of Music, Univ. of Denver. Fall 1994.

Lornell, Kip, and Anne K. Rasmussen, eds. *Musics of Multicultural America.* New York: Schirmer Books, 1997.

Loza, Steven. *Barrio Rhythm: Mexican American Music in Los Angeles.* Urbana: Univ. of Illinois Press, 1993.

Robb, John Donald. *Hispanic Folk Music of New Mexico and the Southwest: A Self-Portrait of a People.* Norman: Univ. of Oklahoma Press, 1980.

Roberts, John Storm. *The Latin Tinge: The Impact of Latin American Music in the United States.* New York: Oxford Univ. Press, 1979.

Singer, Roberta. "Tradition and Innovation in Contemporary Latin Popular Music in New York City." *Latin American Review* 4.2 (Fall–Winter 1983).

Stark, Richard B. *Music of the Spanish Folk Plays in New Mexico.* Santa Fe: Museum of New Mexico Press, 1969.

Stevenson, Robert. *Music in Aztec and Inca Territory: Contact and Acculturation Periods.* Berkeley and Los Angeles: Univ. of California Press, 1977.

Steward. Sue. *¡Música!: The Rhythm of Latin America.* San Francisco: Chronicle Books, 1999.

Waxer, Lise, ed. *Situating Salsa.* New York: Routledge, 2002.

5. Diverse Traditions: French, Scandinavian, Arab, and Asian

Allen, William Francis, Charles Pickard Ware, and Lucy McKim Garrison, eds. *Slave Songs of the United States.* New York, 1867. New York: Oak, 1969.

Asai, Susan M. "Cultural Politics: The African American Connections in Asian American Jazz–Based Music." *Asian Music* (Winter–Spring 2005): 87–108.

Bergmann, Leola Nelson. *Americans from Norway.* Philadelphia: Lippincott, 1950.

Cable, George Washington. "The Dance in Place Congo" and "Creole Slave Songs." Reprinted in *The Social Implications of Early Negro Music in the United States.* Ed. Bernard Katz. New York: Arno, 1969.

Garland Encyclopedia of World Music: Vol. 3. The United States and Canada. Ed. Ellen Kosoff. New York: Garland, 2001.

Garrett, Charles Hiroshi. "Chinatown, Whose Chinatown? Defining America's Borders with Musical Orientalism." *Journal of the American Musicological Society* 57.1 (Spring 2004).

Lornell, Kip, and Anne K. Rasmussen, eds. *Musics of Multicultural America.* New York: Schirmer Books, 1997.

Wang, Oliver. "Between the Notes: Finding Asian America in Popular Music." *American Music* (Winter 2001): 439–65.

Whitfield, Irène Thérèse. *Louisiana French Folk Songs.* New York: Dover, 1969.

Yang, Mina. "Orientalism and the Music of Asian Immigrant Communities in California, 1924–1945." *American Music* (Winter 2001): 385–416.

Zhang, Wei-hua. "Fred Wei-han Ho: Case Study of a Chinese-American Creative Musician." *Asian Music* 25.1–2 (1993–94): 81–114.

6. Folk Music as an Instrument of Advocacy

Boucher, David. "Images and Distorted Facts: Politics, Poetry, and Protest in the Songs of Bob Dylan." *The Political Art of Bob Dylan.* Ed. David Boucher and Gary Browning. Houndmills, Basingstoke, Hampshire (UK) and New York: Palgrave Macmillan, 2004.

Denisoff, R. Serge. *Sing Me a Song of Social Significance.* Bowling Green, OH: Bowling Green State Univ. Press, 1983.

Hampton, Wayne. *Guerrilla Minstrels: John Lennon, Joe Hill, Woody Guthrie, Bob Dylan.* Knoxville: Univ. of Tennessee Press, 1986.

Jackson, George Pullen. *Spiritual Folk-Songs of Early America.* 1937. New York: Dover, 1964.

Marqusee, Mike. *Chimes of Freedom: The Politics of Bob Dylan's Art.* New York and London: The New Press, 2003.

Wilgus, D. K. *Anglo-American Folksong Scholarship Since 1898.* New Brunswick, NJ: Rutgers Univ. Press, 1959.

7. Country Music

Cash, Wilbur J. *The Mind of the South.* New York: Knopf, 1941.

Gentry, Linnell, ed. *A History and Encyclopedia of Country, Western, and Gospel Music.* 2nd ed. Nashville: Clairmont, 1969.

Giddins, Gary. Notes. *Shake, Rattle & Roll: Rock 'n' Roll in the 1950s.* New World 249.

Green, Archie. "Hillbilly Music: Source and Symbol." *Journal of American Folklore.* July–Sept. 1965.

Malone, Bill C. *Country Music, U.S.A.* Rev. ed. Austin: Univ. of Texas Press, 1985.

8. The Blues

Baraka, Amiri (LeRoi Jones). *Blues People.* New York: Morrow, 1963.

Cohn, Lawrence, ed. *Nothing But the Blues: The Music and the Musicians.* New York: Abbeville, 1993.

Cook, Bruce. *Listen to the Blues.* New York: Scribner's, 1973.

Gillett, Charlie. *The Sound of the City: The Rise of Rock 'n' Roll.* New York: Dell, 1970.

Handy, W. C., ed. *Blues: An Anthology.* New York, 1926. New York: Macmillan, 1972.

Keil, Charles. *Urban Blues.* Chicago: Univ. of Chicago Press, 1966.

Oliver, Paul. *The Meaning of the Blues.* New York: Macmillan, 1960.

Patoski, Joe Nick, and Bill Crawford. *Stevie Ray Vaughan: Caught in the Crossfire.* Boston: Little, Brown, 1993.

9. Rock Music

Barlow, William. *Voice Over: The Making of Black Radio.* Philadelphia: Temple Univ. Press, 1999.

Bowman, Rob. "Rock: Rock and Roll." *Garland Encyclopedia of World Music: Vol. 3. The United States and Canada.* Ed. Ellen Kosoff. New York: Garland, 2001.

Charlton, Katherine. *Rock Musical Styles: A History.* Dubuque, IA: Wm. C. Brown, 1989.

Dawson, Jim. *Rock Around the Clock: The Record That Started the Rock Revolution!* San Francisco: Backbeat Books, 2005.

Gracyk, Theodore. *Rhythm and Noise: An Aesthetics of Rock.* Durham and London: Duke Univ. Press, 1996.

Harrison, Daniel. "After Sundown: The Beach Boys' Experimental Music." In *Understanding Rock: Essays in Musical Analysis.* New York: Oxford Univ. Press, 1997.

Hoskyns, Barney. *Glam! Bowie, Bolan and the Glitter Rock Revolution.* London: Faber and Faber, 1998.

Rose, Tricia. *Black Noise: Rap Music and Black Culture in Contemporary America.* Hanover and London: Wesleyan Univ. Press, 1994.

Shaw, Arnold. *Honkers and Shouters*. New York: Macmillan, 1978.

Starr, Larry, and Christopher Waterman. *American Popular Music: From Minstrelsy to MTV*. New York: Oxford Univ. Press, 2003.

Stuessy, Joe. *Rock and Roll: Its History and Stylistic Development*. Englewood Cliffs, NJ: Prentice Hall, 1990.

Szatmary, David P. *Rockin' in Time: A Social History of Rock-and-Roll*. 5th ed. Upper Saddle River, NJ: Prentice Hall, 2004.

Walser, Robert. "The Rock and Roll Era." *The Cambridge History of American Music*. Ed. David Nicholls. Cambridge, UK: Cambridge Univ. Press, 1998.

10. From Psalm Tune to Rural Revivalism

Buechner, Alan. Annotations. *The New England Harmony*. Smithsonian/Folkways 2377 LP.

Chase, Gilbert. *America's Music*. Rev. 3rd ed. Urbana and Chicago: Univ. of Illinois Press, 1987.

Johnson, Charles A. *The Frontier Camp Meeting*. Dallas: SMU Press, 1955. 64–65.

Lovell, John, Jr. *Black Song: The Forge and the Flame*. New York: Macmillan, 1972.

McKay, David P., and Richard Crawford. *William Billings of Boston: Eighteenth-Century Composer*. Princeton, NJ: Princeton Univ. Press, 1975.

Patterson, Beverly Bush. *The Sound of the Dove: Singing in Appalachian Primitive Baptist Churches*. Urbana and Chicago: Univ. of Illinois Press, 1995.

Stevenson, Robert. *Protestant Church Music in America*. New York: Norton, 1966; paperback, 1970.

11. Urban Revivalism and Gospel Music

Abbott, Lynn. "Play That Barber Shop Chord: A Case for the African-American Origin of Barbershop Harmony." *American Music* 10.3 (Fall 1992).

Anderson, Robert Mapes. *Vision of the Disinherited: The Making of American Pentecostalism*. New York: Oxford Univ. Press, 1979.

Boyer, Horace Clarence. "Black Gospel Music." *New Grove Dictionary of American Music*. Vol. 2, 254–59.

———. "C. A. Tindley: Progenitor of Black-American Gospel Music." *Black Perspectives in Music* 11.2 (Fall 1983).

———. "A Comparative Analysis of Traditional and Contemporary Gospel Music." *More Than Dancing*. Ed. Irene Jackson. Westport, CT: Greenwood, 1985.

Du Bois, William E. B. *The Souls of Black Folk: Essays and Sketches*. Chicago: McClurg, 1903.

Ferris, William, and Mary L. Hart, eds. *Folk Music and Modern Sound*. Jackson: Univ. Press of Mississippi, 1982.

Heilbut, Tony. *The Gospel Sound*. 3rd Limelight Ed., 1989.

Ives, Charles. *Ives—Memos*. Ed. John Kirkpatrick. New York: Norton, 1972.

Malone, Bill C. *Southern Music: American Music*. Lexington: Univ. Press of Kentucky, 1979.

Oliver, Paul. *Songsters and Saints*. New York: Cambridge Univ. Press, 1984.

12. Secular Music in the Cities from Colonial Times to the Age of Andrew Jackson

Anderson, Gillian. *Freedom's Voice in Poetry and Song*. Wilmington, DE: Scholarly Resources, 1977.

Crawford, Richard. Notes. *Music of the Federal Era*. New World 80299.

Mates, Julian. *The American Musical Stage Before 1800*. New Brunswick, NJ: Rutgers Univ. Press, 1962.

McKay, David. "Opera in Colonial Boston," *American Music* 3.2 (Summer 1985).

Sonneck, O. G. *Early Opera in America*. 1915. New York: Benjamin Blom, 1963.

Southern, Eileen. *The Music of Black Americans*. 2nd ed. New York: Norton, 1983.

Wolfe, Richard J. *Secular Music in America, 1801–1825: A Bibliography*. New York: New York Public Library, 1964.

13. Popular Musical Theater and Opera from the Jacksonian Era to the Present

Bean, Annemarie, et al., eds. *Inside the Minstrel Mask: Readings in Nineteenth-Century Blackface Minstrelsy*. Hanover, NH: Wesleyan Press, 1996.

Bordman, Gerald. *American Musical Comedy from "Adonis" to "Dreamgirls."* New York: Oxford Univ. Press, 1982.

Clark, J. Bunker, ed. "The Composer and Performer and Other Matters: A Panel Discussion with Virgil Thomson and Philip

Glass, Moderated by Gregory Sandow." *American Music* 7.2 (Summer 1989): 181–204.

Cockrell, Dale. *Demons of Disorder: Early Blackface Minstrels and Their World.* Cambridge, UK: Cambridge Univ. Press, 1997.

Dizikes, John. *Opera in America: A Cultural History.* New Haven and London: Yale Univ. Press, 1993.

Gilbert, Douglas. *American Vaudeville.* Reprint, New York: Dover, 1963.

Hamm, Charles. "Opera and the American Composer." *The American Composer Speaks.* Ed. Gilbert Chase. Baton Rouge: Louisiana State Univ. Press, 1969.

———. *Yesterdays: Popular Song in America.* New York: Norton, 1979.

Lahr, John. "Spellbound." Rev. of *Sunset Boulevard. The New Yorker,* 26 July 1993: 74–76.

Lott, Eric. *Love and Theft: Blackface Minstrelsy and the American Working Class.* New York: Oxford Univ. Press, 1993.

Nathan, Hans. *Dan Emmett and the Rise of Early Negro Minstrelsy.* Norman: Univ. of Oklahoma Press, 1962.

Southern, Eileen, ed. *Readings in Black American Music.* 2nd ed. New York: Norton, 1983.

Stearns, Marshall. *The Story of Jazz.* New York: Oxford Univ. Press, 1956.

Toll, Robert C. *Blacking Up: The Minstrel Show in Nineteenth Century America.* New York: Oxford Univ. Press, 1974.

14. Popular Song, Dance, and March Music from the Jacksonian Era to the Advent of Rock

Cockrell, Dale. *Excelsior: Journals of the Hutchinson Family Singers, 1842–1846.* Stuyvesant, NY: Pendragon, 1989.

Crawford, Richard. *The American Musical Landscape.* Berkeley and Los Angeles: Univ. of California Press, c. 1993.

Hamm, Charles. *Yesterdays: Popular Song in America.* New York: Norton, 1979.

Heaps, Willard A., and Porter W. Heaps. *The Singing Sixties: The Spirit of Civil War Days Drawn from the Music of the Times.* Norman: Univ. of Oklahoma Press, 1960.

Johnson, James Weldon, ed. *The Book of American Negro Spirituals.* New York: Viking, 1969.

Moseley, Caroline. "'When Will Dis Cruel War Be Ober?' Attitudes Toward Blacks in Popular Song of the Civil War." *American Music,* 2.3 (Fall 1984).

Sanjek, Russell. *From Print to Plastic: Publishing and Promoting America's Popular Music (1900–1980).* I.S.A.M. Monograph no. 20. Brooklyn: Inst. for Studies in American Music, 1983.

Schwartz, H. W. *Bands of America.* Reprint, New York: Da Capo, 1975.

Shaw, Arnold. *Black Popular Music in America.* New York: Schirmer Books, 1986.

Spaeth, Sigmund. *A History of Popular Music in America.* New York: Random House, 1948.

Tawa, Nicholas. *A Music for the Millions.* New York: Pendragon, 1984.

Turner, Martha Anne. *The Yellow Rose of Texas: The Story of a Song.* El Paso: Western Press of the Univ. of Texas Press at El Paso, 1971.

Wilder, Alec. *American Popular Song: The Great Innovators 1900–1950.* New York: Oxford Univ. Press, 1972.

15. Ragtime and Precursors of Jazz

Allen, William Francis, Charles Pickard Ware, and Lucy McKim Garrison. *Slave Songs of the United States.* 1867. Various publishers.

Badger, J. Reid. "James Reese Europe and the Prehistory of Jazz." *American Music* 7.1 (Spring 1989).

Berlin, Edward A. *Ragtime: A Musical and Cultural History.* Berkeley and Los Angeles: Univ. of California Press, 1980.

Blesh, Rudi, and Harriett Janis. *They All Played Ragtime.* 4th ed. New York: Oak, 1971.

Cook, Bruce. *Listen to the Blues.* New York: Scribner's, 1973.

Gushee, Lawrence. Notes. *Steppin' on the Gas: Rags to Jazz 1913–1927.* NW 269.

Hasse, John, ed. *Ragtime: Its History, Composers, and Music.* New York: Schirmer Books, 1985.

Lomax, Alan. *Mister Jelly Roll: The Fortunes of Jelly Roll Morton, New Orleans Creole and "Inventor of Jazz."* 2nd ed. Berkeley and Los Angeles: Univ. of California Press, 1973.

Shaw, Arnold. *Black Popular Music in America.* New York: Schirmer Books, 1986.

Southern, Eileen. *The Music of Black Americans: A History.* 2nd ed. New York: Norton, 1983.

———. *Readings in Black American Music.* 2nd ed. New York: Norton, 1983.

Stearns, Marshall. *The Story of Jazz.* 1956. New York: Oxford Univ. Press, 1974.

16. Jazz

Gridley, Mark. *Jazz Styles: History and Analysis.* 6th ed. Englewood Cliffs, NJ: Prentice Hall, 1996.

Jones, LeRoi. *Blues People.* New York: Morrow, 1963.

Kofsky, Frank. *Black Nationalism and the Revolution in Music.* New York: Pathfinder, 1970.

Mezzrow, Mez, and Bernard Wolfe. *Really the Blues.* Garden City, NY: Anchor, 1972.

Morgenstern, Dan. Notes. *Bebop.* NewWorld 271.

Morris, Ronald L. *Wait Until Dark: Jazz and the Underworld 1880–1940.* Bowling Green, OH: Bowling Green Univ. Popular Press, 1980.

Roberts, John Storm. *Black Music of Two Worlds.* New York: Schirmer, 1972.

Schuller, Gunther. *Early Jazz: Its Roots and Musical Development.* New York: Oxford Univ. Press, 1968.

———. "Third Steam Revisited." *Musings.* New York: Oxford Univ. Press, 1986.

Shaw, Arnold. *Black Popular Music in America.* New York: Schirmer Books, 1986.

17. The Search for an American Identity

Beveridge, David R., ed. *Rethinking Dvořák: Views from Five Countries.* Oxford: Clarendon Press, 1996. Particularly the essays by Richard Crawford, Thomas L. Riis, and Charles Hamm in Part VII, "The Impact of Dvořák on America."

Bomberger, E. Douglas. *"A Tidal Wave of Encouragement": American Composers' Concerts in the Gilded Age.* Westport, CT, and London: Praeger, 2002.

Chase, Gilbert. *America's Music: From the Pilgrims to the Present.* 3rd ed. Urbana: Univ. of Illinois Press, 1987.

Ciucevich, David. Notes. *William Grant Still: Afro-American Symphony; In Memoriam; Africa (Symphonic Poem).* Naxos 8.559174.

Copland, Aaron. *The New Music, 1900–1960.* Revised and enlarged edition. New York: W. W. Norton, 1968. Previously published in 1941 under the title *Our New Music: Leading Composers in Europe and America.*

Crawford, Richard. *America's Musical Life: A History.* New York and London: W. W. Norton, 2001.

Davis, John, Ricky Jay, Oliver Sacks, and Amiri Baraka. Notes. *John Davis Plays Blind Tom, The Eighth Wonder of the World.* Newport Classic NPD 85660.

Farwell, Arthur. "An Affirmation of American Music" (1903), reprinted in Gilbert Chase, ed., *The American Composer Speaks.* Baton Rouge: Louisiana State Univ. Press, 1966. 91–93.

———. "A Letter to American Composers." *The Wa-Wan Press*, vol. 1. Reprint, New York: Arno Press/New York Times, 1970.

Farwell, Brice, ed. *A Guide to the Music of Arthur Farwell.* Privately printed by Brice Farwell, Briarcliff Manor, NY, 1972.

Gottschalk, L. M. *Notes of a Pianist.* New ed. Trans. with notes by Jeanne Behrend. New York: Knopf, 1964.

Horowitz, Joseph. *Classical Music in America: A History of Its Rise and Fall.* New York and London: W. W. Norton, 2005.

Kenny, Herbert. Notes. *Mrs. H. H. A. Beach/Arthur Foote.* NW 268.

Knight, Ellen. "Charles Martin Loeffler and George Gershwin: A Forgotten Friendship." *American Music* 3.4 (Winter 1985).

Loft, Abram. "Richard Wagner, Theodore Thomas, and the American Centennial." *The Musical Quarterly* 37.2 (April 1951).

Lowens, Irving. *Music and Musicians in Early America.* New York: Norton, 1964.

Root, George F. *The Story of a Musical Life.* Cincinnati: John Church, 1891.

Sears, Ann. "Keyboard Music by Nineteenth-Century Afro-American Composers." *Feel the Spirit: Essays in 19th Century Afro-American Music.* Ed. George Keck. Westport, CT: Greenwood, 1988.

Southern, Eileen. *The Music of Black Americans: A History.* 2nd ed. New York: Norton, 1983.

18. Twentieth-Century Innovation and the Contemporary World

Adams, John. "Living on the Edge: The Composer in a Pop Culture." Address, California State University, Sacramento, 9 November 1996.

Bruno, Anthony. "Two American Twelve-Tone Composers." *Musical America* 71.3 (Feb. 1951).

Cage, John. *A Year from Monday*. Middletown, CT: Wesleyan Univ. Press, 1963.

———. ed. *Notations*. New York: Something Else Press, 1969.

———. *Silence*. Cambridge: MIT Press, 1966.

Chase, Gilbert, ed. *The American Composer Speaks*. Baton Rouge: Louisiana State Univ. Press, 1966.

Cope, David. *New Directions in Music*. 4th ed. Dubuque, IA: William C. Brown, 1984.

Cowell, Henry, and Sidney Cowell. *Charles Ives and His Music*. Rev. ed. New York: Oxford Univ. Press, 1969.

Crunden, Robert M. "Charles Ives's Place in American Culture." *An Ives Celebration*. Ed. H. Wiley Hitchcock. Urbana: Univ. of Illinois Press, 1977.

Dreier, Ruth. "Minimalism." *The New Grove Dictionary of American Music*. Vol. 3. London: Macmillan, 1986. 240.

Ives, Charles. *Charles E. Ives: Memos*. Ed. John Kirkpatrick. New York: Norton, 1972.

———. *Essays Before a Sonata, and Other Writings*. New York: Norton, 1961; paperback, 1964.

Krenek, Ernst. "Serialism." *Dictionary of Contemporary Music*. Ed. John Vinton. New York: Dutton, 1971.

Layton, Billy Jim. "The New Liberalism." *Perspectives of New Music* 3.2 (Spring–Summer 1965).

Nyman, Michael. *Experimental Music: Cage and Beyond*. New York: Schirmer Books, 1974.

Oja, Carol J. *Making Music Modern: New York in the 1920s*. New York: Oxford Univ. Press, 2000.

Partch, Harry. *Genesis of a Music*. 2nd ed. New York: Da Capo, 1974.

Reich, Steve. *Writings about Music*. New York: New York Univ. Press, 1974.

Rockwell, John. *All American Music: Composition in the Late Twentieth Century*. New York: Knopf, 1983.

Schwartz, Elliott, and Barney Childs, eds. *Contemporary Composers on Contemporary Music*. New York: Holt, Rinehart & Winston, 1967.

Thomson, Virgil. *American Music Since 1910*. New York: Holt, Rinehart & Winston, 1970.

Varèse, Edgard. "Freedom for Music." *The American Composer Speaks*. Ed. Gilbert Chase. Baton Rouge: Louisiana State Univ. Press, 1966.

19. Film Music

Darby, William, and Jack Du Bois. *American Film Music: Major Composers, Techniques, Trends, 1915–1990*. Jefferson, NC, and London: McFarland, 1990.

Hoover, Kathleen, and John Cage. *Virgil Thomson: His Life and Music*. New York: T. Yoseloff, 1959.

Neumeyer, David, James Buhler, and Rob Deemer. *Music in Sound Film: An Introduction*. Forthcoming.

Prendergast, Roy M. *Film Music, a Neglected Art: A Critical Study of Music in Films*. 2nd ed. New York and London: W. W. Norton, 1992.

20. Tales of Two Cities: Austin, Texas, and Sacramento, California

Albrecht, John Theodore. "German Singing Societies in Texas." Ph.D. diss., North Texas State University, 1975.

Candelaria, Lorenzo. "Dvořák, Austin, and the All-American Concert Movement." Unpublished paper read at the conference *New Worlds: Dvořák in Search of America*, University of Texas at Austin, 2004.

———. "Silvestre Revueltas at the Dawn of His 'American Period': St. Edward's College, Austin, Texas (1917–1918)." *American Music* 22.4 (Winter 2004).

McGowan, Joseph A. *History of the Sacramento Valley*. 2 vols. New York and West Palm Beach, FL: Lewis Historical Publishing, 1961.

GLOSSARY

accent Emphasis placed on a single note or chord.

acoustic Not powered by electricity. Refers to an instrument that produces sound naturally when it is plucked, strummed, bowed, struck, or has air blown through it.

acoustics The scientific study of the production and perception of sound.

afterbeat A beat that follows the metrically stronger pulse in a bar of music—for example, beats 2 and 4 in 4/4 meter (march time).

atonal Without a tonal center. Describes music that does not center on any particular key.

augmentation An increase in the duration of a note.

backbeat A strong accent on a beat that is normally in a weaker position—for example, oom-PAH-oom-PAH rather than OOM-pah-OOM-pah in 4/4 meter (march time).

bar A unit of musical time (also called a *measure*) consisting of a certain number of pulses that have been grouped together. In written music, the boundaries of these units are indicated by vertical marks through the staff called barlines.

beat A steady pulse that divides musical time into even segments.

bending A technique used with stringed instruments (especially the guitar) in which the sound of a note is made higher or lower by pulling on the string as a note is sounding.

binary form Two-part form. Describes a musical work that is made up of two complementary sections.

break A brief instrumental interlude that occurs in an ensemble piece; often an improvised solo passage in a work for a group of instruments.

bridge A transitional passage that connects two more musically important sections.

cadence A point at which melodic and harmonic activity comes to a pause or a halt.

chord Two or more notes sounded simultaneously.

chord progression A succession of two or more chords.

chromatic scale A collection of twelve adjacent rising pitches or twelve adjacent falling pitches in which the distance between each pitch and the next is a half step.

clef A sign placed on the musical staff that indicates the positions and names of pitches.

color The character and quality of a note. Also called *timbre*.

consonance Describes pitches that sound stable and agreeable.

counterpoint The art of combining two or more independent melodic lines.

cross-rhythm A rhythm in which the regular or expected pattern of accents in a measure is contradicted by a new and conflicting set of accents.

diatonic scale A collection of seven adjacent rising pitches or seven adjacent falling pitches in which the whole steps and half steps are arranged to form the major scale or the minor scale.

diminished triad See *triad*.

diminution A reduction in the duration of a note.

dissonance Describes pitches that sound unstable and in need of resolution.

dominant The fifth pitch (ascending) of a scale in any given key. A chord built on this pitch is the dominant chord.

dotted rhythm A rhythm in which the addition of a dot after a note has augmented the note's value by half. The effect is such that pulses that usually unfold evenly and steadily are altered to unfold in staggered, uneven time values.

drone A long, sustained sounding of one or more fixed pitches.

dynamics The degrees of loudness or softness in music.

falsetto A high, soprano-like voice produced by an adult male.

form The organization of a musical work as composed by the artist or as perceived by the listener.

genre A "type" of music as determined by factors including style, form, performing medium, and performance venues.

ground bass A pattern of notes in the lowest part of a musical work for two or more voices or instruments that is repeated over and over.

half step The smallest interval in Western music. On the piano, this interval is sounded by any two immediately adjacent keys (white or black).

harmonic progression See *chord progression*.

harmony Pitches sounded simultaneously (chords) that provide support for a melodic line or create the overall soundscape of a work.

heterophony A musical texture in which two or more versions of the same essential melody are sounded simultaneously.

homophony A musical texture in which the melodic interest is invested in one voice or instrument while other parts provide a subordinate accompaniment.

indeterminacy Music created at least in part by random, or chance, elements. Also called chance music or aleatory music.

interval The distance between two pitches.

intonation In theory, a system of tuning; in performance, the degree to which a musician sounds a pitch accurately; also, the first few introductory notes in a piece.

key A tonal center built on a fundamental note called the tonic.

major scale A collection of seven notes that ascend in the following order of whole steps and half steps: 1–1–½–1–1–1–½. The character of this scale might be described as bright or happy.

major triad See *triad*.

measure See *bar*.

melody A distinctive series of pitches forming a recognizable, often memorable, musical unit. This is usually what we whistle or hum in recalling a piece of music.

meter Musical time organized into groups of steady pulses. Most pulses in Western music are organized into groups of two (duple meter) or groups of three (triple meter). Unusual groups not equally divisible by two or three (groups of five or seven pulses, for example) are called asymmetrical meters.

metronome A mechanical or electronic device that sounds steady beats as clicks or beeps, which help musicians keep steady time while practicing or recording a piece.

minimalism A style of composition in which only the smallest amounts of musical materials are used and repeated over and over, sometimes with only very subtle variations between repetitions.

minor scale A collection of seven notes that ascend in the following order of whole steps and half steps: 1–½–1–1–½–1–1. The character of this scale might be described as dark or sad.

minor triad See *triad*.

modal A term often used to describe the character of a musical work that does not fall neatly into the soundscapes of either the major scale or the minor scale. See also *mode*.

mode The quality or character of a scale (pitches organized into fixed ascending and descending patterns of half steps and whole steps). The primary modes in Western music are major and minor.

modulation The process of changing from one tonal center (key) to another.

monody Music that consists of a single melodic line.

monophony A musical texture in which there is one melodic line with no accompaniment.

monotone A single pitch on which a text is recited.

motive A short, sharply defined melodic idea that can stand alone—for example, the four notes that open Beethoven's well-known Fifth Symphony.

offbeat Any subdivision or a beat other than the initial one, which is usually the strongest.

ostinato [Italian, "obstinate"] Any musical figure (it can be a particular melody, motive, chord, or rhythm) that is repeated over and over.

overtones Secondary tones that naturally emanate from a fundamental pitch when it is sung or played on an instrument. Also called harmonics.

pentatonic scale A collection of five pitches that ascend and descend in a fixed order. Its characteristic sound may be heard by playing any five consecutive black keys on the piano.

phrase A self-contained musical idea that forms part of a larger unit of expression, such as a melody or a theme.

phrasing In performance, the realization of self-contained musical ideas that form part of a larger unit of expression, such as a melody or a theme.

pitch A musical sound that can be represented as a single point on a measurable range from high to low—for example, a single point on a staff or in a scale.

pitch class Designates all pitches having the same name, without regard to their relative positions, low or high. For example, the pitch named C sung by an adult male and the pitch named C sung by a child are in two different ranges; thus, strictly speaking, they are not the same pitches. They are both Cs in the most general sense, however, and therefore belong to the same pitch class.

polyphony A musical texture in which several independent melodic lines are presented simultaneously in counterpoint.

program music Any musical work that aims to re-create in sound the events, characters, emotions, and overall impressions of a non-musical source, such as a story, a painting, or the experience of walking through the woods.

recitative A dramatic form of speech that is musically heightened by placing emphasis on natural rhythms and inflections.

refrain A block of text and/or music that is repeated at regular intervals in the course of a piece.

rhythm Organized patterns of movement through time.

riffs Short, sometimes stereotypical, melodic phrases that are repeated over changing harmonies either as the main tune or as an accompaniment.

ritornello [Italian, "little return"] The section of music (most often presented at the beginning of a work) that comes back in part, or in its entirety, in the course of a performance.

scale A collection of pitches organized in a fixed ascending and descending pattern of whole steps and/or half steps.

scat singing A virtuosic manner of vocalizing nonsensical syllables that tends to emphasize fast, complex, "tongue-tying" rhythms.

score A written representation of a musical work in which the notated parts for all instruments and voices involved in its performance are shown simultaneously.

serial music Music in which pitches, rhythms, or other components are arranged in a certain order (series), then redeployed in that exact order throughout a composition.

solmization A manner of designating pitches by a set of syllables rather than fixed letter names—for example, do-re-mi-fa-sol-la rather than C-D-E-F-G-A. Solmization is a useful tool in the instruction of singing, because the syllables indicate where the half steps and whole steps occur.

staff The graph of five horizontal lines upon which pitches and rhythms are indicated.

stanza A unit of song text or poetry usually consisting of at least four lines of verse unified by a regular rhyme scheme and meter.

strophe See *stanza*.

strophic form A form in which successive strophes or stanzas are set to the same music.

subdominant The fourth pitch (ascending) of a scale in any given key. A chord built upon this pitch is the subdominant chord.

syncopation The momentary contradiction of a prevailing meter brought about by placing accents on beats or parts of beats that normally would not receive strong emphasis.

tempo The speed at which beats move forward through time.

texture The musical "fabric" of a composition—that is, how individual lines interact with one another. Basic textures include monophony, heterophony, homophony, and polyphony.

timbre See *color*.

tonal Having a tonal center. Describes music that centers on a key.

tonality The organization of tones (pitches) around a definite key center.

tone A sound that has a definite and consistent pitch. When this term is preceded by an adjective, it describes the character or quality of sound produced by a musician with the voice or on an instrument (e.g., smooth tone, uneven tone).

tone cluster A very densely packed and dissonant collection of pitches. Its characteristic sound may be heard by simultaneously pressing several keys on a piano with the full palm or even the forearm.

tonic The first pitch (ascending) of a scale in any given key. A chord built on this pitch is the tonic chord. The tonic pitch (and the chord built upon it) is the most important in any given key—all harmonies and melodies gravitate toward it.

triad A chord consisting of three pitches with adjacent pitches separated by the interval of a third. A major triad is composed of a major third between the bottom and middle notes, and a minor third between the middle and top notes; its sound could be described as bright or happy. A minor triad is composed of a minor third between the bottom and middle notes, and a major third between middle and top notes; its sound could be described as dark or sad. A diminished triad is composed of two minor thirds; its sound is very tense and unstable.

tuning A system of pitches arranged according to certain intervals; also, the act of adjusting the sounds produced by the voice or an instrument to bring them into accord with predetermined pitches.

vibrato The ornamental wavering or wobbling of a pitch to intensify and enrich the sound quality.

vocables Utterances that are used in an ornamental fashion.

whole step An interval made up of two half steps.

PHOTO CREDITS

p. 3 © State Historical Society of Missouri, Columbia

p. 9 © Eric Schaal/Time Life Pictures/Getty Images

p. 12 © Bettmann/CORBIS

p. 15 © Tim Mosenfelder/Getty Images

p. 18 © National Commission for Museums and Monuments, Ita Yemoo, Ife, Nigeria. Heini Schneebeli/Bridgeman Art Library

p. 20 © Bettmann/CORBIS

p. 24 Lomax Collection of Folk Music/© CORBIS

p. 26 The Granger Collection, New York

p. 32 © CORBIS

p. 34 Drawing by Seth Eastman for *Information Regarding the History, Conditions, and Prospects of the Indian Tribes of the United States*, Henry R. Schoolcraft, 1851. © CORBIS

p. 38 Painting by Robert Lindneux, 1838. The Granger Collection, New York

p. 39 The Granger Collection, New York

p. 45 Painting by Carl Nebel. Published in *The War Between the United States and Mexico, Illustrated*, 1851/MPI/Getty Images

p. 49 © Jan Butchofsky-Houser/CORBIS

p. 52 OMAR TORRES/AFP/Getty Images

p. 57 Frank Driggs Collection/Getty Images

p. 64 © Philip Gould/CORBIS

p. 65 © Minnesota Historical Society/CORBIS

p. 67 © Ed Kashi/CORBIS

p. 72 Shane Sato

p. 74 © Rainer Fehringer www.rainerstudio.com

p. 76 Engraving by Frank Bellow for *Leslie's Illustrated Newspaper*/Photo © Bettmann/CORBIS

p. 78 © Bettmann/CORBIS

p. 82 © Jay Dickman/CORBIS

p. 84 © Bettmann/CORBIS

p. 85 © Bettmann/CORBIS

p. 89 © Buddy Mays/CORBIS

p. 91 Eric Schall/Time Life Pictures/Getty Images

p. 94 The Granger Collection, New York

p. 99 © Bettmann/CORBIS

p. 101 © Underwood & Underwood/CORBIS

p. 103 Frank Driggs Collection/Getty Images

p. 105 © Neal Preston/CORBIS

p. 109 © Henry Horenstein/CORBIS

p. 113 Frank Driggs Collection/Getty Images

p. 117 Hulton Archive/Getty Images

p. 118 The Granger Collection, New York

p. 123 Frank Driggs Collection/Getty Images

p. 125 © Steve Jennings/CORBIS

p. 130 © Topical Press Agency/Getty Images

p. 133 © Bettmann/CORBIS

p. 136 © Bettmann/CORBIS

p. 138 © Douglas Kent Hall/ZUMA/CORBIS

p. 142 © Denis O'Regan/CORBIS

p. 147 © Bettmann/CORBIS

p. 154 The Granger Collection, New York

p. 162 © CORBIS

p. 165 © CORBIS

p. 169 © Bettmann/CORBIS

p. 172 The Granger Collection, New York

p. 173 Hulton Archive/Getty Images

p. 179 © Ted Williams/CORBIS

p. 181 Frank Driggs Collection/Getty Images

p. 183 © Flip Schulke/CORBIS

p. 184 © Gary Hershorn/Reuters/CORBIS

p. 189 © CORBIS

p. 196 From E. Boyd Smith's *Story of Pocahontas and Captain John Smith*, 1906. Photo © Blue Lantern Studio/CORBIS

p. 200 © CORBIS

p. 206 State Historical Society of Missouri, Columbia

p. 210 Keystone/Getty Images

p. 213 Fred Fehl/Museum of the City of New York/Getty Images

p. 217 Ray Fisher/Time Life Pictures/Getty Images

p. 225 MPI/Getty Images

p. 227 MPI/Getty Images

p. 234 Painting by Victor Gilbert [1867–1935]/ © Christie's Images/CORBIS

p. 241 Hulton Archive/Getty Images

p. 247 Paul Thompson/War Department/National Archives/Time Life Pictures/Getty Images

p. 250 Frank Driggs Collection/Getty Images

p. 254 Gjon Mili/Time Life Pictures/Getty Images

p. 258 © Philip Gould/CORBIS

p. 262 Frank Driggs Collection/Getty Images

p. 264 Frank Driggs Collection/Getty Images

p. 267 Frank Driggs Collection/Getty Images

p. 272 Frank Driggs Collection/Getty Images

p. 275 Metronome/Getty Images

p. 281 © Andrew Lichtenstein/CORBIS

p. 283 Kean Collection/Getty Images

p. 292 Hulton Archives/Getty Images

p. 297 New York Times Co./Getty Images

p. 301 © Bettmann/CORBIS

p. 305 New York Times Co./Getty Images

p. 308 Grey Villet/Time Life Pictures/Getty Images

p. 317 © Bettmann/CORBIS

p. 318 © Roger Ressmeyer/CORBIS

INDEX

H